Winning Our Freedoms Together

African Americans and Apartheid, 1945–1960

NICHOLAS GRANT

The University of North Carolina Press   Chapel Hill

© 2017 The University of North Carolina Press
All rights reserved
Set in Charis and Lato by Westchester Publishing Services
Manufactured in the United States of America

The University of North Carolina Press has been a member of the
Green Press Initiative since 2003.

Library of Congress Cataloging-in-Publication Data
Names: Grant, Nicholas, author.
Title: Winning our freedoms together : African Americans and apartheid,
    1945–1960 / Nicholas Grant.
Other titles: Justice, power, and politics.
Description: Chapel Hill : University of North Carolina Press, [2017] |
    Series: Justice, power, and politics | Includes bibliographical
    references and index.
Identifiers: LCCN 2017015853| ISBN 9781469635279 (cloth : alk. paper) |
    ISBN 9781469635286 (pbk : alk. paper) | ISBN 9781469635293 (ebook)
Subjects: LCSH: African Americans—Political activity—History—20th
    century. | Anti-apartheid movements—United States—History—
    20th century. | Anti-apartheid movements—South Africa—History—
    20th century. | United States—Foreign relations—20th century. |
    South Africa—Foreign relations—20th century. | Cold War—Influence.
Classification: LCC E185.61 .G74 2017 | DDC 323.1196/0730904—dc23
    LC record available at https://lccn.loc.gov/2017015853

Cover illustration: Detail from Council on African Affairs, "A Call from
the heroic peoples of Africa to Negro and white Americans," 1954.
W. E. B. Du Bois Papers (MS 312), Special Collections and University
Archives, University of Massachusetts Amherst Libraries.

Portions of chapter 3 were previously published as "Crossing the Black
Atlantic: The Global Anti-Apartheid Movement and the Racial Politics of
the Cold War," *Radical History Review* 119 (2014): 72–93. Republished with
the permission of Duke University Press.

Portions of chapter 8 were previously published as "The National Council
of Negro Women and South Africa: Black Internationalism, Motherhood,
and the Cold War," *Palimpsest: A Journal of Women, Gender, and the Black
International* 5, no. 1 (2016): 59–87. Used here with permission.

For my parents

Contents

Illustrations

Acknowledgments

This book has taken me from the United Kingdom to the United States to South Africa and back again. On each of these journeys, and over eight years of researching and writing, I have had the privilege of meeting many incredible people and have racked up countless debts.

I have learned from a number of exceptional scholars who have been incredibly generous in giving up their time to read and engage critically with the entire manuscript as it has developed over the years. I owe a special debt of gratitude to Kate Dossett. Kate first challenged me to think about African American history from a transnational perspective when I was an undergraduate student at the University of Leeds. Since then, she has been a constant source of intellectual inspiration, pushing me to think more critically about the past, as well of the responsibility of the historian to uncover and accurately represent marginalized voices. Kate's incisive feedback on numerous draft chapters has greatly strengthened this project and I can't thank her enough for her unwavering support as well as her friendship. Shane Doyle's knowledge of African history and analytical eye was invaluable as I wrestled with the historiography of the anti-apartheid movement, while his calmness under pressure helped me to believe that it was possible to actually get this finished. I am also incredibly grateful to Alex Lichtenstein for the time he has taken to critically engage with this work. Alex has significantly enhanced my understanding of the global anti-apartheid movement and his insightful feedback on how best to revise the book has been invaluable. He has also offered a great deal of support and mentorship over the last five years. Simon Hall should be praised for pushing me to think more about the broader significance of this research. Specifically, his insistence on historical rigor has challenged me to think more deeply about my arguments as well as the possibilities and pitfalls of transnational history.

I am lucky to have had the support and encouragement of a number of colleagues and friends, all of whom have generously given up their time to read and discuss my research. Bill Booth, Antonia Brown, Vincent Hiribarren, Matthias Freidank, Say Burgin, Gina Denton, John Munro, Tom Davies, Julio Decker, Althea Legal Miller, Elisabeth Engel, Bevan Sewell, Kaeten

Mistry, Brandy T. Wells, Emma Long, Becky Fraser, and Jackie Fear Segal have all read sections of this manuscript. A shout out too to Michelle Coghlan and Nick Witham for their collegiality and for answering so many questions about the publishing process. Thank you too to Hazel Goodwin, whose remarkable life story taught me so much about 1950s South Africa. Collectively, these individuals have shared their knowledge, recommended resources, pushed me to make bold arguments, and helped me avoid a number of scholarly pitfalls. Brandon Proia at the University of North Carolina Press has been patient and understanding. He has made this process much less stressful than it might have been and I am grateful for all of his work in pushing the manuscript forward. I'd also like to thank Jad Adkins at UNC Press for all of his work on the manuscript. Finally, I owe a special debt of gratitude to Heather Ann Thompson, who supported this project in its early stages. While the input of all of these individuals has been invaluable, any errors that remain within this manuscript are, of course, my own.

Librarians and archivists are often the unsung heroes of historical research. I would have been completely lost without the knowledge, insight, and frequent tip-offs from staff at the Manuscripts Division at the Library of Congress, the Schomburg Center for Research in Black Culture at the New York Public Library, the National Archives for Black Women's History (especially Kenneth Chandler), the Moorland-Spingarn Research Center at Howard University, Manuscripts & Archives at the University of Cape Town, the National Library of South Africa in Cape Town, the National Archives in Pretoria, and the Historical Papers research archive in the William Cullen Library at the University of Witwatersrand (especially Gabriele Mohale). I would also like to thank Bob Edgar for agreeing to meet with me in Cape Town to discuss my research plans—his encyclopedic knowledge of South African archives helped me locate materials that I otherwise would have missed. The multi-archival and international nature of this research was only made possible by financial support from the Arts and Humanities Research Council in the United Kingdom. The John F. Kennedy Institute for North American Studies at the Freie Universität Berlin provided me with valuable thinking space and time as a postdoctoral fellow in 2012.

The opportunity to carry out scholarly research is always a privilege, but it can sometimes be a lonely business. However, I have been lucky to have met people whose kindness and company have made these past few years so much more enjoyable. In the United States, I am extremely grateful to those at the Kluge Center who provided me with a "home" for six months and made it possible for me to access research materials housed at the Library of Congress. I would especially like to thank Mary Lou Reker, whose warmth and personality helped make my time at the Kluge so enjoyable. In South Africa, the generosity of Nigel Worden, who trusted me to house-sit in Cape Town, cannot be understated. Nigel also put me in touch with people who gave up their time to meet and talk with me. Nick Southey in particular was fantastic when it came to raising my spirits after frustrating days in the archives and to encouraging me to experience the sights and sounds of South Africa.

It is also a great pleasure to be able to put down in print my sincere thanks to my friends and family. Thank you to all my friends in Leeds, London, and Norwich who have put up with me talking about my research for so long and have often been brave enough to ask, "how's the book going?"—knowing full well that the response might be longer and more drawn out than they had bargained for. I would especially like to thank Bill Booth and Vincent Hiribarren for their continuing friendship and for always raising my spirits.

I could not ask for a more loving and supportive family. My brother David never fails to cheer me up and has always taken an interest in what I am doing. I would also like to give a special mention to Edwina and John Pearson, members of our extended family, who have always encouraged me to "go for it" and have been incredibly kind over the years. I cannot stress enough how thankful I am for the unwavering support, patience, and love of my Mam and Dad. I could not ask for more caring and understanding parents. This book is dedicated to them. Finally, Heather Knight has perhaps lived with this book more than anyone else. She is my best friend and has made me smile every day for the last twelve years. She has encouraged me at every step and I am constantly inspired by her wit, intelligence, and grace. Thank you Heather—for your enduring love, understanding, and, perhaps most importantly, your remarkable ability to put up with me.

Abbreviations in the Text

ACFS	African Children's Feeding Scheme
ACOA	American Committee on Africa
AFSAR	Americans for South African Resistance
ANC	African National Congress
CAA	Council on African Affairs
CNA	Committee for the Negro in the Arts
CORE	Congress of Racial Equality
CPSA	Communist Party of South Africa
CRC	Civil Rights Congress
ESU	English-Speaking Union
FSAW	Federation of South African Women
HUAC	House Un-American Activities Committee
MDAA	Mutual Defense Assistance Act
NAACP	National Association for the Advancement of Colored People
NACW	National Association of Colored Women
NCAW	National Council of African Women
NCNW	National Council of Negro Women
NNC	National Negro Congress
NUSAS	National Union of South African Students
PAC	Pan-Africanist Congress
PIC	Peace Information Center
SACP	South African Communist Party
SAIC	South African Indian Congress
SAIRR	South African Institute of Race Relations
SCLC	Southern Christian Leadership Conference

SNYC	Southern Negro Youth Congress
Soweto	South Western Townships
STJ	Sojourners for Truth and Justice
UN	United Nations
WIDF	Women's International Democratic Federation

Winning Our Freedoms Together

Introduction

· ·

The October 1949 edition of *New Africa*, the monthly anti-imperial bulletin of the New York–based Council on African Affairs (CAA), featured a cartoon depiction of Eric Louw.[1] The image shows Louw, a leading apartheid official and South African representative to the United Nations, dressed in a schoolmaster's gown and mortarboard standing before a group of white South African students, declaring that "if it's good enough for America, it's good enough for us." Looming behind him, scrawled across the blackboard, is the figure of a hooded Ku Klux Klan member clutching a cross.[2]

This satirical drawing was a response to comments Louw had recently made to the National Union of South African Students (NUSAS) citing the policies of the U.S. government as providing a precedent for National Party efforts to "register and supervise" all "ultraliberalistic and leftist organisations" in the country.[3] A key figure in the Department of External Affairs and South African foreign minister between 1957 and 1964, Louw was one of the most visible defenders of apartheid on the international stage. Reflecting his suspicions of the language of human rights and decolonization, his comments show how apartheid policymakers regularly insisted that efforts to criticize South Africa, whether domestic or international, were in fact orchestrated by Soviet-inspired radicals.[4]

Printed at a time when struggles for black self-determination collided with the politics of anticommunism, the cartoon reveals two interconnected networks that shaped anti-apartheid politics between the United States and South Africa in the late 1940s and 1950s. First, the image hints at how the transnational operation of state power was used to stifle movements for black liberation on both sides of the Atlantic. The idea that the National Party was directly inspired by the policies of the U.S. government when dealing with political dissent reveals the extent to which state repression was reinforced across national borders during the early Cold War. This era witnessed the development of a close political, military, and economic alliance between the United States and South African governments.[5] Based around anticommunist beliefs and racist assumptions, this relationship had important implications for black protest movements on both sides of the Atlantic. Second, by drawing comparisons between race discrimination in each country, the cartoon also illuminates how activists continued to work together to draw parallels between apartheid rule and Jim Crow. Indeed, this same cartoon had originally appeared in South Africa's *Guardian* newspaper—a radical anti-apartheid publication that maintained links with the CAA right up until its demise in 1955.[6] This book traces the complex interplay between these two sets of political exchanges. It sheds new light on the disruptive effect that the Cold War had on the development of the global anti-apartheid movement, as well as the extent to which African Americans and anti-apartheid activists in South Africa continued to call attention to the transnational operation of state power in ways that reaffirmed their commitment to tackling racism on a global scale.

Decolonization, the rise of new superpowers, and the formation of newly independent states in Africa and Asia all resulted in "local" black protest being invested with an additional "global" meaning at this historical moment.[7] Although limited by the dual forces of racism and anticommunism, activists in both countries collaborated to critique and challenge the ties that existed between the United States and apartheid governments.[8] As African National Congress (ANC) activist Alfred Hutchinson wrote in an open letter to Autherine Lucy, the first black student to attend the University of Alabama, "The brave wind of freedom is blowing—the wind which must destroy the house built on the shifting sands of inequality, hatred, suspicion and prejudice. Everywhere new suns are rising and, comrade-in arms, our dawn cannot be far away."[9] Notwithstanding the setbacks and restrictions they faced, activists in the United States and South Africa engaged with one another's struggles throughout the 1940s and 1950s. African Americans—operating across the political spectrum—found ways to engage with the nascent anti-apartheid movement in varied and complex ways. Their actions speak to how black activists forged alliances across national borders in the most testing of circumstances, as well as the extent to which these exchanges continued to inform their respective struggles against racist oppression. Ultimately, the emergence of the global anti-apartheid movement and the racial politics of the Cold War serve to remind us of the accuracy of literary scholar Amy Kaplan's contention that the cultural and political ideas we think of as being "domestic or particularly national" are, in fact, "forged in a crucible of foreign relations."[10]

Resisting White Supremacy in the United States and South Africa

The 1940s and 1950s saw the development of resistance against organized white supremacy in the form of mass civil disobedience in the United States and South Africa. At the same time, diplomatic ties between the nations were rapidly expanding.[11] These two trends helped bind the racial politics of both countries together, while further emphasizing that the struggle against racism required international action. The postwar period ushered in a new phase in South African politics.[12] The ANC, pushed by figures in its Youth League, greatly expanded its membership, moved in a more radical direction, and began to embrace mass action as a political strategy.[13] Responding to the extension of white power, black activists took to the streets in a succession of protests that reverberated around the world.[14] The 1952 Defiance Campaign saw over 8,000 protesters arrested and jailed for openly defying apartheid laws.[15] Later, in 1955, the ANC and its allies in the Congress Alliance gathered in Kliptown on the outskirts of Johannesburg to sign the Freedom Charter, which condemned apartheid and set out a multiracial vision of a democratic South Africa.[16] Black South African women were particularly active in the anti-apartheid movement throughout this period, and in 1956 the Federation of South African Women (FSAW) opposed efforts to force women to carry government-issued passes by organizing a march to the Union Buildings in Pretoria that attracted over 20,000 people from across the country.[17] In 1957, mirroring the protests that had convulsed Montgomery, Alabama, black South Africans in Alexandra Township boycotted busses in protest of fare increases. The boycott lasted six months, spreading across the Transvaal, and at its peak involved over 70,000 people.[18] Later in the decade, the Pan-Africanist Congress (PAC), formed in 1959 and led by Robert Sobukwe, embarked on campaigns aimed at undermining the apartheid state through boycotts, marches, and deliberate arrests.[19]

U.S. race relations also entered a new phase at this historical moment. As African Americans returned from World War II with government declarations of freedom and democracy still ringing in their ears, the black community mobilized with renewed vigor against state-sanctioned segregation and racial discrimination.[20] Although the radical roots of civil rights had been established earlier, it was in the postwar period that the movement gained momentum.[21] Inspired by the battle against fascism, African Americans challenged Jim Crow through grassroots protests, boycotts, legal action, and individual acts of civil disobedience. The National Association for the Advancement of Colored People (NAACP) worked to challenge discriminatory employment, housing, and education practices in the courts. The association's membership grew eightfold in the 1940s as staff members, including Ella Baker and Thurgood Marshall, launched campaigns for black voting rights in the South.[22] Organizations such as the National Negro Congress (NNC), Southern Negro Youth Congress (SNYC), and Civil Rights Congress (CRC) challenged race discrimination from the left, while liberal groups, including the Congress of Racial Equality (CORE) and Martin Luther King Jr.'s Southern Christian Leadership Conference (SCLC) called for a nonviolent dismantling of Jim Crow throughout the United States—North and South.[23] Though there was certainly no wholehearted embrace of race equality by either the U.S. government or white America, the desegregation of the U.S. Army (1951), *Brown v. Board of Education* (1954), the Montgomery Bus Boycott (1955), as well as the 1957 Civil Rights Act struck a series of practical and symbolic blows to legalized segregation. Inspired by black protest in South Africa and further afield, African Americans ensured that race discrimination in the United States came under organized and widespread attack.[24] Although white supremacists utilized racial violence and intimidation in an attempt to hold the color line, the days of Jim Crow segregation appeared to be numbered.

In contrast to the civil rights gains made by black Americans, black South Africans were ultimately prevented from achieving their vision of a country that, as envisaged in the Freedom Charter, "belongs to all who live in it, black and white" and where "the rights of the people shall be the same, regardless of race, colour or sex."[25] As the U.S. government was being pushed toward an official policy of desegregation, South Africa moved rapidly in the opposite direction.[26] The National Party won power from the United Party of Jan Smuts in the narrowest of election victories in May 1948.[27] This victory for Afrikaner nationalism radically altered the racial landscape of South Africa, as segregation and race discrimination, already the norm throughout large parts of the country, became rigidly enshrined in government policy. Under the leadership of Daniel François Malan, the National Party passed a series of acts designed to further racial separation and the dominant position of South Africa's white population. The Mixed Marriages (1949) and Immorality (1950) Acts made it illegal for two people from different racial groups to engage in sexual and marital relationships. The Group Areas Act (1950) aimed to make the residential separation of the races compulsory, while the Natives (Abolition of Passes and Co-ordination of Documents) Act of 1952 made it mandatory for all Africans over the age of sixteen to carry "reference books" that detailed an individual's address and employment history as well as their dealings with the police. As the National Party turned its slim parliamentary majority into a 157-seat majority in the 1953 election, the government intensified its control over the country's African, "Coloured," and Asian population.[28] The election of the uncompromising Johannes Gerhardus Strijdom as prime minister in 1954 resulted in the disenfranchisement of South African Coloureds and the extension of "pass-laws" to African women. This era also saw the rise of "Separate Development" as a political ideology. Pioneered by minster of Native Affairs and future prime minister Hendrik Verwoerd, Separate Development led to the removal of Africans from white urban areas to designated rural and deindustrialized "Bantu Homelands."[29] These efforts to regulate black movement ultimately brought about the destruction of communities through forced removals, most dramatically in Sophiatown, Newclare, and Martindale in Johannesburg, resulting in the relocation of around 70,000 Africans to the South Western Townships (Soweto).[30]

Despite this divergence in the relative fortunes of white supremacy and black protest, the racial politics of both nations would continue to be interlinked. The National Party did its utmost to position itself as an invaluable ally of the West during the early Cold War. Apartheid policymakers presented South Africa as a politically stable white settler state, committed to clamping down on communist subversion and eager to open up the country to American businesses. This was an appealing message for U.S. officials and led to the strengthening of America's political, economic, and military ties with National Party. All this had ramifications for black protest in both countries in that it shone an uncomfortable spotlight on America's Cold War claims that it stood for freedom and democracy on the world stage.[31] Ultimately, it would be this gap between the high-minded language of the Cold War and the continued oppression of the black population of both countries that shaped the character of black international engagements between the United States and South Africa at this time.

African Americans and Anti-Apartheid

Throughout the nineteenth and twentieth centuries black activists in the United States and South Africa engaged in a political dialogue that informed their respective struggles against race discrimination.[32] This was a two-way conversation. African Americans responded to the actions of anti-apartheid activists and were inspired by the scale and apparent unity of their protest. As the internationally famous actor, singer, and CAA chairman Paul Robeson stated in an article entitled "A Lesson from Our South African Brothers and Sisters," "Here we are pushing for civil rights now, for performances not promises, and over there—well, they're really rolling."[33] Robeson's belief in the interconnected nature of black protest at home and abroad, as well as his insistence that African Americans could learn from the anti-apartheid struggle in South Africa, gives a sense of the collaborative and transnational character of black protest.

Here, it is important to remember Laura Chrisman's observation that, within this transatlantic framework, black America did not necessarily represent "a modern vanguard to lead black South Africa."[34] Writing in response to Paul Gilroy, who she argues privileges the United States as *the* major reference point for black cross-cultural exchange, Chrisman demonstrates how the actions of black activists in South Africa demanded recognition throughout the black diaspora.[35] African efforts to undermine apartheid following the election of the National Party in 1948 captured the imagination of African Americans, inspiring a range of activists into action and prompting even greater recognition of the significance of African liberation for the freedom dreams of black America.[36] However, just as the defeat of fascism and the prospect of African decolonization prompted African Americans to look overseas for inspiration in their own struggles against white supremacy, the repressive politics of the Cold War worked to contain global visions of black protest. This was not limited to the black freedom struggle in the United States.[37] Instead, anticommunism represented a powerful global ideology that was used to legitimize the hounding of black activists by the state in a number of geographical locations. In the early 1950s, exaggerated threats of communist subversion were used to exacerbate political divisions between black activists and dismantle transnational anticolonial networks—making it increasingly difficult to challenge the domestic and foreign policies of the U.S. government and its allies.

The historian Penny Von Eschen has argued that Cold War anticommunism "domesticated" African American anticolonialism, resulting in the "collapse of the politics of the African diaspora."[38] She shows how black liberals responded to the repressive politics of the era by embracing Americanism and often held back from criticizing U.S. foreign policy. Von Eschen argues that, in the final analysis, "using the Cold War as a rationale for fighting discrimination left no room for the internationalism that had characterized black American politics from the late 1930s through to the mid-1940s."[39] It is certainly true that many African Americans turned away from the politics of diaspora in order to prioritize the struggle for civil rights at home. However, it is important to remember that the civil rights movement in the United States and anticolonial politics of black America rarely operated on entirely separate plains. Although they faced numerous obstacles, African Americans from across the political spectrum worked tirelessly to link up with South African activists and condemn apartheid on the global stage. Even as Cold War anticommunism disrupted anticolonial networks and exacerbated political tensions, there remained an unwavering belief among a range of black activists on both sides of the Atlantic that their respective struggles against race discrimination were linked. Anticolonial movements transformed the way many African Americans viewed the African continent. As James Meriwether has noted when tracing the responses of African Americans to Ghanaian independence in 1957, African movements for political independence challenged many black Americans to expand their political vision to embrace Pan-Africanism and a broader sense of Afro-diasporic unity.[40] Forty nations, with a combined population of over eight hundred million people, won their freedom in the fifteen years following World War II.[41] As a number of scholars have explored, this landmark shift not only represented a profound challenge to white supremacy, but also ensured that race would play an important role in significantly shaping the course of international politics during the early Cold War.[42] While South Africa did not offer the same uplifting vision of black self-determination, the brutal nature of apartheid still played a significant role in informing anticolonial politics in the United States. The militancy and scale of the early anti-apartheid movement continued to capture the attention of African American activists across the political spectrum.[43]

Noting how anticommunist repression often resulted in the erasure of leftist contributions to the black freedom struggle, scholars have paid close attention to the anticolonial worldview of black radicals throughout the twentieth century.[44] The African American left played a prominent role in supporting the struggle against apartheid in South Africa. Founded in 1937, the CAA was by far the most militant of the U.S. organizations interested in South Africa. Dedicated to the dismantling of "fascist imperialism" in Africa and often adhering closely to the Communist Party line, the CAA was led by prominent black radicals including William Alphaeus Hunton, Paul Robeson, and W. E. B. Du Bois. Through its publications *New Africa* and *Spotlight on Africa*, as well as pamphlets, speeches, petitions, fundraising campaigns, and mass meetings, the CAA roundly condemned South African racism.[45] CAA leaders also established contacts with the ANC, South African Indian Congress (SAIC), and the Communist Party of South Africa (CPSA). The organization's radical anticolonialism incorporated scathing criticism of Jim Crow with full-blooded calls to halt America's growing imperialist ambitions in Africa. As McCarthyism was used to declare war on the left in general and the black popular front in particular, the CAA and its supporters were treated with increasing suspicion.[46] Ultimately, after a sustained campaign of government-led censorship and harassment, the CAA was forced to disband in 1955.

Importantly, anti-apartheid activism in the United States did not begin and end with the black left during the early Cold War.[47] More moderate organizations, including the NAACP, the American Committee on Africa (ACOA), and the National Council of Negro Women (NCNW), were part of a broad-based coalition of black liberals dedicated to the eradication of South Africa's white settler regime. The historian Carol Anderson has stressed the need to recognize the important efforts of the NAACP in resisting white South African territorial claims over South West Africa (present day Namibia) in the late 1940s and early 1950s. More broadly, her work challenges historians to fully acknowledge the energetic anticolonial efforts of black "moderates" in the United States.[48] Black liberals did not turn their back on South Africa during the early years of the Cold War. Although they would have to adopt a careful and considered approach to avoid being labeled "un-American," African Americans who distanced themselves from the left advanced an anticolonial agenda that forced key government agencies and international organizations to debate and occasionally reassess their ties with the apartheid government.

African American organizers associated with the ACOA and the NCNW played a particularly important role in questioning apartheid on the international stage. The ACOA grew out of the Americans for South African Resistance (AFSAR), an ad hoc committee formed in response to the Defiance Campaign in 1952.[49] Led by the white peace activist and Methodist minister George Houser, who served as the organization's executive director from 1955 to 1981, the ACOA was an interracial organization committed to American solidarity with Africa.[50] There was an important African American presence within the organization, with Martin Luther King, Philip Randolph, James Farmer, Bayard Rustin, and Jackie Robinson all involved with the national committee during the 1950s.[51] The ACOA collected funds for the Defiance Campaign and Treason Trial defendants, picketed the South

African consulate, lobbied the UN in opposition to apartheid, and disseminated information on South African affairs through its publication *Africa Today*.[52] The ACOA leadership also had close ties to anti-apartheid leaders in South Africa, including Chief Albert J. Luthuli, Walter Sisulu, Oliver Tambo, Z. K. Matthews, and Manilal Gandhi.

The NCNW's work in South Africa also followed the moderate, anticommunist model advanced by the ACOA. Founded in 1935 by Mary McLeod Bethune, the NCNW was dedicated to promoting a united voice for black women and, through its membership organizations, racial uplift through community organizing. Historians have often overlooked the global political outlook that informed much of the organization's work.[53] In the postwar period, the NCNW became increasingly interested in African affairs and dedicated much of its organizational and educational program to covering independence movements on the continent. Under the national presidency of Vivian Carter Mason, 1954–1957, the council began to work closely with African women on exchange programs and made a clear effort to expand the organization overseas. One of the NCNW's early black international initiatives was its work with the African Children's Feeding Scheme (ACFS), based in Johannesburg. Sanctioned by the State Department, the NCNW used its government connections to secure contacts with black women throughout Africa and the wider diaspora. Although this organization was not without its shortcomings, its involvement with the ACFS provides an insight into many aspects of black international protest during the early Cold War.

Winning Our Freedoms Together examines the anti-apartheid stance of black moderates alongside the activism of the CAA and the Left more generally. Neither approach to anticolonial organizing was without its limitations. However, all of this work to connect the struggle for black freedom in the United States and South Africa mattered. Although their ideas and arguments often differed, African Americans from across the political spectrum launched pioneering efforts to try to respond to the call of black South Africans. Members from the CAA, NAACP, ACOA, and NCNW were involved in fundraising, picketing, and lobbying efforts that questioned the morality of apartheid rule. They wrote articles and pamphlets, gave speeches, opened up regular networks of communication with anti-apartheid leaders—sometimes even sponsoring their travel to the United States—that helped to internationalize the anti-apartheid struggle. Although their labor did not directly result in the dismantling of apartheid, African Americans were part of a broad and multifaceted effort to isolate South Africa in the global political arena. By repeatedly attempting to offer direct support to African liberation movements and emphasizing the need to end America's political and economic ties with white South Africa, their actions made life difficult for white politicians in ways that that would continue to inform the global anti-apartheid movement beyond the Sharpeville massacre of 1960.[54] This argument is not meant to downplay the disruptive influence that anticommunism had on black politics. Rather, it is designed to shift the focus onto the ways in which black activists with different political visions responded to state power so that the urgent anticolonial calls of African leaders would not go unanswered.

The National Party realized the potential disruption that could be caused by these connections and was forceful in its efforts to stifle international opposition to apartheid. So far, most scholars have been silent when it comes to tracing how South African foreign policy influenced the racial politics of the Cold War. Instead they have focused on how American policymakers viewed the apartheid regime as well as how the U.S. government repeatedly prioritized strategic political, economic, and military interests in southern Africa over the rights of colonized subjects.[55] The actions of the National Party in the international political arena reveal another side to this story, one that makes clear the extent to which anticommunism was bound up with white supremacy at this particular historical moment. The South African government worked hard to present a positive image of apartheid in the United States. Targeting politicians and (white) members of the public, the National Party defended white settler rule by playing on unsubstantiated fears of communist subversion. Anticommunism was used as a political facade to secure investment and trade, and to deflect international criticism of the apartheid system at the United Nations. Even as increased violence damaged South Africa's international reputation, and despite internal divisions within the State Department, the U.S. government resisted calls to put in place any meaningful sanctions against the apartheid regime throughout the 1950s. The South African government's foreign policy initiatives give us insight into the global nature of anticommunism, further complicating our picture of the Cold War as a bilateral conflict between two emergent superpowers vying for global hegemony. The actions of South African diplomats and policymakers highlight how the racial politics of the Cold War played out in different locations, as well as how white settler regimes tried to harness the political rhetoric and strategic aims of the United States to pursue their own domestic agendas. The apartheid government recognized the interrelated nature of the Cold War and the African American freedom struggle, and deliberately played up the threat of the Soviet Union in ways that associated anti-apartheid protest with communist subversion. That 2016 brought long-awaited confirmation of the CIA's involvement in the capture and arrest of Nelson Mandela in 1962 shows the extent to which anticommunism brought the political interests of the U.S. and South African governments into alignment. As Donald Rickard, the former U.S. vice consul in Durban and CIA operative, recalled when he was asked about his role in alerting the South African authorities to Mandela's whereabouts, "He could have incited a war in South Africa. . . . We were teetering on the brink and it had to be stopped, which meant Mandela had to be stopped. And I put a stop to it."[56] Operating transnationally, anticommunist ideology represented a powerful tool that could be used to stifle black protest on both sides of the Atlantic.

Anti-Apartheid and Black International Activism

The South African anti-apartheid campaign was multiracial in character—incorporating African, colored, Indian, and white South Africans opposed to Afrikaner rule. The global anti-apartheid movement was equally diverse. South Africa's Indian population called for sanctions to be brought against the apartheid regime, often in collaboration with the Indian delegation at the United Nations.[57] White activists in the United States also raised awareness of the anti-apartheid struggle. Indeed, the British clergyman Michael Scott was at the forefront of the campaign to prevent the annexation of South West Africa at the UN, while the executive director and perhaps the key driving force behind the ACOA, George Houser, was a white pacifist inspired by the principles of Gandhian nonviolence.[58]

These were vital and politically important contributions that encouraged international opposition to apartheid. However, the primary focus of *Winning Our Freedoms Together* is the symbolic and practical ties that connected the activism of African Americans and black South Africans. The link between the United States and South Africa represents a key historical nexus that has informed how people of African descent have interpreted racism as a global problem. Black activists have long recognized the comparable and interconnected histories of white supremacy in both countries, agitating to bring white settler colonialism into conversation with Jim Crow. Although they acknowledge that different forces shaped racism on either side of the Atlantic, there has been a historical readiness to view apartheid and Jim Crow as being two sides of the same coin—correspondingly immoral systems of control that linked American racism to colonial power in Africa.

In the United States, in the 1940s and 1950s, black leftists and liberals talked about these connections in different ways, with the latter group frequently drawing attention the ways in which racism diverged in both countries by acknowledging the U.S. government's oppositional stance toward legalized segregation.[59] As the African American union and civil rights leader A. Philip Randolph wrote in support of the ACOA 1957 "Declaration of Conscience on South Africa," "Whether in Little Rock, Levittown or Johannesburg, the struggle for racial equality is universal and inexorable. There is, however, a fundamental difference between the struggle at home and that in South Africa. Despite the disgraceful incidents of Little Rock, the laws of this nation—backed by the overwhelming sentiment of the American people and the action of the Federal Government—protect the rights and liberties of all citizens, we are bridging the gap between ideal and practice."[60] Noting that the same could not be said of South Africa, Randolph's statement is broadly representative of the faith that black liberals publicly placed in the transformative character of American democracy. This analysis of racism in the United States and South Africa differed greatly from the anticapitalist and anti-imperialist pronouncements of the black American left. Statements made by Robeson and the CAA that "fascism in South Africa is a direct threat to the struggle to preserve and extend our own democratic rights in America" and the belief that "united support for our brothers' struggle in Africa is an integral part of our task in achieving freedom for all Americans and peace for the world," tied together white supremacy in both countries in an uncompromising manner.[61] In the end, black radicals on both sides of the Atlantic concluded that "Negroes in the Southern States suffer all the viciousness of apartheid."[62]

Throughout the early Cold War, the black left made a series of forthright pronouncements on the links that existed between American capitalism and imperialism, challenging the federal government's narrative that the United States served as the guarantor of freedom and democracy throughout world. In comparison, African American liberals were largely hesitant when it came to questioning U.S. foreign policy. However, this does not mean that they were either unable or unwilling to engage with the antiapartheid struggle. In fact, Randolph's statement on behalf of the ACOA suggests that moderate black leaders continued to view racism as a global issue throughout the early Cold War. Comparing race riots in the United

States—North and South—with the situation in Johannesburg, Randolph symbolically linked the ongoing struggle for racial justice in both countries. Black liberals argued there was no place for the apartheid regime among the nations of the "free world." Although often muted in their criticism of America's diplomatic relationship with South Africa, they continued to advance a politics of black internationalism that saw African liberation and the fight against Jim Crow as being connected.

Black internationalism is a varied and contested political framework. It has primarily been associated with individuals and organizations looking to move beyond the oppressive white nation state, incorporating heterogeneous political agendas such as black nationalism, black bolshevism, Pan-Africanism, and Ethiopianism.[63] As Michael O. West, William G. Martin, and Fanon Che Wilkins assert, "The black international . . . has a single defining characteristic: struggle. [It] is a product of consciousness . . . the conscious interconnection and interlocution of black struggles across man-made and natural boundaries—including the boundaries of nations, empires, continents, oceans, and seas."[64] This has often taken revolutionary or insurgent political forms that have insisted on the global character of the African American struggle.[65] These black organizations and individuals have attempted to overturn the racially exploitative practices of the white nation state by forging transnational anti-imperial alliances dedicated to realizing W. E. B. Du Bois's vision of a "future world" where people of African descent would no longer have to suffer the "insults of Europeans."[66] The revolutionary drive that informed black international politics should not be overlooked or in any way diminished.

Yet, it is also important to recognize that global struggle against racism did not always involve an outright rejection of liberal democracy or the policies of the U.S. government. This was especially true during the early Cold War, when intense state repression meant the global struggle against race discrimination was often articulated in more reformist terms, through efforts to engage with and modify the workings of the nation state in ways that made possible the development of anticolonial alliances between people of African descent. African Americans in the NAACP, NCNW, and ACOA all worked to influence U.S. foreign policy "from the inside" and in the process established connections with black South Africans in ways that continued to emphasize their shared experiences of race discrimination. Even as they sometimes stressed the differences that existed between the United States and South Africa, there remained a clear recognition that racism was a global problem that required a response from black America. This was distinct from, but also related to, more revolutionary strands of black internationalism. African American liberals continued to struggle to engage with Africa through a shared anticolonial agenda, constructing symbols and identifying markers that not only challenged apartheid but also continued to point out the existence of a shared racial identity across borders.

The prospect of civil rights in the United States therefore did not necessarily result in African Americans turning their back on Africa.[67] Black liberals continued to recognize that the global struggle against white supremacy would bolster and enhance their struggle for citizenship in the United States. Although distinct from the black internationalist politics that emerged out of the Pan-African Congress Movement, Garveyism, and black engagements with the Communist International, they engaged with the anti-apartheid movement in South Africa in ways that sought to make colonialism irreconcilable with the politics of the Cold War.[68] Calls for racial equality in the United States and efforts to integrate African Americans into the nation overlapped with, and were informed by, a series of transnational efforts to create anti-racist solidarities beyond the boundaries of the nation. Operating within tightly controlled spaces, African American liberals reimagined the American state in ways that they hoped would lead to civil rights advances in the United States and help create an international climate that was conducive to the demands of the anti-apartheid movement. Through their anti-apartheid activism, they attempted to ensure that the American government lived up to its self-proclaimed anticolonial politics. This approach involved compromises and produced political silences. However, the political strategies they adopted played an important role in promoting an anti-apartheid agenda in America, emphasizing the international character of the struggle against racism and questioning the strategic foreign policy aims of the United States in southern Africa.

At the same time, it is undeniable that the embrace of American liberalism by prominent black leaders added to the political vulnerability of the African American left. Government officials tried to silence radical voices that pointed to how the flow of capital and shared strategic interests bound together race discrimination in both countries. Specifically, white policymakers resented how black leftists on both sides of the Atlantic continued to stress the colonial character of Jim Crow and criticized American imperialism in Africa.

Denouncing American imperialism has always been a dangerous under-taking. However, during the early years of the Cold War, this was an increasingly perilous stance for activists to take. In the United States, in the era of McCarthy and the second Red Scare, a clear and consistent line was drawn connecting those who condemned the American government and suspected communist subversion. This stifled and restricted black international engagements that drew attention to the ways in which American foreign policy strengthened the position of the apartheid regime. Anticommunism sought to narrow the terms of black internationalism, stripping it of its most fervent and radical critiques and attempting to prevent leftists from lending practical support to one another. The perceived need to prevent the spread of communism provided a dubious political framework that was used to justify the dismantling of organizations as well as the harassment, arrest, and imprisonment of black activists who questioned the authority of the state. The fight against communist "subversion" in the United States also provided a model for the apartheid government. Ever attuned to the racial politics of the Cold War, the South African government realized that it was useful to have an alternative and more internationally acceptable ideological justification for apartheid, aside from its unshakable faith in white supremacy.

Given the obstacles they faced, it is easy to present a bleak picture of radical black internationalism during the early Cold War. However, this analysis obscures the ways in which black leftists challenged apartheid from ever more limited and restricted spaces. Indeed, shared experiences of oppression were sometimes used to bring together the struggle against apartheid and Jim Crow. As Eslanda Robeson insisted in her 1952 article "The Cry Freedom Rings Through Africa," "When their leaders are arrested and jailed, exiled and killed, the movements grow in strength and numbers, the protests become more numerous and widespread."[69] For Robeson the fact that the state had to resort to repressive measures provided further evidence that radical black activists were engaged in a correct and morally justifiable struggle. Repression often provided a shared language through which black international alliances could be forged. Black radicals deliberately drew attention to what they saw as similar experiences of state repression, using this as a means to draw further connections between racial practices in South Africa and the United States. These were relatable incidents that provided a stark reminder of how the Cold War could be used to stifle black efforts to challenge white supremacy around the world.

Following the lead of the historian Dayo Gore, who has documented how the radical activism of African American women survived the Red Scare, *Winning Our Freedoms Together* shows that the black left fought to maintain their transnational political vision throughout the 1940s and 1950s.[70] Whether resisting the revocation of passports, responding to the imprisonment of black leaders, or repeatedly pointing to the imperialistic behavior of the United States government in newspapers, pamphlets, speeches, and publications, black radicals continued to place pressure on white politicians and policymakers in the United States and South Africa. The ability of black activists to navigate the repressive politics of the Cold War should not be underestimated. In the United States, a committed group of leftists worked hard to ensure that anti-imperial politics would continue to play an important role in the black freedom struggle throughout the 1950s. Ultimately, the response of the African American left to the early anti-apartheid movement provides an important lens through which to explore how black activists maintained their agency and engaged with and negotiated with state power.

Bringing in anticolonial voices from across the political spectrum provides a valuable insight into the changing nature of black internationalism at this historical moment. This book assesses how activists responded to the repressive politics of the Cold War in ways that underline black political agency and challenges the declension narrative that has often dominated scholarship on the black international outlook of African Americans in this era. Instead, it reveals how the anti-apartheid movement in the United States emerged from challenging circumstances and tightly controlled spaces. It also documents how the political constraints of the Cold War negatively affected transnational black activism as African Americans struggled to combine their domestic political agenda with a broader international commitment to racial justice.[71]

To this end, *Winning Our Freedoms Together* is organized into four parts, each of which examines a different aspect of the multifaceted interconnections between the Cold War, anticommunism, and black international activism. Part I documents how black activists and white governments responded to the racial politics of the Cold War. Chapter 1 provides context to the foreign policy ties that existed between the U.S. government and the National Party, tracing how transnational black networks intersected with and attempted to challenge this mutually beneficial political, military, and economic relationship. Chapter 2 extends this analysis by documenting South African foreign policy responses to the civil rights movement in the

United States, as well as the National Party's engagement with the racial politics of the Cold War. Part II, "Travel, Politics, and Cultural Exchange," explores a range of cross-cultural connections and transnational exchanges that helped mold the relationship between African Americans and black South Africans that existed throughout the 1940s and 1950s. Chapter 3 reconstructs the important transatlantic journeys that brought African Americans and black South Africans into contact with one another, while chapter 4 stresses the importance of culture in maintaining feelings of solidarity between black people in both countries. Part III, "Challenging Anticommunism," and Part IV, "Gender and Anti-Apartheid Politics," use specific case studies to call attention to the challenges and opportunities that shaped anti-apartheid politics between the United States and South Africa. Noting the similarities that existed between the ways in which anticommunism was harnessed to stifle black anticolonial activism in both countries, chapters 5 and 6 document how African Americans and black South Africans responded to state repression by establishing the prison as a key site of black international protest. Finally, chapters 7 and 8 examine the activism of black women on both sides of the Atlantic as well as the gendering of anti-apartheid protest. Documenting the gendered language of Pan-Africanism alongside activities of the National Council of Negro Women and the Federation of South African Women, we see how black women critiqued Pan-Africanist ideology, and questioned masculinist articulations of political leadership within the international anti-apartheid movement in ways that emphasized the political significance of black motherhood.

In December 1954, a message from Paul Robeson was read aloud at the ANC annual conference at the Bantu Social Centre in Durban. His eloquent letter, passed to the gathering by Oliver Tambo, underlined both his embrace of Pan-Africanism and his continued commitment to the struggle against apartheid: "I know that I am ever by your side, that I am deeply proud that you are my brothers and sisters and nephews and nieces—that I sprang from your forbears. We come from a mighty, courageous people, creators of great civilizations in the past, dreamers of new ways of life in our own time and in the future. We shall win our freedoms together. Our folk will have their place in the ranks of those shaping human destiny."[72] The circumstances in which this message was delivered to ANC delegates draws attention to the contradictory forces that determined the relationship between African Americans and the nascent anti-apartheid movement. At the time of the conference, Robeson had been without his passport for four years. Fearful that it would be politically dangerous if he was given the opportunity to criticize Jim Crow and American foreign policy overseas, the State Department continued to prevent Robeson from leaving the United States until 1958. His anticolonial work with the CAA was cited as justification for this measure, preventing Robeson—and many of his allies on the left—from addressing ANC delegates in person. The state-constructed barrier that was placed between African Americans and black South Africans was representative of the extent to which Cold War anticommunism restricted black international opportunities and worked to effectively reinforce white settler rule in Africa. Indeed, in practical terms, Robeson's message of support achieved little. It did not reconfigure the domestic and international forces that opposed the anti-apartheid movement; neither did it alter any laws or usher in a new political moment.

Nevertheless, that this message of support arrived in South Africa at all is politically important. It is significant that black South African leaders demanded this expression of solidarity from Robeson and his allies, and that African nationalists heard these words at a time when the apartheid state was clamping down mercilessly on anti-apartheid protest. This was a fleeting but powerful moment of Pan-African solidarity, an optimistic assertion that the struggle for rights and freedom would be successful on both sides of the Atlantic—a hopeful insistence that the ANC and the Congress Alliance would overthrow apartheid rule and that a free and democratic South Africa would assume its place alongside the free nations of continent. Ultimately, Robeson's statement to the ANC is illustrative of the perseverance of black activists and their belief that the struggles against racism in South Africa and the United States were interrelated. It is suggestive of how black activists responded to state repression, continued to speak truth to power, and found spaces where they could maintain their political agency when confronted with the most testing of circumstances.

On its own, Robeson's transatlantic call to arms may have mattered little. But when considered alongside the array of politically diverse efforts that black Americans employed in order to question the legitimacy of apartheid rule, this statement shows that it was still possible to engage with the politics of black internationalism even when faced with the most testing of circumstances. Although they adopted different strategies and had a different relationship with the U.S. government, African American leftists and liberals gathered their limited resources and formulated a range of strategies that they hoped would contribute to the pariah status of South Africa on the world stage. Evoking the spirit of Robeson's message, *Winning Our Freedoms Together* traces this organizational work, noting the complexity of these transnational black exchanges, as well as their achievements and limitations. Despite the best efforts of government officials, the bonds that connected African Americans and black South Africans ultimately survived the repressive politics of the early Cold War.

Part I   **Cold War**

....

1 South Africa, the United States, and the Racial Politics of the Cold War

In 1953, the Council on African Affairs was accused of subversion under the McCarran Internal Security Act. In response, Paul Robeson, the organization's chairman, posed the following question, which found its way into the pages of the anti-apartheid press in South Africa. "Is it 'subversive,' " Robeson wondered, "not to approve our Government's action of condoning and abetting the oppression of our brothers and sisters in Africa and other lands?"[1] In this case, in the eyes of both the U.S. and South African governments, the answer was a resounding "yes." The CAA's commitment to African freedom, condemnation of American imperialism in Africa, and close ties with anticolonial activists overseas moved the organization beyond what the state defined as acceptable black protest during the early Cold War. Robeson's criticism of the State Department offers an insight into how the governments of the U.S. and South Africa responded to black international criticism during the early Cold War. Transnational black activism was highly suspect; to attempt to establish links with other oppressed people of African descent was often interpreted as sedition; to provide assistance to those subjected to the kinds of racial injustices that you yourself faced could be defined as treason.

Anticommunism worked to place severe restrictions on black internationalism. The exaggerated fear of Soviet subversion was symbolically linked to black protest in ways that limited opportunities to challenge both American racism and South African apartheid. Acutely attuned to the politics of the era, South African policymakers also played a significant, and often overlooked, role in promoting apartheid as a political system that would prevent the spread of communism in southern Africa. How they attempted to do this is telling, shedding further light on the Cold War as a complex and multifaceted conflict that not only shaped debates about race in the United States but around the world. Crucially, African Americans and black South Africans ensured that repressive Cold War policies would not go uncontested. As leftists, like Robeson, denounced the anticommunist connections that existed between the United States and the apartheid regime as imperialistic, black liberals worked to ensure that people of African descent were not excluded from the Cold War rhetoric of freedom and democracy.

The politics of anticommunism was used to stifle black protest on both sides of the Atlantic.[2] In the United States, legislation such as the Smith Act (1940), Mundt-Nixon Bill (1950), McCarran Act (1950), and McCarran-Walter Act (1952) placed limitations on African American protest, making it illegal to advocate for the overthrow of the U.S. government, forcing the registration of communists with the U.S. Office of the Attorney General, and preventing the immigration of politically "undesirable" individuals.[3] As McCarthyism took hold in the early 1950s, the American government actively pursued black activists whom they believed represented foreign and subversive elements within the American nation.[4] Bodies such as the House Un-American Activities Committee (HUAC) were used in conjunction with anticommunist legislation in order to limit and control black protest in the United States.[5]

In South Africa too, the rise to power of the National Party in 1948 meant white supremacist and anticommunist ideology became increasingly intertwined. The Suppression of Communism Act (1950) mirrored anticommunist legislation in the United States in that communist organizing was effectively made illegal. In 1951 the act was extended to enable the banning of individuals or organizations judged to be instigating "any political, industrial, social or economic change in the Union by the promotion of disturbances or disorder."[6] More expansive and repressive than the American legislation on which it was modeled, this extremely broad definition of communist organizing was used to mercilessly suppress anti-apartheid protest. Specifically it enabled the banning of prominent individuals and organizations that challenged government power. All too aware of the problem of selling white supremacy to the world following World War II, the National Party regularly framed the containment of black protest in South Africa in the language of anticommunism. As Prime Minister D. F. Malan outlined his "African Charter," it was essential that Europeans throughout the continent "come to an understanding, an agreement, to suppress communistic activity wherever it appears."[7] As the Cold War began then, the National Party responded by justifying its racial practices as being a key part of its strategy to prevent the spread of communism in what was a strategically important region to the United States.[8]

Historians have largely failed to explore the extent to which the South African government engaged with the racial politics of the Cold War.[9] White politicians in South Africa made a concerted effort to justify their racial policies to those they viewed as potential overseas allies. As a result, National Party officials attempted to sell apartheid to both the U.S. government and the American public, stressing their credentials as an effective bulwark against the spread of communism across southern Africa. The ideological fervor of the Cold War meant that apartheid policymakers would have to be receptive to the way in which white supremacy was viewed and consumed by a global audience. Increasingly concerned with how African American protest would affect how the apartheid state was perceived globally, South African officials based in the United States also monitored the development of the civil rights movement. Compiling detailed reports, South African diplomats configured the United States, and the American South in particular, as a key foreign battleground in the struggle to legitimize apartheid rule in the eyes of the world. As scholars such as Marilyn Lake, Henry Reynolds, and Ann Laura Stoler have noted, state racisms have been produced in exchange, through transnational expressions of white racial solidarity that have been used to obstruct a range of racial reforms.[10] Anticommunism often acted as a conduit for these interactions, a global ideology that helped reinforce and legitimate white supremacy in the United States and South Africa. Global anticommunism shaped the character of black freedom struggles in South Africa and America, increasingly circumscribing and hemming in radical black politics and placing significant obstacles in the way of more moderate movements for racial equality.[11]

Analyzing the global contours of anticommunism and white supremacy is key to understanding the interrelated nature of state power and transnational black activism during the Cold War. Despite the repressive local and global forces they faced, black activists in both countries maintained an extensive global outlook throughout this period. The rapid development of anticolonial nationalism provided new opportunities for activists to establish race as an important international issue. Indeed it was this tension between anticommunist repression and the desire to challenge racism on a global level that characterized black activism in the postwar period. For individuals pushing for black self-determination in the United States and South Africa, the politics of the Cold War and the politics of race were fundamentally interconnected—part of the same overlapping processes and operating simultaneously throughout the black diaspora. Anti-apartheid activists often viewed black America through the lens of the United States' bold Cold War ideological claims. As an article in the anti-apartheid press commented in regard to the lynching of Emmett Till in 1955, "America's diplomats in Asia boast of the absence of racialism in the United States. The Till case has demonstrated to the world the falsity of this claim. Negroes in the Southern States suffer all the viciousness of apartheid."[12] Here the claims of freedom, democracy and racial equality made by American government officials and the vicious murder of the fourteen-year-old Emmett Till for "improperly" addressing a white woman in Mississippi are compared and contrasted.

The international response to the Till case is just one example of how African Americans and black South Africans set out to expose the connections between anticommunism and white supremacy, while challenging the idea that South Africa's ideological opposition to the Soviet Union in any way justified the apartheid system. American racism and South African apartheid could be challenged through the political and ideological debates of the Cold War.[13] Global tensions between Cold War rhetoric and the continuation of racial discrimination provided important international opportunities for black activists in the 1940s and 1950s. In spite of the state clampdown on radical black politics, the Cold War would also produce contradictions, anomalies, and inconsistencies around which black international connections could be launched. It was certainly true that black internationalism was dealt a series of heavy blows by the rise of anticommunism after World War II; however it was often these very setbacks that fostered an increased awareness of the global nature of racism. African Americans regularly addressed the issues of white supremacy in South Africa, explicitly tying this to their own experiences of racism in the United States. The same in reverse was true of anti-apartheid activists in South Africa, where publications such as *Liberation*, *Fighting Talk*, and the *Guardian* provided spaces in which American involvement with Africa could be denounced as imperialistic and where contradictions between Cold War rhetoric and white racism in South Africa were exposed.

"From U.S. Steel to Coca Cola—They're All in South Africa": Black Protest and the U.S.–South Africa Cold War Alliance

During the Cold War the racial politics of the United States and South Africa, each with comparable histories of racial discrimination, became even more closely interconnected. South Africa took its place alongside the United States as one of the nations of the so-called free world, becoming an important political, economic, and ideological ally for the United States against the Soviet Union in Africa.

This strategic alliance, based on free-market capitalism and mutual military interests, was driven by the fact that South Africa, a country rich in raw materials and precious metals, also boasted a vast supply of uranium ore.[14] The American government's pursuit of uranium in order to realize its nuclear weapons–building program, coupled with the need of the South African government to attract funding and investment to make its vast reserves of raw materials profitable, brought both countries together during the early Cold War. Just as it seemed that legalized racial discrimination and segregation was on its way out in the United States, the American government was investing heavily in the apparatus of a rapidly expanding white supremacist state. Although it is perhaps too much of an overstatement to say that U.S. investment in South Africa directly funded apartheid, American trade and loans to South Africa were certainly central in propping up National Party policies and legitimizing the apartheid economy.[15] Both the Truman and the Eisenhower administrations failed to mount any sustained criticism of the apartheid regime. As thousands of black South Africans took to the streets to protest attempts to fully exclude them from the workings of the state and as African Americans simultaneously challenged segregation en masse, millions of U.S. dollars were being directed toward the apartheid state. Indeed, anti-apartheid activists would have to wait until 1958 for the U.S. government to nominally challenge white supremacist rule in South Africa, when the American delegation to the UN voted in favor of a resolution condemning apartheid laws.[16] The Cold War initially helped bring the economic and political objectives of the United States and South Africa increasingly into alignment. Extensive trading links were established, military treaties signed, and loans agreed.[17] As a CAA pamphlet noted in 1953, "From U.S. Steel to Coca Cola—They're All in South Africa."[18]

Following World War II, American corporations invested heavily in South African industry and, in particular, the extraction and processing of raw materials. Overall trade with sub-Saharan Africa between 1945 and 1960 expanded almost sixfold, a statistic that is indicative of the rapidly increasing importance of Africa to the world economy.[19] South Africa quickly became the most important site for U.S. business on the African continent. This economic relationship was highly profitable for both countries and helped to drastically reshape the nature of South African industry. For the National Party the development of the South African economy was of vital importance. Despite South Africa's extensive reserves of valuable raw materials, it desperately needed investment in industrial mechanization in order to turn these natural resources into profit.[20] Although

Britain would remain the largest economic investor in the region, the U.S. presence increased dramatically in the postwar period and briefly, in 1948, American companies traded more with South Africa than their British counterparts. In that same year, foreign investments in the country yielded average profit margins of 42 percent, and while this had fallen to around 35 percent by 1960, profit rates remained substantially higher than in most developed capitalist countries.[21] The South African government did everything it could to encourage foreign investment, signing an agreement with the United States that granted special privileges to American investors, including making them exempt from taxation in the Union of South Africa.[22] Mining companies found South Africa to be particularly profitable. By investing in existing mines or setting up new operations in the region, companies such as Newmont Mining, Morgan, and Kennecott Copper were able to access large quantities of metals and minerals, including gold, diamonds, chrome, manganese, iron, copper, and steel.[23] Between 1946 and 1949 South Africa exported around $1.2 billion worth of gold to the United States, while in 1953, it was estimated that nine out of every ten diamonds sold in the United States were imported from the region.[24] For the National Party this investment greatly contributed to the modernization of South Africa's industrial economy.[25] American investment, trade, and industrial expertise contributed to the practical development of the economy of the apartheid state in the 1940s and 1950s. Motivated by the prospect of large returns on their investments, American businesses, often aided by the U.S. government, helped bolster and develop an economic and social system based on access to cheap black labor.[26] Strategic interests and financial opportunism contributed to the U.S. government's failure to strongly condemn apartheid in the international arena. As U.S. embassy official Joseph Sweeney commented in 1950, "No one in the Department of State paid any serious attention to South Africa except as a source of strategic minerals."[27]

By tracing links between the U.S. government, colonial power, and exploitative business practices in Africa, black activists questioned the meaning of "American Democracy." In the United States, the CAA offered the most scathing critique of ties between American capital and apartheid. From its founding in 1937 in New York, the CAA had been vocal in its support for black self-determination in Africa. The organization focused much of its attention on the racial situation in South Africa until its eventual demise in 1955.[28] As one of the leading figures in the CAA, William Alphaeus Hunton perhaps made the greatest contribution to the fight to expose the economic connections between the United States and the apartheid state. Hunton joined the CAA in 1943 as educational director, giving up his professorship at Howard University the following year in order to move to New York to serve full time in this capacity.[29] With his academic background and his encyclopedic knowledge of the African continent, Hunton led the council's criticism of U.S. economic ties with South Africa. In particular, he emphasized the U.S. government's role in the exploitation of black African labor in ways that fundamentally questioned American foreign policy aims during the early Cold War. In an article that resonated with Sweeney's observation, Hunton highlighted the empty rhetoric of white politicians in both countries, noting that "when these gentlemen speak of preserving their 'free world' they mean maintaining the freedom to exploit other peoples."[30]

Hunton's radical anticapitalist analysis made it clear that American notions of freedom rested on the exploitation of black workers both at home and abroad. The trade in raw materials, justified by both governments as part of a mutually beneficial Cold War economic and strategic alliance, was exposed as a form of imperial exploitation carried out by white businesses in the African continent. The CAA drove home this argument in their response to a proposed U.S. loan to South Africa valued at £375 million (over a billion dollars). As an article in *New Africa* stated, "The question at issue is whether the United States will use its economic powers to further the aims of Anglican-American imperialism, incidentally strengthening the power of the most reactionary segment of the population within South Africa itself."[31] Hunton and the CAA argued that any investment in the South African state and its industry would help shore up white supremacist rule. Extracts from this article were reprinted at length in the anti-apartheid press—a transnational exchange that is indicative of how radicals on both sides of the Atlantic saw American finance as being key to the continuation and extension of racial inequality.[32] In the absence of U.S. government criticism of South Africa, and in recognition of the clear role that American investment was playing in strengthening the apartheid state, the Council on African Affairs emphasized how the global flow of capital underwrote racism in both countries.[33] As Hunton asked in a 1953 pamphlet that documented American business interests in the country, "Can we separate the problem of Jim Crow in America from the problem of Apartheid in South Africa? Can the octopus of racism and fascism be killed by simply cutting off one menacing tentacle? Do profitable investments and strategic raw materials have priority over the freedom, the rights, the very lives of millions of human beings in South Africa whose skins are not white? Again we ask, how much of the blood of South Africa's oppressed black people is on America's own hands?"[34]

Adopting a global analysis of white supremacy, Hunton and the CAA played a key role in raising African American awareness of white supremacy in South Africa while also providing practical and ideological support for anti-apartheid activists throughout the 1940s and 1950s. Through news reports, pamphlets, campaigns, marches, and demonstrations, the council helped establish South Africa as a key site in the black diasporic consciousness of African Americans. In carrying out this work the CAA also raised concerns over the expansion of American power around the world. Ultimately they asked the dangerous question—to what extent was the United States behaving as an imperial power? While the council's questioning of American foreign policy and the corrupting influence of capitalism ultimately ensured the organization's untimely demise, this assertion that America needed to live up to the nation's self-professed values represented an increasingly important resistance strategy for African Americans pushing for racial equality during the Cold War.

Anti-apartheid activists in South Africa often echoed the CAA's insistence that American capitalism and the interests of white settlers were intimately connected in the region. Illustrative of this is an article written by Nelson Mandela titled "A New Menace in Africa," published in *Liberation* magazine in 1958. Noting increased levels of American investment in South Africa, Mandela observed how "American interest in Africa has in recent years grown rapidly. This continent is rich in raw minerals. It produces almost all the world's diamonds, 78 percent of its palm oil, 68 percent of its cocoa, half of its gold, and 22 percent of its copper. . . . It is regarded by the U.S.A. as one of the most important fields of investment."[35] For Mandela, and for many of his associates in the Congress Alliance, U.S. involvement in the South African economy amounted a new form of imperial enterprise on the African continent. He went on to state, "American capital has been sunk into Africa not for the purpose of raising the material standards of its people but in order to exploit them as well as the natural wealth of their continent. This is imperialism in the true sense of the word."[36] Mandela also drew an explicit connection between American investment and the further exploitation of African people through the rush to secure access to raw materials. Denouncing the contradictory nature of American power, he went on to argue that the United States "masquerades as the leader of the so-called free world in the campaign against communism."[37] Figures such as Mandela and Walter Sisulu—alongside African American leftists—were united in exposing the inconsistencies between the Cold War claims of the U.S. and South African governments and the reality of race discrimination in both countries.[38] They saw a direct correlation between the development of the diplomatic and economic ties between both governments and the continued denial of black citizenship rights.

The Cold War, Uranium, and "Mutual Defense"

The pursuit of uranium was perhaps the most important factor driving American political and economic investment in South Africa. By the mid-1950s South Africa had replaced the Belgian Congo as the world's largest producer of uranium ore.[39] It was estimated at the time that South Africa's total uranium reserves amounted to 1.1 billion tons.[40] In addition to this, the U.S. government viewed South Africa as a safer and more secure source for uranium than the Belgian Congo. White-ruled South Africa appeared as a rigidly "pro-West," anticommunist, and relatively stable political ally.[41] Despite mounting black protest, the National Party was growing in strength and made the decision to openly court American friendship. It seemed to the United States that South Africa would provide a steady and uninterrupted supply of uranium for its rapidly expanding nuclear weapons programs.[42]

This relationship was pursued with renewed vigor after the Soviet Union detonated its first nuclear device in September 1949, and by 1950 both nations concluded a contract that guaranteed American access to South Africa's uranium reserves.[43] The trade in uranium initiated the flow of vast sums of money into South Africa.[44] In 1951 both nations reached a loan agreement involving a variety of U.S. banks that secured an initial $10 million for South Africa with an additional revolving credit of $20 million.[45] American companies were also heavily involved in uranium production and it was estimated that by 1953 American businesses had already invested around $120 million in South African uranium mines.[46] The first South African mine capable of extracting uranium was built almost entirely by U.S. money to the tune of £4,500,000 (at the time $12,600,000).[47] By 1953 South Africa's export of radioactive materials were valued at £15,000,000 ($42,000,000), a figure that was expected to more than double by the end of the decade as the newly built refining plants reached full production.[48] The United States officially prohibited South Africa from developing nuclear weaponry out of this agreement, instead framing this relationship in terms of nuclear energy production. However, American technology and investment greatly enhanced South Africa's nuclear capabilities, and by the mid-1970s it was widely acknowledged that the National Party had successfully developed its own nuclear weapons.[49]

The presence of uranium within its borders gave the South African government significant room to maneuver in terms of its relationship with the United States. As long as this relationship appeared consistent with both anticommunism and the Cold War rhetoric of the free world, both parties hoped they could sidestep criticism of their record on race.[50] In a letter to the secretary for External Affairs in Pretoria, for instance, South African embassy officials stressed the continued reluctance of the United States to criticize South Africa too forcefully: "The Americans are fully aware of the Union Government's well-known attitude on domestic jurisdiction as well as on the fact that we continue to be an important source of strategic materials. Moreover, it is becoming increasingly clear to me that the United States authorities attach great importance to the supplies of uranium which they hope to obtain from South Africa."[51] This exchange between embassy officials demonstrates how South African officials believed that their country's central role in manufacturing uranium would ensure respect for its domestic jurisdiction with regard to race. The Cold War and the language of anticommunism therefore provided South Africa with an opportunity to attempt to bridge the gap between its own oppressive racial policies and its claims to be allied with the Western nations of the free world. By making repeated appeals to anticommunist rhetoric, South Africa framed its relationship with the United States as part of a Cold War imperative aimed at Soviet containment in Africa.[52]

The trade in uranium also went hand in hand with American investment in both the South African military and the economic infrastructure of the apartheid state. Of particular importance was Truman's 1949 Mutual Defense Assistance Act (MDAA), which was used to establish military alliances between non-Soviet nations. In a key agreement designed to safeguard U.S. access to the country's uranium supplies, South Africa signed up to the MDAA in 1951. The agreement also guaranteed that the United States would have regular access to the country's strategically important ports, shipping lanes, airstrips, and military bases.[53] This Cold War military alliance was further strengthened by Malan's decision to send a squadron of Mustang fighter jets to aid American forces during the Korean War.[54] The Flying Cheetah squadron, as it was known, would fly more than 12,000 sorties in

Korea between 1950 and 1953.[55] However, perhaps the most striking aspect of the U.S.–South Africa mutual defense agreement was the sale of $112 million worth of U.S. weapons to the South African military in 1952.[56] This trade in arms, framed by both nations as a measure designed to protect against Soviet influence in the region, is a clear example of how the Cold War priorities of the American government helped legitimize the oppressive practices of the apartheid state. The National Party frequently and deliberately conflated anti-apartheid activism with communist subversion, insinuating that one could not exist without the other. However, in reality it was the nation's black majority, not an international communist conspiracy, that the South African government needed to defend itself against.

John Pittman, an African American labor organizer writing for the *Daily Worker*, noted parallels between the military ties that existed between the United States and South Africa and the exploitation of black workers in both countries. Arguing that American capitalism underwrote racist practices in South Africa and the American South, Pittman concluded that "every Atomic Bomb made in the United States will henceforth contain as an essential ingredient the blood and sweat of African workers."[57]

Paul Robeson echoed the anticapitalist pronouncements of Pittman in a speech on South Africa. Tying together racism, global capitalism and Cold War politics Robeson commented, "Jim Crow is the twin brother of Colonial exploitation. And so, whether we realize it or not, we Americans *are* involved in the same struggle with our African brothers and sisters. Their enemy is the same as our enemy. The enemy thinks of Africa in terms of super profits, in terms of strategic war materials like uranium, in terms of bases of manpower for the global war which they are plotting. . . . We Americans therefore have a profound obligation to join hands with our African brothers in the fight for their freedom and our own—in the fight for a world of democracy and peace for all humanity."[58]

For African American radicals such as Pittman and Robeson, the trade in uranium between the United States and South Africa was intimately tied to the racial and capitalist exploitation of the black population of both nations. This view was shared by the radical press in South Africa, which condemned the uranium trade as a manifestation of American imperialism aimed at the "super-exploitation of South Africa's non-white labour" and as a crucial factor that enabled the continuation of white supremacy in the country.[59] Embracing anti-imperial and anticapitalist politics that drew attention to the interrelated workings of black exploitation in both countries, these radical voices represented a timely and uncompromising challenge to America's relationship with apartheid South Africa. Black leftists worked hard to expose the extent to which global capitalist interests fueled racism in ways that resonated with the emergence of the boycott, disinvestment, and sanctions campaigns that underpinned anti-apartheid activism in subsequent decades.

The National Party responded to these criticisms by reasserting its commitment to preventing the spread of communism in southern Africa. In newspaper articles, press releases, and government memoranda, apartheid officials stressed their commitment to fighting communism wherever they found it, both locally and globally. Addressing the assembled media at an event celebrating the start of production at South Africa's first uranium mine, Prime Minister D. F. Malan emphasized his country's willingness to join ranks with the Western powers in the fight against the apparent communist threat: "The source of a considerable quantity of uranium lies in South Africa. We have shown actively in the past that we are determined to make our contribution to the cause of the Western Powers, as instanced by our contribution to the struggle in Korea. We have not hesitated, even to the extent of straining our resources, to make a further contribution to that cause by undertaking the production of uranium on a large scale."[60]

Recognizing America's newfound status of global superpower, Malan was eager to firmly position South Africa as a "friend of the West" in order to attract further foreign investment from abroad. In public declarations of this sort, racism was brushed aside and the focus shifted to the key role South Africa was capable of playing in the global disputes of the Cold War. This was reinforced in a communication between the South African embassy in Washington and Malan's office in Pretoria, concerning the potential purchase of weapons from the United States. The memo stated that the weapons South Africa was hoping to receive would principally be used to fight communism in the region: "It will be recalled that it was previously announced that the policy of the Union Government is to range itself in the event of a war against communism alongside the anti-communistic powers in the defence of Africa and with a view to ensuring that its military forces are properly equipped with modern arms in the Union approached the United States . . . for the procurement of its requirements which cannot be manufactured in this country."[61] It was argued that these arms, far from being used by South Africa's military forces to maintain white racial power, would strengthen nation if they were required to take up arms in a hypothetical conflict with the Soviet Union.

Anticommunism provided a convenient and up-to-date political ideology around which South Africa's domestic racial policies could be justified to the outside world. The United States often framed its engagements with South Africa in these terms, as both the Truman and Eisenhower administrations struggled to bring together America's ideological commitment to freedom and democracy with the practical implications of its foreign policy. How could the United States simultaneously be the leader of the free world while supporting white supremacy in South Africa? And how could the National Party justify its racial policies to a nation in the process of slowly dismantling its own foundations of legalized race discrimination? The obvious answer for both countries in the 1950s was to claim that the relationship, despite its obvious inconsistencies and contradictory nature, was central to the containment of the communist threat in sub-Saharan Africa. On the surface any alliance between the United States, with its self-proclaimed anti-imperial stance, and the white settler regime in South Africa was a blatant contradiction. However, while black international activists never allowed the paradoxical nature of this alliance to fully disappear, anticommunism continued to provide an important and malleable ideology that both governments could use to justify their political relationship.

South African officials were responsive to American foreign policy initiatives and made a concerted effort to justify apartheid to their American allies.[62] Recognizing this helps us to move away from traditional narratives of the Cold War that predominantly focus on Washington and the actions of American policymakers.[63] Accounting for the ways in which South African officials defended apartheid overseas demonstrates how the interrelated histories of the civil rights movement and the Cold War shaped racial politics beyond the United States.[64] The foreign policy initiatives of the National Party also provide an insight into the transnational character of anticommunism.[65]

Anti-Soviet politics did not just shape the contours of the American civil rights movement; they also influenced the ways in which white settler regimes responded to anticolonial movements in Africa. As we shall see in the next chapter, the apartheid government was far from isolationist during the early Cold War and would become increasingly concerned about the effect the African American freedom struggle would have on both its domestic policies and its diplomatic relationship with the West. The National Party therefore invested a considerable amount of time and effort in making its apartheid policies palatable in the United States. Framed in stridently anti-communist terms, the South African government engaged in a sustained propaganda campaign in the United States, designed to stress apartheid's compatibility with America's founding ideals as well as the broad similarities that existed between racial discrimination in South Africa and the United States. White supremacist thought became increasingly intertwined with anticommunist ideology, as the National Party sought to ensure that apartheid would not impinge on its profitable Cold War relationship with the United States.

Selling White Supremacy in the United States

. . . .

After sixteen months as the U.S. ambassador to the Union of South Africa, Waldemar J. Gallman reported back to Washington that on many occasions "South Africans have turned to me and said: 'You can understand our race problem. You have the same problem in the States.'"[1] The idea that the "Negro problem" and "Native problem" were one and the same informed a number of South African foreign policy interactions with the United States. Personally sympathetic to this argument, Gallman noted in a later dispatch that, while white South Africans had "made mistakes and are making mistakes . . . in trying to work out their relations with the Native," this had prompted a great deal of "soul searching" and some "constructive" racial policies. He concluded by informing the State Department that "all that should be remembered before we, in our part of the world, judge them. We in the States should above all remember that the reports we see in our news-papers at home are spotty, with all too often only the more sensational events made available."[2] This last comment gets to the heart of the dilemma facing the National Party regarding its international standing in the 1940s and 1950s. South Africa had an image problem. The practical steps taken to address this issue not only show the lengths the apartheid government went to maintain a positive relationship with the United States, but also speak to the centrality of race in shaping the trajectory of the Cold War.[3] As civil rights victories were won in the United States and anticolonial move-ments challenged political hierarchies in Asia and Africa, apartheid in-creasingly appeared as an anathema to journalists, activists, and politicians around the world. This changing racial landscape threatened the legitimacy of white supremacy in the Cold War world and would eventually force pol-icymakers in America and South Africa to rethink how they justified the political and economic ties that existed between both nations.

The National Party did not shy away from challenging negative portray-als of apartheid. In the United States, South African diplomatic officials mounted a systematic propaganda campaign in order to correct "miscon-ceptions" and present the apartheid system in a positive light.[4] Operating through the South African embassy in Washington and the consul general in New York, apartheid officials played on the political and public sympathies that Gallman articulated in his memo. This involved an extensive monitoring of the American press as well as the literature produced by anti-apartheid groups based in the United States. Public criticisms of apartheid would then be countered by the production and dissemination of materials that presented the National Party as a modernizing force in southern Africa, with apartheid depicted as a benign system designed to promote racial uplift and manage cultural differences within an otherwise "uncivilized" country. South African ambassadors worked hard to bolster this mythical version of the apartheid state, delivering public lectures that promoted white racial solidarity between both nations and yet reasserted the anticommunist credentials of the National Party. This pro-apartheid public relations campaign was further strengthened through the use of American advertising companies, as well as efforts to secure the travel of prominent African Americans willing to speak out in defense of apartheid. This strategy was designed to provide a counternarrative to the nascent international anti-apartheid movement. In the early 1950s, it was not a foregone conclusion that South Africa would become a pariah on the world stage. This white settler state, apartheid policymakers argued, had much to offer the West and the United States in particular. For them, the rhetoric of the Cold War and white supremacist ideology were not necessarily mutually exclusive.

As African American protest intensified in the wake of World War II, South African diplomatic officials spent more and more time monitoring the racial situation in the United States. A voluminous stream of paperwork, reports, memos, and correspondence flowed between Washington, New York, and Pretoria, as South African officials attempted the increasingly difficult task of presenting a positive image of South Africa in the United States.[5] The aim of this public relations effort was to ensure that white supremacy in South Africa was accepted in the United States, if possible among the general public, but most definitely in the eyes of potential American government officials and investors. Embassy officials wrote letters, released statements, published pamphlets, gave lectures, and even sought assistance from professional public relations companies, in an effort to present a more positive picture of South Africa's racial policies to the world. By equating black protest with communist subversion, South African diplomats were engaged in a deliberate and sustained effort to make the survival of white supremacy in southern Africa a Cold War imperative.

The Defiance Campaign illuminated many of the issues and concerns that shaped the South African government's public relations efforts in the United States. As thousands of black South Africans took to the streets in 1952 to engage in widespread civil disobedience, the South African government in Pretoria was faced with unprecedented levels of international criticism.[6] Negative publicity generated by these protests sparked fears among government officials over the future of the U.S.–South African alliance. The South African ambassador, Gerhardus Jooste, expressed concerns that the government's often-violent response to acts of civil disobedience would have negative implications for South Africa on the world stage. As he observed in a letter to the Secretary for External Affairs at the height of the 1952 protests, "There is increasing talk by newspapers in the United States about the possibility of the United States Government bringing pressure to bear on the Union Government to alter its present policies." He concluded by noting that there was a very real possibility that President Truman would be forced to officially rebuke Malan during the Defiance Campaign, "warning him that South African Government policy was inimical to the interests of the Western World."[7] These concerns, brought to the fore by the actions of anti-apartheid activists, caused real fear in Pretoria that negative portrayals of the racial situation in South Africa could damage the nation's political, economic, and military alliance with the United States.

The South African government was also particularly wary about the effect the Defiance Campaign protests would have on its standing in the United Nations. In another cable to Pretoria in 1952, Jooste stated, "I cannot escape the conclusion that the apparently deliberate attempt of the press to represent South Africa as the 'plague spot' in Africa may serve to estrange other Governments with interests in Africa from us—at least temporarily. Should this happen, our position in the United Nations would, of course, become increasingly difficult."[8] These concerns provide an insight into the various issues that shaped South Africa's diplomatic strategies in the United States. Pretoria feared that negative international press coverage of its handling of the Defiance Campaign would leave South Africa isolated both politically and economically. Without the support of its economic backers, Britain and the United States in the UN, South Africa ran the risk of becoming isolated from the Western world. Perversely, the political and economic interests of the apartheid regime were predicated on South Africa maintaining close ties with the nations of the free world.

The South African government believed that if they wanted to continue to attract foreign investment and ward off international criticism, they would have to make the political and economic benefits of apartheid clear to the nation's potential allies. South African embassy officials worked hard to make its racial policies palatable to the United States, challenging what they saw as "vicious" and "biased misrepresentations" of South Africa in the U.S. media.[9] Although criticism of South Africa was by no means uniform or comprehensive throughout the period, newspapers such as the *New York Times* published articles—including "Maligning Malan" and "New Outrage in South Africa"—that were critical of apartheid rule.[10] Judging by the repeated references in departmental communications, South African officials were particularly concerned about *Time* magazine, which printed an exposé on black life under apartheid in June 1950.[11] South Africa's press attaché summed up the potential detrimental impact this article might have by commenting "It is . . . easy to realise what sort of distorted picture must develop in the mind of an editorial writer when he has to base his comment on what he reads in a magazine such as 'Time.' "[12] *Time* and its readership seemed to embody the section of white, middle-class, and politically moderate Americans that the South African government hoped could be persuaded to accept apartheid as a necessary component of America's Cold War strategy in Africa.[13] Prime Minister Johannes Strijdom summed up the National Party's public relations strategy in the United States, stating, "We don't ask people to always agree with us," however, "we would like to see them [white American newspapers] give an objective view of South Africa to the Americans."[14]

African American publications provided the most consistent and vigorous opposition to the oppression of black South Africans. However, their coverage of apartheid was often constrained by the politics of the Cold War.[15] Benjamin E. Mays, president of Morehouse College, argued that racism in South Africa provided perfect conditions for the spread of communism in the region. In contrast to black leftists associated with groups such as the Council on African Affairs, Mays stressed the need for an American model of race relations in South Africa: "Negroes have not turned to communism in the United States mainly because they see hope for their future in this country. We can see tremendous gains. . . . This in part explains the reason that there are so few Negroes in America who are Communists. They see progress. Such progress cannot be seen in South Africa. The future is dark there."[16] For Mays, communism was the inevitable byproduct of race discrimination and white supremacy.

The African American press challenged the anticommunist claims of the National Party and argued instead that the discriminatory nature of apartheid would strengthen Soviet influence in southern Africa.[17] This represented a clear effort to harness the politics of Cold War in order to promote an antiracist agenda both at home and abroad. Anticolonial protests and cases of colonial violence featured prominently in the African American press. However, this reporting often viewed these incidents through an anticommunist lens, a rhetorical shift that appeared to signify that racial injustice in and of itself was no longer enough to justify African American engagements with African anticolonialism.[18] By constructing a narrative of racial progress at home, Mays's criticism of apartheid also bolstered the moral legitimacy of American democracy, downplaying the parallels between racial capitalism in the United States and apartheid in South Africa.[19]

Other articles were perhaps more open about the United States' own unenviable record of race relations when commenting on apartheid in South Africa. Homer Jack, a white American pacifist and social activist, published a series entitled "South Africa Uncensored" in the *Pittsburgh Courier*, arguing that the United States would have to drastically change its ways so that South African racism could be defeated. He concluded that "we Americans, finally, must continue to eradicate racism and Jim Crow here in our democracy so that we can be a more persuasive example to South Africa—and the rest of the world. . . . At present, our shortcomings are powerful Communist propaganda. A race riot in Cicero, or a race killing somewhere in Florida occupies a more prominent place in the newspapers of South Africa than of America."[20] Jack's comments show how much of the mainstream African American press viewed anticolonialism through the lens of the Cold War in southern Africa. By pointing out that race riots and lynching in the United States occupied a "prominent place" in the white South African press, the article implies that unless this was completely eradicated, the United States would never live up to its vision of itself as the self-proclaimed leader of the free world.[21] This approach had its limitations in that it established antiracism as a symbolic byproduct of the Cold War, as opposed to a key human rights issue that had international importance in and of itself. Nevertheless, this strategic reasoning did provide a powerful counternarrative to South Africa's insistence that apartheid rule and anticommunism went hand in hand. Racism was still the enemy throughout the black diaspora, but reporting on Africa in the African American press often gave the impression that discrimination could only be eradicated through anticommunism and U.S. interventionism. On the surface, these warnings about the possible spread of communism in South Africa echoed the official line of the South African government. However, while the National Party attempted to establish racial hierarchies as a necessary part of an anti-Soviet future in South Africa, African American newspapers used the language of anticommunism to argue that racism and Cold War freedom narratives were incompatible. When reporting on South Africa, the mainstream African American press worked to redefine anticommunist politics in the global arena. By challenging apartheid practices and arguing that they were not conducive to the United States' Cold War aims, black Americans suggested that anticommunism should put an end to white supremacy and colonialism on a global scale.

Unsurprisingly, South African government officials in the United States emphasized a more repressive and restrictive version of anticommunism. White supremacist and anticommunist ideologies were folded into each other in South Africa's public relations efforts in the United States. An important part of this strategy were the efforts of embassy officials to encourage National Party sympathizers in America to publicize their pro-apartheid views.[22] This often took the form of letter writing to U.S. publications that defended South Africa from criticism.

Throughout the 1950s the embassy kept a file entitled "Public Reaction to South African Bantu Affairs—Favourable" in which positive American press and public responses toward South Africa were collected.[23] Among these clippings were letters that cast the South African government as a staunch Cold War ally of the United States and argued that any criticism of the National Party's racial policies was the work of communist agitators.[24] Representative of this was a letter in the *American Mercury* claiming that "the propagandists who also fight for the repeal of the McCarran Walter Act are most active in spreading Untruth about our ally at the Cape." Defending the National Party, the letter also noted that articles published in the American press that criticized apartheid were probably "Communist inspired."[25] Government officials would then attempt to contact the authors of these statements so that they could supply them with further material on South Africa designed to assist them in their efforts to defend apartheid in the U.S. print media. As South African press attaché H. Moolman told J. R. Rousseau of Florida, who had written to the *Pensacola Journal* in support of apartheid, "it is heart-warming to have such a staunch and understanding friend of South Africa as yourself striking a blow for one's land wherever the opportunity occurs."[26] Moolman supplemented his thanks with leaflets, pamphlets, and transcripts of speeches that provided "interesting and helpful" information relating to population patterns and "the story of the advance of civilization in South Africa." Copies of the ambassador's speeches, and a pamphlet on the "life and policy of D. F. Malan" were also sent along for good measure. All of the documents emphasized South Africa's anticommunist stance and were intended "for possible presentation to receptive minds in your [Rousseau's] area."[27] It was also noted that the embassy was making "a substantial distribution" of these materials to "editors, commentators, universities, libraries, etc., in the hope that they will draw on this material for reference rather than on the distortions of *Time* and kindred publications."[28]

South African officials tried to mobilize public support for apartheid throughout the United States. They spent a great deal of time and effort identifying and contacting those who they believed were sympathetic to the idea that racial segregation and white political control would nullify subversive influences in the country. Diplomatic staff believed that if they could publically establish South Africa as an anticommunist ally, negative headlines that drew attention to state violence and human rights violations might well be overlooked.

While working in the press office of the consul general in New York, Conrad Norton compiled a detailed report assessing the public relations problems South Africa faced in the United States. The document concludes that the problem of bad publicity was caused by "the fact that, generally speaking, the newspapers of America . . . have very little factual information on which to base their editorial articles."[29] To solve this problem, Norton proposed measures that would form the basis of South Africa's efforts to influence public opinion in the United States. He suggested that more embassy staff be assigned to the task of supplying American newspapers with "complete, factual, background material on South Africa designed specifically for the libraries of newspapers"; that every attempt be made to supplement private newspaper libraries with official government publications in the hope that they would be used as reference materials in any future articles concerning the country; and that all government publications clearly stress "the American angle" when addressing developments in South Africa, particularly when it concerned uranium production.[30]

The propaganda strategies outlined by Norton all emphasized the necessity and benefits of having an anticommunist power in South Africa while counteracting any critique of white supremacist rule. The Union of South Africa Government Information Office based in New York regularly published materials that drew attention to the anticommunist efforts of the apartheid government. In the August 1950 issue of "Facts for Filing," a fact-sheet designed to promote the official state line in the United States, special attention was paid to the passing of the South African Suppression of Communism Act in the same year. The piece boasted that "South Africa was one of the first nations in the world to outlaw communism. Legislation passed by the 1950 session of the Union parliament made the Communist Party "including every branch, section or committee thereof" illegal throughout South Africa and South West Africa."[31] In many ways racial violence in South Africa was the elephant in the room. The National Party hoped that, as long as it could maintain the focus on anticommunism, Americans might be willing to turn a blind eye to white supremacy in South Africa and focus their attention instead on the central role the country played as a bulwark against the Soviet Union's feared encroachment into Africa.

Government efforts to legitimize apartheid during the Cold War were further strengthened by Max Yergan's tour of South Africa in 1952. After controversially breaking from the CAA in 1948, Yergan aligned himself with the U.S. government and would go on to publicly avow a strict anticommunist stance throughout the remainder of the Cold War.[32] His past political credentials made his turn to the right surprising. Yergan had cofounded the CAA on returning from South Africa in 1937, where he had been a close associate of prominent ANC leaders Z. K. and Frieda Matthews at Fort Hare University.[33] Up until 1948, he had been at the forefront of the CAA's efforts to publicize and challenge race discrimination in South Africa, using his contacts in the country to strengthen the organization's ties to the ANC.[34] As a committed Browderite, Yergan watched with dismay as William Z. Foster took control of the Communist Party USA in 1945, and, finding himself increasingly marginalized within the party, agreed to speak to the FBI about his communist associates in August 1948.[35]

After his split from the CAA Yergan used his new anticommunist credentials to secure travel to Africa in 1949, 1952, and 1953.[36] On his second trip, Yergan was given permission to enter South Africa. At this time it was common for South African External Affairs to consult with the FBI in order to prevent "undesirables" from traveling between the countries and to determine "whether applicants for visas for the Union had engaged in subversive activities and whether their political sympathies were communistic."[37] After undergoing state vetting, Yergan was initially refused entry to South Africa in 1950 and had to reapply for a visa.[38] In response he worked to actively ingratiate himself with the South African government. In a meeting with a representative from the South African consul general in New York, Yergan provided information on his former colleagues in the CAA and named union organizer Solly Sachs as a key contact of the organization in South Africa.[39] He would later denounce the CAA's South Africa Relief Fund as communistic and provided evidence that South Africa's *Guardian* newspaper received information and support from known communists in the United States.[40] In order to confirm Yergan's claims, South African government officials wrote to the U.S. secretary of state, who duly informed them that his new anticommunist credentials were genuine.[41] In the light of this information Ambassador Jooste, reporting to Pretoria on the suitability of Yergan's application for a South African travel visa in 1952, stated that "there is . . . no reason to believe that Dr. Yergan is not sincerely honest in what he professes and it may well be that refusal to grant him a visa would expose our attitude . . . and lose us the support of a potentially strong ally in the sphere of good race relations. In these circumstances I transmit his application for favourable consideration."[42] Despite an initial wariness of his political past, the state-sanctioned visit of Yergan—an African American who was openly committed to preventing the spread of communism in South Africa—represented a potential propaganda coup for the National Party.[43]

Confidential arrangements were made to facilitate Yergan's trip. With the onset of the Defiance Campaign, the South African government now viewed the trip as being particularly pressing as officials worked to counteract negative overseas coverage of the country's racial policies. Reflecting on a personal meeting with Yergan, Jooste observed that "he feels that it is his mission as a Negro of standing to influence other non-white leaders in the direction of seeking their own way of advancement by way of consultation and goodwill rather than by way of aggressive demands." Expanding on this he added, "At the same time he feels he has had sufficient first-hand experience of the evils of Communism to warn Native leaders of its deadly implications."[44] It was believed that a visit by Yergan had the potential to undermine anti-apartheid protests in both South Africa and the United States. Yergan would represent a model of black anticommunist restraint, averse to radical influences and wary of making antagonistic demands.

South African officials also hoped that a visit by Yergan could have potentially beneficial effects in terms of maintaining foreign investment in the country. Yergan's connections to big business were known to Jooste, who remarked, "I understand, in confidence, that his trip is to a large extent sponsored by certain American and French investment interests who are feeling concern over the possible spread of Communism over African territories."[45] Yergan himself confirmed this role, observing that, "I freely agree that every individual who represents the American Government, American business, philanthropic or missionary interests, should be effective spokesmen for the democratic, free world point of view, and therefore an equally effective opponent of the Communistic propaganda and Communist practices in Africa."[46]

For the South African government and Yergan, anticommunism and the development of American interests in Africa went hand in hand. Because Yergan was a prominent African American leader and newly anointed adversary of global communism, it was hoped that his trip to South Africa could be used to allay the fears of potential American investors while acting as a racial signpost that could be used to dismiss criticism of South African racism. In striking contrast to black leaders critical of American and South African government policies, whose mobility was restricted through arrest, imprisonment, banning, and blacklisting, as well as the refusal to issue them passports and visas, Yergan's new-found anticommunist credentials meant he was free to move between both countries.

His trip to South Africa received condemnation from black leaders in South Africa. Noting that the timing of the visit coincided with the intensification of the Defiance Campaign protests, Nelson Mandela commented, "I was struck with the fact that Mr. Yergan made no attempt to meet the Non-European leaders and discuss the Defiance Campaign with them directly." He added that Yergan "said not a word of condemnation for the Malan Government which, from a man professing to be active in his people's struggles in his country, seemed to us very strange. His warning to us in our activities sounded far more like the warnings of a United States government spokesman than from a Negro participating in any movement for Negro rights."[47]

Black activists in the ANC were fully aware of the government reasoning that facilitated Yergan's visit and saw it as a direct attempt to undermine the legitimacy of black protest in South Africa. Yergan's trip was also beyond the pale for the majority of African Americans and received widespread criticism from across the U.S. political spectrum. From a moderate stance, Walter White of the NAACP commented on the visit, "I know that Dr. Yergan's break with the Communists was a traumatic experience and that he has been basely and bitterly slandered by his former associates. But this is no excuse for his loss of perspective or for his equating of anticommunism with support of the advocates of 'white supremacy.'"[48]

Attracting dismay from black leaders in the United States and South Africa, Yergan's 1952 tour provides evidence of how the U.S. and South African governments collaborated in order to limit black international activism. As David Anthony and Glenda Elizabeth Gilmore have pointed out, Yergan was a complex character whose betrayal of his former comrades was, at least in part, the result of intense governmental pressure.[49] Yergan had made the "terrible, disgusting mistake" of extorting money from a former lover, which the FBI then used to threaten him with charges of extortion unless he agreed to testify against suspected subversives.[50] As Gilmore concludes, by the late 1940s, "the FBI owned Max Yergan."[51] Yergan's tour of South Africa and the extensive efforts of the U.S. and South African governments to ensure he publically endorsed their policies are illustrative of the way in which anticommunism and white supremacy operated across national borders during the Cold War.

Similar collaboration between the U.S. and South African governments resulted in William Nkomo's arrival in the United States in 1959. A founder of the ANC–Youth League, Nkomo had turned his back on revolutionary politics in the early 1950s.[52] When visiting the United States as part of the Moral Re-Armament Summit Strategy Conference held Michigan in 1959, Nkomo stated, "World Communism is determined to keep the pot boiling in Africa and to exploit any divisions to separate us from Europe and America. . . . America with the right ideology can become the leader of the free world, the hope and salvation of mankind."[53] Nkomo, like Yergan, traveled across the Atlantic to vocally oppose communism and argue that segregation was a workable strategy that could reduce racial conflict in South Africa. The travels of black anticommunists were highly symbolic propaganda tools that helped counteract international criticism of South Africa. Through diplomatic cooperation the U.S. and South African governments sought to control black mobility in ways that cast their Cold War relationship in a positive light.

South African diplomats also worked hard to strengthen the bonds of friendship between both countries, making regular public appearances designed to promote South Africa in the United States. In 1947, the South African press attaché gave a lecture as part of the Toward a Better World series at the Museum of Natural History in New York extolling the virtues of modern South Africa. The event attracted around five hundred high school pupils (and uninvited members of the CAA).[54] A later speech, delivered by Ambassador Harry T. Andrews to members of the English-Speaking Union (ESU) in New York, gives a sense of the arguments put forward at these public events. Reflecting the elitist, colonial-style aims of the ESU, the talk was the fifth in a series of lectures by ambassadors from British Commonwealth nations and is largely representative of the embassy's public relations efforts.[55] Andrews, who was also South Africa's permanent representative to the United Nations, focused his lengthy address on the history of South Africa and its parallels with the development of the United States. Throughout his speech he made explicit connections between the development of white supremacy in both national contexts.[56] Referring to the Union of South Africa as "the other U.S.A.," Andrews opened his remarks by commenting:

> If one takes even only a cursory glance at the history of our two countries, it is surprising how many coincidences, how many parallels there are in the story of our respective beginnings and in our story along the pioneering path of progress and civilisation. We are indeed both *pioneering peoples*, and the problems, experiences and perils of the early settlement of our forefathers in what were then uncivilized lands, among wild and war-like savages, were very similar in their nature. Perhaps in that very fact lies the fundamental reason why Americans and South Africans have so many characteristics in common, and why the South African way of life is today so comparable in so many respects to your own American way of life. For it is a significant and noteworthy fact that the people and nations who came from Europe to settle and make new life on this American Continent, were almost exactly the same stocks as have basically gone into the making of our present-day South African nation.[57]

Addressing the largely white audience of American elites, Andrews argued that there are racial ties that bind the United States and South Africa together.[58] He viewed the frontier mentality of its pioneering founders, who risked life and limb to bring civilization to barbaric lands, as proof that white Americans and South Africans shared a common identity. Passing over the ethnic diversity of the first European settlers to arrive in both America and South Africa, Andrews forged a shared racial identity for whites on both sides of the Atlantic divide. Later in the address he emphasized the Dutch influence on the development of both regions, raising the role of the Dutch East India Companies in establishing both New Netherland and the Cape Colony in the seventeenth century.[59] The speech also challenged negative portrayals of South Africa in the American media, as well as dismissing the criticism of anti-apartheid activists. While claiming that

South Africa's "native policy" was guided by the principles of "trusteeship," "Christianity," and "justice,"[60] Andrews asked his audience to "bear in mind, when you read your newspapers or listen to the radio, on matters relating to South Africa and events in South Africa, that the people about whom you are reading, are most similar in nature and character to yourselves—that they came from much the same national stock."[61]

Conflating ideas of race and nation, Andrews argued that it was the shared responsibility of whites to bring civilization to "unruly" lands full of "savage" natives. Reiterating this point, he stated, "Just as America came to be called the 'New World of the West,' so South Africa in later years came to be described as 'the New World of the South.'"[62] In effect Andrews proposed an alliance between the United States and South Africa based on notions of white racial supremacy and Western civilization. He stressed that the "bonds of friendship" that had always tied both countries together "must be maintained and expanded in these post war years."[63] For Andrews it was their shared racial histories, based around white dominance over blacks and myths of the civilizing mission, that connected the United States and South Africa in the contemporary Cold War world.

As racial violence escalated in South Africa, the apartheid government stepped up its efforts to defend its policies in the United States. Recognizing that legalized racial segregation was coming under increasing pressure, officials enlisted the assistance of public relations companies to promote South Africa among sympathetic whites. Reports were requested and compiled by the Institute of Motivational Research in New York, led by pioneering psychologist and marketing expert Ernest Dichter, who claimed his organization could, through psychometric testing and psychological research, change the image of South Africa in the average American mind.[64] South African officials also met with Kenneth Buchanan of Julius Klein Public Relations, with the view that the company would work toward counteracting negative press coverage of South Africa's racial policies. It was proposed that Julius Klein, who also handled PR for the governments of West Germany and Panama, would work for the South African government to "provide the American communications media with accurate information about the Union of South Africa and to promptly correct false rumors, misconceptions, misinformation and biased information which may come from improper sources."[65] The firm also claimed that it would lobby to maintain and increase private American investment in South Africa, expand tourism, and promote good will for the country within the American government. South Africa would be established as a key American ally through an "intensive program" that would "bring home to important leaders of American opinion the urgency of a stable and secure Government in South Africa, as a bulwark in the West's defences against Soviet penetration and entrapment of the African continent."[66] Anticommunist ideology framed how white supremacy in South Africa was marketed in the United States. However, as the Cold War and black protest developed, shaping the political landscapes of both countries, it would become increasingly difficult for the South African government to argue that apartheid strengthened America's strategic interests in Africa.

The brutality and violence exhibited by the South African state compromised the efforts of the state to present apartheid as a benign system designed to promote the development of African "Natives." In reviewing the challenges faced by the South African diplomatic services during the Defiance Campaign, Ambassador Jooste surmised

> The Embassy is doing what it can here in order to combat this misrepresentation of and hostile comment upon developments in South Africa. . . . Lectures given by the Press Attaché and myself on South African racial and economic affairs have been well received, but our audiences, while admittedly important, necessarily constitute a very limited section of the population and our efforts, cannot therefore, offset the effects of the flood of criticism to which the Union Government has recently been subjected. Our only hope is to persevere in our efforts and endeavour to ride out the present storm.[67]

Anti-apartheid activism disrupted the public diplomacy strategies of the South African government. Black activists forced South African policymakers to rethink how they framed their diplomatic relationship with the United States and were successful in bringing about a tenser, and occasionally confrontational, relationship between the apartheid regime and the American government.[68] Indeed, the United States broke from its usual stance of refusing to criticize South Africa at the UN by endorsing a watered-down General Assembly resolution in October 1958 that expressed "regret and concern" over South Africa's failure to guarantee the "fundamental freedoms" outlined in Article 56 of the United Nations Charter.[69] State Department officials were worried that apartheid repression would have the effect of increasing communist influence within African nationalist movements while further damaging the U.S. government's reputation with newly independent nations in Asia and Africa.[70] This is not to say that the strategic Cold War alliance between both nations was damaged beyond repair. Again, American criticism of apartheid was moderate and there appeared to be no genuine desire to completely cut political, economic, and military ties with Pretoria.[71] Nevertheless, black protest in South Africa and the United States guaranteed that calls for racial equality and black self-determination would continue to play an important role in the international politics of the early Cold War. In response, Union representatives at the embassy and consul general developed a more hostile stance when it came to their public relations strategy in the United States. Through the monitoring of the press (both black and white) and of civil rights protests across America, South African officials began to compile detailed reports on major racial flashpoints in the United States in the 1950s. The aim was to deflect criticism of South Africa's racial policies by exposing the contradictions that existed between America's foreign and domestic policies when it came to race.

Lessons in Humility: South African Monitoring of the Civil Rights Movement

The anticipated march toward race equality in the United States and escalating racial violence in South Africa had a profound effect on the nature of the Cold War alliance between both states. As the historian Jason Parker points out, the mid-1950s marked a sea change in international racial and colonial affairs. The 1955 Bandung Conference, which brought together representatives from twenty-nine African and Asian nations united in their calls for self-determination, and the emergence of the nonaligned movement forced policymakers to reassess the effects that decolonization was having on American foreign policy during the early Cold War. When combined with developments in the civil rights movement in the aftermath of the *Brown* decision, the Bandung gathering clearly demonstrated how a rhetorical embrace of an antiracist and anticolonial agenda could benefit American efforts to expand its political and economic influence in the world.[72] While this certainly did not result in a new and enlightened foreign policy approach toward Africa, these landmark events raised ideological questions over the place of apartheid in the era of decolonization. Responding to this apparent divergence in the racial politics of both countries, South African policymakers remolded their public relations campaign to suggest that it would be contradictory for the American government to condemn white supremacy overseas when racism was still alive and well in the United States.

South African officials took a keen interest in American race relations throughout this period, extensively monitoring black protest and noting the often-violent public responses to civil rights organizing. Evidence of race discrimination was collected and analyzed by officials working at South African diplomatic missions in the United States. The South African state reasoned that if it was to be condemned internationally for its racial attitudes, the United States should also be held to account for its own dismally poor racial record. The thinking behind this monitoring of American race relations was summed up by South African ambassador Wentzel C. Du Plessis, who commented, "It is time that events within their own country should be a lesson to the Americans in the grace of humility when expecting other countries to achieve what they themselves have difficulty in doing."[73] National Party representatives argued that any criticism of South Africa should be considered alongside America's inability, both past and present, to deal with racial conflict within its own borders. By drawing attention to racism in the United States, the South African government sought to establish white supremacy as an inevitable, and indeed excusable, feature of multiracial societies. Although criticizing the United States was a risky diplomatic strategy, it was driven by the desire of South African policymakers to draw attention to how both countries were united by a longstanding commitment to white supremacist politics.

The U.S. government was increasingly aware that the fight against Soviet totalitarianism abroad would be undermined by disturbances at home.[74] In this context, supporters of black self-determination and white supremacy criticized the United States in order to push their different ideological agendas. Mary L. Dudziak, while deliberately stopping short of stating that the politics of the Cold War were actively conducive to the civil rights movement, argues that America's need to claim the moral high ground in the conflict with the Soviet Union provided an "imperative for social change" for the U.S. government.[75] However, the high ideals expressed by the United States during the Cold War were appropriated by oppressed peoples around the world pushing for their own political freedom. In South Africa, the anti-apartheid press published articles such as "Race Terrorism against U.S. Negroes: Washington Charged with Genocide" and "Legal Lynching in United States: Six Negroes Sentenced to Death." These reports, documenting in detail cases of racial violence in the American South, became a means of pressuring the United States into condemning white supremacy at home and abroad.[76] International bodies and gatherings, such as the UN and Bandung, also made it possible for the newly independent nations of Africa and Asia to internationally criticize the continued presence of racial prejudice in the United States.[77] By drawing attention to racial abuses throughout the diaspora black activists challenged America's own perceptions of its role in the Cold War, arguing that racism was incompatible with its global agenda as leader of the free world.[78] Anticolonial activists made just this point at the 1958 All-African People's Conference held in Ghana. Attended by black leaders from across Africa and the wider diaspora, this Pan-African gathering was representative of the new global political presence of independent Africa nations.[79] The conference called for black self-government in Africa and an end to race discrimination throughout the world. In regard to South Africa, conference representatives recommended a boycott of all Union products and the establishment of a committee to aid oppressed African peoples.[80] Anticolonialism and decolonization meant that the U.S. government was under great political pressure to tackle white supremacy within its borders. The fear that newly independent nations would ally themselves with the Soviet Union meant that the American government had to be receptive to the demands of black activists from across the political spectrum.

For the National Party, with its grand social and economic plans, decolonization represented a serious threat. As the South African ambassador to the United States commented on the boycott of South African goods proposed at the All-African People's Conference, "If ever anybody were foolish enough to implement it, [it] could indeed strike a serious blow to South Africa's economy."[81] Fearful of the effect that these new shifts in international politics would have on their political and economic alliances with the wider world, the South African government began to criticize the United States for preaching the need for democracy abroad while failing to uphold these ideals at home. Cases that caused racial strife, such as Autherine Lucy's admission to the University of Alabama and the Little Rock crisis, were catalogued and then put to use by South African officials in order to shield the apartheid government from external interference in its domestic affairs.[82]

By 1959, as South Africa faced unprecedented levels of international criticism, the Department of External Affairs sent out a memo to its foreign missions stressing on the need to "adopt a more aggressive attitude toward our detractors by giving publicity to their own shortcomings."[83] It formally instructed embassy officials to ensure that they collected any materials that showed critics of the Union in a negative light and that "could be used effectively by Union delegations to the United Nations."[84] The type of material specifically asked for by the Department of External Affairs included "discriminatory practices in regard to race, colour, class, caste, religion, politics or sex. Restrictions or limitation on the freedom of movement, of speech, of religion, of political expression etc. In this regard information on the lengthy incarceration without specific charges or trial would be of interest. . . . Friction between racial groups . . . [and] the economic, political and social conditions in which lower income groups, and/or unfavoured racial groups live."[85] As thousands were bundled into jail cells for violating apartheid laws, African Americans continued to face racial violence throughout the country and in the South in particular. White supremacy was a global ideology, and in the United States many white South Africans still thought they could see at least part of their own reflection. This internal memo goes some way toward clarifying the thinking behind South Africa's attempts to manage international criticism of its racial practices. By outlining the continued existence of racism in the United States, the South African government made it hard for the U.S. government to criticize apartheid. The hope was that by documenting the prevalence of racial violence in its own back yard, America would find it increasingly difficult to fully promote a nonracial, truly anticolonial, foreign policy.

Segregation and violence against African Americans in the 1940s and 1950s provided ammunition for the South African government's propaganda efforts in the United States. Through the State Information Service in South Africa and the Government Information Office in New York, the National Party used civil rights clashes to publicly defend its own record of race discrimination.[86] If the United States could not achieve racial harmony, then South Africa, where whites were in the minority, could not be expected to accomplish the same task. As a South African representative commented after being questioned about apartheid by the American undersecretary of state and secretary of the treasury, "You're criticised for your Negro policies; we for our Native policies. . . . It is as if you had five hundred million Negroes in the States."[87]

American policymakers were concerned that this line of attack might yield results. As the U.S. chargé d'affaires William Maddox noted in 1957, "It would be difficult to establish South Africa as the only country in the world where, in some form or another, or by one authority or another, segregation is sanctioned." With the Little Rock crisis still fresh in the public's memory, he reminded Washington that "in this respect, we ourselves are not without fault. For although segregation is contrary to the law and policy of our national government, we remain internationally responsible under the Human Rights Charter for the delinquencies of state and local governments."[88] As the civil rights movement laid bare the virulent nature of segregation and white supremacy in the United States to a global audience, some policymakers acknowledged that America might in fact have more in common with apartheid South Africa than they would like to admit.

In response, officials at the South African embassy worked hard to draw attention the hypocritical nature of American criticism of racism overseas. In an aide-mémoire, press attaché J. J. Coetzee compiled information he hoped would expose the similarities between race relations in the United States and South Africa, stating that "in selecting the material I have tried to show that a pattern of race relations exists in America which closely corresponds to the somewhat distorted (indeed, almost wishful) picture of South African race relations which critics in America have tried to sketch. This seems to me to point to a basic human psychological motivation of South Africa's critics to distract attention from personal embarrassment."[89] Coetzee hoped, by documenting similarities between race discrimination in both countries, to force the United States to deal with its own racial affairs instead of criticizing the policies of other nations. His report, which incorporated numerous U.S. press clippings and quoted extensively from NAACP sources, concluded that "general race prejudices . . . Negro poverty and squalor, crime, police brutality, violence, mounting tension in Negro slums adjoining privileged White residential areas, and growing Negro nationalism hostile to White Supremacy" were all factors present in race relations in the United States.[90] When analyzing American race relations, National Party officials believed that they could see many of the same discriminatory practices that they themselves were criticized for maintaining in South Africa. The United States and South Africa represented two sides of the same coin.

Of course, black activists on both sides of the Atlantic had long since come to the same conclusion. In South Africa the struggle for civil rights in the United States took on an almost heroic significance as black South Africans looked abroad for events that would give momentum to their own movement. In much the same way that the South African Defiance Campaign, Freedom Charter, women's marches, and bus boycotts inspired and informed African American protest, the civil rights movement provided inspiration for black activists in South Africa who saw themselves as being involved in essentially the same struggle but on different sides of the Atlantic.

This shared racial consciousness can be clearly seen in an article by ANC activist and educator Alfred Hutchinson. Writing in *Fighting Talk*, a key outlet for the Congress Alliance, Hutchinson penned an open letter to Autherine Lucy, the first black student to attend the University of Alabama in 1956. Lucy was hounded out of the institution by segregationists shortly after her graduate course in library science began. Opening the letter with "Dear Miss Lucy," Hutchinson drew clear comparisons between segregation in the United States and apartheid in South Africa. Focusing on black education, he observed that her treatment "could have happened in this race-benighted country—at any of the colour-bar universities—Pretoria, Stellenbosch, Potchefstroom."[91] However, Lucy's bravery and commitment to attaining a "first-rate" education was, Hutchinson argued, a source of pride and inspiration for black South Africans striving to achieve the same goal. He ended his letter on a powerful and optimistic note:

> But there is no cause for despair. Perhaps that is why this letter is not written to console you. And, if I may, it is meant to exhort you and the youth of the United States to take up the fight for equality with redoubled effort; it is written to say that we are with you every inch of the road—thorny though it be. . . . There are brave men and women in our countries. . . . The brave wind of freedom is blowing—the wind which must destroy the house built on the shifting sands of inequality, hatred, suspicion and prejudice. Everywhere new suns are rising and, comrade-in-arms, our dawn cannot be far away.[92]

Just as segregation in the United States provided the National Party with a readymade defense for its own racist practices, the struggle of African Americans for civil rights also provided inspiration for black South Africans resisting apartheid. For South African officials the Lucy affair was not a sign that white supremacy was on its way out in the United States. Instead, this flashpoint provided further evidence of the deep-seated racial tensions that continued to shape American society. Reflecting on the event Ambassador Holloway observed that "most of us are aware of a tendency in American diplomacy and indeed in American thinking as a whole, particularly manifest in recent years, to regard the United States as a country which is well on the way to surmounting its major problems and which is therefore entitled to assume the role of doctor to the world's moral ills. . . . It must now be clear to many thinking Americans that deep-seated social conflicts have lain hidden under the gloss of prosperity and that these conflicts will continue to plague the country for many years to come."[93]

For both black activists and white supremacists alike, racial politics in the United States and South Africa were intimately connected. The political, economic, and military ties that brought both nations together during the early Cold War meant that the racial futures of both nations were also bound up with one another. White supremacist thought operated globally and often relied on cross-cultural interactions in order to further legitimize its existence. It is clear apartheid policymakers realized at an early stage that apartheid was a globally attuned system which could either be weakened or reinforced, depending on the international political climate.

From the mid-1950s onward, the National Party generally reacted with enthusiasm whenever American race relations seemed to be turning sour. This partisan stance comes through in many of the embassy reports monitoring the civil rights movement. When examining calls for desegregation, John Edward Holloway, South Africa's ambassador between 1954 and 1956, expressed sympathy for southern segregationists and their firm opposition to legalized race equality. The language used in these reports evokes memories of the Civil War and the Confederate cause. Pretoria often viewed American race relations through the lens of Southern distinctiveness, arguing that events in the region were especially significant as they exposed the historical depth of public hostility toward race equality. Predicting widespread "violence and disorder" if integration were to be thrust on southerners "bred" on generations of white supremacy, Holloway stated, "Socially and economically, racial segregation in this region has withstood the pressure of the years, and the Yankee propaganda from the north, and the question of integration, which strikes at the heart of the Southern tradition, will inevitably lay bare passions which are not far below the surface."[94]

Holloway's reports to Pretoria were overtly hostile toward civil rights activists and the federal government. The use of the phrase "Yankee propaganda" shows a deep cultural understanding of America's racial past and deliberately evokes the issue of states' rights.[95] Indeed, government officials seemed to take delight in the prospect of increased racial conflict in the United States. As Holloway claimed in the aftermath of the *Brown* ruling, "secessionist feeling is stronger in some parts of the deep South than before the Civil War," adding that white southerners "will resist school integration to the very last and with all the means at their disposal."[96] He continued to hint at the willingness to break away from the North, stating that "for many years at least six States and probably more will stand in angry discord with the rest of the Union. . . . The Federal Government must then use the force at its disposal or permit a situation in which the highest court of the land is defied."[97] Divisions over race in the United States were a source of hope for those supportive of apartheid in South Africa. In their analysis of the movement toward desegregation in the United States, South African diplomats took on the role of honorary Confederates as they worked to prevent the American government from openly criticizing apartheid in the international political arena.

The National Party tried to predict as best it could the global implications that might follow the attainment of civil rights for African Americans. In its view this could only lead to increased racial tension and ultimately violence that would further undermine America's moral position on the world stage. The intensification of racial violence and black protest in the United States gave the South African government more room to maneuver in terms of its foreign policy. America's failure to address racial inequality was used to justify the continuation of white supremacy in South Africa. As long as the United States continued to struggle to occupy the moral high ground with regard to race, there appeared to be little reason to end the mutually profitable relationship that existed between the United States and South Africa during the Cold War. Both nations were therefore bound together by their racial problems as well as their strategic Cold War concerns.

While the South African government's reporting of the civil rights movement was comprehensive, it would be the events at Little Rock Central High School in 1957 that generated the most sustained analysis and paperwork.[98] The violence and intimidation on display in Arkansas generated unprecedented levels of international press coverage.[99] The Little Rock crisis ensured that the United States' own unenviable racial record was laid bare for all to see as the heroic struggle of, and violent reaction to, the black freedom movement resonated around the world.[100] The U.S. government's apparent inability to deal with racial violence within its own borders significantly undermined America's reputation overseas.[101] As angry white crowds gathered and the U.S. military had to be called in so that nine black students could attend Little Rock Central High School, the South African government busied itself by drafting a series of detailed reports that came to inform the way in which it responded to international criticism of its own racial policies and envisioned its Cold War alliance with the United States. A flurry of memos and reports traveled between South African officials abroad and in Pretoria, all geared toward assessing how Little Rock would shape American race relations.

Unsurprisingly, the South African government positioned itself firmly on the side of the American segregationists at Little Rock. Mirroring similar debates taking place in South Africa, government reports expressed support for the separation of the races in schools. Ambassador Wentzel C. Du Plessis expressed grave concern that white children would be denied an adequate education as long as the government's desegregation efforts continued. He predicted that many high school seniors would find it impossible to go on to college, adding that thousands of white pupils would "not be able to make up these deficiencies in their education."[102] Showing no concern for the educational development of African American students, Du Plessis argued "their education can be provided for quite easily" under the existing system. Echoing the concerns of white conservatives in America, who predicted that white teachers would leave the public school system in droves, he stressed that the collapse of the Southern education system would generate "a new dimension to racial feeling and discord" in the United States.[103] The debates surrounding the Little Rock crisis resonated clearly with many of the issues faced by apartheid policymakers. Access to quality education was a privilege reserved for whites in South Africa and the period witnessed a determined effort by the National Party to remove funding from African schools and to limit black education to labor and industrial training.[104] Little Rock and the broader effort to integrate American schools ostensibly challenged the apartheid government's ideological insistence that certain educational privileges should be reserved for whites.[105]

Ultimately though, Little Rock provided a lesson for the National Party on how to deal with international criticism of apartheid—a lesson they would have to increasingly rely on as tolerance of South Africa waned around the world. Embassy reporting of the Little Rock crisis questioned "the legality of President Eisenhower's continued military intervention in the particular circumstances existing in Arkansas," while at the same time highlighting "the role of States Rights in the enforcement of Federal court injunctions."[106] The reliance of U.S. segregationists on the sanctity of states rights mirrored the manner in which South Africa would deal with international criticism of its own practices of racial segregation. As Du Plessis noted with apparent glee, "If the constitutional issue can be isolated from the race problem—and there is every indication that segregationists are assiduously manoeuvring in that direction—the conclusion is inescapable that the esteem of the Presidency will be embarrassingly strained."[107]

The South African government responded to criticism of apartheid by asserting its right to govern without outside interference.[108] Engaging with the language of the Cold War and the principles of the United Nations, both of which stressed the right to national self-determination, South Africa argued that foreign calls for the end of apartheid interfered with its right to self-governance. For example, in 1955, the secretary for external affairs instructed all heads of missions that South Africa's official response to international criticism should be to stress that "no self-respecting sovereign state can tolerate such interference in its domestic affairs."[109] South African officials chose to evoke the language of self-determination to prevent foreign meddling in its domestic affairs. As anticolonialism spread throughout Africa it became increasingly difficult for the South African government to speak convincingly about an exclusively white right to self-determination. However, the denunciation of outside "interference in domestic affairs" continued to provide a useful barrier to counteract international anti-apartheid protest.

The *Brown v. Board of Education* decision and the integration of Little Rock Central High School were turning points in terms of both the civil rights movement and South Africa's relationship with the United States. This was recognized by Ambassador Du Plessis, who commented that for the United States "the virtue of their anti-colonial and anti-racial policy is perhaps enhanced by the fact that by legislation, or rather by Court Order, they are bringing about a stage of racial integration in the face of traditional and violent opposition within their own country."[110] Little Rock had inevitable global implications that would in turn shape the relationship between the United States and South Africa. Du Plessis's observation that America's antiracial and anticolonial credentials may actually end up being "enhanced" by the government response to the crisis demonstrates how closely racial conflict in the United States and South Africa were intertwined. Assessing the international forces generated by Little Rock and what they meant for the U.S.–South Africa Cold War alliance, Du Plessis concluded, "All this has had inevitable repercussions on the international plane; and even in this country there is a widespread realisation that events have played into the hands of the Soviet and Bandung groups, and embarrassed the United States in the development of its own 'anti-colonial' policy. . . . If this is correct then it does not seem reasonable to expect that there will be modification of American policy of a nature which might bring it more into accord with the needs of our own policy."[111] Du Plessis acknowledged the possibility that the United States might have to sever its close ties with South Africa on the grounds that the latter's racial policies were no longer compatible with American Cold War aims. Anticommunism provided a powerful language through which the National Party could ingratiate itself with American power brokers and deflect criticism of its apartheid policies. However, as African decolonization gathered pace, it became increasingly clear that this strategy would not be enough to legitimize apartheid in the eyes of the watching world.[112] As news of the Sharpeville massacre came across the wires on March 21, 1960 and sixty-nine peaceful black protestors lay dead at the hands of South African police, international outrage at and condemnation of apartheid came to a head. Sharpeville effectively foreclosed any possibility of South Africa successfully presenting its racial policies as acceptable practice to the majority of American citizens.

Tracing how South African diplomatic officials engaged with the United States offers an additional global perspective on the political, economic, and military links that helped mute American criticism of apartheid. The Department of External Affairs in Pretoria and diplomatic officials based in the United States used the language of anticommunism to try to justify South Africa's oppressive racial policies. Later, in response to "negative" headlines generated by the state's response to anti-apartheid protest, the South African government worked hard to draw attention to segregation and racial violence in the United States, realizing that this was America's Achilles' heel in what was a rapidly decolonizing world.[113] These efforts to prevent any international interference in its domestic politics reflected a realization within the National Party that the international political climate was changing. Such criticisms also amounted to a last-ditch attempt to appeal to a specific version of America, one that reflected the beliefs of white segregationists, which the National Party believed would be more sympathetic toward its apartheid policies.

These diplomatic exchanges and public relations initiatives were a response to the actions of anti-apartheid activists in both countries who repeatedly questioned the morality of this mutually beneficial Cold War relationship. It is therefore important to remember that anticommunism was a contested ideology. Black radicals in South Africa and the United States vigorously denounced anticommunism as evidence of U.S. imperialism, proof that American-style race and class discrimination was to be exported around the world. In contrast, African American liberals actively engaged with the politics of anticommunism in an attempt to push the

U.S. government further on anticolonial issues. This more "progressive" view of anticommunism emphasized the need for America to hold firm to the values of freedom and democracy in order to defeat Soviet totalitarianism. The Cold War had a contradictory effect on black protest. Red-baiting had severe consequences for black activists whose international outlook overstepped the mark of what was deemed respectable by the state. However, anticommunism also represented a global ideology through which many black activists viewed Africa and the wider world. This was a powerful political language that would have to be reckoned with if transnational networks dedicated to the dismantling of apartheid were to be maintained.

Part II Travel, Politics, and Cultural Exchange

· ·

3 Crossing the Black Atlantic

Travel and Anti-Apartheid Activism

· ·

The transatlantic journey of Miriam Makeba in 1959 from Johannesburg to New York via Venice and London was a key event in the development of the international anti-apartheid movement. For African Americans, Makeba became one of the most prominent black South Africans in the United States.[1] Widely known as "Mama Africa" during her thirty years of exile from South Africa, Makeba grew into a living symbol of anti-apartheid protest. She was a cultural and political ambassador whose actions abroad helped articulate the reality of black life under apartheid to an international audience.[2] As Makeba's former husband and fellow jazz exile in the United States, Hugh Masekela, commented, "I think that there is nobody in Africa who made the world more aware of what was happening in South Africa than Miriam Makeba. . . . People realised what she was talking about. The more interviews she did, the more people found out about SA. I think that's the way Miles [Davis], Dizzy [Gillespie], [Harry] Belafonte, [and] Max Roach got to know. . . . By the time I got to the States, Miriam had educated, unwittingly, African-American and other artists like Bing Crosby, even Frank Sinatra."[3]

Here Masekela, who himself traveled to the United States in 1960 to attend the Manhattan School of Music, acknowledged the effect that black travel had on the development of international anti-apartheid activism. Transatlantic journeys between the United States and South Africa shaped how African Americans and black South Africans related to one another and developed a sense of their struggles being interconnected. Through her performances Makeba informed and educated her growing American audience about black South African life. Arriving in the United States on November 11, 1959, she quickly became a symbol of black defiance against an apartheid state that appeared to be winning its battle against organized mass civil disobedience.[4] Performing on the same bill as Harry Belafonte's "Belafonte Folk Singers," Makeba made her first television appearance just weeks after her arrival in the United States, becoming an overnight success.[5] Initially reluctant to talk about conditions under apartheid, fearful of what effect this would have on her family and ability to return home, Makeba would go on to regularly criticize the National Party during her time in the United States.[6] Her early political performances included a fundraiser for African students and, in April 1960, she performed at a mourning service in Harlem for the sixty-nine peaceful black protestors killed by South African police at Sharpeville.[7] Reflecting on the nature of her performances Makeba asserted that "I've always said, 'I don't sing politics; I sing the truth.' I sang about the suffering we endured. It was not political. It was *honest*."[8] Although Makeba denied that she was ever a politician, her fame in the United States was inextricably bound up with her views on apartheid.[9] Makeba's life in exile demonstrates the extent to which the lines between politics and culture were often blurred within the global anti-apartheid movement, while her insistence in challenging racism around the world reminds us of the importance of travel to the development of black international connections between African Americans and black South Africans.[10]

Makeba's time in the United States also sheds light on the ways that the American and South African governments worked to control and restrict transnational black protest during the early Cold War. Significantly, Masekela also recalled how Makeba's performances and statements infuriated the authorities on both sides of the Atlantic: "The American government was very upset but couldn't do anything about her fame, [be]cause they were allies of SA, and the whole western world. . . . When we arrived in the States we already had secret files on us, [t]hat [said] we were communists. . . . It's amazing that we made it, given the odds. But I think Miriam carried the torch for this country, and I think she kept the names of the Oliver Tambos, Robert Sobukwes, Nelson Mandelas alive in people's minds all that time."[11] Makeba's international travels were closely monitored. In late 1960, as she attempted to return to South Africa for her mother's funeral, she found that her South African passport had been revoked.[12] Later, she would cite the harassment she received from U.S. authorities as the motivation for her move to Guinea in the late 1960s.[13] The U.S. and South African governments were fearful of black activists and went to great lengths to ensure that they did not criticize domestic race relations when traveling abroad.

Black travel between South Africa and the United States demonstrates the mechanics that shaped how African Americans and black South Africans related to one another's struggles. The lesser-known transatlantic journeys of Canada Lee, Sidney Poitier, and Z. K. and Frieda Matthews reveal how black individuals who traveled between the United States and South Africa in the 1950s served as important cultural translators that physically connected the struggle against racism in both countries. While these mobile black figures could never completely free themselves from the controlling gaze of the state, their efforts to forge links with black activists overseas posed a number of problems for white politicians on both sides of the Atlantic. The extent of state fear over the disruptive potential of black travel is made clear by the U.S. State Department's decision to withdraw the passports of a number of black radicals who were engaged in anticolonial struggles in Africa.[14] However, it is equally important to note that efforts to control black mobility were challenged in both countries. A focus on the international response to Paul Robeson's campaign to win back his passport demonstrates how experiences of state repression could be negotiated in ways that further strengthened bonds of solidarity between African Americans and black South Africans. By engaging with Robeson's struggle, anti-apartheid activists in South Africa would assert that their right to citizenship was part of a broader global struggle against race inequality.

Filming *Cry, the Beloved Country*

In July 1950 the African American actor Canada Lee traveled to South Africa to star in the film version of white South African novelist Alan Paton's *Cry, the Beloved Country* (1952). A number of black actors from the United States and Caribbean were involved in the production, including a twenty-three-year-old Sidney Poitier.[15] Lee was a fierce critic of white supremacy. As an actor he was selective in the roles he took and sought to challenge white racist stereotypes through his performances.[16] Politically aware and outspoken, he used his fame to advance the black freedom struggle in the United States. Lee worked closely with a number of civil rights organizations and traveled in the same political circles as black radicals such as Paul Robeson, whom he regularly appeared alongside at rallies and counted as a close friend.[17] He was a prominent figure in the Committee for the Negro in the Arts (CNA), an organization tied to the CRC that fought for dignified roles for black performers throughout the 1940s. This work brought him into contact with advocates for African independence in the United States, and he lent his support to a number of campaigns organized by the CAA.[18] Given his political background, Lee's time in South Africa appeared to represent an anticolonial opportunity, one that could potentially be used to challenge apartheid and call into question the U.S. government's ties with the National Party. In Johannesburg and Durban, Lee glimpsed firsthand the poverty and brutality of the apartheid system. Both he and his costars were subjected to segregation during filming and under strict instructions not to mix with the "Natives," racial indignities that served to reinforce Lee's view of Jim Crow and apartheid as interrelated systems of racial oppression. As he wrote in a telling letter home that addressed the racial situation in South Africa, "For the Natives, it is as bad as our South—only worse."[19]

However, despite his obvious disdain for white supremacy at home and abroad, Lee found it incredibly difficult to speak out publicly against apartheid. In fact, toward the end of filming, quotes from Lee emerged that praised the "cordial hospitality" he had received in South Africa. In an open letter that appeared in the U.S. and South African press, he strongly dismissed claims that he was "disgusted" with the racial politics of the country, asserting that, "contrary to popular belief abroad I have had a wonderful time in South Africa."[20] Though Lee never went so far as to praise the National Party, observing that things were not "perfect" in the Union, his comments distorted the realities of life under apartheid. By emphasizing his personal encounters with liberal whites and largely ignoring the hardships black, colored, and Indian people faced, he failed to publicly air his private criticism of the white supremacist state. When shooting the film's interior scenes in London, Lee again defended the production from rumors in the British press that, in order to enter South Africa, he had had to be listed as the "bonded servant" of the film's white director Zoltan Korda.[21] In a special bulletin released by the South African government, he stated that he had "just read in the *Observer* that our treatment in S. Africa was abominable. It seems someone was grossly misinformed." Adding that he had lived in luxury in South Africa as a guest in the houses of affluent whites, Lee concluded, "What was abominable to me was that in England, the land of freedom and justice, I was refused accommodation at two leading hotels in London, only because my skin was black, and this is not misinformation."[22]

Lee's controversial public remarks are illustrative of the extent to which state repression shaped black transnational activism during the early Cold War. The pressures placed on African Americans to distance themselves from the black left narrowed what was considered acceptable civil rights discourse and dramatically reduced possibilities for transnational anticolonial organizing.[23] As Richard Iton has commented, state authorities worked to "domesticate blackness" during the Cold War by deliberately preventing the interaction of racial subjects across borders.[24] Although travel across the black Atlantic had the potential to raise uncomfortable questions regarding the interconnected nature of racism in the United States and

South Africa, these journeys were closely monitored in ways that made it difficult to question the legitimacy of the apartheid state.[25] Lee's apparent reluctance to condemn the National Party should therefore be seen within the broader context of the dismantling of the black popular front and mounting anticommunist repression. It is too simplistic to read his public comments as evidence that he walked out on his allies on the left. Instead, a series of political and personal factors combined in ways that that made it increasingly difficult to openly articulate his personal abhorrence of the apartheid system. In the United States, Lee had been denounced as a "fellow traveler" of the Communist Party and was struggling to find work.[26] Produced in Britain, *Cry, the Beloved Country* represented a means to potentially escape this difficult situation. Suffering financial hardship and ill health, Lee saw the leading role in a major motion picture as a valuable opportunity to survive the anticommunist blacklist. In addition to this, as foreign black actors working in South Africa, both Lee and his costar Sidney Poitier were woefully exposed to the demands and the political agenda of the South African government. Indeed, the National Party exerted a great deal of control over the entire production of *Cry, the Beloved Country*, believing that the film could be used to present apartheid in a positive light to a watching world. After signing up to the movie, both men would face intense political pressure from South African officials and the studio not to rock the boat during filming.

Written by the white South African novelist Alan Paton in 1948, *Cry, the Beloved Country* tells the story of the black Anglican priest Stephen Kumalo and his wayward son Absalom, who has been accused of murdering a white man in a burglary attempt gone wrong. In the London Films production Canada Lee plays the lead role of Kumalo, while Poitier takes on the part of Reverend Msimangu, a young priest who assists him as he searches for his son in Johannesburg. Although the film received generally positive reviews in the white press upon its U.S. release in 1952, the African American playwright and activist Lorraine Hansberry wrote that "in the whole movie there is not one word of protest. Not one hint of dissatisfaction, hatred or movement for change. Indeed, the only angry words are between black men."[27] For Hansberry, *Cry, the Beloved Country* conformed to negative racial stereotypes that emphasized the need for forgiveness and black submission.[28] As she wrote in relation to the film's climactic scene where Canada Lee's character attempts to come to terms with his son's conviction for murder, "*He*, the black man, falls to *his* knees, on *his* African earth, to ask the white man's forgiveness. . . . There is, according to the film, no wrath against the Malan government or the international financiers who have turned the beautiful country into a fascistic nightmare of oppression."[29]

Many black South African writers and critics shared Hansberry's view of *Cry, the Beloved Country* as a novel. As Rob Nixon and Andrew van der Vlies have noted, the story's "missionary ethos of white trusteeship" cemented its position as a "cardinal counter-text" for young black South African writers living and working in Johannesburg.[30] However, despite the problematic nature of the source material, it at first seemed as if the cinematic reimagining of *Cry, the Beloved Country* might offer a radical new interpretation of Paton's original narrative. Gerald Horne has noted how Zoltan Korda approached John Howard Lawson, the "Dean of the Hollywood Ten," to write the first treatment of the film's script. Identifying some of Lawson's trademark dramatic tropes in the final version of the film, Horne concludes that his involvement resulted in a "powerful" production that helped establish anti-apartheid drama as a cinematic genre.[31] However, despite Lawson's contribution, the final cinematic version of *Cry, the Beloved Country* ultimately failed to deliver any revolutionary challenge to white supremacy in South Africa. Black characters are generally portrayed as passive, submissive, and struggling to come to terms with modern life, whereas black urban areas are represented as slums, areas of vice and violence—proof that black South Africans were intrinsically unsuited to city life. Such images closely reflect the thinking of Afrikaner Nationalists and were used throughout this period to justify policies such as the 1950 Group Areas Act that further entrenched solidified racial segregation in urban areas.[32]

That the film should so closely follow National Party views on the need for complete racial separation was no coincidence. The South African government was acutely aware of the extent to which the foreign-produced film had the potential to shape global public perceptions of apartheid. On first hearing of the planned production, the South African secretary for native affairs wrote to the state information officer in Pretoria, commenting that "such a film would give the widest publicity to whatever it portrayed— whether true or false—of Native conditions in the Union and it would, therefore, be of considerable importance to the Government to have a fair and balanced picture portrayed showing that while there are slums and some hardships for Natives to cope with, there are also model townships and a growing set of social services."[33]

This image of a South Africa where for every "slum" there was a "model township" chimed with the National Party's broader efforts to present apartheid as a benign, even reformist, presence in the Cold War world. Speculating on how this problematic vision of South Africa might be realized, the secretary suggested discreetly contacting London Films to let it be known that the government would "be willing to assist in making the picture authentic provided undue stress were not laid upon hardship and suffering."[34]

Over the ensuing months, the South African government exerted its control over various aspects of *Cry, the Beloved Country* in its pursuit of an "authentic" vision of apartheid. Despite Zoltan Korda's claims to the contrary, London Films representatives liaised at length with high-ranking government officials and even Prime Minister D. F. Malan in order to secure permission to film in South Africa.[35] In the summer of 1949, Korda himself delivered an early treatment of the script to South Africa House in London, after which the director of public relations, Julian Mockford, reported to Pretoria that the "right treatment is being developed, that the possible political snags have been avoided, and that the film, if interpreted on these lines will do the White man's cause in South Africa good not harm."[36]

The extent of the National Party's influence over the film is further illustrated by the government's reaction to press reports that Paul Robeson had been approached to play a starring role in the production.[37] Alarmed at the rumors that such an outspoken critic of the apartheid regime had been linked to the project, the South African government immediately postponed discussions with London Films while the South African embassy in the United States quickly cabled Pretoria, noting that "the danger of permitting Robeson to enter our country on any pretext whatsoever, will be apparent to the Government, I am sure."[38] Negotiations only resumed after London Film's founder and Zoltan's older brother, Alexander Korda, gave his personal assurances that rumors about Robeson's hiring were "quite inaccurate."[39]

The National Party's close involvement with the production of *Cry, the Beloved Country* is typical of the practical steps that were taken to limit international criticism of the apartheid regime. This was part of the South African government's broader efforts to transform its image in the international arena in the 1950s. The National Party hoped that *Cry, the Beloved Country* could be used as a tool to deflect criticism away from its racial policies and strengthen its Cold War relationship with the West.[40] That two prominent black actors based in the United States ended up playing the central roles in such a racially divisive film was highly symbolic in this context. By traveling to South Africa, Canada Lee and Sidney Poitier effectively became enmeshed in a political project that was deliberately designed to counteract efforts to mobilize global opposition against apartheid in the 1950s.

Filming for *Cry, the Beloved Country* began in South Africa on August 3, 1950. The three months of shooting in Natal and Johannesburg took its toll on the film's foreign actors. Reflecting on his arrival in the country, Sidney Poitier commented in his autobiography, "I was barely through customs when I noticed signs saying 'Bantu' and 'White.' Damn, I thought, nobody told me this."[41] It didn't take long for Poitier to experience South African race discrimination firsthand. When he was walking home one night after filming, police descended on him, demanding that he produce his pass, suspicious that he was not in the townships or the reserves.[42] Poitier and Lee quickly found that their fame and status did not make them immune from the strict racial hierarchies of the apartheid system, while their experiences in South Africa are testament to bell hooks's observation of how, for many African Americans, "to travel is to encounter the terrorizing force of white supremacy."[43]

During his stay in South Africa, Canada Lee corresponded regularly with his white fiancée, Frances, in New York. In his early letters, it is clear he struggled to come to terms with the "poverty, filth and squalor" he witnessed. Like other African American travelers, including Richard Wright and Era Bell Thompson, he appeared to find the realities of African life to be somewhat alien.[44] As he wrote when describing his defiant response to being denied access to a whites-only public toilet, "I'm from America, I'm no bloody native."[45] Understandably keen not to be subjected to the same treatment as the majority of black of South Africans, Lee took refuge in his identity as an American citizen in order to resist apartheid regulations. These efforts to lift himself above the apartheid system can again be seen in his response to Frances's request for more information on South Africa. Ignoring the similarities that existed between apartheid law and segregation in the American South, he stated, "You want to know about this place? Well they've passed a law here which is called the immorality law. This law says that anyone of non-European extraction (African, Indian, Colored) . . . caught in the company of [a] European (white person) of opposite sex can be jailed. . . . That's the kind of country this is. Isn't it horrible to live here? Just imagine if we were to come here we would be put into jail just because we were in love with each other."[46] From personal experience, Lee would have been all too aware of how miscegenation laws and lynching culture still pervaded the United States. However, his seemingly selective memory effectively enabled him to position himself as being out of reach of white supremacist control on both sides of the Atlantic. Thousands of miles from home, Lee initially attempted to dissociate himself from his hostile surroundings. Through his correspondence to his white partner at home in New York he remained defiant, creating an autonomous space in which he could continue to assert his agency in the face of white supremacist power.

Although Lee occasionally tried to rhetorically distance himself from the racial situation in South Africa, his correspondence home also demonstrates the extent to which he read apartheid through the lens of race discrimination in the United States "It is much worse here for the natives than it is for the negro in the South," he noted in another letter to Frances, adding that "the greatest fear is contained in the whites who are afraid to educate the Native because it might raise their standards and of course their salaries. . . . It is really funny that the philosophy of the Southern white and the South African white is the same."[47] By articulating the similarities between racism in South Africa and the American South, Lee made exactly the type of connection that the governments of both countries wished to prevent. Although both he and Poitier faced immense pressure not to publicly voice their opinions, this private recognition of the global significance of apartheid is telling. The process of traveling to South Africa gave both men new perspectives on race discrimination in the United States, prompting them to think about how this related to other systems of oppression overseas.

As an international production, *Cry, the Beloved Country* served as a potential site of cross-cultural exchange, providing the physical means through which foreign black actors and South Africans could meet and converse. Lee and Poitier worked alongside a number of local black actors on the film—including Lionel Ngakane, who went on to have a successful acting career in Britain—and regularly socialized with extras after filming.[48] In addition to this, and despite clear instructions "not to speak to the natives about politics," both actors covertly sought out a number of South African anti-apartheid leaders.[49] Poitier talked of being received in the homes of African and Indian congress members, "in a real cloak-and-dagger manner," recalling how these South African activists "overwhelmed us with facts and figures relating to their constant struggle against a political system that considered both Indians and blacks to be less than human."[50] Reflecting on these clandestine meetings in his autobiography, he explains how the individuals they met had "leaped at the opportunity to outline in detail every aspect of their struggle—their aims and aspirations and what they had so far cost in human life and suffering," adding that, "with a casualness peculiar to men who live their lives dangerously, they apologized for the extensive briefing by saying, 'You must excuse our long-windedness, but since we may never meet again, given the politics of our lives in South Africa, we would appreciate it if you could in the fullest sense tell our friends in America about our struggle.' "[51]

Although there were significant obstacles preventing them from speaking out against apartheid, it is clear that the friendships Lee and Poitier formed during filming provided them with a much more detailed and nuanced understanding of South African politics. After the completion of filming Lee maintained contact with a black South African whom he referred to as "Uncle." Writing to this unnamed associate about the recent banning of black South Africans from the University of Witwatersrand, almost a year after Lee left the country, he commented, "I don't see any chance of black people getting anywhere there unless they can throw off this prejudice that the white man has given him against each other, by giving privileges to one and not to the other because of the color of his skin. And sticking together in a new order of solidarity. Black hand in Black hand marching together towards freedom, as every group in the world is doing—*except the Black man.* . . . A lot of people are going to die for liberty in S.A., but it is worth it."[52] Lee's understanding of apartheid policy and firm support for direct action against the National Party demonstrates how, by traveling to South Africa, he became personally connected to the anti-apartheid struggle. Through their firsthand experiences of racism abroad as well as the friendships and alliances they formed, both Lee and Poitier left South Africa determined to lend their support to the global anti-apartheid movement. By deliberately defying both London Films and the South African government, they became increasingly aware of the global dimension of race discrimination as well as the need for organized international opposition against apartheid. This feeling of solidarity with the anti-apartheid struggle is clear in one of Canada Lee's last letters home at the end of filming, where he wrote, "I love the political atmosphere of the country. Revolution is in the air. The Indians, the Colored People and the Native African are uniting. That spells trouble. It's about time."[53]

Immediately on his return to the United States, Sidney Poitier gave Paul Robeson's radical Harlem-based newspaper *Freedom* an interview about his time in South Africa. In the article, which was later reprinted in the anti-apartheid press, he roundly condemns the National Party, describing in detail how black South Africans were forced to live in "miserable shantytown ghettoes" and noting how he was explicitly "warned not to speak to the natives about politics."[54] Poitier concluded that "the Native African has a deep and solid hatred for white rule. For him, the white man is a symbol of oppression, starvation and the worst form of cruelty."[55] This frank assessment of apartheid differed greatly from Lee's public statements and contributed to what the young up-and-coming actor described as a "dry spell" in terms of his own career in the mid-1950s.[56] While roundly praising Poitier, South African activists condemned Lee for his failure to come out publicly against the apartheid regime. As the SAIC leader Yusuf Dadoo commented, "It is most surprising and no less shocking to learn that Canada Lee disagrees with statements on the condition of Non-Europeans in South Africa. . . . During his stay in South Africa, Canada Lee in discussions he had with groups of Non-Europeans and with me personally, very bitterly condemned the plight and suffering of Non-European people in South Africa."[57] The disparity between Lee's private and public statements should be understood in relation to the severe personal and professional demands he was under during the early Cold War. As an established actor and star of the film, he was expected to market the production and ensure that the public viewed it positively, a responsibility that as a supporting cast member Poitier was largely able to escape. The fact that Lee had so much invested in the success of the film meant he was in an impossible position. As the National Party extended its considerable influence over the production, he was under great pressure to remain silent and toe the official line.

On his return to the United States things did not get much better for Lee. In spite of the critics largely praising his performance in *Cry, the Beloved Country*, work still remained hard to come by.[58] In what would be one of his last acts of defiance before he passed away from severe hypertension in May 1952, he finally spoke out publicly against apartheid two months after the film's U.S. release. No longer tied to London Films, Lee met with George Houser of the AFSAR in order to discuss his experiences in South Africa, and later followed Poitier's lead by condemning the apartheid regime in articles and interviews.[59] His involvement with the AFSAR, an avowedly anticommunist organization, is both illustrative of Lee's enforced break from radical politics and his continued determination to criticize white supremacy wherever he found it. In a final act that symbolically challenged the blacklist and the National Party's influence over *Cry, the Beloved Country*, he appeared as a main speaker at an AFSAR mass meeting at Adam Clayton Powell's Abyssinian Baptist Church, marking the announcement of the Defiance Campaign on April 6, 1952. There Lee boldly condemned white supremacy in South Africa before heading downtown to join an anti-apartheid rally held outside the South African consulate.[60]

Z. K. and Frieda Matthews: Defying Apartheid in the United States

As Canada Lee took to the stage in Harlem to denounce the apartheid regime, on the other side of the Atlantic the black South African educator Z. K. Matthews was in the process of finalizing plans for his own transatlantic journey. Professor of social anthropology at Fort Hare University, Matthews was scheduled to take up the role of Henry IV Luce Visiting Professor of World Christianity at the Union Theological Seminary in New York City in the summer of 1952. Somewhat fortuitously, his departure for the United States coincided with the start of the Campaign for the Defiance of Unjust Laws. Organized by the ANC and SAIC in response to the implementation of a number of apartheid laws, the Defiance Campaign sent political shockwaves around the world and left the National Party facing unprecedented levels of international criticism. The historian James Meriwether has demonstrated how African American activists were particularly inspired by these mass protests against apartheid.[61] Recalling the intense interest in the Defiance Campaign that he found in the United States, Z. K. Matthews stated, "People—especially the Negro sections of the community—were anxious to know what was happening. . . . The word apartheid was being bandied about and people wanted to know what it meant, and what its implications were for the black folks of South Africa."[62] Matthews's wife Frieda joined him in New York in September, and this husband and wife team both became spokespeople for the anti-apartheid movement in the United States. Faced with an audience eager to learn about the explosive political situation in South Africa, they both made a significant contribution to increasing international awareness of and support for anti-apartheid protest.[63]

Frieda Bokwe and Zachariah Keodirelang Matthews married in 1928. The daughter of the famous minister, journalist, and composer John Knox Bokwe, Frieda was a graduate of Lovedale Missionary School and Adams College in Natal. She was a talented writer and musician, and an outspoken critic of South African racism, particularly in relation to the issue of Bantu education.[64] The first black student to obtain a bachelor's degree from a South African university, Z. K. first traveled to the United States in 1929 to complete his master's at Yale University.[65] At Yale, he worked under the direction of Professor Charles Loram, the white South African director of the Department of Culture Contacts and Race Relations, touring many of the United States' leading black educational institutions and meeting the likes of Robert Moton, Mordecai Johnson, Ralph Bunche, Alain Locke, and Charles H. Wesley.[66] A leading intellectual figure in South Africa, Z. K. was involved at various points with bodies such as the Natives' Representative Council and the South African Institute of Race Relations (SAIRR). In 1949 he became president of the ANC's Cape Province branch and was a moderate but active influence on the organization's policymaking at a national level. Perhaps reassured by the aura of religious respectability that surrounded Z. K.'s visiting position in New York, South African officials apparently granted the Matthewses their documents for travel without much difficulty.

This decision backfired on the National Party almost immediately. From their arrival in the United States, Z. K. and Frieda spoke publicly about the Defiance Campaign and South African race relations, condemning white supremacy on a global scale in the process. Recognizing that his presence overseas could aid their cause, the joint committee of the ANC and SAIC made Z. K. an official plenipotentiary of both organizations in the United States.[67] With this role in mind both Z. K. and Frieda worked closely with the AFSAR, developing a lasting personal relationship with George Houser.[68] The couple were also introduced to many prominent NAACP members during their stay and would continue to correspond with the organization's executive director, Walter White, on their return to South Africa.[69]

Perhaps most significant though, given the group's subversive status in both the United States and South Africa, was the Matthewses' involvement with the CAA. Z. K. had been a close associate of the council's founder Max Yergan, who had worked as a missionary at Fort Hare in the 1920s and 1930s. Although Yergan had turned his back on radical black politics by this time, he had been instrumental in bringing together African American and black South African activists.[70] Z. K. had lent his vocal support to a number of CAA campaigns in the 1940s, including its fundraising efforts for the 1946 Ciskei famine and opposition to the annexation of South West Africa. In 1949, as the CAA faced charges of subversion, Z. K. wrote to the organization to state his "appreciation of the service which the Council on African Affairs is rendering to the cause of African freedom."[71] In New York, Z. K. developed these connections in person, meeting with Paul Robeson, W. E. B. Du Bois, and William Alphaeus Hunton in order to discuss and develop the CAA's ongoing work in South Africa.[72] The Matthewses appeared to mediate the Cold War left-liberal divide during their time in the United States, forging diverse political alliances in order to secure widespread overseas support for the Defiance Campaign. The scramble to host Z. K. and Frieda also provides a reminder of how both black radicals and anti-communists attempted to legitimize their support for the anti-apartheid struggle by forging tangible links with black South African activists.

Often invited to speak at two or three meetings per day, Z. K. and Frieda made numerous public appearances during their time in the United States.[73] Recalling the demand there was for information about South Africa, Z. K. stated, "The telephone in my flat was constantly ringing with people from all-over the USA trying to make appointments to come and see me, or inviting me to participate in some Adult School Forum, University group discussion, or Women's League Meeting. When my wife joined me in September she was also pressed into service and often we went in different directions to fulfill engagements, which became so overwhelming that we had to refuse to take on more than a few each week."[74] When delivering these addresses Z. K. and Frieda repeatedly stressed the readiness of black South Africans for full political independence. For example, speaking at an Urban League "Sounding Off" dinner in New York in November 1952, Z. K. stated that "with or without your assistance, the Africans will get their freedom in this century. The first half of the century belonged to Asia; the second half belongs to Africa."[75] Z. K. wrote a number of articles calling for African independence in African American publications such as the *Chicago Defender, New York Amsterdam News,* and *Freedom,* while his comments on South Africa were also quoted in press reports covering the progress of the Defiance Campaign.[76] Finally, toward the end of 1952, at the behest of the ANC, attempts were made to secure an appearance for Z. K. before the United Nations. With the assistance of prominent figures in the AFSAR, NAACP, and CAA, Z. K. lobbied to address the ad hoc political committee of the UN on the subject of apartheid and the current political unrest in South Africa.[77]

Frieda Matthews's activism in the United States is particularly significant given the way in which black women's contributions to the global anti-apartheid movement have often been neglected. Although Frieda dissociated herself from more revolutionary strands of anti-apartheid protest, she had been introduced to a number of radical anticolonial activists during her time as a student in London in the 1930s.[78] Partly as a result of these personal links, she had hosted the African American writer and activist Eslanda

Goode Robeson at her home in South Africa in 1936.[79] As Erik S. McDuffie and Dayo F. Gore have documented, in the early 1950s Robeson was part of a small but dynamic community of radical black women in New York committed to challenging race and gender discrimination across national boundaries.[80] Along with individuals such as Louise Thompson Patterson and Beulah Richardson, Eslanda played an active role in the Sojourners for Truth and Justice (STJ), a short-lived organization that worked to forge ties with female anti-apartheid activists.[81] It is unclear whether Frieda spoke at meetings organized by the Sojourners, but given her public presence and existing personal connections it is likely that she would have influenced the organization's views on South Africa. As a politically active black South African woman in the United States, Frieda represented a highly visible alternative to the masculinist articulations of black internationalism as advanced by her husband and individuals such as Lee and Poitier.[82]

The Matthewses' work in publicizing the Defiance Campaign and asserting the need for African independence soon attracted the attention of South African government officials. South African consulate employees often attended the public meetings at which they spoke, reporting back to Pretoria on their statements.[83] Z. K.'s attempts to address the UN especially angered the South African government, eventually setting in motion a diplomatic tug-of-war aimed at the immediate return of the Matthewses to South African soil.[84] The *Advance* newspaper in South Africa reported that Z. K. was picked up from his New York apartment and driven in a Cadillac to the South African consulate where he was "grilled" for two hours. Arguing that any appearance in front of the UN would constitute a "breach of faith," South African officials sought assurances from Matthews that he would refuse any such invitation if extended. He was also warned that any involvement with the UN would be regarded as a "hostile act" that would have "dire consequences" for himself, his family, and his professional career.[85] George Houser recalls how, on one occasion, he arrived at the Matthewses' Morningside Heights apartment to be met by two FBI agents who, it transpired, had called in to stress the U.S. government's disapproval of Z. K.'s efforts to petition the UN.[86] In the African American press it was also reported that the Matthewses received a visit from a representative of the U.S. State Department, who warned of the potential problems that the couple would face upon their return to South Africa if Z. K. were to appear before the UN committee.[87] The pressure placed on Z. K. by the U.S. and South African governments highlights the vulnerability of black activists who traveled internationally during the Cold War. Through surveillance, harassment, and intimidation, both governments made it perfectly clear that the Matthewses' continued criticism of apartheid would not be tolerated.

The efforts to secure Z. K.'s appearance before the international delegates of the UN ultimately ended in failure, with the head of the organization's political committee concluding that there was "no precedence" for such an address.[88] However, this incident, the suspicion it caused, as well as the treatment the Matthews received at the hands of the South African authorities on returning home are all illustrative of the bureaucratic processes used to restrict global anti-apartheid protest. Like Poitier and Lee in South Africa, the Matthewses were subjected to a form of state surveillance deliberately designed to deny them a public platform from which they could challenge apartheid. That U.S. and South African officials pressured Z. K. and Frieda to abandon their political activities is especially significant given the shared interest both governments had in silencing black international criticism of apartheid. Traveling between both countries, these politically minded individuals all had the potential to directly challenge the legitimacy of the U.S.–South Africa Cold War relationship, a situation that both powers found intolerable.

Unsure of their immigration status in the United States after the passing of the McCarran Act and hopeful of extending their stay, Z. K. and Frieda Matthews applied to Pretoria for a six-month passport extension in April 1953.[89] However, their political activities in the United States, and the anger that this had generated among the South African authorities, all but guaranteed that this request would be denied. Almost immediately, the South African Department of the Interior cabled the consul general in New York that "Interior not, repeat not, prepared to approve renewal passports [for] Professor Matthews and wife."[90] Although this cable was sent on April 9, 1953, over a month before the expiration of their original travel permits, the couple failed to receive any official confirmation from South African government representatives that their request had been denied.[91] The Matthewses, and those close to them in the United States and South Africa, believed this failure in communication to be a deliberate ploy by government officials to trap them into traveling without valid documentation. If they failed to return to South Africa before the expiration of their passports, the South African government would have sufficient grounds to arrest and detain them.[92] In response to this attempted bureaucratic entrapment, friends and supporters in the United States raised enough money for Z. K. and Frieda to fly home, rather than travel by ship and risk missing the passport deadline.[93] Despite arriving back in South Africa on time, the couple received a rough welcome home.[94] They were greeted on landing by the police, their possessions were thoroughly searched, and their private documents were confiscated. They were placed under surveillance and an investigation of Z. K.'s activities while abroad was started by the CID.[95]

Z. K. Matthews was highly critical of his and Frieda's treatment at Jan Smuts Airport. Talking to the *Chicago Defender* about his harassment as well as the government's failure to notify the couple that their passports would not be extended, he commented, "I take the strongest exception . . . as I do not know of any crime I have committed to warrant this."[96] His crime, in the eyes of the South African state, was to criticize apartheid abroad and to attempt to publicize the plight of black South Africans to African Americans in the United States. As the South African justice minister Charles R. Swart angrily claimed in parliament, the Matthewses' actions in the United States amounted to an active incitement of African Americans against the Union of South Africa through the forceful promotion of ideas of "Africa for the Africans."[97] As Z. K. himself noted in his autobiography, "Ever since my return from the United States in 1953 I realized that I had become *persona non grata* with the Government. I had not behaved as they thought I would during my visit to the States."[98] Z. K. Matthews would attempt to travel to the United States on two more occasions in the 1950s. However, in both instances he was denied a passport.[99] Instead, for both him and Frieda, the years following their return were marked by increased police harassment and government persecution.[100]

Taking place at a key moment in the struggle for racial equality on both sides of the Atlantic, the journeys of the Matthewses, Canada Lee, and Sidney Poitier encouraged African Americans and black South Africans to think about white supremacy in global terms. Whether their experiences took the form of a more personal political awakening or involved actively raising public awareness of the anti-apartheid protest overseas, their transnational movements laid bare the commonalities that existed between different systems of racial segregation, while helping to promote the formation of black identities that transcended the narrow boundaries of the nation-state.[101]

Significantly, these journeys also tell us about the mutually constitutive relationship between transnational black activism and the development of state mechanisms designed to stifle global anti-apartheid protest. As a centralized and coercive entity, the Cold War state monitored, circumscribed, and controlled black movements in ways that restricted global black responses to apartheid policy. The U.S. and South African authorities worked hard on this front, assigning government officials to harass, intimidate, and generally place restrictions on its citizens who traveled overseas—a strategy that, as we have seen, had a particularly devastating effect on radical anticolonial organizing. The control the National Party exerted over *Cry, the Beloved Country*; Canada Lee's initial inability to criticize apartheid and his ultimate failure to break the blacklist; the harassment of Z. K. and Frieda Matthews by the South African consul, U.S. State Department, and FBI are therefore all illustrative of the ways in which anticommunist and white supremacist power merged in order to limit black freedom during the early Cold War.[102]

The time, money, and effort spent policing these journeys can be read as evidence of the pervasive power of the apartheid state *and* its continuing susceptibility to transnational black activism.[103] While often underlining the vulnerability of mobile black subjects to state power, these transatlantic travels demanded a response from white governments eager to maintain their political legitimacy in the Cold War world. Whether it was from the floor of a public meeting, through the press, or in personal letters to loved ones, Lee, Poitier, and the Matthewses all managed to find spaces through which they could challenge apartheid in the global political arena. While the apartheid regime was largely able to deflect their criticisms, each of these journeys points to the National Party's concern over how South Africa was perceived overseas. This provided an opportunity for those African Americans and black South Africans who were eager to support one another in their struggles for racial justice.

Paul Robeson's Passport Case and Anti-Apartheid Protest

Although it may appear counterintuitive, travel restrictions placed on black activists occasionally provided opportunities to challenge racism across national borders. The South African response to the U.S. State Department's decision to withhold Paul Robeson's passport provides a case in point.[104] Along with other radical black activists, including his wife Eslanda, Robeson was denied the right to travel due to his insistence that Jim Crow exposed the imperialist character of American capitalism.[105] John Torpey has documented how the passport has been central to the development of the mechanisms of the modern nation state. As a method of establishing identities, passports have played a central role in determining national citizenship through the regulation of an individual's mobility.[106] Indeed, Robeson argued that his inability to access this document amounted to the withdrawal of his rights as an American citizen and a sign that he was effectively an exile within the country of his birth.[107] The international support Robeson received in his struggle to regain his passport demonstrates how black activists on both sides of the Atlantic positioned the right to travel as a key marker of freedom.

The potential embarrassment that could be caused by Robeson publicly denouncing American racism and U.S. imperialism overseas was cited by the State Department as the key factor in their decision to deny him his right to travel. In 1950 Robeson was offered his passport on the condition that he refrain from criticizing the U.S. government abroad and sign a so-called noncommunist affidavit.[108] In a legal brief submitted to the court of appeals in 1952, the State Department publicly affirmed that Robeson's passport had been revoked "in view of applicant's frank admission that he has been extremely active politically on behalf of the independence of the colonial peoples of Africa." The document concludes that "the diplomatic embarrassment that could arise from the presence abroad of such a political meddler, travelling under the protection of an American passport, is easily imaginable."[109] In 1955, government officials reiterated this stance. U.S. attorney Leo A. Rover told an appeals court that Robeson's passport should continue to be denied to him on the grounds that in the past "during the concert tours of foreign countries he [Robeson] repeatedly criticized the conditions of Negroes in the United States."[110] The U.S. government, clearly aware of their vulnerability on the issue of American racism, went to excessive lengths to attempt to isolate Robeson from his allies and supporters abroad.[111]

As travel opportunities became increasingly limited, African Americans and black South Africans responded creatively. Through letters, statements, newspaper articles, and pamphlets, black activists in both countries asserted that the ability to travel freely amounted to a fundamental human right—incontrovertible proof of one's citizenship and all the rights that this guaranteed. African Americans and black South Africans used Robeson's passport case to assert their right to citizenship on a global level. Nationalism and internationalism are not mutually exclusive terms. By protesting racial discrimination in a national context, activists used this case as a stepping-stone to a broader black international identity.

From the outset Robeson's mistreatment at the hands of the U.S. government was used to demonstrate how global forces worked to prevent black liberation.[112] In his position as head of the Committee to Restore Paul Robeson's Passport, William L. Patterson wrote to the editor of the *Daily Worker*, encouraging the newspaper to give further publicity to the case. Patterson argued that "the far-reaching significance of the Robeson fight lies in its unifying potential." Outlining Robeson's continuing commitment to freedom and democracy throughout the world, he affirmed that "today the voice of Paul Robeson is sorely needed as the Negro people launch their winning fight for democracy and justice. People must be rallied to support him actively. The victory of the Negro people in America will have a mighty impact upon liberation struggles of all mankind and especially Asia and Africa. As this fight develops, America grows stronger, the demoralizing myths of white superiority grow weaker and thus the cause of peace is furthered. The Robeson passport fight is just beginning. The voice of Robeson must be heard throughout the world."[113] The restrictions placed on Robeson's mobility had the potential to unify black activists and provided a common cause around which black international connections could be established. As Patterson commented in a circular letter to prominent Asian and African leaders at the Bandung conference, "I respectfully submit that colored peoples everywhere have an interest in this matter [Robeson's passport case], and that, in the spirit of Bandung . . . it is in order that the peoples of Asia and Africa lend their influence and voice in behalf of justice for a beloved people's leader and artist."[114]

Robeson himself drew clear links between the right to travel, the black freedom struggle, and the attainment of citizenship rights. As he noted defiantly in *Freedom*, "The right to travel is a Constitutional right. And there is nothing in that document that says you have to be muzzled before you pack your bag."[115] By denying him his passport, the State Department had stripped Robeson of what both he and his supporters viewed as a key constitutional right. He therefore became a symbolic reminder of the interconnected forces that worked to stifle black protest—both in the United States and further afield.

Robeson talked about being "exiled in the United States" throughout this period, a rhetorical phrase that established his natural position as being beyond the confines of the nation-state while emphasizing his lost citizenship status.[116] Significantly, pamphlets protesting the refusal of Robeson's passport cast his situation as a form of domestic detention. The front cover of the pamphlet *Lift Every Voice for Paul Robeson* by Lloyd L. Brown depicts Robeson as being bound down to the American soil by men wielding ropes, as the Statue of Liberty weeps in the background.[117] This image of Robeson tightly bound, straining to break free, deliberately evokes the memory of slavery. The restrictions that were placed on Robeson provide a reminder of the historical struggle of African Americans for full citizenship and the white supremacist forces that sought to deny them civil rights. Robeson himself also alluded to his situation as a form of domestic enslavement. In an article that focused on the detention of black South African protestors during the Defiance Campaign, he commented that in the United States "there are invisible chains too—like denying me a passport because, as the government noted in one brief, 'Robeson has been active politically on behalf of the independence of the colonial peoples of Africa.'"[118] The shared chains that bound Robeson and African activists together, an image so closely associated with the transatlantic slave trade, were used to establish the interconnected nature of the struggle for black self-determination in both countries.

Robeson also noted how the right to travel has been intimately connected with ideas of freedom for enslaved black peoples.[119] As he reflects on his passport case in his autobiography *Here I Stand*, "From the days of chattel slavery until today, the concept of *travel* has been inseparably linked in the minds of our people with the concept of *freedom*. Hence, the symbol of the railroad train recurs frequently in our folklore—in spirituals and gospel songs, in blues and ballads—and the train is usually 'bound for glory' and 'heading for the Promised Land.' And there are boats, too, like the 'Old Ship of Zion' and the 'Old Ark' that will take us over the waters to freedom and salvation."[120] For Robeson the right to travel was a vital part of how people of African descent interpreted and proclaimed their freedom. He also acknowledged the important role foreign travel had played in the abolition of slavery, noting how some runaway slaves went abroad to "gain liberation for their kinsmen in chains" and recognizing the "precious heritage" that had been established by "those early sojourners for freedom who crossed the seas to champion the rights of black men in America."[121] The travel restrictions he faced provided compelling evidence that racism was alive and well in the United States. Robeson invoked historical memories of slavery to argue that unrestricted travel was part of the broader struggle for full black citizenship. For African Americans especially, he commented, "the right to leave one state and go to another, or to go abroad—has been of vital importance throughout our history. . . . Conditions today in Mississippi and elsewhere in the South make it clear that this right is of continuing importance to our people," concluding that "it is highly significant that the right of American citizens to travel is embodied in the 14th Amendment—our legal guarantee of equal citizenship."[122] During slavery African Americans secured their independence by making the dangerous journey from the South to North. Measures such as the 1793 and 1850 Fugitive Slave Acts were introduced to prevent this.[123] Robeson's references to slavery recall this link between travel and black freedom, updating this to reflect the nature of white supremacy in the twentieth century. Whereas African American slaves crossed state borders from South to North in order to claim their freedom, Robeson claimed that it was his constitutional right to transcend national borders as a free man.

Robeson therefore deliberately positioned his passport case as a significant issue for oppressed peoples of African descent around the world. As he commented in relation to a verdict by the court of appeals, "Democratic opinion at home and abroad has greeted the historic decision of the U.S. Court of Appeals which affirmed 'the right to travel . . . is a natural right.' I am here to insist that the right to travel is also an *equal* right, and, as the Negro press has made clear, that is the way the Negro citizens of this country see it. Indeed, colored peoples all over the world will see here a basic test of democratic principles."[124] The right to travel was positioned a cornerstone of any free and democratic society, an important indicator of the progress made by African Americans, Africans and all black peoples scattered throughout the diaspora marching toward freedom. Reflecting on his determination to denounce racism both at home and abroad, Robeson defiantly declared that, "I have criticized those conditions abroad as I have at home, and I shall continue to do so until those conditions are changed. What is the Negro traveler supposed to do—keep silent or lie about what is happening to his people back at home? Not I! Furthermore, as long as other Americans are not required to be silent or false in reference to their interests, I shall insist that to impose such restrictions on Negroes is unjust, discriminatory and intolerable."[125] Robeson's black cosmopolitan status—his standing, in the words of Shirley Graham Du Bois, as a "citizen of the world"—was threatened.[126] The prevention of black travel was used to punish those who were deemed to have transgressed racial boundaries and designed to limit the geographical contours of black protest. This, Robeson and his supporters argued, required an international response. It is clear that many anticolonial activists in Africa and throughout the black diaspora shared his view. As a group of South African and West African students based in London wrote to Robeson in 1954, "We regard the denial to grant you passport facilities—tantamount to imprisoning your voice—a flagrant breach of elementary human rights. And this action by a government which claims to be the world's leading democratic nation, underlines the very hollowness of the boast."[127]

While by no means confined to one country, anti-apartheid activists in South Africa openly condemned Robeson's treatment by the State Department and led calls for his passport to be returned to him.[128] Robeson was a popular and well-known figure in the country, and his activities during the 1940s and 1950s were regularly reported on, particularly in antigovernment publications.[129] South African press reports noted Robeson's decision to change the lyrics of "Old Man River' from "tired of living and scared of dying" to "I must keep fighting until I'm dying" and provided readers with a detailed account of how he mounted "one of the bravest stands ever taken before the notorious un-American activities committee." South Africans were also informed of his cultural performances and were regularly updated on the progress of his passport case.[130] Robeson's stance on racial oppression, engagement with the politics of anticolonialism, and self-assurance when facing government oppression meant that he became a symbol of defiance for many black South Africans throughout the 1950s. As Essie Robeson commented on her husband's passport problems in 1952, "Paul Robeson, while still living, has become a symbol and a challenge. . . . When [he] . . . sings songs of sadness, people weep; when he sings songs of hope, they take heart; when he sings songs of protest, guilty governments worry."[131]

Made publicly and often directly addressed to the U.S. government, the majority of South African statements in support of Robeson argued that it was their right, as people committed to political self-determination, to see and hear him speak and perform. As a message on behalf of the leading organizations of South African civil disobedience campaign stated, "We salute Paul Robeson as one of the most outstanding artists of our time, a great champion of the oppressed people and a brave fighter for peace. . . . [He] is a beloved citizen of the world and the United States authorities have no right to deprive us of the privilege of listening to his gifted and magnificent voice."[132] By demanding to hear his voice, South African activists reinstated Robeson's cosmopolitan status and claimed him as one of their own. In 1954, Robeson received another public letter that was signed by a number of prominent South African activists, including Walter Sisulu, declaring, "When the United States Government deprived you of your passport, they deprived the people of the world of your wonderful voice. It is not a personal move against you—it was a political move of worldwide importance. This is why we here in South Africa are interested in the action now being taken by the Americans to try and get your passport restored to you. We want to hear you sing. We have heard you on records. We want to see you, and hear you yourself."[133] The global messages of support sent to Robeson reinforced political and ideological connections between African Americans and the anti-apartheid struggle in South Africa. They restated Robeson's status as a black international icon, and in the process questioned the construction of bureaucratic boundaries designed to isolate him from the politics of African anticolonialism.

Many of these messages directly called attention to the similarities between state oppression in the United States and in South Africa. An article in the June 1954 issue of *Advance* directly criticized the U.S. government in regards to the Robeson passport case. Yusuf Dadoo, in an article entitled "A World Wide Campaign to Free Paul Robeson," written "on behalf of the progressive forces in South Africa," notes that

> ten million oppressed Non-Whites and European democrats in South Africa condemn the action of the U.S. Government in refusing a passport to Paul Robeson to go abroad as yet another blatant example of the way in which aggressive American imperialists are attempting to trample underfoot the hard-won and cherished rights and cultural heritage of the American people. It exposes the claim of the American rulers that they are the champions of freedom as a hollow sham and mockery. The world acknowledges the voice of Paul Robeson as the voice of democracy, and as long as the U.S. administration stifles this voice so long will the U.S. ruling class be condemned by peace-loving people all over the world. We in South Africa support wholeheartedly the world-wide demand to see and hear Paul Robeson, the world's great artist and fighter for peace and freedom.[134]

Robeson's passport case provided anti-apartheid activists with an issue through which they could condemn what they saw as America's imperialist foreign policy as well as the government's failure to eradicate racism at home. Dadoo interprets Robeson's treatment by the U.S. government as a challenge to the American creed and the long-held assertion that the United States acted as the guarantor of democracy throughout the world.[135] With the global politics of the Cold War firmly in mind, the article extends the warning that "as long as the U.S. administration stifles this voice so long will the U.S. ruling class be condemned by peace-loving people all over the world."[136] Another message received by the CAA from the Congress Alliance echoes this sentiment, saying of Paul Robeson that "to us you represent the real America, the true America—not of the H-Bomb, McCarthy, blood and thunder comics and Mickey Spillane—but of the love of peace and real culture that we know exists among ordinary people everywhere. By preventing you from travelling, your government is depriving itself of its finest ambassador."[137] Through Robeson, South African protestors imagined an alternative version of America, one that was free from violence, intimidation, and prejudice.[138] Engaging with the patriotic language of the era, they challenged America to live up to its self-proclaimed democratic ideals by denouncing anticommunist abuses.

Transnational solidarities generated in response to Robeson's plight were further strengthened by the fact that his baritone voice had, on occasion, provided backing to anti-apartheid protests. In his autobiography, Robeson notes that although he was "exiled" within the United States, "through the written word, by recordings and filmed interviews" he strove to maintain his links with his supporters abroad.[139] In articles and through recordings, his voice traveled across the Atlantic and was relayed to black South Africans actively defying apartheid laws. Even as news came through in 1949 that his records had been banned by the National Party, Robeson remained optimistic and defiant, asserting that "I would expect one who belongs to the Hitler tradition to do that [ban his records], but I know it won't keep my voice from reaching my people in Africa."[140] Indeed, as has already been outlined in the introduction to this book, his insistence that African Americans and South Africans would win their "freedoms together" was read aloud at the forty-second ANC annual conference in 1954.[141] In addition to this, Robeson's songs provided the soundtrack to mass rallies and acts of defiance in the country. During the Defiance Campaign a *New York Times* article reported that "several thousand non-whites marched into Fordsburg Freedom Square to the tune of Paul Robeson songs played over a loudspeaker. They carried banners reading, 'Down With Apartheid' . . . and 'Down With Passes.'"[142] Robeson was particularly proud of this fact, commenting on black South African protest that "these South Africans aren't afraid of baiting. They march in thousands with raised clenched fists. They sing their songs of protest (including some of mine, may I modestly add). . . . They say quite sharply and plainly they want their youth alive to struggle for the independence of Africa."[143] Through the singing of his protest songs, Robeson was able to imaginatively march alongside South Africa's black resisters, in spite of his enforced physical absence. As he commented in a message to the ANC, "I have been very happy to learn that my recorded voice is heard among you, and has perhaps contributed in some small way to your great courage and strength in carrying forward your banner in the face of the most cruel persecution and oppression. But I wish that my contribution, that the contribution of all of us here in the United States who support your just cause could be much greater."[144]

Robeson's written statements of support and protest songs appeared to anti-apartheid activists as visible declarations of black international solidarity between African Americans and black South Africans. Technological innovations in recording, distribution, and communication meant that performances and the recorded voice could be transmitted around the world and popularized. Robeson's cables and recordings traveled to South Africa while he, the performer, remained stationary. To those who heard his voice, he ceased to be a distant figure confined to the United States. Instead, through the technological reproduction of his words and performances, he became a symbolic part of black protest in South Africa. Through black print culture and the mechanical reproduction of his performances, Robeson's national detention was challenged and his black cosmopolitan status reasserted. Anti-apartheid activists in the United States and South Africa ensured that it was impossible to fully silence Robeson in the international arena. On the contrary Robeson, albeit in increasingly restrictive circumstances, maintained his global presence and radical anticolonial politics, exposing the excesses of racialized anticommunism along the way.

Robeson's passport case enabled African Americans and black South Africans to challenge race discrimination on a global level. The way in which this was achieved—the metaphors that were employed and the alliances that were formed—help us to better understand how black activists responded to the restrictions placed on their activism during the early Cold War. By drawing attention to the way in which white supremacist politics had historically operated to restrict black mobility, African Americans and black South Africans invested an oppressive situation with certain emancipatory possibilities. Robeson's struggle demonstrates how the right to travel was central to ideas of black freedom in both countries. A historically contested issue that resonated with African Americans and black South Africans, the ability/inability of black individuals to physically cross national borders exposed the symbiotic relationship between black international protest and the transnational power of white governments.

4 African American Culture, Consumer Magazines, and Black Modernity

· ·

Cultural exchange provided another vitally important avenue through which black South Africans engaged with, understood, and were influenced by African American life.[1] Through newspapers, magazines, film, and music, black Americans regularly appeared in South Africa as modern citizens, models of black achievement who lived, worked, and thrived in the urban environment. Although such representations of black life abroad were caricatured and oversimplified, they nevertheless carried an important political significance. Images of black cultural and economic success from across the Atlantic directly challenged a number of white supremacist assumptions, providing black South Africans with a lens to assess the extent to which their lives were constrained and circumscribed by the modern apartheid state. These cross-cultural connections featured heavily in the pages of South African consumer magazines, specifically the popular monthly publication *Zonk!*. The magazine's transatlantic coverage gives an insight into how black South Africans envisioned African American life and culture in the wake of World War II.

First published in 1949, *Zonk!*, the "African People's Pictorial," provided black South Africans with a highly selective glimpse of black America. The publication was filled with articles that covered the lives of film stars, singers, musicians, and athletes, alongside pieces that emphasized the importance of family values and the ideal of respectability. *Zonk!* has often been neglected by historians of this period, who have instead largely focused on the literary output of *Drum* magazine.[2] Indeed, when writing about the 1950s as the "*Drum* Decade," Michael Chapman argues that *Zonk!* was a "politically non-contentious" publication that failed to engage with black resistance.[3] It is certainly true that the magazine avoided addressing black protest or mass civil disobedience and repeatedly refused to question National Party policies. However, the narrative content of *Zonk!* provides a useful lens through which it becomes possible to examine not only how blackness was constructed under apartheid, but also how consumer texts helped foster a global understanding of racism among black South Africans.

Like its more illustrious counterpart, *Zonk!* was a white-owned publication with a large black and colored writing staff.[4] At its peak in the early 1950s it consistently outsold the newly established *Drum* magazine.[5] By 1959 its circulation stood at about 68,000 per month, and it was estimated that at least five more people would go on to read each copy sold as it was passed around among family members, friends, and neighbors.[6] Despite its wide circulation, however, *Zonk!*'s contribution to black South African journalism, and its role in shaping black cultural identity, has often been overlooked.[7]

Zonk! was both informed by and reflected black consumer culture as it emerged in South Africa in the 1940s and 1950s. Fueled by foreign investment and inspired by the "Americanization" of the South African marketplace, white-owned businesses began to deliberately target potential black consumers.[8] Just as the National Party was rapidly expanding the mechanisms of the apartheid state, publications like *Zonk!* were asking black South Africans to buy into notions of economic mobility and development.[9] The growth of consumer culture had a profound influence on how black modernity was envisioned in South Africa while, at the same time, providing a clear reminder of the capitalist structures that fueled the development of the apartheid state. As Tsitsi Ella Jaji has observed, the glossy, modern, and often black American images that stared out at the readers of South African consumer publications clearly illustrated the race and class inequalities that were inherent within the apartheid system.[10] Although readers used the disparity between these images and the realities of black life to question a range of discriminatory practices, South African magazines that tied black success to economic consumption were often problematic.[11] The freedom and mobility portrayed in consumerist images were inaccessible for the vast majority of black South Africans living under apartheid.[12] Even as black consumer magazines provided an important medium through which a transatlantic black consciousness could be forged, these ties were distorted by global capitalist forces that relied on the exploitation of black labor while simultaneously selling mythical visions of black freedom.[13] The African American figures that appeared in the pages of *Zonk!* are therefore representative of both the possibilities and the limitations of consumer culture as a medium through which transnational black solidarities could be forged.

Zonk! envisioned an ideal black identity based around hard work, material wealth, and individual achievement. Articles and images within the magazine were also highly gendered, often focusing on family life and privileging middle class notions of female domesticity. The promotion of

American-style consumer capitalism was important in this regard.[14] This can be seen clearly in an advertisement for Coca Cola in the February 1960 issue of *Zonk!*, which provided the reader with a sleek image of a social gathering of young black professionals. Dressed in smart, expensive clothes and standing as couples, the group collectively beams at the arrival of the party's host carrying a full tray of the sparkling soft drink. These young, well-dressed individuals are positioned as modern black citizens. There is no indication whether this scene is from the United States or South Africa. Indeed, the implication is that with Coca Cola national differences and geographical distances are collapsed. Through the consumption of American products, black South Africans accessed a respectable and modern form of black citizenship that was far removed from common white supremacist notions of African "backwardness" and "primitivism."[15]

This idea that racial advancement could be secured through consumption did not go unchallenged. Indeed, black South African leaders used examples of rampant materialism and individualism to question white claims of racial superiority. Arguing that consumption was part and parcel of a Western project of colonization meant to undermine an authentic African way of life, Chief A. J. Luthuli, leader of the ANC from 1952 to 1967, commented in his autobiography, "What we want now is to be ourselves, to retain our personality, and to let our soul, long buffeted by the old scramble for Africa, grow free. African leaders must be wary of the material enticement of her people. We do not live by bread alone. However alluring the sight of bread may be to the hungry."[16] Warnings against materialism and individualism were, at times, used to advocate for a specifically African brand of politics that warned against buying into notions of white privilege. However, as the articles and adverts that filled the pages of *Zonk!* demonstrate, consumer culture continued to be a powerful force that mediated black identity and popular representations of blackness in South Africa.[17]

Zonk!'s engagement with the United States provided its readers with exciting new social and cultural forms. However, these images were inextricably part of a culture of capitalism that privileged consumption and individual achievement over more militant networks of political solidarity. It is this tension—between consumer capitalism and the agency of the black reader—that is at the heart of *Zonk!* magazine. Even as consumer capitalism established distinct race and gender hierarchies, it also provided spaces through which new racial discourses could be forged and the white supremacist status quo could be questioned.[18] The African Americans who appeared in *Zonk!* played an important role in this process, prompting black readers to imagine new individual and collective identities that destabilized the racist logic of the apartheid state.

Apartheid Policymakers and the "Ideal" Urban African

For black South Africans caught up in the forced removals of the 1950s and the destruction of racially diverse communities such as Sophiatown, urban and cosmopolitan identities associated with black America directly spoke to the issue of black mobility under apartheid.[19] The belief that Africans were unsuited to city life had a long history in terms of racial segregation in South Africa.[20] Such ideas were at the heart of racist arguments that promoted the superiority of white Western civilization and sought to prevent the intermixture of different racial groups. During the 1950s, as biological explanations of racial inferiority/superiority came under repeated attack, segregationists responded by asserting that racial difference was, in fact, the result of a range of cultural, environmental, and historical factors. This emphasis on the cultural incompatibility of specific racial groups was both a response to and reworking of African nationalism, as white settlers sought to justify racial separation in postwar South Africa.[21] This segregationist cultural turn ran through the apartheid government's language of "separate development" and would play a key role in shaping Verwoerd's Bantustan policy.[22]

Central to this language of separation was the belief that Africans were unsuited to living in urban environments. Indeed, it was argued that cities posed a threat to traditional tribal customs and that these places of liquor, prostitution, and crime would be a corrupting influence on supposedly underdeveloped African minds.[23] According to this segregationist logic, the urban was a site of higher Western civilization that would "disorient, demoralize, detribalize, and ultimately de-Africanize raw Natives," destroying the traditional African way of life.[24] In contrast, rural environments were often viewed as "natural" and "tribal" sites where Africans could remain "in a state of 'unspoilt' primitive dignity."[25] Afrikaner nationalists repeatedly invoked these ideas as they responded to the legacy of large-scale black urban migration during World War II.[26] The urban character of African American culture presented in the pages of *Zonk!* therefore provided an important rejoinder for black South Africans that the city, along with the "modern" values it was perceived to embody, was not a space solely reserved for whites.

This ideological split between the urban and the rural was complicated by the apartheid economy's need for cheap black labor, which continued to attract Africans to urban areas. Responding to this dilemma of racial capitalism, early apartheid policymakers embarked on large-scale urban planning initiatives designed to create what the anthropologist Jason Hickel has referred to as the "ideal urban African."[27] Forced removals and policies such as the Group Areas Act therefore went hand in hand with the adoption of modern planning techniques that the government believed could tackle the problems associated with urban African communities.[28] During the 1950s, the National Party worked to establish model townships designed to house "natives" living and working in close proximity to white urban areas.[29] Inspired by European modernist architecture and design, apartheid policymakers believed that urban planning could be deployed to both "civilize" and control Africans.[30] As Hickel argues, the construction of planned townships can be seen as a form of "reluctant colonialism" that amounted to "an unwilling embrace of the civilising mission."[31]

Administrators believed that the development of modern township settlements, such as Meadowlands near Johannesburg, would prevent the crime and moral decay that many whites associated with black urban communities. This "scientifically" constructed Native Housing provided self-contained dwellings with limited public amenities that prioritized private space and discouraged community interaction. Rows of four-room NE 51 (Non-European 51) model houses were built to encourage the development of the nuclear family as well as to prevent communal living and overcrowding.[32]

This was all part of a broader effort to exert power over and pacify the urban African population. It was believed that proper urban planning and community development would tackle a variety of social ills, create productive workers and even protect against subversive political influences.[33] As Secretary of Native Affairs W. W. M. Eiselen argued, "Only with the provision of adequate shelter in properly planned Native townships can full control over urban natives be regained."[34] This paternalistic policymaking privileged modern Western ideals associated with the nuclear family, literally constructing spaces that the apartheid state believed would produce docile and domesticated Africans.[35]

The African Americans who appeared in South African consumer magazines to a certain extent reflected this ideal of the modern and urban black family. For example, a series of adverts for Blue Seal Vaseline, common in the late 1950s, carried the tagline "This American family insists on the very best." Alongside appeared an image of a mother, father, and daughter all dressed in their Sunday finery, beaming at the camera, each clutching their own individual pots of the product.[36] African Americans were presented as professional, discerning consumers with a stable work and home life.[37]

This focus on separate spheres within the African family were, of course, severely limiting for black women who were expected to take on the role of housewife and mother. According to this type of advertising the urban home, presided over by the caring and nurturing African mother, was the basis of successful and autonomous family life. Such images closely corresponded with the National Party's faith in separate development, as well as its paternalistic assumption that only modern European values could "civilize" the urban African.[38] The modern lifestyles that were reflected in *Zonk!* also resonated with the white government's claims that it was committed to the social welfare and development of the native population.[39] The idea that the National Party was working to protect Africans from the dangers of detribalization provided a useful, modernist defense of segregation. Although apartheid administrators made it clear that black South Africans would never be able to attain a level of civilization reserved for white settlers, they argued that Western liberal values could be used to help black South Africans adapt to modern urban environments. To a certain extent then, in articles and advertisements, *Zonk!* privileged the lifestyles and social arrangements that apartheid planners had envisioned for the urban African. Representations of black modernity that ran through the publication constituted a useful propaganda tool, proof that black South Africans could develop under the modernizing influence of the apartheid government.

Zonk! therefore operated as a contradictory text within the cultural and political climate of 1950s South Africa. On the one hand, the magazine affirmed the white state's faith in urban planning, providing visual evidence that a respectable and domestic black middle class could develop under the apartheid system. However, in accepting this view that *Zonk!* merely mimicked the segregationist mythmaking of the National Party, we run the risk of underestimating the interpretative agency of the black South African reader. It would have been difficult for black readers not to compare black life abroad with the reality of their day-to-day lives in South Africa. Inevitably, many would have found the apartheid government's paternalistic message of racial uplift and development wanting.[40]

Black American Culture and *Zonk!*

There are striking similarities between the race, class, and gender politics of *Zonk!* and those of *Ebony* magazine published in the United States.[41] In-

ZONK'S London Correspondent

Gonny Govender Interviews

Fabulous
EARTHA
KITT

"JUST AN OLD-FASHIONED GIRL"

Eartha as she appeared in the recent Royal Command Performance, before Her Majesty the Queen, the Duke of Edinburgh and Princess Margaret. She received rounds of Royal applause for her rendering of "Just An Old-Fashioned Girl."

ORSON WELLES called Eartha Kitt "the most exciting woman in the world." The world obviously respects Mr. Welles' judgment, for it, too, has acclaimed the exciting qualities of this woman. When I went to see her at the Mayfair Hotel, where she stayed during her brief visit to London, it was not to find out how accurate Mr. Welles' description of her was, but to talk to her and see for myself what the ingredients are that go to make up the world's most exciting woman. For female

"No Newspaper man has dared speak to me like that before"

— Eartha to Gonny

readers eagerly awaiting my revelation of the secret formula, let me say right away that I don't have it in my pocket, for it seems that excitement like beauty lies in the eyes of the beholder. This is not to disagree with Mr. Welles, but just to say that Eartha did not have such an impact on me as she obviously had on him and millions of her admirers throughout the world — from Madras to Manchester. Perhaps Miss Kitt was tired and not her usually exciting self when I saw her; perhaps this is a garb that she wears on special occasions. I am inclined though to use three words to describe her — they are not mine, but were used to describe Jayne Mansfield — Eartha Kitt like the curvaceous wife of the former Mr. Universe is mean, moody and magnificent. She has undoubted sex appeal; a voice that is bewitching; a figure like a goddess; and eyes that see through you, and enslave those who look into them. These are, by themselves, great assets, but they also go with an income of £85,000 a year, some of the finest mink coats from the world's top fashion houses, and jewellery whose value it is very difficult to estimate. Eartha Kitt wasn't born into all this; poverty was her world. But it was obvious that her birth was the harbinger of good fortune — her father, a small farmer, reaped a rich harvest after her birth — hence her name Eartha. Her parents died several years later, and the little girl was taken in by poor farming neighbours. When she was eight, she came to live with an aunt in New York. As in the South, poverty stalked the household. Many believe that Eartha's standoffishness which has caused people to describe her

Continued on page 29

"Fabulous Eartha Kitt," *Zonk!*, March 1959. Source: Courtesy of the Beinecke Rare Book and Manuscript Library.

deed, the white director of *Zonk!*, Ike Baruch Brooks, visited the Chicago offices of the Johnson Publishing Company in 1956 in order to learn from the successful African American publication.[42] Despite its liberal integrationist view of race relations in the United States, *Ebony* also played an important role in enhancing African American awareness of and "concern for his fellow Negroes on the Dark Continent."[43] Alongside occasionally clichéd articles that cast Africa as exotic and mysterious were accounts of African life that emphasized black political agency and self-determination.[44] Pieces such as "African Art for the Americans" and "Africa's Greatest Artist" deliberately promoted a positive view of African culture.[45] They provided African Americans with facts that challenged ideas of African primitivism through stories that reminded readers of the fact that "when white men in Europe still lived in caves . . . an abundant, advanced, early civilization flourished in Africa."[46] Other articles stressed the inevitability of African independence and the readiness of black Africa for freedom. *Ebony* promoted the idea that the future of black America was bound up with political and cultural progress in Africa.[47] As an article on racism in South Africa and decolonization in Africa concluded, "With it [African independence] will disappear the myth of racial superiority." In this period of anti-colonialism and decolonization, African Americans regularly looked to Africa for inspiration in their fight for civil rights at home. Africa was moving toward freedom and this development, a number of black leaders argued, would have inevitable consequences for the civil rights movement in the United States.

Just as *Ebony* provided African Americans with visions of African independence that informed civil rights activism in the United States, *Zonk!* magazine exposed black South Africans to imagery of racial uplift from abroad. This process of cultural exchange encouraged black South Africans to imagine alternative racial identities and challenge patronizing racist discourses. By looking toward the United States, and African American celebrity culture in particular, *Zonk!* presented respectable, urban, and modern black identities that could be used to question the ideologies and policies of the apartheid government.

The glossy pages of *Zonk!* regularly featured profiles of prominent African Americans, including Marian Anderson, Louis Armstrong, Adam Clayton Powell, Ralph Bunche, Joe Louis, Jackie Robinson, Harry Belafonte, Sidney Poitier, Dorothy Dandridge, Hazel Scott, and Eartha Kitt, to name just a few. On the whole, the majority of the Americans that appeared in the magazine were actors, musicians, and athletes. However, well-known black political figures occasionally made an appearance too. African Americans also provided *Zonk!* readers with an impressive list of black firsts. Black South Africans heard about the first black women's Wimbledon tennis champion, the first black major league baseball star, the first African American Nobel Prize winner.[48] Other African American celebrities were described in glowing terms that emphasized their skill, professionalism, and success. "With her dazzling smile, expressive eyes, hands, and graceful figure," Lena Horne, the publication proclaimed, was "probably the most beautiful singer appearing in movies, theatres, hotels, night clubs or concert halls. This, plus her superb voice, remarkable sensitivity and resourceful presentation stamps her as a truly great artist."[49] Some articles retold personal stories such as those of the jet fighter pilot Daniel "Chappie" James, "an American Negro who lives with danger" and one of the only men to "have had a jet plane explode under him, crashed in it, and not only walked away from it but saved his student pilot from being burnt to a cinder."[50] Readers were alerted to the fact that "millions of baseball fans in the United States are marvelling over the sensational play of the star centre fielder of the New York Giants professional team, the 23-year-old effervescent Willie Mays."[51] They could "learn how to box with Joe Louis" or immerse themselves in the details of the sprinter and hurdler Harrison Dillard's "longest winning streak in United States track history."[52] *Zonk!* relayed tales of African American heroism, bravery, success, and triumph against the odds to a black South African readership. African Americans were represented as thoroughly modern, urban, and respectable individuals, whose success was indicative of their hard work, perseverance, and professionalism.

Americanized culture permeated South Africa in the 1950s, influencing the younger generation of black South Africans in particular.[53] For example, the journalist Bloke Modisane's autobiographical account of life in Sophiatown, *Blame Me On History*, is full of cultural references to the United States. Modisane tells of an urban world saturated with American film, jazz, and the latest stateside fashions; a time and a place where Miriam Makeba and the Manhattan Brothers would regularly attract crowds to the Odin cinema for concerts, and infamous *tsotsi* gang members were known by names taken directly from the latest Hollywood releases.[54]

Black culture imported from the United States pervaded urban areas in South Africa, influencing and shaping alternative cultural sites while at the same time undergoing important transformations. Black South Africans were not helpless victims of American cultural imperialism. Instead, American influences were used, adapted, and reinterpreted within a specifically

South African context.[55] As Laura Chrisman eloquently argues, the black transnational political and cultural flows between the United States and South Africa "cannot be prematurely converted into the conclusion that Africans were uncritically modeling themselves on African-Americans, nor that African America supplies a vanguard global class."[56] That black South Africans did not simply embrace dominant American ideas of black culture leads Chrisman to conclude that "to read modern South African political culture exclusively in terms of its relations with African America is to distort that culture by neglecting its formation through and against European colonialism."[57] The appearance of African American cultural forms in publications such as *Zonk!* were therefore transformed and reinterpreted by black South Africans seeking to intervene in, and act on, their own domestic experiences of white colonialism.

Central to this process was the way in which *Zonk!* complicated dominant political narratives of race and modernity in South Africa. Specifically, the publication encouraged black readers to question, redefine, and sometimes claim Western standards of modernity. Writing about this period, Kevin Gaines demonstrates how the diverse migratory experiences of black subjects, coupled with the development of communication technologies, "provided the basis for a global culture of black modernity linking colonies with metropolitan centers."[58] This, together with the global flow of commerce, meant that African Americans and black South Africans were often confronted with similar ideas of what constituted a modern black identity.[59] Historically, black South Africans have looked to the United States in order to reinforce their understanding of black modernity in Africa. As Ntongela Masilela argues, prominent black South African figures such as R. V. Selope Thema and Solomon Plaatje "appropriated the historical lessons drawn from the New Negro experience within American modernity to chart and negotiate the newly emergent South African modernity."[60] Although this was not a simple one-way configuration, these transnational links were central to shaping black conceptions of modernity across national borders.[61]

Paul Gilroy's influential claim that the political and cultural flows of the black Atlantic amount to a counterculture of modernity continues to offer a provocative starting point from which to think through the complex and fraught relationship between the African diaspora and the West. Black subjects were part of, and perpetually engaged in a conversation with, narratives of European modernity. At various times and from a range of political standpoints, black intellectuals pushed for inclusion within dominant narratives of modernity while regularly criticizing its violent excesses.[62]

Michael Hanchard outlines the extent to which non-Western populations have been historically excluded from European narratives of modernity. Pointing to "the inequalities of temporality that result from power relations between racially dominant and subordinate groups," Hanchard highlights how racialized understandings of time have been used to cast nonwhite groups as backward and to justify their exclusion from a range of institutions and resources of European modernity.[63] According to Hanchard, black subjects have often responded to the construction of these temporal inequalities by configuring different forms of "Afro-Modernity." Broadly defined, Afro-Modernity describes a specifically black vision of what it means to be modern that references, while being set apart from, dominant ideas of modernity in Western Europe and North America. Drawing on political and cultural practices associated with African and black diasporic identities, Afro-Modern subjects forged alternative visions of modernity that directly challenged white supremacist assumptions. As Hanchard argues, "Dialectically, Afro-Modernity can be seen as the negation of the idea of African and African-derived peoples as the antithesis of modernity."[64]

A particular version of Afro-Modernity emerged in the pages of *Zonk!* magazine. Its black readers were confronted with representations of modern black subjects that were shaped by, but also distinct from, the structures of white European modernity.[65] Although modernity was defined in stereotypically Western terms—with references to technological advancement, individual achievement, and capitalist success—*Zonk!* also offered black readers the opportunity to claim modern identities as a means of resistance. In particular, by depicting African Americans as modern black citizens, the publication challenged racialized notions of time that associated blackness with the primitive past. The world of *Zonk!*, inhabited by black movie stars, musicians, and athletes from the other side of the Atlantic, allowed readers to adopt a diasporic black identity that questioned and occasionally transcended domestic racial hierarchies. The magazine's focus on black celebrity provided a forum through which its readers could imagine alternative forms of citizenship. In consuming the lives of famous African Americans, it was sometimes possible for black South Africans to question the immediate realities of life under apartheid by imagining themselves as a modern global citizenry connected to the broader black diaspora.

This potential for black international solidarity can be seen in the regular *Zonk!* feature, "Picture News from the U.S.A.," which showcased the lives and achievements of a range of famous African Americans. As one article explained, "About one tenth of the citizens of the United States are of African descent. Few sections of the population have advanced as rapidly as Negroes during the last 25 years. Ralph Bunche, Marian Anderson, Mary McLeod Bethune and many other Negroes, famous in America and throughout the world, have made valuable contributions to international understanding, in the field of entertainment, and to community welfare."[66] By recounting the achievements of prominent African Americans, the series promoted a pan-African conception of identity that reinforced cultural and political connections between *Zonk!*'s South African readers and the wider black diaspora. This message of uplift appealed to ideals of racial respectability across the Atlantic. Articles featured the "outstanding Negro statesmen" Ralph Bunche, who it was argued "upheld the highest ideals of American citizenship"; champion boxers such as Joe Walcott whose unshakable religious belief made him pray "with tears in his eyes" and appeal to God "for strength and guidance"; season MVP Jackie Robinson, the baseball star who "devotes much of his time to youth work"; Marian Anderson, who was performing for kings, queens, and presidents; and Sugar Ray Robinson, who had just donated the $33,000 purse of his latest world title fight to a New York cancer charity.[67]

The African Americans featured were dressed in suits, the uniforms of their profession, or the latest modern fashions. They were often shown either hard at work or at home with their loving families. These were more than images of black success and achievement. They depicted a particular type of modern black identity, one that promoted the respectable principles of hard work and professionalism, as well as community and family values. As David Goodhew points out, the ability to claim a form of respectability was a politically powerful tool for many black South Africans throughout the 1950s. Respectable black identities were more malleable in South Africa than in the United States, as the severity of state sanctioned apartheid made distinctions between the black working and middle classes increasingly precarious.[68] Black South Africans from different backgrounds therefore asserted their shared respectability as a form of political unity that challenged the apartheid state. Indeed, as the National Party sought to destroy and uproot African communities, displays of black respectability provided an important rallying call for a number of individuals and organizations opposed to these policies.[69] With its popularity and wide circulation, *Zonk!* promoted a public philosophy of racial respectability that was central to the way it conceived of black modernity. The publication's use of famous African American figures to emphasize economic independence, individual

Picture News From The U.S.A.

Film Star

Carnival Queen

"Picture News from the U.S.A.," *Zonk!*, June 1952. Source: Courtesy of the Beinecke Rare Book and Manuscript Library.

success, and stable family relations gave its readers the opportunity to question racial stereotypes that undermined black autonomy and cast black South Africans as being unsuited to the trappings of modern life. Representations of racial respectability in *Zonk!* therefore provided an alternative model of how to be black that challenged longstanding white supremacist assumptions.[70] Through the selection and representation of internationally famous African Americans, the magazine advanced a respectable black internationalism that asserted the modernity of people of African descent.

Respectable values, such as patience, self-discipline, and hard work, often appeared to be all too closely aligned to the government's vision of a docile and productive African population. However, black American culture still had the potential to disrupt racist imagery and to challenge assumptions of white superiority within this context. The presence of African Americans in consumer texts complicated entrenched racial hierarchies and racist ideology in South Africa. They provided proof that in the realms of politics and culture, black South Africans did not need to accept white power and control. African American celebrities and politicians continued to provide a powerful reminder of black equality.

Zonk! and Black International Communication

These tensions among consumer capitalism, apartheid politics, and black internationalism often came to the fore when African Americans addressed black South Africans in the pages of *Zonk!* Early editions of the magazine contained a relatively short-lived feature called "American Letter," in which a series of famous African American figures appeared each month. The series provided a space for black international communication between both countries. The thoughts, comments, and supportive words of these famous African American individuals often gave the impression that black lives in the United States and South Africa were closely interconnected. These messages were meant to inspire, reminding South African readers that they too could share in these stories of racial uplift. Yet while many of the "American Letters" emphasized the values of hard work and perseverance, they did so in ways that tended to overlook the structural inequalities of the apartheid system. Again, these cross-cultural exchanges were limited and reflected the efforts of the state to stifle black international criticism of apartheid.

"American Letter" segments were made up of a full-page spread that contained a large photograph and a short piece of text outlining the professional achievements, activities, and personal lives of certain African American celebrities. Representative of the item's tone was the following message from the United States: "It is with great pleasure that I extend my heartfelt greetings to the African people. I and fifteen million other American people share the same aims for a happy, prosperous and peaceful life. Sincerely, Lena Horne."[71] Here, in the first issue of the magazine, Horne—a radical representative of the black freedom struggle in the United States—delivers a direct message to the black South African population.[72] This emphasis on her personal ties to Africa, as well as the assertion that black South Africans had the support of 15 million African American allies living across the Atlantic, functioned as a rare message of pan-African solidarity within the magazine. Writing as a representative of African Americans on the international stage, Horne's words were both an extension of black international friendship and an acknowledgment that the relative fortunes of both groups were interlinked. Marian Anderson, Adam Clayton Powell, Hazel Scott, and the president and editor of the *New York Amsterdam News*, C. B. Powell, were among the other prominent figures featured in "American Letter."[73] Again, each of these individuals boasted strong activist credentials and were vocal advocates for civil rights in the United States as well as black self-determination overseas.[74]

Marian Anderson, perhaps most famous for her 1939 performance at the Lincoln Memorial, after being refused access to Constitution Hall in Washington, D.C., on racial grounds, offered readers another striking example of black defiance.[75] In her message of support to black South Africa she emphasized the values of hard work and professionalism. As *Zonk!*'s editorial staff framed part of her "American Letter," "Marian Anderson's message is addressed on the surface to all stage performers—but applies equally to every kind of work. She says: 'You want to do your level best every time you perform. Sometimes, for reasons you cannot explain, things do not come off the way you want. You wait then for the next time and then go back to redeem yourself.'"[76] This message, that hard work and perseverance would ultimately result in redemption, was illustrative of the focus on racial uplift and respectability that the publication projected to its readership. Although black South Africans (and most black Americans for that matter) were constrained by political forces and socioeconomic structures that prevented them from emulating the lives of these famous individuals, they were asked to follow the values that they embodied, to have pride in their work, and to continue to persevere under difficult conditions.

This connection between individual hard work and racial uplift came to the fore again in an interview with Althea Gibson, the first black woman to win a grand slam on the world tennis tour. Reflecting on a meeting with Gibson in 1958, Gonny Govender, *Zonk!*'s London correspondent, "told her that the readers of ZONK! had read about her and were very proud of her achievements as the only Coloured woman player of world standard. She thanked me and said that she would do her best to live up to the high hopes that the nonwhite community had placed in her. 'I will of course do my best,' she told me, 'and please thank your readers for their expression of good wishes.'"[77] By stressing the "high hopes" that the black South African community had placed in Gibson, the article directly connected Gibson's own individual success to the collective fate of racially marginalized groups in South Africa. Gibson was living proof that whites could be taken on and defeated in any arena. Her sporting achievements represented an important challenge to the global color line.

Nevertheless, even as "American Letter" articles offered inspiring words and hinted at a shared racial identity between African Americans and black South Africans, they consistently refused to openly acknowledge or criticize the structurally embedded inequalities that shaped race relations in the United States and South Africa. Significantly, the ideals of hard work, perseverance, and individual success embodied by these prominent African Americans furthered the illusion that opportunities for black economic development existed under the system of apartheid. Articles that featured famous African American figures often worked to reinforce the apartheid government's narrative that the political and economic isolation of black South Africans represented a positive opportunity for self-governance. Indeed, images of African American success that were used to rouse and inspire black readers sometimes made it easier to cast apartheid policies as benevolent and compatible with notions of black advancement.

However, this view of *Zonk!* downplays the ability of black South Africans to read against the grain in ways that recognized why the "American Letter" feature rarely tackled the issue of apartheid head on. Black South African readers engaged with these famous African Americans from tightly regulated spaces, in which open political dissent was forbidden and journalistic censorship was the norm. Black readers were well aware of these structural limitations. In response, they would have read "American Letter" critically—with skepticism—investing certain images or quotes with additional meaning while deliberately suppressing aspects of the publication that reflected the policies of the government. The presence in the magazine

many more opportunities would not come her way. How well the 5 ft. 11½ in. tall Althea won can be seen in these results. In the quarter final she beat South Africa's Sandra Reynolds 6-3, 6-4. In the semifinal she crushed Britain's Christine Truman 6-1, 6-1, and in the final she trounced her fellow American, Darlene Hard, 6-3, 6-1.

Together with Darlene Hard Althea was on the winning side of the women's doubles, when they beat the Australians, Thelma Long and Mary Hawton 6-1, 6-2. What a triumph for the Harlem-born girl who learned her tennis on the sidewalks of New York. When she returned home New York laid on the traditional "hero's welcome." Driving down lower Broadway, in an open car, Althea was cheered to the echo by thousands upon thousands of spectators, while the ticker tape snow fell from the sky scrapers.

ALTHEA is WORLD'S No. 1 WOMAN TENNIS PLAYER
— New York gives her traditional "hero's welcome"

New York's Althea Gibson became the first Non-white woman to win the singles final of the All England Tennis Championship, in all the long history of the Wimbledon championships, which is recognised as the tennis championships of the world. Before leaving on a world tennis tour last year, Althea stated that her goal for 1957 would be the winning of the Wimbledon and United States women's singles titles. During the championships in England, Althea often made herself unpopular by her single-mindedness of purpose and ruthlessness on the courts — to win the championship was all that interested her, and at 29 years of age she knew that

"Althea Is World's No. 1 Woman Tennis Player—New York Gives Her Traditional 'Hero's Welcome,'" *Zonk!*, August 1957. Source: Courtesy of the Beinecke Rare Book and Manuscript Library.

of figures like Horne, Anderson, and Gibson continued to disrupt a range of white supremacist beliefs with clear and contemporary visual reminders that white racial superiority was based on a series of myths, including that African Americans—and by extension black South Africans—could achieve success in a number of white dominated arenas.

This feeling of black pride and international solidarity often comes to the fore in *Zonk!*'s music journalism. This appears clearly in an interview with Louis Armstrong that appeared in the June 1959 edition of the magazine. The centerpiece of the interview, again carried out by Gonny Govender, was a meeting between Armstrong and the South African jazz musician Pinocchio Mokaleng in London.[78] As Penny Von Eschen outlines in her study of State Department jazz tours, Armstrong was a strong advocate for African independence.[79] Aware of the problematic nature of his role as an African American ambassador for a government that continued to deny civil rights to its black citizens, he used the travel and performance opportunities such tours offered to promote a "global way of thinking" about race.[80] Reflecting on the meeting between Mokaleng and Armstrong, Govender commented, "I thought the little South African was going to cry with joy. Satchmo shook his hands and Mokaleng handed him a book. It was a copy of Father Huddleston's "Naught for Your Comfort" and contained the signatures of many other famous jazzmen."[81]

Mokaleng's uninhibited joy was not simply the product of his admiration of Armstrong as a jazz musician but was also underpinned by a broader sense of racial kinship. Mokaleng's gift of Huddleston's book, an autobiographical account of the radical Anglican churchman's time in Johannesburg, written at the height of the Sophiatown forced removals, served as a powerful metaphor for the way racism had blighted the lives of the black populations of both countries.[82] Keen to foster these links, Armstrong described how on his visit to Ghana he had learned of the links between African folk music and jazz, concluding that it had been his desire to visit South Africa to observe firsthand the "wonderful talent in the Union, and how jazz conscious the different communities were."[83]

Often carrying pan-African messages of solidarity, black American celebrities provided readers with an important counternarrative to the negative representations of blackness that prevailed under apartheid. Presented in this way, tales of African American success in *Zonk!* were designed to inspire the magazine's black South African readership. Cultural manifestations of black internationalism also offered a potential tool for political critique. Messages of black success on the other side of the Atlantic not only helped instill racial pride among black South Africans but also encouraged readers to think about how their lives differed from these glossy African American figures and to ask why notions of freedom and success, mythically embodied by black America, were difficult to imagine in a South African context. It is unrealistic to think that black South Africans embraced images of black success from abroad uncritically. The African Americans that appeared in *Zonk!* were often inspiring figures. However, they also enabled black South Africans to debate and define a distinctly South African form of black modernity.

Zonk!'s focus on jazz also gives us a sense of how black South Africans were inspired by, but not completely beholden to, African American culture when talking about what constituted a modern black identity. Paul Gilroy has famously asserted that the transatlantic flows of music were central to the development of a black "counterculture of modernity."[84] Jazz in particular has been envisioned as a site of black modernity that challenged exclusionary forms of white modernism through the production of alternative cultural forms.[85] The professed musical kinship of jazz musicians from the United States and South Africa exposes an interesting additional dynamic of how black populations constructed modern diasporic identities.[86] Jazz featured heavily in *Zonk!* There were record reviews, profiles of famous jazz performers, and reports of the latest fashion trends from the jazz scene. As Von Eschen shows, jazz musicians from the United States acted as "cultural translators" who shaped global ideas of black freedom.[87]

Jazz performances were also possible sites of racial transgression. For instance Bloke Modisane recognized the importance of jazz as a site of resistance in his account of the Johannesburg shows of the famous white American clarinetist Tony Scott. Modisane described Scott's performance at Witwatersrand University's Great Hall as amounting "to what can only be described—in South African terms—as cultural subversion."[88] Scott's insistence that he would only play before mixed audiences, as well as his surprise introduction of local black South African saxophonist Kippie Moeketsi to play on stage with him, was a rebellious nod to the black roots of jazz that directly confronted apartheid laws. Recalling the defiant performance, Modisane described how the Africans present "offered up silent admiration for the man who had the courage to defy the philosophy of a nation, and we canonised him as the first man who publicly refused to accommodate what we held to be a fundamental wrong."[89]

Although *Zonk!* keenly promoted African American jazz performers, the publication also called for a uniquely South African transformation of "jazz themes and riffs."[90] Carol Muller points out that the historiography focusing on jazz in the United States and South Africa "has been one of the master and its minions—the United States as the superpower, South Africa as derivative of the master narrative."[91] Consequently, there is a need to document how black South Africans responded to African American jazz musicians, their music, and their performances. While *Zonk!* made it possible for famous African American jazz performers to speak to ordinary black South Africans, it also provided a space where black South Africans could assert their own individual voice. As an article in the July 1954 edition of *Zonk!* by P. G. Makaza, "Originality in Jazz?" asserted, the imitation of American jazz performances simply was not good enough. Instead black South African jazzmen had to become accomplished performers in their own right.[92] As Makaza argues, "The African jazzman is safely becoming an end in himself, he copies his favourite American musician. Studying his records judiciously and trying to memorise his phrasing. . . . Without knowing it, he loses his identity and individuality and natural interpretative ability. He copies the external without possessing the spiritual content to back it up."[93] For Makaza imitation resulted in a loss of identity and individuality, and was an indication of a lack of emotional connection with the music. Makaza observed that Louis Armstrong, Fats Waller, and Dizzy Gillespie were at their peak when they "played their own tunes" or "one of the great themes of their race." Makaza argued that aspiring black South African musicians must do the same. To become great performers in their own right South African jazzmen must look inward.[94] The "African jazzman," Makaza asserted, "must turn composer if he is ever to emancipate himself from America and the 'Majuba Beat,' otherwise we, the followers, will never know the common denominator between improvised and composed jazz."[95] The article stresses the need to eradicate both the "Majuba Beat," a traditional African tune closely related to jive music, and American influences that were diluting South African jazz performances. This call to turn composer symbolizes the ways black South Africans transformed external cultural influences in order to both reimagine the African past and respond to their present domestic circumstances.

Zonk!, with its focus on black American celebrity culture, provided a space where black South Africans could respond critically to external cultural forces, engaging with these famous black figures in order to comment on their own cultural and political situation. The desire to break free from imported forms of jazz as well as traditional African modes of performance suggests that *Zonk!* ultimately promoted an alternative version of modern black South African culture. This was informed by, but also set apart from, the cultural influences of black America.

Zonk! reflects both the limitations and possibilities of black cross-cultural exchange in the era following World War II. The publication was a tightly controlled space that reflected the racial beliefs of the apartheid government as well as the desire of white businesses to profit from black South Africans. However, the consumerist focus of *Zonk!* also represented an important site where white supremacist beliefs could be contested and transnational black connections could be forged. As Davarian Baldwin argues in his study of the New Negro in 1920s Chicago, "The very notion of a race discourse was largely circulated and contested within the marketplace."[96] This process of contested consumption is central to understanding the role that *Zonk!* played among aspiring black South Africans in the 1950s. Historically, the consumer marketplace has helped perpetuate a range of race, gender, and class stereotypes.[97] Even so, the ideas and connections articulated through consumer texts could also be used to challenge racial hierarchies. *Zonk!* circulated images and stories that informed efforts to establish a modern black identity and reject racist stereotypes. African Americans played an important role in this process. They emphasized black achievements, promoted racial pride, and, ultimately, embodied a sense of racial possibility. These were politically important messages for *Zonk!*'s black readers as they confronted the day-to-day reality of life under apartheid. Specifically, the magazine provided a space where black South Africans could take on and challenge racist beliefs that emphasized black primitivism. By promoting a sophisticated and urban form of black identity, *Zonk!* encouraged its readers to draw on African American culture as a way of negotiating and claiming a modern black identity in South Africa.[98]

African American culture was privileged in *Zonk!* in ways that encouraged black South Africans to question and redefine dominant standards of modernity, thus wresting this concept away from white colonizers. This represented a selective embrace of Western modernity alongside African American and African culture in order to challenge racial oppression. The heavily stylized representations of African American culture clearly demonstrated that black exclusion from modern everyday life was not inevitable. In addition to this, they reminded *Zonk!* readers that the achievements of whites could be matched, if not bettered, in every sphere of life—if only black South Africans were given the opportunity. The magazine therefore touched on a series of political issues, even as it was heavily censored and motivated by the desire for profit. By presenting black lives in the United States and South Africa as being connected, it drew attention to the racist myths and exploitative practices that oppressed black South Africans. Significantly, the African Americans that appeared in *Zonk!* could be used to challenge the apartheid system rather than acting as icons that promoted separate development. The magazine placed black bodies in spaces usually reserved for whites under apartheid, clearly demonstrating that white superiority was neither natural nor preordained.

The Afro-Modernity running through the pages of *Zonk!* illustrates the unequal way in which notions of sovereignty and citizenship operated in modern South African society.[99] However, this was not about escaping South Africa by imaginatively embracing a black American identity. Instead, black American achievements were used to draw attention to and question apartheid on a local level. Foreign and domestic cultures intersected throughout this era in ways that shaped a specific form of South African modernity that exposed the exploitive racial and labor practices of apartheid. Again, readers had the potential to take this information and use it in ways that suited their own political agenda and outlook. Specifically, the publication encouraged black readers to question and redefine Western standards of modernity. As P. G. Makaza warned in his editorial on jazz, black South Africans should not simply copy "the external without possessing the spiritual content to back it up."[100] This observation provides a metaphor for the cultural significance of *Zonk!* in this era of mass anti-apartheid resistance.

Black American culture could be interpreted and put to use by black South Africans in a number of ways. This had the potential to promote a sense of racial solidarity and citizenship across national borders and could be used to inform a specifically black South African identity that drew attention to the political and economic forces that limited racial progress under apartheid. The lives of African Americans and black South Africans were often very different. *Zonk!* underlined these differences and reminded black South Africans that they were united through their shared experiences of apartheid. African Americans in *Zonk!* therefore also prompted black South Africans to look inward, to search for a deeply rooted and specifically South African spiritual identity that spoke to their local experiences.[101] African American culture was used in a number of ways in apartheid South Africa. It was repackaged to give the illusion of racial development and political economic possibility, while it could also be harnessed in order to critique and challenge the state. Although these messages were often compromised or tightly controlled, they should not simply be brushed aside and dismissed. Doing so would deny the agency of black South African readers and suggest that black consumers uncritically bought into the myths they were being sold.[102]

In April 1963, Miriam Makeba made a particularly telling comment in an interview with the *Chicago Defender*. For an article called "Crossing the Culture Bridge between [the] U.S. and Africam" Makeba was asked how her new life in the United States differed from her life in South Africa. Reminiscing on home and the strangeness she had felt when she first arrived in New York, she replied, "Actually, people [in the United States] know very little about us [black South Africans]. Often they are amazed that I speak English. I am certain that just my appearance on stage is dispelling much of the misconception people had about us."[103] Makeba's statement demonstrates how cultural performances and displays could help bring black people together during the early Cold War. Although white governments tightly policed their mobility, African Americans and black South Africans found alternative ways to cross "the culture bridge" between both countries. Through the consumption of black culture overseas African Americans and black South Africans attempted to challenge white supremacist ideas and claim their identity as consumer citizens.

Part III   Challenging Anticommunism

· ·

5 Black Internationalism, Anticommunism, and the Prison

....

In *Long Walk to Freedom*, Nelson Mandela notes, "It is said that no one truly knows a nation until one has been inside its jails."[1] The prison as an allegory for the nation has been a common theme in the writing of intellectuals, philosophers, and activists. However, in the history of the black freedom struggle, the prison has often acted as a broader metaphor, one that has been used to connect movements for black self-determination across national borders. For many African Americans and black South Africans, the arrest and imprisonment of black political leaders represented a shared experience of racial oppression around which international connections could be forged. Political prisoners on both sides of the Atlantic became icons of resistance, heroic figures through which black international solidarities were launched and maintained. By engaging with the plight of political prisoners overseas, as well as noting parallels between the ways in which incarceration was used to stifle black protest in both countries, anti-apartheid activists worked to turn oppressive situations into emancipatory opportunities.

The prison system has been a central instrument of racial control in both the United States and South Africa.[2] In the postbellum American South, physical detention and the convict-lease system were widely used to reestablish white dominance over newly free blacks.[3] Through vagrancy and anti-enticement laws, the criminal justice system became a key mechanism through which citizenship rights were denied to African Americans.[4] Although the racialized dynamics of the prison system changed over time, incarceration has been used to harness black labor and reassert racial hierarchies, the legacy of which has been traced by a number of groundbreaking historical studies that have documented the rise of mass incarceration in the twentieth century.[5] The prison was also central to the maintenance of racial control in South Africa. In particular, there are striking parallels with the United States in terms of how the criminal justice system was used to secure cheap black labor in the country. Starting in the late nineteenth century, the colonial state implemented a number of legal measures, including the development of pass laws, designed to create an accessible and flexible convict labor force.[6] This production of a vast pool of unfree labor rested on notions of black criminality that cast Africans as socially threatening and in need of control.[7] By the late 1940s and 1950s a growing number of African prisoners were leased to Afrikaner farmers as agricultural laborers. The journalist and activist Ruth First sparked a national scandal when she denounced the rise of farm labor as being "akin to slavery" and published a number of articles exposing how the criminal justice system was being used to exploit black labor.[8] Finally, and perhaps most importantly, South African jails were also filled with those who had fallen foul of the pass laws—responsible for an estimated twenty million African arrests between 1920 and the end of apartheid.[9]

Mirroring practices in the United States, the prison system in South Africa was used to enforce segregation and to maintain racial hierarchies. Incarceration disciplined those who violated apartheid laws and allowed the state to further extend its control over the mobility and labor of black South Africans. As Florence Bernault argues, the "tropical prison" in South Africa "did not seek to separate lawful citizens from marginals and delinquents; it aimed to reinforce the social and political separation of the races to the sole benefit of white authority by assigning the mark of illegality to the whole of the dominated population."[10] The centrality of the prison to the colonization process ensured that it became an important political site for black South Africans struggling to gain full citizenship rights. It is important to note that the experiences of everyday inmates differed greatly from individuals arrested for their anti-apartheid activism. Political prisoners were often housed together and kept apart from prisoners who had been arrested for more conventional crimes.[11] However, the physical space of the prison served as a telling reminder of how easily the brand of criminality could be applied to Africans regardless of their position in society. Even as there were discrepancies in terms of how an individual came to be caught up in the criminal justice system, all who passed through the gates of South Africa's jails were aware of how blackness was criminalized in the eyes of the white settler state.

The prison represented a site where black citizenship claims could be denied and contested. It functioned as a physical space that effectively determined which individuals and groups constituted a threat to the stability of the nation-state. In marking individuals as undesirables within the nation, incarceration played an important role in the construction of boundaries that have distinguished citizens from noncitizens.[12] The production of black criminals through the media, social science, and a range of discriminatory laws effectively dehumanized African Americans and black South Africans, stripping them of any claims to legitimate national citizenship.[13]

All this had important consequences in terms of how black protest—both domestic and global—was framed. A focus on how the criminal justice system was interpreted by activists in both countries not only uncovers important political exchanges between African Americans and black South Africans that were forged throughout the 1950s, but also illuminates how and why these transnational linkages developed. An exploration of how the harsh realities of political imprisonment in both countries were interpreted and challenged provides important insight into how activists connected their own experiences of the prison in order to construct a language of black internationalism that was designed to secure racial justice across borders. Political prisoners in both countries recognized the extent to which they were criminalized. By comparing their treatment at the hands of the state, they challenged their status as criminals and reasserted the legitimacy of their political protest. African Americans and black South Africans saw reflected in one another's legal mistreatment the same mechanisms of power that continued to deny them full citizenship status. The arrest and imprisonment of black leaders in both countries acted as a global indicator of race discrimination. Highly visible and innately recognizable, incarceration became a lens through which black identity could be rearticulated across national borders.

The imprisonment of anti-apartheid activists during the Defiance Campaign (1952) and later the Treason Trial (1956–1961) received a great deal of attention in the United States. The fate of political prisoners in South Africa inspired support from American organizations operating across the political divide.[14] Responding to the mass arrests that accompanied the Defiance Campaign, the CAA launched the Fund for Victims of Nationalist Persecution. Through this initiative the council raised money for the Joint Defence Fund set up by the ANC to post bail money and cover the legal costs of imprisoned campaign leaders.[15] The council's leadership argued that it was "an opportunity to demonstrate in a concrete and meaningful way our friendship for and solidarity with the 10 million oppressed darker peoples in the Union of South Africa who are helping to fight OUR battle against Jim-Crow, fascism and war."[16] In little over five months the CAA raised $2,442.41 for this cause.[17] The organization also collected signatures for a petition to President Truman calling for the U.S. government to condemn apartheid, organized an emergency conference on South African racism, and busied itself by bombarding the South African ambassador to the United States and the consul general in New York "with telegrams and resolutions demanding the immediate release of the hundreds of South Africans jailed for participation in the defiance of unjust laws campaign and under the Suppression of Communism Act."[18]

The newly formed Americans for South African Resistance (AFSAR) also made important financial contributions to the defense of anti-apartheid activists arrested during this era of mass civil disobedience. Corresponding primarily with prominent ANC figures J. L. Njongwe and R. T. Bokwe, the liberal AFSAR sent over $3,000 to "support the families of resisters" imprisoned during the Defiance Campaign.[19] On April 6, 1952, the ANC and SAIC called a National Day of Pledge and Prayer to announce the official start of the Defiance Campaign.[20] Both the AFSAR and the CAA held mass meetings to show their support, and the NAACP wrote to the ANC to express its support for the campaign.[21] With Canada Lee in attendance, the AFSAR's inaugural action was to organize a rally at Adam Clayton Powell's Abyssinian Baptist Church, which ended in protestors marching on the South African consul general to show their solidarity with the anti-apartheid movement.[22] The CAA also marked this event by calling a rival mass meeting in Harlem at the corner of 126th and Lenox that attracted hundreds of supporters who took part in a symbolic two minutes of silence that marked their solidarity with the victims of apartheid.[23]

These fundraising efforts in the United States were regularly reported on in the anti-apartheid press with articles such as "World Action against S.A. Mooted: Humanity's Conscience Outraged by Apartheid" and "Dollars Sent to Help Resistance Victims," stressing the importance of this international support.[24] In the aftermath of the Defiance Campaign, Walter Sisulu wrote to the CAA to thank the organization for its support, stating that "the interest taken by the Negro people in the struggle of the oppressed people both in our country and [in] other parts of the world, their sentimental and historical affiliations to the Continent of Africa, and their contribution the campaign for world peace and international harmony are factors which make them our comrades-in-arms in spite of the considerable distance and space that separates us."[25] The readiness of "the Negro people" to assist black South Africans constituted black internationalism in action. African Americans who offered their support to black South Africans at this time actively demonstrated their commitment to the politics of Pan-Africanism, as well as the anticolonial struggle in Africa. Cases of political imprisonment provided African Americans with a lens through which they could compare and contrast racism in the United States with the repressive system of apartheid. For many the prison became a symbol that underlined the power of white supremacy, providing proof of both the draconian nature of the apartheid regime and the need for people of African descent to come together to push for an end to colonial rule in Africa.

After the dismantling of the CAA in 1955, the liberal anticommunist American Committee on Africa (ACOA) became the largest U.S. organization working to mobilize support for the defendants of the Treason Trial. Emerging out of the AFSAR, the ACOA was an interracial organization and was led by the white pacifist George Houser. The committee had strong links to civil rights organizations and counted prominent black leaders such as James L. Farmer, Adam Clayton Powell, A. Philip Randolph, Bayard Rustin, and James H. Robinson among its sponsors.[26] In response to the arrest of the 156 Treason Trialists, the ACOA established the South Africa Defense Fund, which would go on to raise a considerable amount of money for the accused and their families. In 1957 Martin Luther King Jr. circulated a letter through the ACOA asking for contributions to this fund, concluding, "Your support will help serve justice in Africa today and build our friendship with Africans in the crucial period ahead. We need your help."[27] By the end of the decade the organization claimed to have collected in excess of $50,000 for the Treason Trial Defence Fund, money that was put toward legal costs, bail funds, the support of defendants' families, and international publicity.[28]

A letter from Frieda Matthews to George Houser, written after the arrest of her husband Z. K. Matthews, clearly demonstrates the need for these financial contributions. "I am appealing to all our friends for assistance for all," Frieda writes. "The need for funds is urgent, especially for the purpose of bail which might be granted on the 21st and is likely to be very high. Please tell all our friends [in the United States]."[29] Financial assistance from the United States, to help with bail, legal costs, and loss of earnings, was invaluable for many incarcerated black South Africans and their families. As Chief Luthuli recalls in his autobiography, "The difference which the Fund made to our lives is beyond calculation. . . . It cannot be denied that the character of the people who sponsored the Fund gave the world some inkling of the true nature of the trial, and also brought in observers from overseas."[30] At a time when leftist organizations were being dismantled and black radicals imprisoned, the ACOA provided practical and tangible support for South African political prisoners.

The committee differed from the CAA in that it failed to link cases of political imprisonment in South Africa to the prosecution of black leftists in the United States. Although the organization was critical of America's relationship with the apartheid government, its political vision was restricted by its anticommunist politics and reluctance to recognize the relationship that existed between capitalism and imperial power. Nevertheless, the ACOA made important contributions to the anti-apartheid struggle at a time when South African activists were in desperate need of assistance. Within a reformist and nonviolent framework, the ACOA represented a significant anticolonial lobby that worked with South African activists from across the political spectrum to marginalize the political standing of the apartheid regime in the United States.[31]

Despite this range of responses to the Defiance Campaign and Treason Trial, it was the African American left that most clearly identified with the plight of political prisoners in South Africa. The legal and political processes that led to the imprisonment of South African activists provided a blunt reminder of how anticommunism was used to bolster white supremacist rule and to limit black protest. Indeed, black activists who suffered as a result of anticommunist legislation often interpreted this manifestation of state power as evidence of the interconnected nature of white supremacy on both sides of the Atlantic. Adopting an anti-imperial critique of American power, African American leftists strategically connected white settler colonialism in southern Africa to racism in America.[32] Historical literature has largely focused on the ways in which Cold War anticommunism shaped the civil rights movement in the United States.[33] However, there is also a need to acknowledge the extent to which anticommunism influenced race relations around the world.[34] The National Party's embrace of anticommunism not only was an attempt to win over the hearts and minds of U.S. policymakers but also provided a repressive political framework that could be used to silence black protest.

It is undeniable that anticommunism had disastrous consequences for radical forms of black protest. However, there remains a need to document the tensions and acts of resistance that continued to characterize this period—to examine how black activists on the left responded to the anticommunist harassment they faced and to remember that—for the most part—they came out fighting.[35] This rarely brought large-scale victories and required a great deal of self-sacrifice. Yet for many of these individuals the hardships that they faced reaffirmed their commitment to an analysis of racism that explicitly traced the global contours of white supremacist power.

In other words, we need to look at what black radicals were able to achieve in a repressive climate, as well as focusing on the way in which black protest was stifled at this historical juncture. Black activists were occasionally able to expand their international analysis of racism and imperialism as a result of the state repression they experienced.[36] We need to recognize the agency of black radicals so that they are not simply cast as unfortunate victims of the Cold War. Many individual activists did not capitulate to state repression, even as the organizations and movements that they were part of were dismantled around them. By focusing on the activism of black political prisoners in the United States and South Africa, it is possible to glimpse the ways in which they incorporated state repression and anticommunism into their political critiques of racism and colonialism. Caged and often subjected to the repressive mechanisms of the state, many of these individuals continued to draw connections between the struggle for racial equality in the United States and South Africa.

Anticommunism and Political Imprisonment

Anticommunism narrowed the terrain of the black freedom struggle, as anticapitalist and anti-imperialist critiques of the United States were labelled politically suspect.[37] The notion that black activism and communist politics were interconnected continued to shape a range of government responses to the civil rights movement during the early Cold War. Though the African American left bore the brunt of anticommunist repression, even politically moderate black leaders were viewed with suspicion.[38] Legislation such as the redefined Smith Act (1940) and the McCarran Internal Security Act (1950) meant numerous black activists faced the threat of arrest, imprisonment, and possible deportation due to their alleged communist political sympathies in the 1950s.[39] Although the majority of cases involved white defendants, anticommunist prosecutions had an undeniable racial significance and played a central role in state attempts to critically undermine black protest in the United States. Benjamin J. Davis and Henry Winston were among the eleven CPUSA leaders indicted in the first round of Smith Act prosecutions in 1949 (*Dennis v. the United States*), where defendants were accused of attempting to overthrow the U.S. government.[40] The men received sentences of five years each. The trial defense attorneys, including the leading black lawyer George W. Crockett Jr., were also jailed for six months for contempt of court. Other African American CPUSA members convicted under the Smith Act included James E. Jackson, Claudia Jones,

Pettis Perry, Benjamin L. Careathers, and Claude Lightfoot.[41] In 1951 William Alpaheus Hunton, the education director of the CAA, was also imprisoned for nine months for contempt of court after refusing to reveal the names of donors to the Civil Rights Congress Bail Fund.[42] The deportation of black individuals under the Smith and McCarran-Walter Acts was also common at this time.[43] Among the most famous of the black "subversives" deported were the Trinidadian-born activists Claudia Jones and C. L. R. James.[44]

HUAC became as a permanent standing committee in the postwar period. Fueled by the inflammatory rhetoric of McCarthyism, other investigative committees also emerged to tackle the so-called communist threat, including the Subversive Activities Control Board and the Senate Internal Security Subcommittee.[45] Government-led investigations into "subversive" activities often had an undeniable racial significance and resulted in the harassment and demise of a number of civil rights organizations. As Jeff Woods outlines, anticommunism was an "exportable commodity" that many white Southern politicians drew on when working to defend segregation and discredit the civil rights movement.[46] Prominent HUAC member John Elliot Rankin from Mississippi was well known for his regular racist and anti-Soviet outbursts. Following the Peekskill riots, Rankin referred to Paul Robeson as a "Nigger Communist" and suggested that if he "does not like this country let him go to Russia, and take that gang of alien Communists with him."[47]

House and Senate investigations could result in imprisonment of up to one year if witnesses were deemed to have obstructed the work of the committee they appeared before and were found to be in contempt of Congress.[48] In April of 1954, William L. Patterson, CRC leader and author of "We Charge Genocide," which accused the U.S. government of allowing acts of genocide against African Americans, was sentenced to ninety days in prison on these charges.[49] His treatment in front of the house Lobby Investigating Committee in 1950 shows the extent to which racism and anticommunism were interrelated. During his hearing, Patterson's steadfast refusal to list the names of CRC donors and his defiant stance on the stand enraged Georgian congressman Henderson Lanham. During the proceedings the increasingly irate Lanham hurled insults at Patterson, repeatedly referring to him as a "black son of a bitch," with reports suggesting that he had to be restrained by court police after jumping up and marching to the bottom of the dais in an attempt to assault Patterson after he accused the congressman of presiding over the "legal lynching" of African Americans.[50]

Anticommunist legislation and investigative committees unambiguously raised the prospect of imprisonment for those who continued to openly critique the government's stance on race relations. The fact that accusations of communist subversion could feasibly result in the jailing of black leaders and members caused many prominent civil rights leaders and organizations to distance themselves from the black left.[51] In the context of the Second Red Scare, African Americans who denounced American democracy and emphasized the socioeconomic roots of racism were effectively criminalized by the state. Through accusations of subversion, treason, and the threat of incarceration, anticommunist politics greatly restricted the ability of African Americans to confront racism on a local and global level.[52]

The South African government was also acutely aware of the ways in which anticommunist and white supremacist ideologies spoke to one another. Indeed, in their strident opposition to communism, the National Party invoked a global language that it believed could be used to secure the continued existence of white supremacy in an era of anticolonialism and growing calls for black self-determination.[53]

Anticommunism had a long history in the country.[54] Prior to the election of the Nationalist government in 1948, Jan Smuts invoked the dual specters of bolshevism and communism in order to delegitimize the growing labor movement. Smuts's attitude toward potential communist subversion pervaded the broader public consciousness of white South Africa. This can be seen in the publication of pamphlets like *In The Menace of Red Misrule* by the journalist Hedley Chilvers, who in the aftermath of the 1922 general strike expressed grave concern at "how earnestly the South African 'Reds' are endeavouring . . . to reproduce Russian conditions in this country."[55] This general fear of communism among the white ruling elite would be firmly established, and indeed given legal credence, by the National Party. As early as 1937, the Cape Province Congress of the NP openly called for a response to the communist threat through the implementation of new immigration, deportation, and censorship laws.[56] These earlier manifestations of South African anticommunism culminated in the Suppression of Communism Act in 1950. The centerpiece of National Party attempts to control and prevent black protest, the act banned the CPSA and was used against the leaders of the mass civil disobedience campaigns of the 1950s.[57]

The use of anticommunist politics to justify the arrest and imprisonment of black activists was made clear during the 1952 Defiance Campaign. Over eight thousand protesters were jailed over the course of the protests, leading the *Chicago Defender* to conclude that this organized civil disobedience would have South African jails "overflowing within a week."[58] Whereas the majority of protestors were arrested for deliberately entering whites only spaces, the leadership of the ANC and SAIC were charged with violating the Suppression of Communism Act.[59] This was a deliberate effort to cut off the head of the anti-apartheid movement and to tarnish the mass protests by denouncing them as acts of sedition instigated by outside agitators.[60] It was not uncommon for black activists to be members of both the ANC and the CPSA. Indeed, the majority of black leaders refused to distance themselves from communist organizers, even after this was made illegal. Less than six months into the campaign, more than twenty prominent members of the ANC and SAIC, including the organization's leaders Dr. James Moroka and Yusuf Dadoo, were found guilty under charges of furthering communism in South Africa.[61] Issued with two-year suspended sentences, these leaders faced nine-month prison terms if they were to organize or appear at any future antigovernment protests.[62]

The subsequent years saw an intensification of such practices. In an urgent call to ANC members in 1953, Chief A. J. Luthuli commented that "almost daily reports are appearing about fresh bans and further restrictions imposed upon this or that leader of the ANC for alleged promotion of feelings of hostility between Black and White."[63] The act's extremely broad definition of communism meant virtually all anti-apartheid protest could be labeled communistic.[64] If found guilty of violating the act, individuals could be sentenced to up to five years in prison, were banned from attending or addressing public meetings, faced travel restrictions, were heavily fined, and could even be deported from the country.[65] In 1956 the act was again used to prosecute 156 of the most prominent anti-apartheid activists for treason. Although all the defendants were eventually acquitted, the Treason Trial lasted almost five years and was highly damaging to the anti-apartheid struggle. The Suppression of Communism Act was used to nullify calls for black self-determination and drastically compromised the anti-apartheid leadership. While there is no doubt that any questioning of the white supremacist status quo could result in imprisonment, the international language of anticommunism made this process easier. Anticommunist politics transformed legitimate protests into acts of communist subversion and was used to justify the most repressive measures of the apartheid state.

Anticommunist prosecutions in the United States also provided a model for the prosecution of South African anti-apartheid activists. Tellingly, Brian Bunting, the editor of the South African *Guardian* newspaper and member of the CPSA, drew parallels between the policing strategies of the South

African Special Branch and the FBI in their targeting of communist "subversives." As he recalled, "Not a public meeting was held by the Congress organizations without the presence of a battery of note-taking policemen. Telephones were tapped and correspondence tampered with, whilst the latest electronic devices used in detection were imported from the United States."[66]

American legal practices also influenced the way in which the National Party targeted anti-apartheid activists. The South African government prepared for the Treason Trial by meticulously following Smith Act prosecutions in the United States. This overlooked connection demonstrates how anticommunist ideology was informed and reshaped transnationally during the Cold War. Prior to the trial, the South African embassy in the United States approached the Washington-based law firm Dow, Lohnes, and Albertson for legal information on the workings of the Smith Act prosecutions. The South African Department of External Affairs had initially cabled the South African embassy requesting a detailed legal report on *Dennis vs. the United States*, as well as the full investigation into the "number and nature of cases" involving the Smith Act "or Communism as a whole." The cable surmised, "Generally speaking what the authorities want are legal decisions which will be quoted in South African Courts as to the evidence available and admissible to prove Communistic activities."[67] Responding to this, John R. Sims, a representative of Dow, Lohnes, and Albertson, wrote directly to Attorney General Herbert J. Brownell on behalf of the South African government to request the availability of "certain legal memoranda on, and briefs of, the various cases which have been prosecuted by your department under the Smith Act."[68] Noting the similarities between the Smith and Suppression of Communism Acts, as well as enquiring as to whether his work would require his registration under the Foreign Agents Registration Act, Sims stated that any information supplied would be used in relation to the Treason Trial, "to assist them" (the National Party) "in their preparation for the trial of these defendants."[69]

The South African government also contacted a variety of experts, including academics and leading civil servants, on the workings of communism. This brought South African officials into contact with John Lautner. Described by Howard Fast as "a person of small and shabby character, dubious morals, and little repute," Lautner was a former head of the State Control Commission of the New York Communist Party, turned government informer and regular state witness in prosecutions involving the Smith Act.[70] Lautner's role in the communist witch hunt became a transnational one when, in 1957, he was invited by the South African government to give evidence on behalf of the crown in the Treason Trial.[71] In this role, it was proposed that he would liaise with Professor Andrew Murray, a so-called expert on communism at the University of Cape Town, in order to advise him on the nature of communistic activity. It was also suggested that he might be called on to appear as a special witness in the trial at the South African Supreme Court in mid-1958.[72] Lautner was asked to prepare a detailed questionnaire that would act as a kind of anticommunist factsheet for the South African prosecutors and provide additional expert evidence to Professor Murray's prosecutors. South African government sources stated "The review of Prof. Murray's evidence will serve to establish a relationship between the professor's theoretical knowledge and Mr. Lautner's practical experience. Where he differs from Prof. Murray, he should expound in detail. Should he wish to expand on certain aspects, he would be welcome to do so."[73]

Accusations of communist subversion in the United States and South Africa, occurring simultaneously and often interlinked in the minds of government officials, demonstrate how anticommunist legislation was used to target black leaders across national borders. The American influence on the prosecution of 156 of the most prominent anti-apartheid leaders shows the extent to which anticommunism shaped race relations on a global level. Those seeking to protect white racial privilege put the geopolitical machinations of the Cold War to good use.[74] Anticommunism provided an updated, modern, and seemingly nonracial language that could be employed to defend a range of white supremacist practices.[75] By embracing and deliberately exaggerating the threat of communism, the National Party attempted to discredit the mass civil disobedience campaigns of the 1950s as well as establish the legal structures that made it simple to arrest and imprison key anti-apartheid leaders.

African American leftists facing jail—in contrast to black liberals—recognized the extent to which anticommunism was used to prevent racial progress and came out fighting. For example, when protesting his imprisonment under the Smith Act, Harlem councilman Benjamin J. Davis asserted that his detention was the result of his opposition to white supremacy. In a leaflet calling for his release he stated, "In the name of my grandfather who was lynched, and of my grandmother who felt the whiplash of the Southern white master, I will continue to battle for my people until the last drop of blood is drained from my body and until the last breath has left my lungs. I know you will stand with me. YOU FREED THE SCOTTSBORO BOYS

AND HERNDON, YOU SAVED THE TRENTON SIX. I KNOW YOU WILL FREE ME AND MY COMRADES. I AM CONFIDENT YOU WILL SMASH THIS HITLER-LIKE ATTEMPT TO OUTLAW MY PARTY AND THE BILL OF RIGHTS."[76]

Davis directly compared his incarceration to the physical restrictions African Americans faced under slavery. By referencing infamous cases that resulted in the wrongful imprisonment of African Americans, including campaigns where he himself had served as a defense lawyer, he positioned himself as being part of a longer history of black persecution through the courts. The arrest and imprisonment of prominent black leaders was proof of the fascistic tendencies embedded within American politics. Such cases were framed as a rallying call for African Americans, a key battleground in the long history of white supremacy and black resistance in the United States. Black leftists worked to establish their incarceration as a key issue in the struggle for racial equality. As William L. Patterson argued in response to his treatment on the stand by Congressman Henderson Lanham, "This attempt to jail me is part of a pattern of terror against Negro people and those who are leading their fight for civil and human rights. Congressman Lanham, who illegally holds his seat in Congress through the denial of the vote to Negro citizens in his Georgia constituency, is leading the fight to get me. His attitude to the Negro people was clearly indicated three weeks ago when he called me a 'Black S.O.B.' "[77]

Patterson's treatment at the hands of the investigating committee caused widespread outrage from most black commentators.[78] Despite their general wariness of the African American left, both the mainstream black press and the NAACP condemned Lanham's behavior.[79] Significantly, Patterson's insistence that his arrest was not simply a civil rights but a human rights issue amounted to an effort to connect his personal predicament to the plight of oppressed races around the world. He was also aware of how his own incarceration served as a reminder of the broader political forces used to marginalize black Americans as a group. In a 1953 newspaper article, "Prison figures Show 'Brand of Criminality' Placed on Negroes," Patterson examined the links between the operation of incarceration and race discrimination. Noting that between 1939 and 1952 of the 366 people executed on charges of rape in the United States 328 were black, and that African Americans made up 72 percent of prisoners executed in the Southern states in the same period, he concluded that, "In my opinion" these figures "tell a fantastic story of the inhuman persecution of a people. It is a story for the free world apostles to explain, a picture for those who propagate the unprecedented virtues of the democracy of America's ruling class to interpret."[80]

For Patterson, a man who had organized numerous defense campaigns for black activists, the imprisonment of African Americans provided further evidence that white supremacy was alive and well in the United States.[81] Once again, this was uncompromisingly configured as a broad human rights issue that emphasized the democratic deficiencies of the country. For radicals like Patterson, the systematic incarceration of African Americans and the silencing of black political leaders directly contradicted the American government's assumed ownership over the values of freedom and democracy during the Cold War.

The imprisonment of anti-apartheid activists also influenced how apartheid was characterized and challenged in South Africa. Press reports detail how, on the opening day of the trial of twenty-eight Defiance Campaign leaders, thousands of people converged on the Magistrate's Court in Johannesburg. Swarming the corridors, courtyards, and adjacent streets, protestors sang "Nkosi Sikelel' iAfrika," thumbs raised in the "Afrika" salute. As the CAA's *Spotlight on Africa* reported, "In the throng were hundreds of black and brown school children of all ages from six to eighteen who quit their classes and went to court carrying banners proclaiming 'HANDS OFF OUR LEADERS' and 'SOUTH AFRICA IS A VAST PRISON.'"[82] Given the expansion of the apartheid state and National Party's unabashed commitment to white supremacy, public support for these imprisoned activists was notably more widespread than in the United States.

The Treason Trial hearings prompted similar scenes of mass protest. Black demonstrators, wearing signs that read "WE STAND BY OUR LEADERS," lined the streets surrounding the courthouse.[83] The Treason Trialist Alfred Hutchinson described the defendants' journeys back and forth from Johannesburg's Fort prison to the courthouse: "They are singing, and I am singing too: **Izokunyathela i Afrika** . . . Africa will trample you underfoot. Unrepentant. People seen through the mesh: surprise and dawning understanding. The thumb raised in reply. **Mayibuye i Afrika!** . . . The world is lovely though seen through mesh. . . . There are crowds, huge crowds, outside the Drill Hall and their warmth beats on you like strong sunlight after rain—planting life. And you know, as you never knew before, that you could never be lost: that if you fell another would take your place: that the struggle could never be lost. It could never have been in vain."[84] For Hutchinson, the court and the prison were where new political solidarities could be made. To go to jail was an act of defiance; the support of political prisoners provided evidence of the righteousness of the struggle against apartheid, proof that the Congress Alliance had the backing of the African, Colored, and Indian majority.

"We Stand by Our Leaders," 1956 Treason Trial protests. Source: Eli Weinberg, UWC–Robben Island Museum Mayibuye Archives.

Women lead Treason Trial protests outside Drill Hall, Johannesburg, December 1956. Source: Eli Weinberg, UWC–Robben Island Museum Mayibuye Archives.

Imprisoned black leaders often viewed the prison cell as a site of resistance. Chief Luthuli recalled how at Johannesburg's Fort prison, after an impromptu religious service led by fellow inmate Rev. James Calata, the treason trialists "all stood around in a great circle and sang some of our freedom songs. I led the prisoners in our pledging ourselves to solidarity in the cause of liberation. . . . There was no doubt about it, we had not languished in gaol, our morale was very high."[85] Luthuli, like Hutchinson, transformed the oppressive site of the prison into a place where collective resistance and anti-apartheid solidarity flourished under the most testing of circumstances.[86]

The prison was also a site where potential interracial connections could be formed. Although cells were strictly segregated spaces, political prisoners regularly commented on the opportunities for racial mixing that resulted from extended periods of detention and long drawn-out trials. Inside the confined spaces of the prison and the courtroom, the barriers established by apartheid could be undermined by interracial groups.[87] In a letter to ACOA General Secretary George Houser, Z. K. Matthews underlined the political significance of this unintended integration, commenting that "in this country where the colour line is so rigidly drawn in every sphere of life, the accused in this trial sit together as a mixed group without regard to race. I suppose the intention is to show that this is a group beyond redemption . . . but we see it as a picture of the South Africa of tomorrow for which the best sons and daughters of our country have longed and worked for generations."[88] What the apartheid state saw as evidence of the criminal nature of the Treason Trial defendants was, for Matthews at least, a sign that a politically enlightened and multiracial South Africa was possible.

Many anti-apartheid activists echoed Matthews's views during this period of civil disobedience. In the immediate aftermath of the mass arrest of the treason trialists, a headline in *New Age* declared that "There's No Ethnic Grouping in Jail."[89] In his autobiography Chief Luthuli noted of his imprisonment, "At last I could meet a really representative cross-section of *my* South Africa. . . . The conditions of our lives in Johannesburg gave us the chance to meet such men and women, both eminent and lowly, and to find within us all common allegiance—and a common refusal to bow to the totalitarian threat. The colour-bar dropped away like the fictitious and beastly thing it is, within the borders of the unexpected world which the Trial had created."[90]

The suffering that imprisoned black activists experienced in South Africa was transformed into an opportunity for resistance through the development of political solidarities, friendship, and camaraderie.[91] By arresting and detaining anti-apartheid leaders of all races, the National Party had inadvertently created a space in which the enemies of apartheid, regardless of their political and racial background, could further develop their common opposition to the practice of white supremacy. The transformation of the prison cell into a place of resistance is indicative of the way in which black activists made political opportunities out of oppressive situations. For many, the prison represented the nation in that it was a physical site that epitomized both white racial control as well as the need for collective resistance against the power of the state.[92] The prison came to be viewed as a proving ground for the struggle, a place where activists could establish their credentials as national leaders and form political solidarities through their mutual understanding of what it meant to suffer for the cause.[93] Brutal, dehumanizing, and disruptive, the shared experience of imprisonment nevertheless provided an important focal point for black protest. The experiences of political prisoners also had implications for black protest on a global level, shaping the ways in which activists in the United States and South Africa related to one another's struggles for racial justice.

"The Wrong Negro for the F.B.I. to Pick On": Political Prisoners and Anti-Imperialism in the Cold War

In February 1951, W. E. B. Du Bois appeared in a Washington courtroom charged with failing to register the Peace Information Center (PIC) under the Foreign Agents Registration Act. The PIC, chaired by Du Bois, was an antiwar organization committed to the promotion of nuclear disarmament.[94] The image of a then eighty-three-year-old Du Bois in court, handcuffed to a fellow defendant, facing spurious charges of subversion, sparked condemnation of his treatment from African Americans across the political spectrum.[95]

The harassment of one of the most prominent, distinguished, and instantly recognizable black leaders in the United States also resonated beyond the borders of the United States. As the famous African American poet Langston Hughes observed after Du Bois's arrest, "If W. E. B. Du Bois goes to jail a wave of wonder will sweep around the world. Europe will wonder and Africa will wonder and Asia will wonder. And no judge or jury will be able to answer the questions behind their wonder. The banner of American democracy will be lowered another notch, particularly in the eyes of the darker peoples of the earth. The hearts of millions will be angered and perturbed, steeled and strengthened."[96]

Hughes's contention that the imprisonment of Du Bois would do irreparable damage to America's standing around the world—and among people of color in particular—directly spoke to the racial politics of the Cold War. As a statement, it is representative of the ways in which African Americans strategically made visible their persecution to a global audience in an attempt to shame the U.S. government into guaranteeing genuine democratic rule at home. Again, the black left made this argument repeatedly, often out of personal necessity. Under intense pressure and threatened with jail, African Americans used their harassment to further their anti-imperial criticism of American power and to draw clear parallels between Jim Crow and apartheid. As William Patterson noted when addressing cases of extralegal lynching and racism in the courts, "It is a story for the free world apostles to explain, a picture for those who propagate the unprecedented virtues of the democracy of America's ruling class to interpret."[97]

Incarceration provided African Americans with a stark physical reminder of the extent to which they were denied their freedom in the United States. The fate of black political prisoners also resonated beyond national borders, raising important questions about the nature of American democracy as well as the forces that shaped U.S. foreign policy. As Eslanda Robeson noted, Dr. Du Bois was simply "the wrong Negro for the F.B.I. to pick on," because it was his work that "first directed our attention to Africa, to our kinship with the African people, and with all the Colored peoples of the world."[98] Robeson reasoned that he represented a dangerous target for the government due to his status as a powerful symbol of the worldwide struggle for black self-determination.

Du Bois's court appearance and humiliating treatment was roundly condemned in the South African activist press. As an article in the *Guardian* newspaper entitled "Peace on Trial in the U.S." noted, the defense committee established for Du Bois was in need of "world-wide support"—especially from Africa. The piece reported that concern over the treatment of Du Bois had mobilized South African workers, with the central executive committee of the Food and Canning Workers of Cape Town having "recently adopted a resolution demanding the unconditional release of Dr. Du Bois and his associates."[99] The rhetoric around Du Bois's case provides a small glimpse into how black leftists used the legal mistreatment of political leaders to question notions of American democracy. By associating anticommunist harassment with imperial power, they worked to expose the true character of U.S. foreign policy and connect white supremacy in South Africa with the repressive politics of Jim Crow.

Racism within the American criminal justice system was regularly reported on in the anti-apartheid press. The cases of the Martinsville Seven, Emmett Till, Rosa Lee Ingram, and the Korean War veteran John Derrick were covered in detail in the South African *Guardian*.[100] The newspaper, along with other anti-apartheid publications such as *Liberation* and *Fighting Talk*, argued that the abuses of the American criminal justice system exposed the hollow nature of the U.S. government's claims that it stood for freedom and democracy during the Cold War. As a 1951 article covering the execution in Martinsville, Virginia, of seven African American men accused of raping a white woman stated, "The Martinsville case has gone into history as a part of the American Way of Life."[101] Anti-apartheid leaders in South Africa argued that the failings of the American justice system—alongside the harassment of black leaders—mirrored the political practices that were used to establish white supremacy at home. South African reporting of the systematic nature of racism in the United States amounted to a fundamental questioning of America's role in the world and the implications that this would have for those struggling to free themselves from colonial rule.

Anti-apartheid activists on the left regularly cast the United States as an imperialist power historically committed to the preservation of white power.[102] Indeed, at the height of the Defiance Campaign, Paul Robeson evaluated black protest in the United States and South Africa and concluded that the situation was "so much the same that we ought to compare notes on these two great movements against white supremacy in the two USAs."[103] Stressing the need for a global analysis of racism, he drew attention to the laws that underpinned apartheid in South Africa: "Take some of the laws that they're fighting against over there: the Removal of Colored Voters Act, the Group Areas Act, the Mixed Marriages Act, the Suppression of Communism Act, the Flogging Law." He added, "Sounds mighty like 'down home' doesn't it?—and up North too for that matter."[104] This litany of repressive laws, and the extent to which they resonated transnationally, vividly underlined comparable obstacles black activists in both countries faced during these years.

This criticism of the United States, and the parallels drawn between Jim Crow and apartheid, were often accompanied by the explicit denial that black leftists were blind followers of the Soviet Union. As the CAA declared in 1953 in response to accusations that the organization's anticolonial activities were "furthering the objectives of the Communist Party . . . this allegation and others contain an implicit insult to the Negro people for they rest upon the racist assumption that Negroes do not and cannot think for themselves, are not intelligent enough to determine their own opinions and attitudes on the basis of the experience of their daily lives, and merely follow like sheep wherever they are led."[105]

This point is significant, especially considering the long and complicated relationship between black activists and leftist politics.[106] Historically, the structures of the Left have provided African Americans with a political framework through which they have articulated calls for black self-determination globally.[107] Indeed, at this time, South African communists forged personal relationships and political networks that provided an important link between black American activists, the ANC, and the broader Congress Alliance.[108] These connections were driven by a genuine commitment to the anti-apartheid struggle as well as the belief that African Americans needed to challenge racism and colonialism on a global scale. Statements that called attention to the imperial character of the American foreign policy or insisted that apartheid and Jim Crow were interconnected systems of oppression did not amount to a simple rehashing of Soviet propaganda. Instead, they represented a politically vital assessment of the links between American power, capitalism, and racism. Focusing in on the plight of political prisoners made it possible for black activists to demonstrate how anticommunist politics were used to nullify antiracist politics in ways that protected white capitalist interests in and in-between both countries. This represented an important and much-needed attempt to limit the effects of the Red Scare on the black freedom struggle. If racism was to be eradicated and human rights attained, black activists on the left argued, progressive forces around the world would have to grapple with the imperial character of the United States. Anticommunism was denounced as a global ideology that reinforced racism on both sides of the Atlantic.

The CAA made this argument clearly when comparing how the United States and the South African state dealt with political dissent: "It is apparent, by the magistrate's logic," they noted in a pamphlet, "that anyone who advocated racial equality [in South Africa] is ipso facto a Communist. They do not say things quite so bluntly here in the United States; nevertheless, the 'loyalty' quizzing of U.S. government employees here has included questions as to whether they as whites have Negro friends, or as Negroes had white friends."[109] The article makes clear that interracial organizing against race discrimination was politically suspect in both countries. For the CAA, an organization that was understandably very vocal on this subject, anti-communist arrests in the United States and South Africa provided further evidence of the connections that the struggle against apartheid and Jim Crow were interconnected. Black South African activists repeated this argument that oppressive anticommunist practices incorrectly labeled advocates of racial equality as subversive. In a message that noted the "good work and tireless efforts" of the CAA on behalf of African freedom, Walter Sisulu declared, "It is not accidental that your organisation has become the victim of the reactionary Eisenhower-McCarthy ruling clique who are conniving with their imperialists for the oppression and exploitation of millions of colonial and semi-colonial peoples. We are, however, confident the progressive forces the world over, united as they are in their determination to expose and end oppression and domination of one group by another, will triumph for their cause is just."[110]

Sisulu's message is notable for its defiant optimism. Even as possibilities for change and resistance were being systematically narrowed and shut down, black activists maintained their global analysis of race discrimination and anticommunist harassment. Indeed, their shared experiences of oppression informed their black international exchanges in ways that bound together their respective struggles against white supremacy. In 1953, when defending itself from accusations of subversion, the CAA laid bare the contradictory nature of American democracy by choosing to compare the Eisenhower administration to the apartheid government. Alphaeus Hunton, for example, said, "The Malan government of South Africa also regards the leaders and organizations of the people's struggle there for democratic rights as 'political meddlers' and prosecutes them under a so-called Suppression of Communism Act. . . . Will our own government, besides giving financial and military aid to the European imperialists who would keep Africa in chains, also prescribe jails and concentration camps for those Americans who support the cause of African liberation?"[111]

By making a direct comparison between the treatment of black leaders in the United States and South Africa, the CAA insisted that anticommunist repression required a black international response. At their heart, these political exchanges involved an implicit questioning of how American power should be perceived by the rest of the world. As Paul Robeson outlines in a letter to Dr. G. M. Naicker, president of the Natal Indian Congress, "We who are on the side of Peace and Freedom in the United States can well understand the desperate nature of the struggle in which you in South Africa are engaged. For if you have your Malan's and Swart's, we have our McCarthy's and Brownell's. South Africa's notorious suppression of the Communism Act is paralleled by this country's equally notorious Smith Act and McCarran Act."[112] Hunton, Robeson, and their political allies all outlined the extent to which the United States and South Africa embraced analogous methods of colonial rule. In their eyes, this was an anticommunist form of imperial power that resulted in the race and class exploitation of the black population of both countries. For black radicals in the United States, the repressive actions of the state provided further proof that the U.S. government was invested in empire building, both at home and overseas.[113]

Black leftists remained defiant throughout the darkest days of the early Cold War and the entrenchment of apartheid in South Africa. Their experiences of anticommunist harassment fueled their belief that the United States was an imperial power invested in the maintenance of white settler colonialism in South Africa. The arrest and imprisonment of black radicals in both countries provided a particularly vivid illustration of these repressive connections. It is important to remember that the stifling political climate of the early Cold War did not completely obliterate anti-imperial black international networks. Anticommunism was effective in restricting the work of black radicals and limiting their global interactions, but that does not mean this form of anticolonial politics disappeared completely. Black activists continued to resist from tightly controlled spaces. The way in which political imprisonment in the United States and South Africa was reconfigured as an international issue is especially significant in this regard. The incarceration of black activists in both countries was interpreted as evidence of the imperialistic nature of anticommunism. This was a repressive politics that was used to both silence vocal opponents of white supremacy and justify the expansionist policies of nations that denied basic human and civil rights to black people. The African American left deliberately reconstituted the jailing of "communist subversives" on both sides of the Atlantic as part of a sustained white supremacist effort to suppress black freedom across national borders. By stressing the oppressive nature of state-sponsored anticommunism, they claimed the moral high ground and questioned the government's definition of what constituted American democracy.

6 Political Prisoners
Heroic Masculinity and Anti-Apartheid Politics

In 1952 the Council on African Affairs published "South African Honor Roll," an article which documented the actions of activists involved in the Defiance Campaign.[1] Appearing in *Spotlight on Africa*, the article proudly listed the names of a number of black South Africans who had been imprisoned for carrying out acts of civil disobedience. It declared, "It is a commonly understood thing in colonial countries all over the world, but is apt to be forgotten sometimes by people in countries like the United States: to go to jail for refusing to compromise with one's belief in liberty and justice is not a thing of shame but of honor."[2]

As John Iliffe has noted, the politics of honor has a long and complex history in Africa, playing an important role in shaping narratives of colonial rule as well as anticolonial resistance. The remarkably broad concept of honor combines a variety of personal and political ideals—including pride, dignity, righteousness, and respectability.[3] Claiming prison as an honorable site helped the CAA draw explicit connections between imprisoned black activists in South Africa and those in the United States. Both the character and moral fortitude of political prisoners were emphasized in the CAA article. Far from being considered common criminals, they were lauded as individuals whose commitment to racial equality had made them undesirable in the eyes of the oppressive state. As the young African activist Raymond M. Mhlaba stated after his arrest for defying apartheid regulations in a South African railway station, "The proper place today, the only place which South Africa has provided for those who believe in justice, democracy and fair play, is in our prisons."[4] A member of the ANC and Communist Party, Mhlaba himself would spend twenty-five years of his life behind bars. The argument that it was honorable to go to jail for challenging race discrimination cast black activists as heroic and respectable individuals, wrongfully imprisoned for their refusal to compromise their belief and remain silent. Throughout this period, political prisoners on both sides of the Atlantic worked to frame their experiences in ways that promoted the moral legitimacy of their struggle.

However, the CAA's "South African Honor Roll" is also significant in that it documents how male experiences regularly dominated political narratives and international exchanges that were generated around the issue of political imprisonment. Indeed, the vast majority of the names featured on the "Honor Roll" were men. Prominent ANC figures such as Mhlaba, David Bopape, Moses Kotane, Nelson Mandela, J. B. Marks, and Walter Sisulu appeared alongside short descriptions of why they were arrested. The name of just one African woman is featured in the article—Miss Karabo Sello, a "17-year-old Executive member of the A.N.C. Youth League," imprisoned for civil disobedience in Port Elizabeth.[5] The inclusion of Sello in the CAA's reporting hints at the prominent role of black women during the Defiance Campaign.[6] However, the fact that her story stands out in an article that the CAA framed as being based on information "from direct sources in South Africa" highlights the extent to which male experiences dominated black international narratives.[7]

There were many black women that the CAA could have added to this list. African women were extremely active in the mass civil disobedience campaigns of the 1950s, leading militant protests against passes and declaring their willingness to face jail with the call of "No bail, No fines."[8] Black leaders such as Lilian Ngoyi, Bertha Mkhize, Elizabeth Mafeking, Florence Matomela, Annie Silinga, and Frances Baard were imprisoned at this time. However, their stories were largely overlooked in black American reporting of civil disobedience in South Africa. This left African Americans, and the world at large, with a distorted and masculinized vision of anti-apartheid protest—an anticolonial vision that privileged black male leadership and often failed to account for the monumental sacrifices African women made to the black liberation struggle.[9]

In her analysis of anti-apartheid autobiographies, Elaine Unterhalter argues that male activists used their treatment at the hands of the state to construct heroic masculinities that politically empowered black men.[10] She observes how, in these protest narratives, idealized masculine identities were usually associated with political work, male autonomy in the public sphere, and nation building.[11] As Unterhalter notes, "The theme of heroic masculinity that emerges from the autobiographical writings of men, implies a particular conception of work and gender relations."[12] In South Africa, prison was where this heroic vision of black masculinity could be forged. Black political prisoners used their carceral experiences to construct specific gender identities that affirmed their status as political leaders in the public sphere. Articulations of heroic masculinity celebrated the morality, honor, and heroic defiance of black men in order to argue their suitability for political leadership roles.[13] In this configuration, the prison experiences of African women were either neglected or used in ways that reaffirmed the need for strong black male leadership. This led to black women often being cast as vulnerable figures, their imprisonment interpreted as a threat to respectable gender roles that placed women in the domestic sphere as mothers and caregivers. This emphasis on the heroism of black men often resulted in women being denied their autonomy and agency as political activists.[14]

Activist responses to political imprisonment explicitly challenged myths that bound together blackness and criminality in the white imagination. In South Africa, rapid industrialization during the 1930s brought about increased African migration to city spaces, stoking white fears of what became known in public discourse as the "Wandering Native."[15] The anthropologist Kelly Gillespie notes how white liberals and conservatives used this term to describe unemployed, homeless, and potentially dangerous Africans drawn to urban areas by the labor market. Although there was disagreement of how best to deal with the problem of the urban African, there existed a general concern among whites that this pattern of migration would result in Native "detribalization," which would lead to an increase in crime. Ultimately, the concern over the potential for black crime in urban spaces fed into the political climate that gave rise to apartheid and the entrenchment of racial separation.[16]

In 1948 the influential apartheid thinker W. M. M. Eiselen called for the restriction of African migration to cities, noting that, "Major disturbances have occurred, there has been an unprecedented wave of crime and the urban authorities have been unable to cope with the situation."[17] The white press contributed to the idea that black lawlessness was a serious threat, regularly reporting on how urban areas were in the midst of a crime wave and fueling the racist belief that "the natives are rapidly becoming a race of criminals."[18] Later, in the 1950s, fears of tsotsism and juvenile delinquency—shared by whites and Africans alike—reinforced popular perceptions of black criminality.[19] The apartheid government responded to these concerns through the mechanisms of the criminal justice system. As outlined in chapter 5, excessive policing and large-scale incarceration were central to the "management" of the African population and would play an important role in the development of the white supremacist state.

For apartheid policymakers crime and race were inextricably linked.[20] An editorial in the July 1954 edition of the South African *Guardian* drew attention to the relationship between the fear of black crime and the implementation of apartheid laws. Noting that South Africa had the highest rate of imprisonment in the world, the article condemned the National Party's introduction of an ever-increasing "list of statutory crimes by which a man may be sent to prison in South Africa—if his skin happens to be black." Adding that it would be a miracle if any African managed to avoid jail, the editorial concluded that "the Nationalist government bears a heavy load of guilt. They are the makers of criminals. Their laws create poverty, distress, bitter resentment. They drive whole populations below the bread-line and many into crime."[21] As this piece points out, popular and legal myths of black criminality enabled the apartheid state to exert control over the mobility and labor of black South Africans.

Anti-apartheid activists were all too aware of how crime informed racial hierarchies in South Africa. When commenting on their own prison experiences, they therefore worked to overturn myths associated with black criminality in ways that questioned the legitimacy of the apartheid state. This was a powerful tool of rhetorical resistance that worked to emphasize the moral legitimacy of the anti-apartheid struggle both in South Africa and to a wider international audience. In constructing these narratives, political prisoners attempted to challenge racist stereotypes that cast Africans as politically incompetent and of dubious moral standing. Black male leaders transformed the prison into a site of resistance, narrating their prison experiences to an international audience in ways that stressed their autonomy and associated the struggle against racism with masculine strength.[22]

Heroic Black Masculinity and Political Imprisonment

Strength, bravery, self-sacrifice, and respectability were all central to accounts that emphasized the heroic masculinity of imprisoned anti-apartheid leaders. Indeed, these character traits were positioned as key features of a strong and vital black manhood under threat from the apartheid system. As a 1953 article in the African American newspaper the *Pittsburgh Courier* claimed when reporting on the pass laws, "White South Africans are using every means they can to suppress the natural dignity and manhood of Africans."[23] Depictions of black masculine strength and power represented just one way African Americans engaged with iconography of both the South African prison and anti-apartheid protest in general. An example of this was an ACOA pamphlet that detailed the "unnecessary suffering" and "brutal"

"Support the Non-Violent Campaign against Unjust Laws in South Africa,"
pamphlet, American Committee on Africa, April 1953. Source: Library of
Congress, NAACP Records, 1940–1955, Part II, Box A7.

treatment meted out to anti-apartheid activists involved in the Defiance Campaign.

The document, aimed at encouraging American support for anti-apartheid activists, emphasized in striking visual terms the close association between masculinity and the anti-apartheid struggle in South Africa. The front page was dominated by an image of a muscular black man shackled and tethered to the African continent. The chains that bind him to South Africa represent the unjust laws that restricted black freedom in the country, visually evoking the historic chains of slavery that connected racist oppression in the United States and the African continent. The figure of the imprisoned African served as a symbol of restricted black masculine power. The quiet dignity and the restrained muscular strength of the shackled black man suggest that, in order for South Africa to be free, this powerful vision of black masculinity must be allowed to flourish. Manliness and African nationalism, it was argued, went hand in hand.[24]

Bravery and fearlessness were also consistently elevated as masculine traits that positioned black men on both sides of the Atlantic as natural leaders in the fight against race discrimination. As Paul Robeson observed when discussing the black international significance of the Defiance Campaign, "What about that item in the paper the other day that told of how Dr. J. S. Moroka, president of the African National Congress, was arrested . . . because he is one of the militant leaders in the fight against segregation? Makes you think of our own brave Ben Davis, jailed for over a year now under the Smith Act because he led the fight against Jim Crow housing and for equal rights for his people."[25] The fight against apartheid and Jim Crow were symbolically connected through the bravery of these two black men. For Robeson, the shared commitment of Dr. Moroka and Harlem councilman Benjamin Davis to ending race discrimination was further proof of their status as incorruptible and committed race leaders.

Black newspapers and anti-apartheid publications in the United States regularly reinforced this notion of a fearless black male leadership. For example, Joe Matthews was quoted in the *New York Amsterdam News* after his imprisonment during the Defiance Campaign: "I was not afraid, for I am in greater fear of the lingering death of humiliation visited on us Africans over the many years."[26] On his arrest in the same year, Walter Sisulu asserted that he hoped his own defiant example would inspire others to take up the cause of black freedom, commenting in a message that would be heard around the world that "I have full confidence that no matter for how long I am imprisoned, the spirit of liberation has gone deep into the hearts of our people."[27]

Such declarations of courage and defiance stress the willingness of men to sacrifice their own personal freedom for the broader cause of black liberation. J. B. Marks was quoted in the internationally circulated *Bulletin of the Campaign for the Defiance of Unjust Laws* when facing prosecution under the Suppression of Communism Act: "Life is very precious and very valuable, but if for the freedom of our people I must give it up, I will give it up. I will give it for true democracy in this country. I will give my last drop of blood."[28] The willingness to sacrifice oneself placed African men at the heart of the nationalist struggle. As Cynthia Enloe has stated, "nationalism has typically sprung from masculinized memory, masculinized humiliation and masculinized hope."[29] Here, African nationalism is closely bound up with the physical fate of the black men. Threatened with detention, the black male leader often faced restrictions and constraints but nevertheless remained defiant and full of political potential. This self-fashioned and highly gendered account of nationalist struggle took on an international significance as black male leaders sought to legitimize their struggle to a global audience. Johnson Ngwevela, chairman of the Western Cape branch of the ANC, characterized his imprisonment in remarkably similar terms. Writing in the same publication before he was arrested at a mass meeting in Cape Town, Ngwevela declared: "I was elected by my people to lead them to freedom. . . . I would rather die fighting for my rights and for my people's rights than surrender to oppression."[30]

Heroic declarations such as these were frequently reproduced in the African American press and disseminated to organizations such as the CAA, ACOA, and NAACP in the United States. That anti-apartheid leaders were willing to go to jail for their political beliefs served to reinforce their leadership credentials, as well as the legitimacy of the ANC and SAIC's joint action. In many of these accounts political imprisonment was positioned as a form of "redemptive suffering" by anti-apartheid activists.[31] While this was open to both men and women, the prison narratives constructed by activists such as Matthews, Moroka, and Ngwevela consistently prioritized the agency of male leaders. The prison was a place where black men could test their leadership credentials. These experiences were used to establish bravery, courage, strength, and honor as primarily masculine traits. The willingness to go to jail was therefore used to provide proof that black male leaders were ready to give everything, including their lives, to the cause of freedom.

Narratives that dealt with political imprisonment also emphasized the respectable status and moral fortitude of these men in order to challenge myths of black criminality. For example, an article in the Defiance Campaign *Bulletin* responded to the imprisonment of Moses Kotane, Yusuf Dadoo, J. B. Marks, and David Bopape by saying "They were all arrested and are now languishing behind prison bars, where they are treated as ordinary murderers, gangsters, and criminals, there being no provision for political prisoners in South Africa."[32] These men, the article continued, represented a different class of prisoner, whose moral standing and exceptional status were beyond doubt. Class-based thinking informed narratives of heroic black masculinity in ways that associated manly values with resistance.

Surprisingly, this was also true of African American leftists, who, despite their scathing criticisms of incarceration rates in the United States and clear understanding of the role the criminal justice system played in black disenfranchisement, used their prison experiences to bolster their leadership credentials.[33] This can be seen in the campaign to secure the release of Alphaeus Hunton from prison in 1951, which repeatedly emphasized both his and his family's respectable status in the black community.[34] In a letter protesting Hunton's imprisonment, Paul Robeson noted that Hunton was an "honorable" and "worthy citizen" who belonged to a "distinguished American family," a fact that he believed meant that "his continued imprisonment violated the essence of justice and negates the best democratic traditions of our country."[35] Hunton's refusal to hand over the names of contributors to the Civil Rights Congress Bail Fund was cited as further evidence of his noteworthy character and status.[36] Framed as part of the African Americans' "historic struggle" against informers, fifty-four African leaders signed a petition in support of Hunton that proclaimed, "Time and again, leaders in the struggle for Negro democratic rights have been confronted by official and unofficial oppressors with the demand: 'Tell us the names of your associates.' Time and time again these leaders have refused to act as informers for the oppressors of their people, even at the risk of their personal liberty or lives. They have refused so to degrade themselves on the high moral ground that the cause for which they and their colleagues struggle is a just cause, and that to name their associates would be to betray them to the wrath of immoral, illegal and prejudice-ridden forces of oppression."[37] To those who protested his imprisonment, it was unthinkable that Hunton could be considered a criminal. His principles were beyond reproach. Instead the article firmly located Hunton as being part of a long and defiant tradition of black leadership, one that was moral, just, and characterized by a belief in self-sacrifice in order to protect others.

An article by the African American journalist John Pittman in the *Daily Worker* also advanced this view, explicitly comparing Hunton to a series of prominent black male leaders who had suffered at the hands of the state. The piece, which also asked the question, "While Dr. Hunton is in prison what is the Truman government doing to the African peoples?," observed that this preeminent African American leader had "followed the fighting traditions of his distinguished family, and joined the company of other Negro spokesmen who have stood their ground in the face of threats of imprisonment or worse—such a glorious company as that of Vesey, Nat Turner, Frederick Douglass, Dr. W. E. Burghardt Du Bois, Paul Robeson, Benjamin J. Davis, William L. Patterson, [and] Henry Winston."[38] By advancing a selective masculine view of the history of African American activism the article firmly positioned Hunton as a legitimate heir to, and contemporary of, a series of defiant black men who had bravely opposed race discrimination from slavery to the present day. Again, men were positioned as representing the vanguard of the black freedom struggle, their willingness to face prison a vivid indication that they possessed the right character traits required to lead the race.

The separation of political prisoners by their gender further fed patriarchal constructions of black political leadership that marginalized the experiences of black women activists.[39] Male camaraderie was presented as a central aspect of the prison experience of black South African leaders. Noting the spirit of togetherness that existed among his fellow cellmates, Alfred "Tough" Hutchinson compared his imprisonment during the Treason Trial to a continuous political rally and asked, "Is this another Congress of the people—drawing all South Africans together?"[40] In the all-male space of the prison cell, black activists asserted their autonomy as black men and political leaders. Alex La Guma echoed Hutchinson's sentiments, noting that "there are some hard boys in this trial. Tough organizers from the slums and the townships, and the mob who went through the Defiance Campaign, and who can go through this, too, I'm sure. They and the others. Comrades. The spirit of the struggle."[41]

This representation of the hard and rugged masculine character of these anti-apartheid activists was repeated throughout the Treason Trial. Describing the workings of a cell in which the non-European defendants were held, Hutchinson referred to "the fraternity of strong men in the 'lower house' building muscles. . . . Joe Modise in his enthusiasm landing up in the

A Call

from the heroic peoples of AFRICA to Negro and white Americans

"A Call from the Heroic Peoples of Africa to Negro and White Americans," pamphlet, Council on African Affairs, c. 1954. Source: Courtesy of the Department of Special Collections and University Archives, W. E. B. Du Bois Library, University of Massachusetts Amherst Libraries.

prison hospital. Robert Resha taking longer rests than exercise spells. . . . Dr. Naicker and his 'small walks.' The perennial youthfulness of Rev. Gawe, found where the song is thickest and the dancing most spirited. . . . And [Vuyisile] Mini's glorious voice riding the sea of song like an unerring pilot homeward bound."[42] This description hints at an intimate personal relationship and male camaraderie that existed between political prisoners. Mandela would also stress this point in regard to the Treason Trial, detailing in his autobiography the "programme of activities" organized by the prisoners that included lectures by Z. K. Matthews on the "American Negro" as well as the history of "African Music" by Reverend James Calata, while describing the communal cell as "a kind of convention for far-flung freedom fighters."[43] The prison was a gendered space. It was constructed as the heart of the struggle against apartheid, sites where black male solidarities could develop and where incarcerated black men could prove their leadership credentials. By transforming the prison cell into a place of comradeship, learning, and political discussion, black men positioned themselves as the natural leaders of national liberation movements.

Honorable, strong, brave, and respectable—the actions and experiences of political prisoners also inspired the struggle against racism around the world. Internationally circulated reports that focused on the imprisonment of anti-apartheid leaders challenged white supremacist accusations of the criminal and subversive character of these individuals, further legitimizing calls for black self-determination both in South Africa and the United States. However, by establishing strength, power, and self-sacrifice as distinctly masculine characteristics, international accounts of black imprisonment often endorsed class and gender assumptions that privileged male leadership. Men and women were assigned fixed gender roles within national and international narratives of anti-apartheid protest. The heroism of black male activists became a key lens through which African Americans engaged with, and responded to, the politics of anti-apartheid. This gendered vision of black protest was based around a shared belief in strong male leadership, as well as the perceived need to protect supposedly vulnerable black women from the oppressive structures of the apartheid state.

The Incarceration of Black Women: Vulnerability, Protection, and the African Family

Reports in the United States and South Africa focusing on the incarceration of black South African women largely downplayed their militant contribution to the anti-apartheid struggle.[44] Although women were occasionally commended for their bravery, accounts of their actions stressed the dangers that they faced when operating in the public political sphere. African women could only be made "safe," it was often argued, if black male leaders were by their side.[45] Narratives of anti-apartheid protest also used the supposed vulnerability of African women to emphasize the precarious position of the family and, by extension, the African nation as a whole. The status and fate of African women was therefore configured as a call to action for men—a gender rescue paradigm that promoted fixed gender roles within a patriarchal view of the African family.[46]

Press reports, pamphlets, and speeches originating in South Africa and the United States positioned African women as the primary caregivers in the black family. This idealization of strong black motherhood represented a challenge to long-established racist myths that questioned the moral status and stability of the African family.[47] However, it also had the effect of restricting African women to the domestic sphere. Here, the prison experiences of black women were used as a rallying cry. Women needed to be made safe and—if possible—returned to the relative safety of the home. Their vulnerability and suffering were symbolic of the violent nature of apartheid, as well as the need for black men to secure the safety of the African family.[48]

Images of African women at the mercy of police or in jail were strategically used to promote gendered feelings of solidarity between African Americans and black South Africans. Stories of police violence against women filled anti-apartheid press reports on black protest and civil disobedience campaigns in South Africa.[49] The South African *Guardian* and other newspapers associated with the anti-apartheid press carried headlines such as "Pregnant Women Battoned by Police in Uitenhage" and "Police Baton Women, [and] Babies." These sickening stories of police brutality against African women were laid bare for a concerned readership.[50] As the report on the antipass protests of African women in Uitenhage revealed, "Eyewitnesses . . . state that they saw a number of women being mauled by hefty policemen. Some of the women had their scalps broken and blood was flowing freely from the wounds on their heads. Others had weals on their bodies caused by sticks. Pregnant women [were] sprawled on the ground as they defended themselves against the police attacks."[51] The bloody detail of such accounts forced home the vulnerability of black women at the hands of oppressive state forces.

It is also important to note that details of violence are often absent from accounts that focused on black male activism, which instead seemed to favor a narrative of triumph over adversity.[52] The decision to downplay the racial violence that they faced has been strategically used by black South African men as a response to colonial and white supremacist forces that sought to strip them of their masculinity.[53] By deliberately obscuring the brutality of their experiences at the hands of the police, black men shielded themselves from the oppression that they faced and turned imprisonment into a positive political experience. In contrast, the prison conditions faced by black South African women repeatedly stressed their susceptibility to the violent practices of the apartheid state. Articles in the South African press that detailed the "inhuman jail treatment of African women" and exposés such as "Pregnant Women Beaten in Gaol" made it abundantly clear that the South African prison cell was no place for a woman to be.[54]

The very real dangers faced by women engaged in the struggle against apartheid were picked up on by organizations in the United States. Once again, this gendered language spanned political divides, influencing the anti-apartheid activism of both leftists and liberals. Evidence of police brutality against black women provided shocking headlines that presented a gendered call to arms for black Americans. For example, the CAA used examples of police brutality and threats of sexual violence against women to condemn the fascist character of the South African government. As one CAA pamphlet noted, "Police have on a number of occasions been convicted of raping non-white women they had arrested," supporting this observation with an account of the brutal assault of Johanna Skozena while in police custody.[55] Skozena described her assault by a white officer named van der Merwe in detail: "I was taken to a charge office where van der Merwe tied a hosepipe around my neck. Van der Merwe seized one end of the hosepipe and another constable another end, and pulled it. This choked me and I lost consciousness. When I recovered van der Merwe was striking me with the hosepipe over my shoulder and elsewhere on my body. Van der Merwe told me 'I must pray because it was my last day.'"[56]

Accounts such as this tapped into long-established ideas relating to the perceived vulnerability of women that could result from their enforced isolation from male figures and family support structures.[57] The violence perpetrated against women by the South African police provided horrific and visceral insight into the brutality of the apartheid state. One ACOA account of the breakup of a FSAW meeting in Pretoria suggests that the apparent inability to protect women from this type of treatment became an important rallying cry for the nascent international anti-apartheid movement. The report told how police at the meeting "continued to hit at heads, limbs and bodies indiscriminately, and lined the exits so that women trying to escape were also beaten. . . . They did not hesitate to hit women repeatedly even after they had fallen, according to eye witnesses. Children in the crowd were lost and injured, pregnant women also beaten; an elderly grandmother and a girl passing by the hall were among the injured. Men on the Platform were beaten and arrested."[58]

Significantly, the apparent helplessness of African men was outlined in this report. Their inability to defend black women from indiscriminate police beatings vividly revealed the dangers that the African family unit faced. The system of apartheid left women and children exposed to acts of brutality, leaving men unable to fulfill the traditional role of protector associated with dominant codes of masculinity. While women were clearly active in the anti-apartheid movement—indeed the meeting was called to oppose the extension of the pass laws to African women—it was the men at this meeting who were ultimately arrested and taken away by the police. The article therefore calls attention to the dangers that African women faced in the public sphere, as well as the apparent inability of male activists to protect them. Political protest—as it appeared in a range of reports—was perilous work that often placed women in impossible situations. Underpinning much of the language of the anti-apartheid movement was the insistence that women should no longer be exposed to the violence of the apartheid state.

South African appeals for black international support also emphasized the need to shore up the patriarchal structures of the black family. Chief Luthuli recalled how the Treason Trial Defence Fund provided an invaluable lifeline for imprisoned black activists, noting how "the Fund came to the rescue of their dependents." Describing how this money was put to use, he added, "I shudder to think what might have been the fate of parents and families but for this help, and all of us if we had been obliged to do without a brilliant team of lawyers who fought every inch of the ground."[59]

There was a widespread belief that anti-apartheid organizers based in the United States could help protect and care for black families in South Africa, as evident in a letter a black Defiance Campaign leader wrote thanking the ACOA for their financial support: "Many thousands of our men and women have gone to jail. . . . Many more are prepared to do so even at the risk of leaving their own families to starve. It thus becomes the duty of those who can to prevent unnecessary suffering of young and aged."[60]

Z. K. Matthews also stressed the importance of international support to the black South African family, writing to the CAA to thank the organization for the "practical assistance" it provided for those imprisoned black activists "and their dependents" during the Defiance Campaign.[61] Matthews made these gendered appeals to protect the black family when he was based in the United States. For example, in a speech to the Harlem members of the National Urban League in November 1952, he described the experiences of a group of African women jailed during the Defiance Campaign. Addressing a predominantly African American audience, Matthews noted how these women were stripped of their clothes in the prison courtyard where "they were made to stand naked for hours whilst a ferocious African rainstorm pelted their helpless bodies." He concluded that, "the women will never forget this treatment, or the forcible separation of mothers, children, wives and husbands."[62]

Torn apart by the violent mechanisms of the apartheid state, the plight of the African family would have been immediately recognizable to African Americans, who were all too familiar with the way in which white supremacy worked to dismantle black family structures at home. The idea that it was the duty of those who were able to intervene and prevent the suffering of black families animated the international appeals of anti-apartheid activists throughout this period.[63] They represented gendered calls to action through which activists in the United States personally related to the anti-apartheid struggle. The dismantling of the African family provided a way into anti-apartheid politics. For black Americans in particular, this was a clear symbol of the personal and domestic pressures state-sanctioned racism placed on black people on both sides of the Atlantic. Within this configuration, the domestic sphere was idealized as the proper place for African women. When women ventured out of these spaces to participate and lead political protests, they were cast as vulnerable, alone, and—when unable to rely on male protection—at the mercy of the white settler state.

Internationally circulated accounts of the anti-apartheid protest did not shy away from the hardships and violent forces that black women confronted. However, such reports largely failed to recognize African women as autonomous political actors and downplayed their leading role in the early anti-apartheid struggle. Instead, they drew a clear line between the domestic and the public sphere in ways that symbolically connected the ability of African men to protect and control the family with the attainment of political rights.[64] This was a state of affairs that black women's activists would not leave unchallenged.

After the police raided the homes of the 156 anti-apartheid activists who would make up the defendants in the Treason Trial, FSAW released a telling statement. "As women and mothers," the organization declared, "we proclaim that the real treason in South Africa is the betrayal of our children, the denial of the fundamental right of every child to universal education, to a decent home, to comfort and security, to peace and freedom."[65] Black South African women forcefully critiqued the arrest and imprisonment of anti-apartheid activists, condemning these actions in gendered terms that stressed their important position in black self-determination movements. Black women did not need to be rescued by black men from the oppressive forces of the apartheid state. On the contrary, their arrest and imprisonment enabled them to advance their own leadership credentials and refute sexist ideas that claimed a woman's place was in the home. For women activists, familial structures did not necessarily represent patriarchal spaces but instead were reconstituted as important sites of resistance from which they could articulate a militant version of black motherhood.

FSAW members established motherhood as an overtly political identity.[66] In a petition to Johannesburg's Native commissioner opposing the pass laws, FSAW activists argued that any extension of the reference book system would result in the widespread imprisonment of black women: "We are not cattle to be herded into kraals. We are women and mothers. Our children, our families are scattered, and when they need us, we must answer their call. We demand the right to move freely, to come and go as we have always done and we condemn this effort to make us into slaves, to be bought and sold through the labour bureaux."[67] Black female leaders in the anti-apartheid movement discussed their incarceration not as a sign of their vulnerability or need to be protected by black men, but on the contrary, as an oppressive act that highlighted the central role they played in black self-determination movements. The FSAW statement defiantly concluded, "NO!' these things must not be. . . . WE SHALL NOT REST UNTIL WE HAVE WON FOR OUR CHILDREN THEIR FUNDAMENTAL RIGHT TO FREEDOM, JUSTICE AND SECURITY."[68]

The claims of black South African women that their imprisonment would result in the neglect of black children and endanger the black family empowered them politically. They did not accept that their status as mothers meant their concerns were limited to the domestic sphere. Conversely, they expanded their understanding of motherhood in ways that politically empowered black women and enabled them to place their specific concerns at the forefront of the anti-apartheid movement. When faced with the prison cell, African women used this experience to assert their militancy and as evidence of their dedication to eradicating white supremacy.

Black women emphasized their willingness to suffer both for their families and for the cause of freedom. As the ANC-Women's League and FSAW joint pamphlet "Women in Chains" asserted, "Women are not afraid of suffering for the sake of their children and their homes. Women have an answer to the threats to their families and their future. Women will not face a future imprisoned in the pass laws! Women will fight for the right to live and move freely as human beings!"[69] African women leaders talked about their experiences of prison in ways that were reminiscent of their male counterparts' narratives.[70] They too stressed their defiance and established prison as a site of political resistance. ANC-WL National President Lilian Ngoyi stated defiantly, "If the Government deports women in the impending struggle against passes, they will bring new hope to those in whose midst they are thrown in their deportation; if they are sent to jail they will convert the jails into institutions for universal education."[71] Just as imprisoned black male leaders used incarceration as a way to establish their leadership credentials, black women strategically obscured the hardships of prison life in order to assert their determination to resist white supremacy at every opportunity. It is clear that black women in the United States and South Africa did not accept masculinist narratives of anti-apartheid protest. Instead, they worked to challenge depictions of the heroic leadership of black men in ways that placed their own political experiences and gender concerns at the center of the struggle against white supremacy.

Part IV **Gender and Anti-Apartheid Politics**

....

7 Motherhood, Anti-Apartheid, and Pan-African Politics

. . . .

Often denied a political platform by the patriarchal structures that viewed public politics as a male domain, black women in the United States and South Africa drew on their domestic experiences in order to move beyond the private sphere and publicly challenge race and gender discrimination.[1] In the decades following World War II, black women in both countries often argued that their status as mothers placed them at the center of black political and cultural life. By embracing this role, they established their position at the forefront of movements for black freedom.[2] Motherhood provided a way for women to use the patriarchal gender identities assigned them to transcend male-dominated definitions of black political activism.[3] Through maternalist ideals, such as the importance of the home and the care of black children, black women developed a set of mutual concerns that spanned the black Atlantic. This shared "female consciousness" amounted to a form of global black motherhood that influenced the political and cultural connections between their countries.[4]

Global black motherhood can be defined as a form of transnational maternalist politics based around the shared experiences of black women in white supremacist societies. Ideas relating to social position of the black mother have been historically important in terms of shaping narratives of race discrimination and black protest.[5] As Patricia Hill Collins has asserted, "Black motherhood as an institution is both dynamic and dialectical." Noting how representations of black motherhood have been used to inform the "intersecting oppression of race, class, gender, sexuality and nation," Collins documents how black women sometimes embraced this gender role as a means of challenging white supremacist structures.[6]

In the United States and South Africa motherhood was used to enforce race and gender stereotypes, while simultaneously providing a space through which black women could define themselves as self-reliant and independent. Motherhood was therefore both a burden and a potential base for the self-actualization of black women. By claiming ideals of motherhood usually reserved for whites, black women challenged negative gender stereotypes that emphasized the inherent inferiority of the black family.[7] This often involved calling attention to the political significance of the domestic sphere. Exerting control over the home and providing a black space free from the intrusion of the white supremacist state represented an important resistance strategy in the black community. As bell hooks argues, the "homeplace" has been an important site of resistance for African Americans. Recalling her own upbringing in Kentucky she notes, "We could not learn to love or respect ourselves in the culture of white supremacy, on the outside; it was there on the inside, in that 'homeplace,' most often created and kept by black women, that we had the opportunity to grow and develop, to nurture our spirits."[8] For hooks, the transformation of the domestic sphere into a homeplace—a safe space for black families through which they could escape white supremacy—was an overt act of defiance that stressed the self-sufficiency and capability of the black family. Significantly, hooks notes how "this task of making a homeplace, of making home a community of resistance, has been shared by black women globally, especially black women in white supremacist societies."[9] Historically, black women in the United States and South Africa have transformed the domestic sphere into a site where citizenship claims could be made.[10] By privileging their position within the home, as primary caregivers for the black family, they worked to stress the political significance of black motherhood in the global fight against white supremacy.

The Global Black Mother and the Pan-African Family

The African mother has served as a symbolic figure around which black transnational connections were articulated. For an ever-increasing number of African Americans, inspired by the colonial liberation struggles of the era, Africa came to be seen as a motherland—a gendered and racialized location from which all scattered peoples of African descent had once originated.[11] In particular, the idea of the African mother functioned as a central component of Pan-African thought. This amounted to a gendering of the African continent through the construction of an imagined black international family, as well as the establishment of transnational links based around the protection of black women and the care of black children.[12] Defiant, proud, and respectable, the metaphor of the black international family informed the anticolonial outlook of many African Americans throughout the 1940s and 1950s.

Engaging with dominant discourses that assigned men and women specific gender roles, African Americans regularly conceived of the black diaspora in terms of a metaphorical family that connected them to other people
of African descent around the world. An example of this was when the
respected African American union leader, and founder of the March on Washington Movement, A. Philip Randolph, referred to the figure "Mother Africa"
when addressing an audience at an African Freedom Day held at Carnegie
Hall. At the start of his speech he noted how "the hearts and lives of Negro
Americans have been deeply enriched, chastened and strengthened by a
sense of reference, respect, affection and love for our great and ancient
mother Africa—a symbol of suffering surpassing suffering born of millions
of her children being torn from her bosom and transported by the slave
trade over the high sea to become slaves in an ancient land."[13] Continuing
in a similar vein, he described how "the great intuitional wisdom and
prophecy of our black mother, Africa, with her majesty, nobility, beauty and
grace, her sense of history and destiny, enabled her to read in the heavens
the unfailing signs that no night however dark is ever endless and that a
star of promise is never far."[14] For Randolph, a close collaborator with the
ACOA, black American identity had been "greatly enriched" and "strengthened" by its association with an African culture embodied by the universal
"mother Africa." African motherhood was positioned as both a symbol of
suffering evocative of the horrors of the transatlantic slave trade and a figure of strength—a reminder that freedom was "never far" away. By evoking the image of the African mother, Randolph embraced a highly gendered
vision of Africa. Articulated at an event celebrating African independence,
Randolph's words encouraged black Americans to imagine an intimate connection to the continent through the reassertion of familial ties that had
been stripped away by imperial systems of commerce and thought.[15]

The family unit also provided an important metaphor through which African Americans could engage with anticolonial politics in Africa. In her
political writings Eslanda Goode Robeson frequently used the metaphor of
the black African family in order to promote Pan-African solidarities. A
prominent member of the CAA and the STJ, Robeson traveled extensively
in Africa and consistently promoted African independence throughout her
life.[16] A more radical political figure than Randolph, she used similar gendered metaphors to make black international connections with Africa.[17] In
a 1951 speech to a meeting of the Victims of the Smith Act, Robeson listed
all the different families that she had belonged to throughout her life,

commenting in relation to the time she spent on the continent that "when I travelled through AFRICA, I discovered that I belonged to the AFRICAN FAMILY, with 150 million AFRICAN RELATIONS, with an ancient and honorable historic and cultural background."[18]

For Robeson, the African family was a central aspect of her black international thought. Reflecting on her trip to Ghana to attend the All-African People's Conference in 1958, she chose to compare the Pan-African meeting to a family gathering.[19] Robeson viewed the event, held to formulate plans to achieve full-scale African independence, through the lens of the family, an extended African kinship group whose members stretched far beyond the confines of the continent itself. She commented, "The African family, in the large sense, has assembled in Accra for a week (Dec. 5–12) to discuss a family matter, an internal domestic matter of deep concern to all its members: the question of Independence for the family as a whole, not just a few of its members."[20] For Robeson this high point of the Pan-African movement represented a far-reaching family reunion. The first coming together of Africans and people of African descent in an independent African nation brought home siblings who had for too long been separated by colonial and imperial forces. By characterizing the conference as "an internal domestic matter," Robeson strategically transferred the politics of the home to the global political arena, a rhetorical move that collapsed the divides between the domestic and the public, the local and the global.

Here, the metaphor of the African family also affirms that Africans and people of African descent would overcome their ideological and political differences in order to work toward an independent Africa.[21] Toward this end, she stressed that, "as with all family gatherings, there are differences of opinion as to how to proceed, there are aspects of the problem which are very important to some members and unimportant to others; there are minor irritations; but, as with all good families worth the name, when it comes down to a question of survival and well-being of its members, this family is closing ranks in order to present a strong united front (a 200 million strong united front) to the world on the number one question: Independence and Self-Government for ALL the members of the African Family."[22] In Accra, the extended African family, notwithstanding the occasional internal squabble, would put their individual differences aside and work together as a whole. For Eslanda Robeson the idea of the Pan-African family was important in helping establish a common ground in the presence of many diverse political opinions and views. As anticommunism exacerbated political divisions among African Americans, the language of the extended African family made it possible for black activists such as Robeson and Randolph to rhetorically overcome their political differences and present a united front with anticolonial movements in Africa. Black activists in the United States invested domestic sites with an international significance that underlined the political and cultural connections with the wider world. For African Americans across the political spectrum "Mother Africa" and the African family provided instantly recognizable symbols through which they could both identify and engage with African independence movements.

The systematic dismantling of homes and the dispersal of families under apartheid fueled African American interest in and concern for the South African branch of the African family.[23] These repressive practices also enabled African Americans to draw broad parallels with historical and contemporary forces that disrupted black family structures in the United States. U.S. newspaper reports and political publications focusing on apartheid regularly stressed the importance of the black family unit when it came to confronting white supremacist practices. The vulnerability of the black South African family under apartheid was used as a rallying call in the United States and was often read as evidence that African Americans had certain responsibilities to the global black family.[24] Linda Gordon calls apartheid a "deeply gendered system" that sought to control black family structures in order to assert the dominance of the ruling white population.[25] She highlights how white supremacist power pervaded intimate and personal spaces as apartheid laws separated black men and women, "institutionalized 'single' motherhood," and exacerbated gendered tensions that ultimately led to the breakup of black families.[26] State efforts to control familial relationships and harness black reproduction for a system of capitalist exploitation have also been central to the development of race, class, and gender inequalities in the United States.[27] The security of the black family, and the care of children in particular, were therefore often read as experiences though which African Americans could relate to, and potentially get involved in, the anti-apartheid struggle.

Mainstream African American newspapers such as the *Chicago Defender*, *Pittsburgh Courier*, and *New York Amsterdam News* all examined the effect that apartheid had on the black family.[28] In 1953, the *Pittsburgh Courier* ran a series of articles entitled "South Africa Uncensored." Accompanied by photographs, maps, and tables, the series explained to an African American audience what life was like under apartheid through the prism of the black family. In one article Nomple Njongwe, the wife of the then president of the Cape Province ANC James Njongwe, was quoted alongside an image of a black South African holding her small child in her arms saying that, during the Defiance Campaign, "every woman who loves her children must join the ranks of the African National Congress liberatory movement; to do otherwise would be a betrayal of the just claims of the starving African children."[29] Anti-apartheid protest was often framed in ways that stressed the need to care for the black family. Njongwe asserted that women needed to play a central role in the nationalist struggle. However, her motivations for protesting were intimately connected to the politics of the family.

Reports in the African American press regularly encouraged sympathy for families and communities caught up in the apartheid system.[30] A picture accompanying one of the *Courier* articles reinforced this point. Featured in a piece that discussed the relationship between the Dutch Reformed Church and the development of apartheid, the image showed a group of young, unsupervised African children. The caption stated, "Here is young South Africa, a cheap source of labour for the 'herrenvolk' white men under the present way of life in the Cape countries."[31] The children appear without any visible parental care, alerting the reader to how the exploitation of black labor threatened the family. Mining had a devastating effect on African family structures as men worked away from home, for little pay, and women were forced to leave their children as they too sought employment in order to make up the family income.[32]

Images of children in need of care and assistance would have resonated with many black readers all too familiar with the effects that white supremacy and segregation could have on black families.[33] Under slavery, black women had had no legal claim to their children and struggled daily to resist the control of slave owners over the black family. Segregation continued to place economic strain on black families. In the early twentieth century black intellectuals such as E. Franklin Frazier argued that single-parent families represented one of *the* major obstacles to black success in the United States.[34] When confronted with images of the break-up of the black family aboard, African Americans were encouraged to consider the historic economic and social forces that shaped the structure of their own families. Confronted with images of vulnerable children, readers were encouraged to extend their own gendered responsibilities of care to the black families in South Africa. An article in the *Chicago Defender* reinforced this point in its coverage of the 1959 Natal protests against forced removals, reporting that: "News dispatches from South Africa continue to be disturbing and distressing. Hundreds of African women have been arrested since last Friday. . . . These women are hunted down like wild beasts, and clubbed into insensibility, simply because they had the fortitude to strike out against the intolerable injustices of a system that degrades them and their kinfolk."[35] Focusing on the indignities faced by African women, the article served to reinforce sympathetic ties between African Americans and their extended black South African families. The vivid illustration of the abuse these women faced implied that *Defender* readers had a responsibility to prevent the degradation of African women and mothers who were on the streets protesting forced removals and the breakup of their homes. African Americans, it was argued, needed to fulfill their roles as part of the black transnational family and, as the article concluded, "should do something to help."[36]

Leftist organizations such as the CAA used images of the African family for strikingly similar purposes. The council consistently engaged with notions of black motherhood when reporting on and articulating its support for anticolonial movements in Africa.[37] A striking visual example of this was the use of an image depicting an African mother and child that appeared on the front page of the August 1954 edition of *Spotlight on Africa*.[38] Adorning an issue that included articles on "The Voice of Black South Africa," "Some Questions on Kenya," and "How They Voted in the U.N.," the cover provided an instantly recognizable and relatable image through which African Americans could engage with black independence struggles overseas. The publication gave no indication of the origins or location of the mother and child depicted. Instead, this family scene stood in for the African continent as a whole, providing a striking visual representation of black international solidarity across national borders.[39] Images that depicted the African family, or indeed its conspicuous absence, hinted at imagined family ties between African Americans and black South Africans. Most significantly, these representations encouraged African Americans to actively intervene in the lives and the struggle against white settler colonialism as members of the African family, connecting issues of race and gender across the black Atlantic.

The case of Elizabeth Mafeking also illustrates how the fate of the African family was used to generate support for the anti-apartheid movement in the United States. President of the African Food and Canning Workers Union from 1954 to 1959 in the Western Cape, Mafeking was also one of the founding members of the Federation of South African Women and in 1957 was elected vice president of the ANC Women's League. In November 1959, mainly as a result of her illegal travels to attend the Warsaw Youth Festival, Mafeking was issued with a banning order forcing her removal from her home in Paarl in the Western Cape to a small African location on arid land over 600 miles away near the small North Western town of Vryburg.[40] In order to avoid deportation, she fled with her two-month-old baby to Basutoland (now Lesotho), leaving behind her husband and remaining ten children.[41] This tale of exile and the mistreatment of a politically active woman and mother became a rallying cry for those involved in the international anti-apartheid movement.[42] Significantly, it was not Mafeking's extensive travels, her role as a committed labor organizer, or her position as a prominent ANC activist that were used to publicize her case. For the most part, it was her status as a mother, her sudden departure from the home she had made and maintained on her own terms, the forced abandonment of her children, and the escape she made with her two-month old baby that featured in reports condemning the cruelty of the apartheid system. Although her political credentials were occasionally noted, Mafeking's identity as a mother was of the utmost importance to anti-apartheid activists.[43] Her inability, as a result of the oppressive actions of the state, to fulfill all the gendered responsibilities that motherhood demanded became a central issue around which African Americans responded to Mafeking's exile.[44]

The ACOA was particularly vocal when it came to the Mafeking case, issuing press releases and raising money on her behalf. In early 1960 the organization's African Defense and Aid Fund sent money to Mafeking to help her provide for her young child and as "a first sign of American support [for her] in exile."[45] The opening speech of baseball star Jackie Robinson at the ACOA South Africa Emergency Conference, held in the aftermath of the Sharpeville shootings, also explicitly made reference to Mafeking. Using her exile as a lens through which to view white supremacy more broadly in South Africa, Robinson commented,

> Living in South Africa is not joyous for Elizabeth Mafeking, one of
> the outstanding women leaders of the African National Congress. . . .
> Mrs. Mafeking is the mother of 11 children, the youngest only two
> months old at the time of her arrest. Fortunately, she escaped from
> her captors before she was sent to her banishment, and is now in the
> British protectorate of Basutoland. But only one of her children is
> with her, and until change comes about in the South African situa-
> tion, she is doomed to be separated from her family, unless they can
> come to join her.[46]

Mafeking's separation from her children and family provided a way in to South African politics for black activists in the United States. Although Robinson referred to Mafeking as one of the ANC's "outstanding women leaders," her identity as a mother and the plight of her family was ultimately given greater billing than her anti-apartheid activism.

In the end, George Houser would write to the ANC's Duma Nokwe in order to enquire into the likelihood of Mafeking being able to elude the South African authorities and travel to the United States to take part in an ACOA speaking tour.[47] Although the plan never came to fruition, the fact that the ACOA identified Mafeking's exile as a landmark case that would effectively translate to an American audience is significant in terms of the gendered nature of the global anti-apartheid movement. The negative effect that race discrimination had on the black South African family provided ammunition for those seeking to condemn apartheid. Whether designed to encourage African American involvement and intervention in black South African struggles, or to knowingly convey the racial oppression they faced to a global audience, the gendered language of black motherhood permeated coverage of race relations in South Africa. This was often limiting for black women, in that their status as mothers sometimes obscured their contributions as anti-apartheid organizers. However, these gendered images of anticolonial protest helped to promote networks of shared responsibility between African Americans and black South Africans.

Motherhood and Apartheid in South Africa

Motherhood and the role of African women were deeply politicized issues in South Africa. Black women often argued that their status at the heart of the family gave them unique insight into the operation of apartheid power. Using maternalist discourses, they claimed that it was their right to provide a stable home environment for their children.[48] Through their ideological commitment to the care and welfare of their children, black South African women were able to use their identities as mothers to challenge politically the operation of racist practices within South Africa. In part, this was a response to popular representations of black family life that idealized the domestic duties of women in order to make broader political observations about the damaging effects of racial segregation. Under apartheid, domestic spaces were positioned as important sites where the political prospects of black South Africans were debated and assessed.

South African newspapers and magazines were filled with articles and opinion pieces on how to care for black children. The *Bantu World* newspaper in particular stressed the importance of motherhood and the care of children to the development of ideas of black self-sufficiency. Founded in

1932, *Bantu World* was owned by the Argus Printing and Publishing Company, the largest white-owned media publishers in South Africa.[49] Despite its white ownership, the newspaper employed a predominantly black writing staff and was edited at the time by the black educators R. V. Selope Thema and Jacob M. Nhlapo.[50] Its content was almost entirely devoid of coverage detailing political protest and it even expressed outright opposition to the Defiance Campaign. Nevertheless, *Bantu World* played a significant role in shaping the political and cultural outlook of a large section of the black South African population, accounting for 25 percent of African newspaper circulation.[51] The publication carried regular columns dedicated to African women and the preservation of the home. These opinion pieces used the ability of black women to care for their children as a lens through which South Africa's racial problems could be better understood. Often these political points were made through romanticized constructions of the black South African home. This can be seen in the poem "So Long," published as part of newspaper's column "Home Corner for African Women" that appeared throughout the 1940s:

> So long as there are homes to which men turn
> At close of day;
> So long as there are homes where children are,
> Where women stay—
> If love and loyalty and faith be found
> Across those sills—
> A stricken nation can recover from
> Its greatest ills.
> So long as there are homes where fires burn
> And there is bread.
> So long as there are homes where lamps are lit.
> And prayers are said;
> Although a people falter through the dark—
> And nations grope—
> With God himself back of these little homes,
> We have sure hope.[52]

The poem ties the fate of the home to the hopes and fears of a "stricken nation." The ability of every African to access a thriving, respectable, and godly homeplace, where children are cared for, is positioned as a possible solution to racial strife in South Africa. As we have seen elsewhere, the politics of respectability fed black political resistance by asserting the value of

African culture and questioning racial stereotypes that undermined black autonomy.[53] It was within this context that black South Africans made their claims about motherhood, the home, and the African family. Emphasizing the morality and caring nature of the family were ways of asserting self-sufficiency and independence in the face of white supremacy.[54]

Significantly, articles in *Bantu World* occasionally warned that black South Africans were in danger of losing their identity and traditions through their exposure to modern ways of life. For example, in a regular column entitled "Letter to African Motherhood" it was asserted that "we all love beautiful children, with easy smiles and a cheerful face. But it appears that as the African is becoming more and more absorbed in civilised life, he is steadily losing that child who has a plumpy body, with well-built features. We now see bony children with wiry features and ghost like eyes that tell one long sad story of undernourishment, disease and poverty."[55] Here the rush toward civilization is portrayed as a threat to the happy, well-fed, and contented black family. The piece called for black South African women to bolster the African family by looking inward, to traditionally African values of care. This was often limiting in that it reinforced the white supremacist myth that black South Africans could not handle the demands of modern citizenship. However, descriptions of malnourishment and poverty also clearly demonstrated the shortcomings of the white settler state. By and large, pieces that promoted the value of black motherhood argued that traditional African standards of care were in fact superior to those that were endorsed by white society. This was a potentially dangerous argument to make in that it promoted the idea of a separate African way of life that could be used to isolate Native groups in South Africa. However, articles in *Bantu World* consistently established the home as a political site in ways that drew attention to the negative effect that segregation was having on the African community.

Overall, the "Letter to African Womanhood" series argued that a safe homeplace could provide an environment for a powerful and dynamic black population, capable of challenging their inferior status within society.[56] Evoking the political significance of black motherhood, the column insisted that "the African woman has the peculiarly delicate and important task of bringing up a generation of self-reliant, sturdy young Africans who are not afraid to look the world in the eyes."[57] This piece then went on to argue that the knowledge and skills of African women would be crucial when it came to facing the realities of racial oppression. Another article in the series stated, "Modern conditions of life are such that a group that is tame, docile and yielding will always go under and perish, whereas a virile, assertive group will always triumph. We have a duty to bring up confident children who are prepared to face the stiffest trials and overcome superhuman difficulties."[58] It was the duty of African women to raise children capable of facing up to the hardships of South African society. By providing a nurturing and respectable environment, African mothers would produce a new generation, capable of leading the nation to freedom. As this particular "Letter to African Motherhood" concluded, "If we can rear and bring up children of this sort, then we can be certain that we have laid sound foundations for the future of our people. When our leaders say 'Mayibuye i Afrika' they can always count upon a virile youth which can always be trusted in the hour of crisis. The call to African mother is: Give our leaders of tomorrow a self-confident youth and the African will be a free citizen."[59]Articles in *Bantu World* argued that the capacity for social and racial change was inextricably linked to the home and through the raising of black children. It was the job of the African mother to care for the family in ways that would prepare them for the hardships that they would face within an industrialized and white-controlled South Africa. These commentaries implored black South African women to bring up children prepared to fight for the future of black Africa, to push for political rights, and ultimately, to claim political independence.

Discussions concerning the role of women in the African family continued into the 1950s in the pages of *Zonk!*[60] The magazine published a number of articles advising African mothers on how to properly care for their children. Regular columns included "Looking after Baby," in which readers were confronted with messages outlining their parental responsibilities, such as a page given to breast-feeding, "vital because, just when we hear that overseas countries are seeing a great revival of this truly natural form of baby care, we hear of African mothers refusing their babies the breast."[61] The relationship between the African mother and child is revered in the publication. For example, on receiving a photo of a mother and child for the magazine's "beautiful African baby" competition, the editors published the image in full with the comment that the photo "was not quite suitable, but showed such a delightful example of mother and child that we have included it. The mother is Mrs. Daphne Thorpe, an Evaton nurse, with her daughter Goitsemang."[62] The front cover of the magazine was often taken over by images of happy and contented African children. In 1951 an entire cover was dedicated to an image of a smiling African child, accompanied by the caption, "This month our cover shows a typical happy young African, with her face covered in ice cream. The smile is the smile of youth confident in the future. We know that this picture will be loved by parents happy in their love for their children, but we are also confident that it will appeal to all Africans who are known for their great feeling toward the younger generation."[63]

The happy and contented child was used as a unifying image, a symbol of hope and a sign of confidence in their own future.[64] Black South Africans, the magazine suggested, were united in their love and responsibilities towards their children.[65] Later that year, as part of a particularly bizarre front cover, three images of the same African child appeared. The caption attempted to explain, "Three babies or one baby? Well, it's one baby actually, but how many babies does not really matter as long as the influence that is to launch them in life is the mother's love and care so vividly captured by our photographer. This child illustrates just the sort of home that kills Tsotsism and the evil described on page 20 [abandoned babies]. It also illustrates just what most Africans feel about children, and last, but by no means least, it shows what the African man most wants his wife and baby to look like."[66] The literal reproduction of this image—the happy and healthy baby raised on the love of its mother—was brought into conversation with other articles within the issue that focused on the rise of "Tsotsi" criminal gangs and the abandonment of babies.[67] Emotional and practical investments in the structures of the African family were promoted as a potential antidote to a range of social problems perceived to be plaguing the African community.[68] Black South Africans were encouraged to embrace respectable family values in ways that had the potential to contradict white racist assumptions concerning the supposed immorality and inferiority of the black population.

This also reflected a broader shift in gender relations that uncoupled black men from the domestic sphere and that emphasized the role of black women in the home as the primary caregivers of black children during the 1950s.[69] Black motherhood and the fate of the African family therefore offered a lens through which black South Africans viewed and debated their position within the apartheid system. Another *Zonk!* article, "A Study in Misery and Courage," shows how the private concerns of the black family were positioned as an important political issue.[70] The piece opens with a tale of the breakup of the black family: "Meet this family, it's a family that may be found in any big town—maybe it's your family—but beware that it doesn't become a typical African family!" Abandoned by a father who had succumbed to his "craving for strong drink," the mother "is in pain" as she laments the fates and possible futures of her six children. Two of her children have died, her eldest is in jail, another has run away and also turned to crime, while her daughter who is still at home "sells her body to earn the luxuries she craves." The only hope for the African mother is her infant child who she still hopes "will grow up to be a decent, responsible, hardworking young man."[71] This tale, one that "may be found in any big town," warned that the breakup of the respectable family must be avoided at all costs. Documenting the dangers of the modern township, the article criticizes black South Africans who failed to fully embrace their family commitments. Once again, the anti-urban message of the article is closely aligned to apartheid thinking that emphasized the inability of black South Africans to adapt to modern city life. However, despite its problematic nature, the piece clearly outlines the extent to which the apartheid system placed pressure on African communities. The solution to this problem, according to the article, was to strengthen the family unit: "The very meaning of the word 'family' must be reconsidered. The people in a family should live together in love and understanding, helping one another, protecting one another. There is a wonderful beauty about a family who live in such harmony. Let there be an end to the sins that destroys such family happiness. Let every member of the family work together for the good of all."[72]

Zonk!'s message was that the racial uplift of black South Africans would only be secured through the moralizing force of the black family. A well-functioning and harmonious home environment had the potential to protect against further strife and raise a new generation of moral and upstanding individuals capable of finding their way in the world. As "A Study in Misery and Courage" concluded, "If he [the mother's youngest son] grows up to be strong, healthy, upright and decent, then so will millions of other children. But, if he too, is swallowed by the evil around him and turns to crime and vice so will millions of others—and a mother's prayers and tears will have been in vain!"[73] The fate of the African child, it was argued, was central to the future of black South Africa as a whole.

The condition of the black family, its future seen through the figure of the African mother, was invested with a national political significance. Articles in *Zonk!* that commented on the African family were often patronizing and restrictive, especially in the way that they attempted to return black women to the domestic sphere.[74] They also played into racist myths that emphasized the criminal tendencies of Africans and their supposed inability to care for their children. This echoed National Party claims that forced removals and the construction of townships would benefit Africans, securing their welfare and development.[75] However, this moralizing discourse also clearly drew attention to the pressures that black family structures faced under the apartheid system. The magazine's African readers would have understood this criticism in relation to the oppressive structural forces that shaped their lives and personal relationships. By focusing on the fears and concerns of African mothers, *Zonk!* publicly articulated the damaging effects that apartheid had on the black family unit.

Bantu World and *Zonk!*, despite their ambivalence toward organized protest and their relatively conservative outlook, were highly politicized in terms of the commentary they provided on the day-to-day concerns of the black South African population. In the 1940s and 1950s, as both labor migration and the policies of the apartheid state dismantled family support networks, publications with a large African readership repositioned the home as an important political site. African women were expected to play a vital role within this configuration. Articles that imagined the ideal family unit, often presented as a respectable environment that would produce a new generation of upstanding and moral South Africans, placed a great deal of emphasis on black motherhood. Although constrained by patriarchal gender ideas that cast them as the primary carers within the family, African women responded to these concerns by questioning the divides that existed between the domestic and the public political sphere. Reacting to concerns about the future of the African family, black women active in anti-apartheid organizations repurposed the gender roles that were assigned to them by formulating a politicized and militant brand of black motherhood.

The Federation of South African Women: Toward a Militant Black Motherhood

In the mid-1950s the Federation of South African Women began organizing protests against the introduction of new laws that paved the way for the extension of permits and passes to African women.[76] Members of the ANC Women's League, the CPSA, and various trade unions founded FSAW in 1954 as a nonracial alliance of women against apartheid and gender discrimination.[77] There was significant crossover in terms of the aims, membership, and leadership of FSAW and the ANC Women's League in particular. ANC Women's League leaders, including Elizabeth Mafeking, Ida Mtwana, and Lilian Ngoyi, held key leadership positions in the organization. Working alongside white leftists such as Ray Alexander and Helen Joseph, they hoped to achieve the following goals: "To bring the women of South Africa together; to secure full equality of opportunity for all women, regardless of race, colour or creed; to remove social and legal and economic disabilities; [and] to work for the protection of the women and children of our land."[78]

Although somewhat constrained by its ties to the broader Congress Alliance, FSAW provided its members with a political association through which specifically woman-centered politics could be articulated.[79] This was made clear by the organization's Women's Charter, issued on its founding in April 1954. The document, which provided the inspiration for the Congress Alliance's Freedom Charter of 1955, directly challenges the gender hierarchies that oppressed South African women.[80] When addressing the "obstacles to the progress of women" in South African society, the Women's Charter proclaims that "this intolerable condition would not be allowed to continue were it not for the refusal of a large section of our men folk to concede to us women the rights and privileges which they demand for themselves. We shall teach men they cannot hope to liberate themselves from the evils of discrimination and prejudice as long as they fail to extend to women complete and unqualified equality in law and in practice."[81] This document shows how motherhood could be used to challenge patriarchy as well as apartheid rule. As a social category motherhood was subjected to constant reinterpretation as black South Africans embraced, and then transformed, this ideology in order to transcend traditional gender roles.[82]

The proposed extension of passes to African women represented a key issue for FSAW in their fight against race and gender discrimination throughout the 1950s. Cherryl Walker comments that the African women's antipass campaign amounted to "one of the most vociferous and effective protest campaigns of any" launched by anti-apartheid activists in the 1950s.[83] Although black South African women had been threatened with the extension of passes before, most notably in 1913 in the Orange Free State and then nationwide in 1930 and 1937, it was only when the National Party came to power that it became mandatory for black women to carry passes. The decision made in January 1956 to issue black women with reference books sparked unprecedented levels of protest.[84] At the heart of FSAW's antipass campaigns was the political identity of black South African women as mothers.[85] By embracing these gendered roles, FSAW women leveraged the intimate experiences of the black family to advance a militant brand of anti-apartheid politics.

The activism of FSAW was channeled through a form of militant motherhood that gave black women a voice in political protest. Moving beyond the gender ideals presented in *Bantu World* and *Zonk!*, the militant forms of motherhood articulated by FSAW members engaged directly with state power and asserted the right of the black population to equal citizenship within South Africa. Central to this political construction of black motherhood was the willingness of women to sacrifice everything for the care of their children, as Lilian Ngoyi's comments at FSAW's inaugural conference in 1954 make clear: "All mothers are human beings and we must be prepared to face death in life for the rights of our children; it is our duty to die if we have to. We must fight ourselves; Almighty won't do it for us. The history of the past 300 years has proved that."[86] Ngoyi, who would go on to be elected national president of both FSAW and the ANC Women's League in 1956, embraced an activist form of maternal politics that emphasized how African women were willing to give everything in order to secure rights for themselves and for their children. Ida Mtwana, the first national president of FSAW, echoed Ngoyi's words at the same conference: "We have to sacrifice all we have for our freedom. If we do not fight now, it will be too late and our children will curse us for our callousness."[87] If black women were to be judged on their ability to care for their children, FSAW activists argued, they should be willing to take to the streets to secure freedom for themselves and their loved ones.

FSAW members exposed the conditions that Africans faced on a daily basis in order to document the pressures the black family faced under apartheid. In 1955 the organization published *Children of South Africa: A Report Compiled by the Federation of South African Women*.[88] Outlining the relative conditions experienced by children of different races in South Africa, the report stresses that "it is important to understand the extent to which [African] children are left without care."[89] It goes on to detail how passes, labor migration, long working hours, low wages, poor housing, inadequate education, and the absence of state support made it almost impossible for black women to look after their children to the extent that they believed was necessary. Finally the report states defiantly, "Despite the depths of suffering and indignity, the courage and determination of the non-European mother rises triumphantly, going forward to ultimate victory, not for herself, but for her child."[90]

FSAW women used the abuses forced on the African family to push black women to the forefront of anti-apartheid protest. Through her central role in the black family, they argued that the black South African mother was best positioned to expose the brutalities of apartheid rule. FSAW's message of militant motherhood made it possible for black South African women to position their gender concerns at the center of nationalist politics. They escaped the domestic sphere by radically reimagining their gendered responsibilities within the black family and, in the process, dramatically exposed how apartheid not only trampled over political legal rights but also resulted in the day-to-day destruction of black lives.

The most obvious illustration of the power of FSAW's maternalist politics was the 1956 Women's Day protest in Pretoria.[91] Held in the same year that the government officially started to issue passes to women, the Pretoria protest attracted an estimated 20,000 women from all over the country and became a landmark event in the history of the anti-apartheid movement.[92] That so many women attended is even more remarkable considering the cost of transport, the travel restrictions, and the sustained police harassment that threatened the event. In a pamphlet published by FSAW in the immediate aftermath of the Pretoria protest, the organization reflected on the issues that had mobilized African women to such an extent:

> For the women well understand that this is a bitter struggle, demanding everything they can give. They know that there is no refuge for them in their homes; they cannot provide for their children by keeping quiet or "leaving it to the men." Poverty, hardship, insufficient food and clothes, inadequate housing, they have always known. Now they know, as well, that the laws of the country invade what homes they have, walk right into their kitchens, pervert the minds of their children, tear families asunder, demand that a man and his wife must live apart from each other in different areas, hound them day and night. They understand that they, as women, are essential in the struggle of a better life. The road to Pretoria leads forward. The way will be bitter, but there is no turning.[93]

Among the litany of complaints regarding the invasion of apartheid into the home, FSAW warned its members against the dangers of remaining silent and allowing men to speak on their behalf. After the successful Pretoria protests, FSAW continued to argue that women should not be confined to the domestic sphere. In fact it was imperative, FSAW leaders argued, that women take the lead in any movement against white supremacy in South Africa.

Ideas of militant motherhood also shaped black FSAW members' perceptions of the activism of African men and the national liberation movement in general. Writing on gender and protest in South Africa in this period, both Shireen Hassim and Anne McClintock note the extent to which black women were marginalized within national liberation movements. McClintock comments, "Women are represented as the atavistic and authentic 'body' of national tradition (inert, backward-looking, and natural), embodying nationalism's conservative principle of continuity. Men, by contrast, represent the progressive agent of national modernity (forward-thrusting, potent and historic), embodying nationalism's progressive, or revolutionary principle of discontinuity."[94] Indeed, this dichotomy is made abundantly in chapter 6 in terms of the ways in which black men often responded to the issue of political imprisonment. However, an examination of the political language of FSAW demonstrates how black women found agency within these nationalist structures.

By embracing and transforming the ideology of black motherhood, black South African women challenged the male-dominated nature of black self-determination movements in the 1940s and 1950s.[95] Although they continued to stress their key role in the functioning African family unit, FSAW members were overtly critical of black men in the ANC and other organizations. Black women's leaders often made appeals for "the return of their men" while appearing to operate entirely independent of male influence.[96] As FSAW national president Ida Mtwana stated in 1954, "Gone are the days when the place of women was in the kitchen and looking after the children. Today women are marching side by side with the men on the road to freedom. They are beginning to break the chains which have been created by the oppressors to retard the progress of women. Today we have come together to build up one big family."[97] Here, Mtwana seems to simultaneously reject and embrace patriarchal structures of protest that often defined the relationship between black men and women in nationalist movements. However, it is significant that black women were invested with a new mobility in this speech. Mtwana's metaphorical family is removed from its domestic setting as she urges African women to leave the kitchen behind and join with men in the political arena. Interestingly Mtwana also seemed to reject the idea that women should care for their children alone. Although this seems to contradict FSAW's commitment to a maternalist politics, her statement indicates how black women both accepted and at the same time transcended the gender roles assigned to them.

Reflecting on this period in the 1980s, Frances Baard remembered how black women mobilized by FSAW and the ANC Women's League continually pushed to be able to protest alongside black men. "A man would go to jail and the wife would also say, well, I'm going," Baard recalled. Even when this would result in small children being left behind, the response was the same, "No, I'm going."[98] This apparent willingness to leave children at home is not the central message of this statement. Instead, Baard's story demonstrates the willingness of black South African women to openly reject conventional gender roles. This was not a denial or complete rejection of motherhood but rather an assertion that their interpretation of this role stretched beyond the realms of the domestic sphere.

Even as FSAW activists did from time to time deliberately distance themselves from the burdens of care, the majority of their statements reaffirm the need to secure better lives for African children. What remained constant in the activism of FSAW members was their belief that apartheid conditions required women to move beyond the private sphere, to bridge the gap between domestic spaces and public places. In a letter promoting its Conference to Promote Women's Rights, the organization stated: "Women now have the same conditions to contend with as men. . . . Yet in their jobs, as in their lives, women receive inferior treatment. . . . We women, like men, want to be free to move about in the country of our birth, to live where we like, to buy land freely. We want an end to the migrant labour system. We want our own homes, the right to stay in them and not to suffer mass removals, the right to live with our families near our places of work. . . . The battle for democracy and liberation can only be won when women—a half of the whole population—can take their rightful place as free and equal partners with men."[99]

The fight for the home and the family was intimately connected to the "battle for democracy and liberation" in South Africa. Occasionally this desire to achieve both gender and race equality spilled over into outright criticism of African men. For example, when Lilian Ngoyi addressed a crowd gathered at a FSAW conference on rent increases, she said, "I speak to you African women particularly; the others have come to cry with us. Let us be brave; we have heard of men shaking in their trousers, but who ever heard of a woman shaking in her skirt?"[100] Through their criticism and assertion that they were the political equals of men, black South African women claimed a prominent space within the national liberation movement. Their commitment to self-determination introduced a distinctly black feminist voice into anti-apartheid politics.[101]

The criticism, as well as FSAW's effective organizing to challenge the extension of the pass laws, did not go unnoticed by African male leaders. Albert J. Luthuli, leader of the ANC between 1952 and 1967, appeared to be simultaneously impressed and embarrassed by the militancy of African women. Regarding the eruption of women's protests in Natal in 1959, Luthuli commented in an article in *Liberation* that "men should take a leaf from the women in this regard."[102] He added, "Why are the women alone in these demonstrations? . . . Men should positively and constructively meet this women's challenge. But more to the point about women is that it is they, especially in African homes, who bear the brunt of facing daily poverty of the home, since it falls on women to prepare food for the family and see that children are clothed."[103]

Luthuli was encouraged by the militancy of African women and used this to provoke men into action. Recognizing that it was women who bore the brunt of apartheid laws, he called for black men to meet this challenge and join black women on the streets. Although Luthuli appeared to support these protests, he often interpreted the activism of black women in ways that reinforced ideas of masculine dominance. In a speech at an event commemorating the third anniversary of the 1956 Pretoria demonstrations he observed that, in relation to African women, "men seem too cowardly and timid. Women are putting men's traditional dignity and so-called supremacy in great jeopardy. Do African men of our day want to play second fiddle to women?"[104] Luthuli used the political activism of African women to challenge men to reclaim their manhood. There was still no recognition that women were equal within the national liberation movement. In fact "male" and "female" activism continued to be separated in Luthuli's analysis. While the male leadership of the ANC sometimes praised women for their commitment to black self-determination, this did not automatically result in African men accepting gender equality. The belief that women's work should be limited to the domestic sphere was still widely held by African male activists.

The work of FSAW ensured that ideas of African motherhood were placed at the forefront of the anti-apartheid struggle. Black South African women advanced a feminist agenda within the broader struggles for national liberation. They claimed that the ability to care for their children was a fundamental right. However, this promotion of militant forms of black motherhood also had an important transnational significance. Largely overlooked in existing historical accounts of the organization, FSAW leaders engaged with the work of the women's international peace movement in the years following World War II. Although opportunities to travel beyond South Africa were limited, FSAW members made a conscious effort connect their opposition to race and gender discrimination to the struggles of women around the world.

FSAW's global outlook was made clear in the following statement made at the organization's Congress of Mothers: "We are women of South Africa appealing to all women of our country, and joining with the women of every country of the world. We are women who know the joy of having children, and the sorrow of losing them. We know the happiness of rearing our children, and the sadness of our struggle against poverty, illness, ignorance and racial oppression. We stand together with the women of all lands in our fight for happiness for all children and peace for all peoples. We know how mothers in other countries have suffered through the ravages of war. And today, once again, peace is endangered."[105]

Held in the Transvaal in early 1955, FSAW's Congress of Mothers was organized as a precursor to the World Congress of Mothers, due to take place later that year in Lausanne, Switzerland. Hosted by the Women's International Democratic Federation (WIDF), the Lausanne gathering provided a forum for black South African women to express the joy and the sorrow of being a mother in apartheid South Africa. This enthusiasm to link up with women abroad to "fight for happiness for all children and peace for all peoples" established FSAW as an active participant in the women's international peace movement of the 1950s. As Lelia Rupp notes, shifts in international power brought about by the global upheavals of World War II and the development of anticolonial nationalism in Africa and Asia transformed both the membership and outlook of the women's international movement.[106] Although any attempt at international organizing was severely restricted by the National Party, FSAW managed to make important links beyond South Africa.

For a brief but significant period the organization had links with the WIDF, an international alliance of women dedicated to peace and freedom. The WIDF was founded in 1945 at the International Congress of Women in Paris. Organized by the Union des Femmes Français Conference, the WIDF boasted a large international membership and claimed to represent the interests of over 140 million women around the world, including a number of communist-affiliated organizations.[107] The WIDF's radical political ties opened it up to anticommunist censorship and harassment. As a result, FSAW would never officially affiliate with the organization, as this would have inevitably led to its prosecution under the Suppression of Communism Act. Instead, the organization provided the WIDF with regular reports on the status of South African women under apartheid. Through white FSAW leaders Ray Alexander and Helen Joseph, the organization received WIDF materials that detailed the role of women in the international peace movement and condemned race, class, and gender discrimination globally.[108] When the World Congress of Mothers was called, FSAW started planning so that its members would be represented at the gathering. After negotiation with the WIDF, it was decided that Lilian Ngoyi and Dora Tamana would travel as official FSAW representatives.[109]

The WIDF provided an international forum through which it could articulate the grievances and militancy of its members. Helen Joseph commented on FSAW's association with the international organization, "In fighting against passes for women, and for the rights of our children to proper and full education and care, our task is immeasurably strengthened by the support of women of other countries, through the WIDF. We are not fighting alone—140 million women of 66 countries will watch us, support us, give us their encouragement. They know oppression in South Africa is a threat not only to all Africa, but to the world."[110] Recognizing the importance of having allies abroad, FSAW actively sought to cultivate a global network of support among women committed to challenging apartheid rule in South Africa. Representing women's groups from Africa, the Caribbean, and Central America, the WIDF provided opportunities for FSAW members to escape their isolation and connect with other black women internationally.[111]

Ngoyi and Tamana's journey to the World Congress of Mothers was both audacious and illegal. In attempting to escape South Africa, both women tried to stow away, under "white names," on a boat leaving Cape Town; they defied segregated seating on a plane bound for London with the help of a sympathetic pilot; and they finally gained entry to Britain under the pretext that they were traveling in order to undertake a course in bible studies.[112] At Lausanne, Ngoyi presided over the second session of the conference, giving its opening address, while Tamana stood in front of assembled women and mothers from almost every continent and declared, "The Federation of South African Women . . . has joined hands with all organisations fighting for democratic rights, for full equality, irrespective of race or sex." She detailed the hardships faced by South African women to a global audience and appealed for support in bringing freedom and democracy to the nation in the name of the women's international peace movement. FSAW also circulated its official report, *The Life of the Child in South Africa*, at the congress. Engaging with the anti-imperial outlook of the WIDF the report declared that South African whites were "colonisers," before going on to describe the effects of passes on black families, infant mortality, malnutrition, inadequate living conditions, and forced removals.[113] By traveling to the World Congress of Mothers, Ngoyi and Tamana raised the issue of the care of black children in front of a sympathetic international audience. Their presence overseas ensured that issues of race discrimination and capitalist exploitation in South Africa would not be completely absent from the women's international peace movement.

Following the conference Ngoyi and Tamana, as official representatives of the WIDF, traveled extensively throughout Europe over a seven-month period, before heading on to the Soviet Union and China. They eventually arrived back in South Africa as wanted women. In the same year, Elizabeth Mafeking embarked on a separate journey to Poland to attend the Warsaw Youth Festival, following this up by visiting the Soviet Union and China.[114] The subversive potential of travel is illustrated by the punishments meted out to Ngoyi, Tamana, and Mafeking on their return to South Africa. All three women were issued with banning orders, and Ngoyi and Tamana were among those arrested for the Treason Trial in 1956.[115] By making illegal border crossings both women had struck at the heart of the apartheid doctrine that sought to regulate the mobility of Africans at all costs.

As they traversed Europe, passing from London through the iron curtain to the eastern bloc, Ngoyi and Tamana commented on the absence of racism and the potential benefits of communism. Ngoyi observed that the women she met were not black, white, or colored, but mothers, stating, "I was a woman and a mother, my colour was not my problem." Tamana echoed this sentiment: "When I saw all these things, different nations together, my eyes were opened and I said, I have tasted the new world and won the confidence of our future, wonderful."[116] These travels provided a temporary escape from the racial discrimination that infected their lives at home. Mafeking expressed this view when reflecting on her transnational travels in 1955, commenting that away from South Africa "there were no signs such as 'Europeans only' or 'Natives only.' . . . You are bound to forget that you are black when you arrive at a country where you do not find such signs."[117]

By asserting their identity as mothers, committed to peace, freedom, and democracy, each of these women challenged the race and gender hierarchies of the apartheid system overseas. As Dora Tamana stated in her speech at the WIDF conference, "The Government says that we Africans are backward and primitive. Well, I don't quite know what they mean. I wonder whether you think that I am backward and primitive? . . . If it is backward to want good health, a home that is happy or to want freedom of education, to wish for opportunities for our children and peace for everyone—then I suppose we must be classed as backward. But we are not so backward as to be ignorant about what is taking place in the world today."[118]

Tamana directly confronted racist myths that cast black women as uncivilized and unable to properly care for their families. Embracing her motherhood on the global stage, she affirmed that black South African women were part of a broad coalition of progressive women committed to freedom and equality in the Cold War world. As Ngoyi noted when reflecting on their time in Switzerland, "Mothers want to save their children, whatever age they may be. That is why they left their homes, left their dear ones to attend this Congress."[119] The language of motherhood prompted these transnational journeys, uniting women across national borders.

The politicization of the domestic sphere was an important feature of anti-apartheid movement during the 1950s. Black South African women used their gendered association with the family in ways that emphasized their political agency. By embracing their identity as mothers, they drew attention to the distinctive forms of discrimination black women faced under apartheid and questioned masculinist conceptions of leadership within the Congress Alliance.[120] Large numbers of women mobilized in defense of the African family, documenting how apartheid laws disrupted kinship networks in ways that positioned women as important political actors in national movements. Ngoyi and Tamana brought the concerns of black South African women to an international audience. Through their audacious travels, they ensured that the race and gender concerns of black South African would appear before, and be debated by, progressive women around the world.

8 The National Council of Negro Women and Apartheid

· ·

Lilian Ngoyi and Dora Tamana were two of 1,063 delegates who attended the WIDF's World Congress of Mothers in 1955. Participants from sixty-six countries made the journey to Switzerland, united in their insistence on women's rights and readiness to agitate for democracy and peace in the second half of the twentieth century.[1] Ngoyi recalled the interest the issue of apartheid generated among congress delegates, noting that "they asked many questions: What is apartheid? What are the pass laws? What is Bantu Education? What is the position of the African trade unions? To my answers, there were cries of 'Shame!'"[2]

African American women, however, were not involved in these discussions. In fact, there is no evidence that any delegates from the United States attended the congress. This absence provides further evidence of the changing nature of black internationalism during the early Cold War. In 1954, the U.S. delegation succeeded in securing the removal of the Women's International Democratic Federation's official consultative status at the UN. And by 1955, the federation had been classified as a "Communist front" in the United States.[3] The labeling of the WIDF as subversive is just one example of how black transnational networks were shut down at this time. Despite the best efforts of activists, it was extremely difficult for African American and black South African women to collaborate in their struggle for racial equality and women's rights.

The fact that the opportunity to link up with Ngoyi and Tamana at the World Congress of Mothers was lost does not mean that African American women were uninterested in the women's struggle in South Africa. In fact, it is clear that black women activists in the United States were inspired by the militant role played by African women in the anti-apartheid movement throughout the 1950s. The work of the Sojourners for Truth and Justice, a short-lived radical black feminist group based in Harlem, is testament to this.[4] Founded in the autumn of 1951, the STJ included radical figures such as Louise Thompson Patterson, Eslanda Robeson, Shirley Graham Du Bois, Beulah Richardson, and Alice Childress.[5] The STJ had a strong black international focus and lent their support to black South African women during the Defiance Campaign.[6] Louise Thompson Patterson and Charlotta Bass wrote to anti-apartheid activists observing that the lives of black women in the United States and South Africa were "inextricably linked" and declaring that "we salute the women of Africa and hold out our hands to join yours in a solid bond of unity."[7] Bertha Mkhize, ANC Women's League activist and future vice president of FSAW, replied to this message of support, thanking both women for providing the "link we have always wished for [on] this side of the world."[8] However, just as the women's movement in South Africa was escalating, these connections became increasingly difficult to maintain. Under intense surveillance from the FBI and with many of its key members facing jail or deportation, the STJ was unable to properly function and effectively disbanded in early 1953.[9] As the historian Erik S. McDuffie has noted when examining the activism of radical black women in the United States, Cold War repression "severed organizational ties of international solidarity between black women on both sides of the Atlantic."[10] The fate of the Sojourners for Truth and Justice demonstrates how African American women were prevented from forging connections with political figures active in the ANC Women's League and FSAW.

This was the case across the political spectrum. However, an examination of the anti-apartheid stance adopted by the Washington-based National Council of Negro Women reveals how black liberals adapted to the climate of the Cold War when attempting to challenge colonialism overseas. Dedicated to fighting race and gender discrimination throughout the United States, the NCNW sought to expand its international activities in the aftermath of World War II. However, the council eschewed direct political links with women's organizations at the forefront of the anti-apartheid struggle in favor of humanitarian, welfare, and charitable initiatives set up to support black South African women. The NCNW's relationship with the WIDF indicates why the organization adopted this strategy. The council was initially supportive of the federation's work and sent two delegates to its founding meeting in Paris, including future NCNW president Vivian Carter Mason.[11] Both delegates were impressed with what they saw, commenting in their report on the gathering that "the National Council of Negro Women must acquaint women in the Western Hemisphere and in Africa with the great task and opportunity before them—helping in every possible way to organize and expand activities of women in this country and the world."[12] Mason in particular was inspired by the WIDF, and her experiences in France influenced her subsequent efforts to expand the international activities of the NCNW.[13] However, this initial enthusiasm was dampened by the charges of subversion that were thrown at the international women's organization. Critical of the Soviet Union and understandably wary of being accused of subversion in the United States, the leadership of the NCNW severed its ties with the WIDF and its affiliate, the Congress of American Women, a couple of years after the Paris meeting. This political disengagement effectively meant that its members would be denied the opportunity to meet, hear, and learn from Ngoyi and Tamana in Switzerland in 1955.

The NCNW therefore had to find different ways to advance an anticolonial political agenda throughout the repressive climate of the Cold War. Although this meant avoiding direct engagement in mass protests and acts of civil disobedience, the NCNW challenged apartheid in ways that drew attention to the callousness of the apartheid state. The NCNW worked with the U.S. State Department when seeking to expand its overseas activities. Faced with the destabilizing effects of anticommunism, they attempted to engage with, negotiate, and ultimately influence U.S. foreign policy toward movements for colonial independence in Africa. Although the political vision of the NCNW was constrained by its ties to the U.S. government, this stance allowed the council to offer support to black South African women at a time when radical expressions of black internationalism were severely restricted.

The NCNW's Black Internationalism

Mary McLeod Bethune founded the NCNW in 1935. A prominent national civil rights figure, she had been the president of the National Association of Colored Women (NACW) in the 1920s and, in the following decade, served as an advisor on racial issues to the Roosevelt administration.[14] Critical of what she saw as the NACW's old-fashioned policies of race and class uplift, Bethune conceived of the NCNW as a new centralized body capable of bringing about real political change on the national level.[15] Made up of regional and state affiliates, the NCNW brought black women's groups together from across the United States in order to "plan, initiate and carry out projects which develop, benefit and integrate the Negro into the Nation."[16] From their headquarters in Washington, council leaders lobbied a range of federal institutions on behalf of race and gender equality for African American women.[17] As Joyce Ann Hanson has commented, "Bethune's vision was to create a mechanism that would train African American women to be insightful political activists and lobbyists, increase black women's collective political power, and give them greater representation at the highest levels of government."[18] Boasting around 850,000 members by the 1950s, the NCNW worked hard to pressure federal institutions to live up to the rhetorical commitment of the United States to freedom and democracy, running campaigns that addressed inequality in black voting rights, education, employment, and welfare.

Although much of its early practical work was limited to the United States, the NCNW held a distinctly international focus that, in the years following World War II, inspired the council's efforts to develop organizational ties with black women's groups in Africa, the Caribbean, and Latin America.[19] Bethune firmly believed that "progress in one country should stimulate progress in another," and she was acutely aware of the interconnected nature of race discrimination across the world.[20] Her relationship with Africa and her general interest in the plight of black women throughout the diaspora informed both the ideological focus and practical activities of the NCNW. Intensely proud of her own African heritage, as a student Bethune had hoped to "return" to the continent as a religious missionary.[21] She maintained this interest in Africa throughout her life, and during the 1930s and 1940s was a prominent supporter of the CAA.[22] Although she severed her ties with the council after it was alleged that communists had infiltrated the organization, her work with figures such as Paul Robeson, W. E. B. Du Bois, and William Alphaeus Hunton was symptomatic of her early interest in the struggle for African independence.[23]

Bethune's disavowal of the CAA is also symptomatic of the broader shift in African American anticolonial politics during the early Cold War. In 1943, Martin Dies and HUAC publicly accused Bethune of being a communist.[24] Bethune successfully fought the allegations, but the episode provided her with firsthand knowledge of how being labeled a "communist" could ruin lives and destroy hard-earned reputations. Fearful that the NCNW might be tarnished as a result of these accusations, Bethune made a concerted effort to follow the dominant anticommunist political line of the era. The NCNW's anticommunism greatly affected its international outlook. As she noted, commenting on the global responsibilities of African American women in the postwar period, "Currents of minority thought, of national thought, of world thought, are in motion all around us. They stir the lives of every one of us. We must be responsive without being overwhelmed into blind acceptance or equally blind resistance. Sober thought must precede our every action. Leadership, in 1947, will need to be informed as never before."[25] This warning hints at the somewhat constrained nature of the

Dorothy Ferebee and NCNW members meet with Kwame Nkrumah in Washington, D.C., c. August 1958. Source: Image courtesy of National Park Service, National Council of Negro Women Records, Subgroup 1, Series 14. Copyright unknown.

NCNW's global vision. Bethune believed it was imperative that the NCNW made moderate and respectable choices regarding the type of international projects it pursued. The council's global outlook can therefore be seen as a product of the complex relationship between the desire of African American organizations to engage in anticolonial politics and the U.S. government's Cold War efforts to stifle black international criticism of its foreign policy initiatives. For many African American organizers, cooperation with the state appeared to represent a safe and expedient way through which they could work across national borders in order to challenge racism both at home and abroad.

In her 1946 president's message, Mary McLeod Bethune made clear her belief that NCNW women needed to reach out beyond the borders of the United States: "For it is, truly, a new world in which we are now feeling our

Workshop on Africa at annual meeting of the NCNW, December 1954.
Source: Image courtesy of National Park Service, National Council of
Negro Women Records, Subgroup 1, Series 14. Copyright unknown.

way. Barriers of all kinds are crumbling, and many of us are seeing, for
the first time, how close we are to peoples and to problems about which we
have known very little. We shall have to know more; we shall have to face
more; we shall have to do more—and this without flinching."[26] It was this
belief that African American women needed to greatly expand their knowledge of global political affairs that shaped the council's activities following
World War II. As old colonial empires crumbled and the United States
became a full-fledged superpower, the NCNW leadership attempted to position the organization as an international body capable of promoting
political and cultural exchanges between black women around the world.
From their Council House headquarters in Washington, D.C., NCNW members were given the opportunity to keep up to date with the latest international developments, learn about different cultures, and directly engage
with black leaders from Africa, the Caribbean, and Latin America. The

council hosted a series of visiting dignitaries involved in a range of colonial liberation movements. Records show that during the 1950s the NCNW welcomed individuals from Ghana, Nigeria, Ethiopia, Liberia, and South Africa, including prominent political figures such as Kwame Nkrumah and Madame Sékou Touré. As they toured NCNW headquarters, these leaders offered both council members and the wider African American community a striking new image of Africa, one that emphasized black respectability, self-sufficiency, power, and, most importantly, freedom and self-government. The council's annual conventions also had strong international and often specifically African themes. Taking place in Washington every November, these events, attended by invited foreign guests, included workshops, talks, and exhibitions aimed at familiarizing NCNW members with the global issues of the day.[27] The 1954 convention held at the Raleigh Hotel was an especially international affair, culminating with a workshop entitled "Women United in a Program of Action to Help and Understand the Peoples of Africa."[28] Howard University historian Rayford Logan presided, and speakers included the Nigerian activists Babs Fafunwa and Flora Azikiwe, as well as the founder of Operation Crossroads Africa, Reverend James H. Robinson.[29] The African American sociologist E. Franklin Frazier concluded events by providing a detailed summary of the discussions, after which the NCNW formally pledged its intention to forge organizational links with the women of Africa.[30]

Vivian Carter Mason played a particularly active role in the development of the NCNW's international work in this period. A student of political science and social work at the University of Chicago and a former YWCA program director, Mason did a great deal to expand the international activities of the NCNW. When she returned to the United States from the inaugural meeting of the WIDF in Paris, she led the newly established permanent International Committee of the NCNW.[31] Stressing the need for African American women to develop "friendship ties with women of different countries," this working group hoped to forge links with African representatives in Washington, D.C., and suggested a range of activities for local councils, including "international nights" where, as part of study groups, black women could "become more acquainted with what is happening internationally."[32] Mason became the national president of the NCNW in 1953. Building on the work of her predecessor Dorothy B. Ferebee, Mason strengthened the council's organizational structures and made a concerted effort to set up a practical network of women's organizations throughout the black diaspora and Africa over her two terms in office.[33]

Mason made it her priority to forge tangible networks with black women in Africa in particular.[34] In her January 1955 presidential address, she reaffirmed the NCNW's postwar aim "of reaching across the seas to help and work with the women of Africa" and repeatedly stressed that black women in the United States and Africa could learn from one another in their shared struggle for race and gender equality.[35] Mason laid the groundwork for the organization's black international work by developing networks that would bring African women leaders to the United States and eventually enable NCNW members to travel to Africa. She wrote to women in Nigeria, Ghana, Liberia, Ethiopia, Sudan, and South Africa in an attempt to open up lines of communication with African women and attract new affiliate organizations to the NCNW. The 1950s therefore saw the NCNW develop a clear and practical international program. Following Bethune's original vision, council leaders made it their mission to keep African American women educated and informed about international relations. They transformed the NCNW into a cosmopolitan space and made a concerted effort to forge organizational links with black women around the world. Indeed, at a time when black radicals fought accusations of subversion in the courts and the U.S. government successfully closed down a number of global black networks, the NCNW actively expanded its international activities.

The NCNW was deeply concerned by the political situation in South Africa and clearly stated its opposition to the apartheid regime, adopting the following resolution in 1953: "The National Council of Negro Women urges the United States to exercise its strongest endeavors in the United Nations and through direct negotiations to convince the Union of South Africa that it should abandon Apartheid and adopt policies consistent with principles of the United Nations and with the democratic aims asserted by the free world."[36] The NCNW hoped that the United States would take a stand against the apartheid regime by using its influence in the UN to actively condemn racial inequality in the country.

The council's lobbying efforts on this front were backed up by its success in forging connections with black South African women throughout this period. Madie Hall Xuma, the African American wife of former ANC leader Alfred Bitini Xuma, was an important early link for the NCNW in South Africa.[37] A graduate of Columbia University Teachers' College, she had moved to the country in 1940 with her new husband and was active in black women's politics as the first president of the ANC Women's League and the founder of the Zenzele Club movement, which focused on training black South African women as community leaders.[38] Throughout the 1940s, NCNW administrators sent Madie Hall Xuma material and reports on the situation of black women in the United States, which she then disseminated to the Zenzele clubs. Acknowledging the black international potential of the NCNW's interest in the Zenzele movement, Xuma noted, "It really is an inspiration to our people here to know and learn about the Negroes overseas. These articles coming through are very helpful to me for I am able to show them and tell them of current news about our people there [in the United States]."[39]

The idea that black women could inspire one another and work for change across national borders influenced the NCNW's efforts to affiliate with the National Council of African Women (NCAW). An outgrowth of the Bantu Women's League, the NCAW saw itself as a nonpolitical organization dedicated to African women's welfare.[40] Mary McLeod Bethune first approached the NCAW in 1940, corresponding with its leader Minah Soga. In a letter to Soga, Bethune noted the similar problems faced by black women in the United States and South Africa, adding, "We should like very much to have the National Council of African Women become a part of the National Council of Negro Women—incorporated so that together we could work for world freedom for all women."[41] In 1954, Mason wrote to Minah Soga inviting the NCAW to send a delegate to the NCNW 1956 annual convention in Washington, D.C.[42] Although the South African authorities tightly controlled black travel in and out of the country, records show that Gertrude Mdledle, NCAW leader between 1955 and 1956, traveled to the United States to attend the event.[43] Introduced by Mason, Mdledle expressed her "great appreciation" at being invited to the convention and asked that NCNW women "further cement [their] relationship with the women of South Africa."[44]

The NCNW's motivation for establishing links with the NCAW can be seen in a letter Mason wrote to the Pretoria-based organizer Edith Nono Msezane in 1955. Articulating the NCNW's desire to engage with the lives of black South African women, she wrote, "We desire to help in any way that we can. We desire to know about your problems, your activities, your programs, for in doing so we can be helped too by becoming more intelligent and more aware of our responsibilities for the women of your country."[45] Mason believed that NCNW members had a duty to black women in South Africa. Aware that theirs was a black international organization operating from a position of relative privilege in the United States, the council's leadership argued that it was the responsibility of its members to find out about problems black South African women faced under apartheid so that they could offer practical assistance. By communicating with figures such as Madie Hall Xuma, Minah Soga, Gertrude Mdledle, and Edith Msezane, council members built a good working knowledge of the South African racial situation, allowing them to develop a practical program to assist black women living under apartheid.

The NCNW and the African Children's Feeding Scheme

The NCNW's first organized engagement with South African politics was a fundraising campaign in aid of the African Children's Feeding Scheme (ACFS). Founded in 1945, the ACFS was established with the aim of providing black children in Johannesburg with at least one full meal a day.[46] Set up by the white English missionary Father Trevor Huddleston, the initiative was a direct response to the efforts of the apartheid government to slash state-subsidized school meals for nonwhite children.[47] Relying on voluntary contributions and often "on the brink of financial disaster," the charitable organization came to represent a small practical challenge to policies designed to dismantle black educational provision during the early years of apartheid.[48]

By the 1950s, in desperate need of funds and operating in a hostile political environment, representatives of the ACFS began to reach out to overseas organizations that they hoped would offer them financial assistance. As part of these efforts, Feeding Scheme officials approached the NCNW. In a letter to the council written on July 4, 1955, ACFS organizer Pat Sutten pleaded "it is our heartfelt wish that your association give our cause your sympathetic consideration, and help us to combat one of the worst evils—Hunger Amongst Children." Detailing their work in assisting more than five thousand children a day, the letter concluded, "Happily we all know that wherever there are women of goodwill, suffering and misery can be lessened."[49] The NCNW responded to this gendered appeal with enthusiasm. Over the next year, the organization dedicated a significant amount of time to the Feeding Scheme, making it the annual cause of its junior councils in 1955.[50] Its members circulated pamphlets, initiated letter-writing campaigns, and held regular meetings to raise funds for the scheme, while in March 1956 the local Manhattan council hosted Trevor Huddleston at a fundraising event held at the 137th Street YWCA.[51]

The NCNW's involvement with the African Children's Feeding Scheme is illustrative of what this particular brand of anticommunist black internationalism was able to achieve, as well as some of its shortcomings. In their initial response to the ACFS, the NCNW expressed sympathy for the cause but conceded that they would have "to find out from our State Department just what steps must be taken so that neither your group nor mine will be embarrassed."[52] Council leaders then passed on the details of the Feeding Scheme to State Department officials, writing to the South African Desk: "We solicit your advice and assistance in getting this project of help from the United States underway."[53] After a series of meetings and written exchanges, the council was finally given the go-ahead by the government to lend its support to the Feeding Scheme, ultimately receiving confirmation from the U.S. consul general in South Africa that the ACFS was "a most worthy public welfare organization."[54]

The NCNW genuinely believed that it could shape American foreign policy from the inside, ensuring that the U.S. government lived up to its anti-imperialist rhetoric. This, of course, had its limitations, and involved black liberals disassociating themselves from leftist criticisms of American power. However, African Americans who worked with the U.S. government were not passive figures who blindly followed the wishes of the state.[55] Black individuals and organizations that cooperated with the State Department challenged racism at home and abroad, while questioning aspects of U.S. foreign policy within the broader ideological conflict between "Western democracy" and "Soviet totalitarianism."[56] The NCNW represented an important anticolonial lobby in Washington, working to challenge government perceptions of apartheid throughout the early Cold War.

The NCNW's decision to choose an organization dedicated to providing food for black South African children is also significant. At home, in the U.S., the NCNW was dedicated to the well-being and care of children within the black family. They emphasized the need for strong and responsible adult figures for black children if their goal of racial uplift was to be achieved. "Adult behavior," an NCNW report commented, "has a decided effect upon the development of [the] moral character of young people. The environment shapes and molds attitudes. The stress and strain of family living and community life, all have important bearings on the personality and subsequent reactions of juveniles."[57] This respectable view of the black family and gendered notions of care also informed NCNW work in the international arena.

Given the shared race and gendered discrimination black women faced in the United States and South Africa, the council's work with the ACFS provides further insight into the gendered contours of black internationalism. By deliberately embracing their identity as black mothers—and the historical responsibilities and burdens associated with this role as part of the global black family—NCNW leaders expanded their domestic civil rights agenda to the African continent. Hunger and the care of black children ultimately played a key role in shaping the ways in which African American women engaged with Africa and conceived of their racial responsibilities on the other side of the Atlantic.

The work of the ACFS was a much-needed intervention into the lives of black South African families. Its efforts to feed black children and ensure they could attend school directly confronted the white supremacist policies of the National government. Across nine permanent feeding centers and in ten schools, the ACFS provided more than five thousand children with at least one full meal per day, consisting of two slices of fortified brown bread, with peanut butter and glucose, and a pint of skimmed milk.[58] This intentionally protein-heavy food appeared to have a transformative effect, with one Feeding Scheme report noting that "the results have so far been gratifying where figures are available. At any rate there have been no more reports of children fainting in the schools now getting the A.C.F.S. meal."[59]

Claiming that "self-help is our motto," the ACFS also aimed to provide the information and guidance it believed was necessary for black South Africans to look after their children.[60] Armed with a projector and a range of public health films, the organization disseminated information on subjects such as health, hygiene, and nutrition to African children and mothers attending feeding centers and visiting non-European clinics.[61] The ACFS requested a contribution of one pence from the family for every meal their child received. The rest of the cost of a meal, five pence in total, was raised through donations collected by volunteers. Feeding Scheme officials believed that the one-penny scheme would "inculcate a feeling of responsibility" in black South African parents.[62] This language of "self-help" was often paternalistic and at times seemed to echo racist beliefs concerning the perceived failings of African families. However, the scheme's emphasis on grassroots organizing and the empowerment of women within the black community nevertheless played an important role in unsettling the "logic" of apartheid.

Evidence of the confrontational nature of the ACFS can be seen in a letter sent by Pat Sutten to Vivian Carter Mason, in which she outlined the National Party's opposition to their activities. "I regret that our present government are not in sympathy with our work," Sutten commented, adding, "with their policy of Apartheid . . . any attempt to bridge the ever widening chasm between white and coloured races is viewed with suspicion and extreme irritation, to put it mildly."[63] The ACFS established African committees dedicated to organizing and running feeding centers in black locations and promoted "the idea of service in the community" among the black workers they employed.[64] In areas such as Pimville, Moroka, and Kilptown, African women formed "Women's Service Committees," giving up their time on an unpaid and voluntary basis to play a vital role in the day-to-day management and operation of the feeding centers.[65] Furthermore, around 10 percent of the scheme's finances came directly from black South African pockets. Both the one-penny contributions to each meal and general donations meant that black South Africans were investing more than £2,000 per annum into the feeding program at a time when the average yearly wage for an African family was £119.[66]

The Feeding Scheme also encouraged interracial organizing as whites, usually women, worked alongside African volunteers in the townships. Father Trevor Huddleston recalled the daily operation of the feeding centers: "There were thousands of them. But the people who went out and cut up the wholemeal bread and spread the fortified peanut butter, mixed the skimmed milk and opened up at 8:30 in the morning and stayed on until midday were white women from the white suburbs who stood alongside the black ones and did the same thing. And this was a tremendous thing—our committee was very multiracial."[67] By bringing together black and white women dedicated to providing for black children, the ACFS represented a clear challenge to apartheid policies by working to empower black women through interracial cooperation.

This is not to say that the Feeding Scheme was immune from the hierarchies of race and class. On the whole, wealthy white women managed the ACFS, while black volunteers worked in the kitchens or as servers. Additionally, the scheme's insistence that black South Africans needed education and assistance in order to care for their families occasionally resonated with the apartheid government's belief that they were incapable of looking after themselves. While the Feeding Scheme seemed to reinforce ideas that black South Africans needed to be raised up to white standards, its work was invested with an important political meaning within the context of apartheid South Africa. The driving ideological belief behind the ACFS was that black South African children had just as much right to an education as their white counterparts. By launching a program designed to support black South African families with feeding their children, and crucially making black women an integral part of this process, the ACFS ultimately questioned myths of black helplessness that were central to white supremacist thought of the era. The ACFS can therefore be read as a small but practical initiative through which black South African women could symbolically challenge racist ideas about their supposed inability to care for their children.

After receiving the "all clear" from the State Department, the NCNW immediately began to work on how they could best assist black South African children through the ACFS. At the 1955 annual convention, it was announced that the Feeding Scheme would be made the national project of the NCNW's junior councils.[68] Made up of NCNW members under the age of twenty-one, the junior councils took the lead in a national fundraising effort that would be seen as a symbolic gift to the children of South Africa.[69] Although the response was sometimes slow, there is evidence that junior council members responded to this call in a variety of creative ways.[70] Under the direction of Margaret G. Simms, junior members were asked to collect five cents each from schoolchildren in the community as part of the South African fundraising drive.[71] In addition to this, local councils held a range of fundraising events, including food collection drives, white elephant sales, African discussion evenings, art exhibitions, and musical performances, occasionally complete with an appearance from an African student studying in the United States.[72] Simms also circulated ACFS pamphlets, initiated letter-writing campaigns, and held regular meetings to publicize the NCNW's fundraising efforts.

The NCNW's fundraising for the ACFS was not limited to the junior councils. Trevor Huddleston, who had just been forced to leave South Africa due to his political work, spoke about the Feeding Scheme's dire need for donations at the NCNW's Manhattan council.[73] After his talk, Vivian Carter Mason wrote to Huddleston stating that "we want to do everything possible to help and hope this project here in the United States spreads and grows until the committee is able to extend the work because of our concern."[74] At ACFS fundraising events, NCNW members often received donations of tinned food and clothes. Not wanting these to go to waste, the council's leadership met with CARE and the American Friends Service Committee to ensure that these reached South Africa. An NCNW member and former president of the Los Angeles metropolitan council, Artishia Jordan also played an important role in expanding the NCNW's involvement with the ACFS. The wife of AME Bishop Frederick Jordan, she had visited South Africa as a missionary in 1954.[75] As a result of her AME connections, Jordan transported to South

Africa three hundred dollars' worth of clothes that had been collected as part of the Feeding Scheme appeal through Chief Berung Monyake of Basutoland, who was in America attending an AME Church Conference.[76]

In total, after its first year of fundraising between November 1955 and November 1956, available NCNW records show that the organization raised more than six hundred dollars for the ACFS and donated more than four hundred dollars' worth of clothes.[77] While this was by no means inconsequential, Margaret Simms and Vivian Carter Mason both expressed frustration that more money had not been sent and instructed local councils to continue to fundraise over the next year.[78] Despite the disappointing results, fundraising for the ACFS represented a key initiative in the annual program of the NCNW, while the council's leadership repeatedly stressed the worthiness of the cause.

Limited in terms of size and resources, the NCNW's work with the Feeding Scheme had a negligible impact on the racist structures black South Africans faced. However, by choosing to engage in South African politics through the important issue of food, the NCNW made both symbolic and practical contributions to the lives of black South African families in Johannesburg. The NCNW's fundraising on behalf of the Feeding Scheme is particularly significant in terms of understanding the role gender has played in the development of black international networks. As Jacqueline Nassy Brown has noted, it is important to interrogate how particular diasporic practices and processes "come to be infused with gender ideologies (or become 'gendered'), and how such gendering effectively determines the different positionalities men and women can occupy."[79] By asking African American women to assist black South African families, the ACFS effectively brought together the race and gender concerns of black women in both countries.

The African American family has been a key site of racial contestation throughout U.S. history. During slavery, white owners deliberately disrupted black familial ties in order to reinforce strict racial hierarchies, while efforts to maintain these kinship networks were central to black efforts to resist the slave system.[80] In the mid-twentieth century, debates about the family continued to permeate civil rights protests, as black activists challenged racist ideas that excluded African American men and women from what were deemed respectable, white, middle-class gender identities.[81] Many leading civil rights organizations responded to these arguments by promoting an idealized image of the black family that adhered to "traditional" and often white-defined gender roles.[82] As Cold War ideals of "domestic containment" privileged conservative notions of the nuclear family, African American women were encouraged to embrace the identity of the caring, responsible, and respectable mother as a way of advancing the race.[83] Popular black publications reinforced this view, praising the ability of African American women as loving and caring mothers dedicated to the uplift of the black family.[84] As a 1947 *Ebony* editorial entitled "Goodbye Mammy, Hello Mom" put it, when imagining the theoretical return of black women to the home after the war, "The cooking over which the 'white folks' used to go into ecstasies is now reserved for her own family and they really appreciate it."[85] While obscuring the harsh reality of their labor both inside and outside the home, this reified image of the postwar black mother enabled African American women to challenge white racist myths that deliberately denigrated the black family unit and, by extension, to claim political and moral authority in the public sphere.

The NCNW recognized the importance of motherhood as a highly contested political category, and a strong maternalist politics ran through much of the organization's work in the United States. While primarily working to increase the collective political power of African American women as activists on a national level, the NCNW maintained a keen interest in the black family and actively provided care for the extended black community.[86] For example, the NCNW's 1954 annual report bemoaned the erosion of black family structures and, pointing to the high percentage of "neglected" black children in foster care, hoped that this would "challenge every Negro woman into action."[87]

Repositioning the personal as political, African American women embraced an expansive idea of black motherhood that emphasized self-reliance.[88] By assuming the role of the caring, respectable mother they challenged racist stereotypes that positioned black women as immoral, overbearing, and unable to properly care for their children.[89] This notion of "good" black motherhood not only allowed African American women to place themselves at the forefront of civil rights activism in the United States but also provided a universal gender identity around which transnational racial alliances could be forged. Influenced by the traditions of the black women's club movement, the NCNW embraced their identity as mothers in order to actively engage with black domestic life in South Africa. Through their work with the ACFS, the leaders of the NCNW invested the duties and responsibilities of the black mother with global political meaning.

The provision of food to black South African children resonated closely with the council's emphasis on the role of black women as community organizers. Based around gendered assumptions that emphasized the role of women as the primary caregivers of the black family, NCNW members embraced their motherhood in order to transcend the domestic sphere and engage in global discussions about the need for black self-determination. The NCNW's brand of moderate black internationalism promoted ideas of self-reliance and respectability that challenged racist assumptions about the black family both in the United States and South Africa. Like the assumed responsibilities of the black mother, the NCNW's work with the Feeding Scheme represented a conscious effort to extend the political influence of black women to the international arena, which simultaneously placed them at the heart of ongoing discussions relating to the nature of U.S. foreign policy debates.

The NCNW's focus on food in South Africa was especially significant within the context of its gendered black international organizing. Differences between those who could provide for their families and those who could not helped establish racial hierarchies in both the United States and South Africa. Historically, African American slaves, living on meager food allowances on Southern plantations, invested both the attainment and preparation of food with great significance. Taking control over the food they ate was a form of resistance, a way of reclaiming control of a key part of their daily lives.[90] As Doris Witt has demonstrated, this politics of black hunger continued well into the twentieth century.[91] The type of food African Americans consumed, and the circumstances under which they consumed it, continued to be invested with certain social meanings that were used to determine the racial status of an individual or group.[92]

In South Africa, too, food was closely linked to racial politics. Diana Wylie argues that in the twentieth century scientists, policymakers, and the South African state used the dietary deficiencies of the African population to prop up racist myths of black inferiority. Evidence of black malnutrition, she continues, paved the way for segregation in South Africa by propagating "an image of an ignorant, nonscientific Africa that dominated popular attitudes by the 1950s and helped accommodate even non-NP supporters to the policies of apartheid."[93] White officials chastised black South Africans for their "obsolete" methods of securing and distributing food, while pointing to these methods as evidence of the unsuitability of the African for modern life.[94] By the mid-1950s it was found that in the townships around 71 percent of boys and 67 percent of girls were malnourished.[95] The newly elected apartheid government repeatedly denied that the state should bear

the burden of feeding black South African children, arguing that this reduced parental responsibility and brought about "state pauperism."[96]

Black women in particular bore the brunt of this criticism and were often admonished for their perceived inability to properly care for their
children. In the 1950s, black South African women responded to these criticisms by drawing attention to the oppressive race and class structures that
underpinned the pressures placed on the black family. For example, at the
1954 FSAW conference, the organization's vice president, Lilian Ngoyi, outlined how food costs and wage differentials in the Transvaal impacted the
procurement of nutritional foodstuff: "We are told that we must eat proper
food, we must have fats, proteins, vitamins. We should like to have these
things, we want them, but we have to eat mealie meal because we cannot
buy other foods. Although our wages are low, we must pay the same price
for food as the Europeans. . . . The Kaffer will put Malan in *his* place—by
fear. For we, the hungry, do not fear. We want to live and be able to work
like others. And our men must be fed well for their work."[97] FSAW viewed
the ability to access food as both an indicator of racial hierarchies and a
symbolic issue that legitimated black women's protest. In insisting that "our
men must be fed well for their work," Ngoyi and FSAW used their inability
to live up to their status as mothers to challenge the racist political and economic structures of apartheid. The absence of nutritious food acted as a
daily reminder for Africans of the discrimination they faced and helped
drive movements for political change.

The NCNW's work with the ACFS was therefore implicitly tied to broader
racial debates in apartheid South Africa. Concentrating specifically on the
issue of food, council organizers drew on their understanding of themselves
as "good" black mothers dedicated to providing care for black children
both at home and overseas. Vivian Carter Mason wrote about this in a letter
to Artishia Jordan when discussing publicity for the ACFS, stating that: "The
problem of feeding people is certainly one that must find great sympathy
here in America."[98] The political significance of hunger in the United States
attracted the NCNW to the Feeding Scheme. Aware of the ways in which
access to food had been used to further control and disenfranchise African
Americans, the NCNW attempted to challenge these forces both at home
and abroad. This was achieved through a global reimagining of the responsibilities of African American women that encompassed South Africa.

The images associated with the ACFS give further insight into how the
NCNW extended its visions of a global black motherhood to South Africa.
Feeding Scheme pamphlets directly appealed to the ideals of care, social

APPEAL 1955

It is with great confidence that I address this appeal to you.

The African Children's Feeding Scheme of which I have the honour to be chairman, has won a place in the hearts of our citizens second to none amongst Johannesburg's many works of mercy. We have always depended on the generosity and goodwill of the public, and, because our trust has not been misplaced, we have never had to retrench our work. But **we want to expand it further,** in order to combat that evil thing, **hunger amongst children.** So we invite you **to put back some of what you take out of the community.**

What does your money do during the year?

It feeds 1,800,000 African children, with 100,000 lbs. of bread, 50,000 gallons of milk, 80,000 gallons of soup and 25,000 lbs. of peanut butter. We have NINE permanent centres and TEN schools to look after.
I am sure you will want to help us in this really worth-while job.

Trevor Huddleston CR.

Father Trevor Huddleston and feeding scheme volunteers, "African Children's Feeding Scheme Pamphlet," c. 1955. Source: Image courtesy of National Park Service, "African Children's Feeding Scheme," 1955, Subgroup 1, Series 7, Folder 3.

welfare, and racial uplift that informed the NCNW's work in the United States. Disseminated widely among NCNW members through letters, memos, newsletters, and press releases, these materials presented a highly gendered image of its work in Johannesburg.[99] African children were often represented as being without adult supervision. Pamphlets contained pictures that depicted crowds of children at feeding stations, clutching empty containers, underlining the scale of the task facing the ACFS as well as the importance of the organization's work. It was these "motherless" children that NCNW members were being asked to assist. Images of neglect promoted maternal ideas that related to the traditional role of women in the family. In the absence of adult supervision, it was implied that it was up to the supporters of the Feeding Scheme to assist black children in South Africa.

Laura Briggs has identified how images of the foreign "waif" and "Madonna with Child" became increasingly prevalent in American visual culture after World War II. These images questioned the stability of the black

AFRICAN CHILDREN'S FEEDING SCHEME.

(W.O. 300.)

Chairman :
The Revd. Fr. T. Huddleston, C.R.
Vice-Chairman :
The Hon. Colin Stamp.
Hon. Treasurer :
Mr. J. Knox. Tel. 44-2807.
Chairman Fund-Raising Committee :
Mr. A. Vituli. Phone : 33-4423.

Hon. Organising Secretary:
Miss Eleanor Ponsonby. Tel. 33-5965.

P.O. BOX 3624,

9, FRASER STREET,

JOHANNESBURG.

JUL 1953

We are

fighting

malnutrition

The wealth of

the nation is

its children

APPEAL 1953

It is with great confidence that I address this appeal to you.

The African Children's Feeding Scheme, of which I have the honour to be chairman, has won a place in the hearts of our citizens second to none amongst Johannesburg's many works of mercy. We have always depended on the generosity and goodwill of the public, and, because our trust has not been misplaced, we have never had to retrench our work. But WE WANT TO EXPAND IT FURTHER, in order to combat that evil thing HUNGER AMONGST CHILDREN. So we invite you TO PUT BACK SOME OF WHAT YOU TAKE OUT OF THE COMMUNITY.

What does your money do during the year ?

It feeds 1,300,000 African children, with 100,000 lbs of bread, 50,000 gallons of milk, 30,000 gallons of soup and 25,000 lbs of peanut butter. We have NINE permanent centres and TEN schools to look after.

I am sure you will want to help us in this really worth-while job.

Trevor Huddleston CR.

Put Back Some of What You Take Out of the Community.

AFRICAN CHILDREN'S FEEDING SCHEME.

P.O. Box 3624,
9, Fraser Street,
Johannesburg.

(W.O. 300.)

STOP ORDER

Chairman :
The Rev. Fr. T. Huddleston, C.R.
Organising Sec. : Tel. 33-5965.

FOR BANK USE ONLY.

THE MANAGER,

....Bank.

....Branch.

....Town.

Please remit to the credit of AFRICAN CHILDREN'S FEEDING SCHEME (without any charge to me) at Barclay's Bank (D.C. & O.) Ltd., Commissioner Street, Central Johannesburg :

the sum of £ .... per month for twelve months commencing on

.... day of .... , 19......

debit my account accordingly.

NAME..
(In block letters)

ADDRESS..

....

Signed..

Jan. ....
Feb. ....
Mar. ....
Apr. ....
May ....
June ....
July ....
Aug. ....
Sept. ....
Oct. ....
Nov. ....
Dec. ....

Children queue for food, "African Children's Feeding Scheme Pamphlet," c. 1953. Source: Image from the Records of the South African Institute of Race Relations, Part III—Historical Papers Research Archive, University of the Witwatersrand, Johannesburg, South Africa.

family while producing "an ideology of rescue by white people of non-white people."[100] Briggs argues that, adopted by organizations such as UNICEF and regularly reproduced throughout the media, these ubiquitous images of black hunger, poverty, and need were, in turn, used to legitimize U.S. foreign policy interventions during the early Cold War.[101]

It is tempting to see the NCNW's involvement in the Feeding Scheme as being part of this broader narrative of liberal interventionism, used to validate America's foreign policy. At times the pamphlets promote an idea of black African helplessness that seems to privilege the role of the Feeding Scheme's white organizers and undermine the independence of black South African women. The scenes that they present are a far cry from the militant activism of Ngoyi and FSAW, who emphasized how black South African women themselves could overthrow and challenge the racist structures that prevented them from fulfilling their roles as mothers. Indeed, the very fact that the NCNW avoided groups such as FSAW, whose members included communists and trade unionists, is illustrative of the limitations of their moderate internationalism.

However, the NCNW's fundraising efforts on behalf of the Feeding Scheme also demonstrate how African Americans maintained their anticolonial outlook when faced with the repressive politics of the early Cold War. Reluctant to challenge the U.S. government on the international stage, moderate black organizations like the NCNW worked with the state in an attempt to influence American attitudes toward white supremacy in Africa. Small and limited in nature, the NCNW's early engagement with South African politics is representative of how black liberals worked to pressure U.S. policymakers into taking a stand against the apartheid government.[102] By emphasizing their identity and responsibilities as black mothers, NCNW members presented their work as part of an acceptable and respectable endeavor designed to help black South African families living under the apartheid regime.

This organizing is also significant in terms of thinking through the gender politics of black internationalism as it sheds light on the extent to which NCNW leaders were invested in challenging negative portrayals of black motherhood on a global scale. African American women were cast as the dominant partners in this transatlantic relationship; responsible figures with the necessary skills and experiences uplift black South African families. By extending their care across the black Atlantic, African American women had the potential to secure and safeguard the future of black children globally. Often hierarchical, issues of motherhood, care, and family responsibilities traveled and therefore became an important way through which black women could relate to one another across national borders. As Collins suggests, black women often responded to pressures that were placed on the black family by embracing the identity of the "community othermother"—a role that placed them at the center of broad kinship networks. The NCNW's work in South Africa suggests that the concept of the community othermother also had an important diasporic significance.[103]

Throughout its history, the NCNW made efforts to engage with international political issues while actively developing networks between black women across national borders. Although the council's activities in South Africa were limited, both in terms of financial contribution and ability to mount an effective challenge to the rapidly expanding apartheid state, they are nevertheless significant in terms of understanding the changing nature of black internationalism during the early Cold War. As white governments attempted to forcibly remove radical black voices from the global political arena, moderate organizations such as the NCNW were able to expand their international networks. It is therefore tempting to dismiss the NCNW's black internationalism as part of broader, state-directed efforts to tackle communism. However, this line of argument overlooks the ability of African Americans to shape Cold War debates on race and ultimately leaves us with the impression that black activists simply capitulated to the demands of the U.S. government. This was not the case—black organizations consistently lobbied on behalf of oppressed people in Africa and the black diaspora throughout the worst years of anticommunist suppression.

By working with the U.S. government, African Americans attempted to place issues of self-determination at the center of U.S. foreign policy initiatives through their welfare and humanitarian work. Although this was an imperfect compromise, the NCNW's work in South Africa represented an active contribution on behalf of African American women to resist the impact of apartheid on the day-to-day lives of black South Africans. Furthermore, as its first sustained engagement in Africa, the NCNW's work with the ACFS was a pioneering enterprise that helped lay the groundwork for the organization's considerable charitable work on the African continent throughout the second half of the twentieth century.[104]

Finally, the NCNW's particular brand of black internationalism illustrates how highly gendered representations of the African family worked to promote a diasporic consciousness among African Americans. During the 1950s, images such as those of the oppressed African mother, the poor and malnourished African child, and the African family in need of protection were deliberately employed as gendered motifs around which black women could build international alliances. The NCNW's own ideological emphases on social welfare, child care, and religious respectability were reflected in the work of the African Children's Feeding Scheme. This organization, dedicated to tackling apartheid policies that left black children malnourished, called on African American women, as mothers, to extend their organizing in order to assist the South African family. By tackling hunger in South Africa, the NCNW invested in the image of a healthy and self-sufficient black family across national borders.

These activities had important political resonance in both the United States and South Africa in that they challenged white racist images of black incompetence and powerlessness used to maintain racial hierarchies. By contributing to the feeding of black South African children in Johannesburg, African Americans offered an alternative vision of the black family that contradicted the racial ideologies of apartheid. Through the Feeding Scheme, the NCNW articulated a form of global black motherhood that symbolically linked African American and black South African women in ways that reinforced ideals of self-reliance and independence.

Conclusion

· ·

In January 1959 William Gordon, the black American managing editor of the *Atlanta Daily World*, arrived in Johannesburg. In Africa to study in Ghana on an Ogden Reid Fellowship, Gordon had obtained a supplementary grant from the U.S. State Department to fund a tour throughout the African continent.[1] Shortly after his arrival in South Africa, he held a press conference that was attended by a number of African journalists. When asked by one of the reporters whether he had been required to present a pass on his visit, he promptly produced his American passport, asserting, "I think there is none finer than this." Claiming that it represented "Exhibit A" for American freedom, Gordon announced that the Native Affairs Department would be looking after him during his stay in the country. The journalists responded with "a great roar of laughter."[2]

This laughter is telling. It hints at the hollow nature of the benevolent Cold War claims of the U.S. and apartheid governments, while demonstrating the willingness of black South Africans to subvert staged representations of race relations on both sides of the Atlantic. The assembled African journalists knew all too well that U.S. government declarations that the nation's racial problems were consigned to the past were a myth—just as they would have been painfully aware of the irony of characterizing the Native Affairs Department as a compassionate force in South Africa. This, then, was the laughter of knowing resistance. A symbolic indication of how, in a tightly controlled and carefully managed space, defiance was still possible. This brief and seemingly inconsequential exchange helps us to better understand the nature of the relationship between African Americans and black South Africans during the early Cold War. The awkward encounter between Gordon and the black South African press sheds light on how governments worked to counteract international criticisms of their racial policies, as well as how these public relations efforts were generally met with skepticism by people of African descent. It was a meeting that documented both the power that the state exerted over black international exchanges and the continued willingness of black audiences to subvert these narratives.

African American responses to the nascent anti-apartheid movement were constrained by the Cold War. Both the U.S. and South African governments harnessed the politics of anticommunism to stifle criticisms of capitalist imperialism, disrupt anticolonial networks, and ultimately validate the expansion of that apartheid state. As landmark events in the struggle against Jim Crow combined with Asian and African decolonization to undermine the ideological power of white supremacy, exaggerated fears of communist subversion emerged as a useful framework to deflect international criticisms of apartheid. This had a real and damaging effect on activists and organizations committed to defeating white supremacy in both countries. Anticommunist politics made it easier to censor those who questioned state power, bolstered legal mechanisms designed to intimidate, arrest, and imprison activists, and were used to justify the removal of passports from individuals who had the potential to cause diplomatic embarrassment overseas.

All of this points to the need to understand the role of the state in shaping the global contours of black protest during the early Cold War. Networks launched to challenge white supremacy on a global level had to reckon with state authorities that worked hard to nationalize and nullify black protest. It is clear from the relationship between the U.S. and the South African governments that these acts of repression did not always occur in isolation. States learned from one another when it came to tackling black dissent, forging political and ideological ties that exacerbated racial inequality in both countries. The National Party's extensive monitoring of the civil rights movement, its efforts to appeal to segregationist sentiment in the United States, as well as the government's use of the Smith Act during the Treason Trial all speak to this. Efforts to internationalize anti-apartheid protest were therefore in constant negotiation with transnationally organized forms of state power. Indeed, the lengths that state officials went to prevent international criticism of their racial policies make the political connections that were established between African Americans and black South Africans in this era all the more remarkable.

Still, although they were never entirely free from the controlling gaze of the state, anti-apartheid activists in South Africa and the United States continued to find ways to transcend national boundaries to condemn racism and colonialism on a global scale. Through correspondence, print journalism, political rallies, and various cultural exchanges, African Americans and black South Africans continued to navigate the repressive politics of the early Cold War in order to condemn racism and colonialism on a global scale.

If anything, then, this is a book that documents the hope and persever-ance of black activists engaged in the anti-apartheid struggle. It is an ex-amination of how African Americans found ways to challenge apartheid even when this was deemed to be politically dubious by the state. Ideas trav-eled, even if individuals could not. The end of the "diaspora moment" of the early to mid-1940s did not usher in an inward-looking phase in the his-tory of black resistance.[3] It is certainly true that black international poli-tics was divided and less expansive during the early Cold War, but the commitment of African Americans to black freedom on a global scale was not erased entirely. There was simply just too much at stake for black activ-ists in both countries not to be genuinely invested in one another's strug-gles for freedom throughout the 1940s and 1950s.[4] Tracing the emergence of the global anti-apartheid movement therefore requires historians to trace both the disruptive effects of state-sponsored anticommunism *and* the com-plex ways in which black activists responded to these repressive measures. Whether it was through letter writing, travel, print journalism, popular culture, or the lobbying of government agencies, African Americans and black South Africans found ways to connect their struggles for racial jus-tice during the darkest days of the Red Scare.

Indeed, the breadth and political diversity of these exchanges raise broader questions relating to the fate of black internationalism during the early Cold War. Historians have largely interpreted this era as a nadir in the history of black international organizing—a time when African Ameri-cans shed their anticolonial connections with Africa in favor of achiev-ing civil rights at home.[5] However, this interpretation has a tendency to downplay the ability of activists to engage with state power in ways that underlined their continued commitment to anticolonialism. Black leftists responded to the harassment they faced in imaginative ways, often repur-posing their experiences of repression to draw parallels between the U.S. government and the apartheid state. Despite their marginalization from the political mainstream, they continued to forge tangible connections with black anti-apartheid leaders well into the 1950s.[6] Historians should not downplay the damaging effects that Cold War anticommunism had in terms of attacking black voices that called attention to both the capitalist roots of racial inequality and the expansion of American imperial power. However, while anticommunism dismantled organizations and disrupted alliances, it could not fully contain the rebellious character of black radicalism.[7] At the same time, the sincerity and value of the contributions that African American liberals made to the anti-apartheid movement also needs to be recognized. Black organizers working with groups such as the NCNW and the ACOA were capable of embracing "Americanism" while maintaining transnational racial alliances that established white supremacy as a global problem and connected the call for civil rights to colonial independence movements in Africa.[8]

African American liberals worked strategically to steer U.S. internationalism in an anticolonial direction.[9] While they did not offer a sustained criticism of the expansion of American power following World War II, their lobbying efforts made it difficult for the United States to openly endorse white settlerism in Africa while the government wrestled with the damage Jim Crow was doing to America's international reputation. African Americans were largely united in their opposition to apartheid but were often divided on how they should interpret exactly what the expansion of American power around the world signaled for people of African descent.[10] This not only speaks to the range of responses to apartheid at this historical juncture but also forces us to acknowledge the diverse and contested nature of black internationalism as a political ideology.

Recovering these political and cultural connections adds to our understanding of the global character of black protest as well as how racial identities are constructed transnationally.[11] However, the full complexity of black internationalism is only revealed if we trace exactly how and why these connections were formed. This requires an in-depth analysis of how black activists deliberately framed specific issues, events, individual experiences, and movements in ways that evoked global sympathies and contributed to a shared language of oppression that connected geographically distinct struggles against white power. As Tiffany Patterson and Robin D. G. Kelley state, "The linkages . . . that tie the diaspora together must be articulated and are not inevitable."[12] Transnational racial solidarities therefore must grapple with important discontinuities and are necessarily constructed through difference.[13] Even as the racial policies of the U.S. and South African governments diverged, black activists in both countries drew comparisons between their own experiences of oppression and advanced a global vision of black freedom. Incarceration and comparable experiences of political imprisonment played an important role in the forging of a diasporic consciousness between African Americans and black South Africans. Similarly, by invoking the black family organizers drew parallels between the damaging effects that institutionalized racism had on black lives in both countries. Although there were key differences in the racial dynamics of both countries, black activists worked to collapse these distinctions, engaging in acts of "imaginative discovery" and making universal appeals that spoke to vivid and personal experiences of racial oppression on both sides of the Atlantic.[14]

Delving into the language and iconography that was used to launch transnational responses to the apartheid regime also reveals the importance of gender in shaping the politics of black internationalism.[15] The construction of a powerful and mobile vision of black masculinity was a key feature of how anti-apartheid protest traveled. In speeches, political writings, and memoranda, black men were often positioned as the natural leaders of the anti-apartheid movement. They presented themselves as heroic figures, men who had the power to win freedom for oppressed black communities.[16] In the 1940s and 1950s, both the language and imagery of the international anti-apartheid movement reinforced traditional gender roles in ways that promoted a masculinist vision of black freedom. This language enabled black men to maintain their agency in the face of white supremacist and anticommunist repression at the same time it marginalized and domesticated the anti-apartheid activism of black women activists. This gender divide rested on the assumption that both domestic and international politics were primarily a male domain.[17]

Transnational exchanges between African Americans and black South Africans regularly emphasized the vulnerability of black women and, by extension, the African home. Anti-apartheid discourse focused on how the repressive actions of the state prevented women from carrying out the responsibilities and duties associated with idealized forms of motherhood. This relationship between mother and child provided, in the words of the historian Asia Leeds, a "gendered politics of redemption" that shaped how people of African descent engaged with apartheid throughout the diaspora.[18] The vulnerability of the African family was used to expose the violence of the South African government and, in turn, to stress the righteousness of African nationalism.[19] Shared conceptions of motherhood therefore played an important role in establishing black international connections, promoting a sense of "racial globality" that symbolically connected the fate of black families around the world as a response to white supremacy.[20] This diasporic politics of identification further established women as the symbolic guardians of the race both in Africa and throughout the black Atlantic.[21]

Many women in the United States and South Africa steadfastly refused to accept this masculinist vision of black protest. Though their freedom dreams were often frustrated, women in both countries articulated a form of black internationalist feminism.[22] Gender concerns were at the heart of the political activism of individuals such as Mary McLeod Bethune, Vivian Carter Mason, Frieda Matthews, Eslanda Robeson, and Lilian Ngoyi. Each of these women forged political solidarities across national boundaries in ways that connected calls for gender equality and women's rights to the struggle for colonial liberation. Black women collapsed distinctions between the domestic and public spheres, firmly asserting that they were uniquely positioned when it came to challenging racism and comprehending the true meaning of democracy. Although opportunities to engage with one another were limited, this was a view that was shared by black activists on both sides of the Atlantic. Black women struggling against apartheid made sure that they were not relegated to the domestic sphere. Engaging with, criticizing, and attempting to redefine the gender roles often assigned to them by men, they ensured that their concerns were heard within the global anti-apartheid movement. As Eslanda Robeson recalled in an interview in the early 1960s, "The women of Africa have always taken an active part in protests and demonstrations for independence, and against repression. They have come out, with their children, some of them with babies on their backs, to join the men in protest."[23]

The rebellious character and unprecedented scale of anti-apartheid activism meant South Africa was key when it came to shaping the anticolonial outlook of African American activists throughout the 1950s. Nelson Mandela, reflecting on the interrelated nature of black protest in the United States and South Africa, put it like this: "We were part of a worldwide movement. . . . Just as we watched and learned from the continuing struggle within the United States, so too did activists there gain strength from our struggles."[24] The defiant actions of anti-apartheid activists influenced how many African Americans thought about and challenged segregation.[25] As Paul Robeson proclaimed during the Defiance Campaign, "What a challenge these brave African brothers and sisters of ours pose for us!"[26] Expressing dismay at red-baiting and the fragmentation of the black popular front in the United States, he argued that this unified action against apartheid provided a model for African Americans in terms of realizing the potential of black protest at home. "Just imagine if we started something like that in the South—or even in New York, Chicago, St. Louis, Indianapolis, Louisville and Los Angeles," Robeson wrote longingly.[27]

Just as the civil rights movement resonated beyond the borders of the United States, African Americans also gained strength from the efforts to dismantle white settler regimes in southern Africa. Anticolonial struggles in Africa presented a challenge to black America, further underlining the shortcomings of American democracy and reminding African Americans just how far they still had to go in order to secure race equality in the United States. Between 1945 and 1960, a total of twenty-three African nations threw off the shackles of colonial rule and claimed their independence. Although a free and democratic South Africa would remain a distant dream, this was an era when African decolonization set the tone in the global struggle against white supremacy.

The Trinidadian writer and Marxist intellectual C. L. R. James once stated that "the first step to freedom was to go abroad."[28] Appearing in the appendix to *The Black Jacobins*, James's observation demonstrates how moving beyond borders, whether through physical travel or a more figurative journey, has long been an important resistance strategy for people of African descent. By thinking and acting globally, black activists gained a greater understanding of the worldwide operation of white supremacy, as well as a better knowledge of the political potential of black internationalism. As this book outlines, it is clear that white governments also recognized the emancipatory possibilities that such transnational journeys held. Through the denial of passports, visas, and permits, the state played an important role in denying black activists opportunities to travel. Moreover, through censorship, harassment, and intimidation governments have actively sought to erase global themes from black political and cultural thought. It is this tension, between the willingness of black activists to look globally, and the imposition of state power designed to prevent such movements, that shaped early African American engagements in the anti-apartheid movement. Through a number of bureaucratic processes, the U.S. and South African governments made a concerted effort to ensure that black activists would find it difficult to combine their respective struggles for racial justice. However, the time, money, and effort put into policing anti-apartheid protest between both countries suggests that, even in the darkest moments, both nations remained susceptible to black international activism.

These extensive efforts to prevent African Americans and black South Africans from forging political alliances with one another remind us of the accuracy of Stuart Hall's famous observation that "hegemonizing is hard work."[29] Although they did not directly result in a dramatic transformation of racial hierarchies in either country, the persistent efforts of black activists to look abroad forced the U.S. and South African governments to continually reassess their political, economic, and military relationships during the early Cold War. By drawing attention to the oppression they faced, as well as the way in which white supremacy was reinforced across borders, African Americans and black South Africans forced governments to account for their racial policies within the context of Cold War debates regarding the nature of freedom and democracy. It was this dialectical relationship, between state power and black international protest, that was at the center of how white supremacist thought was maintained, questioned, and ultimately undermined during the Cold War.

Notes

Abbreviations

ACOA Records	Records of the American Committee on Africa, Microfilm: Bethesda, MD: University Publications of America
BSCP Records	Records of the Brotherhood of Sleeping Car Porters
Du Bois Papers	W. E. B. Du Bois Papers, Microfilm: Amherst, MA: University of Massachusetts
FRUS	Foreign Relations of the United States Collection
FSAW Records	Federation of South African Women Records
MSRC	Moorland-Spingarn Research Center, Howard University, Washington, DC
NAACP Records	Papers of the NAACP: Frederick, MD: University Publications of America
NCNW Records	Records of the National Council of Negro Women
Robeson Collection	Paul and Eslanda Robeson Collection
Robeson Papers	Paul Robeson Papers
SANA	South African National Archives, Pretoria

Introduction

1. Nolutshungu, *South Africa in Africa*, 53. Eric Louw held prominent diplomatic positions in the United States in the 1920s and 1930s. He became the minister of Economic Affairs for the National Party in 1949 and would become South Africa's minister for Foreign Affairs in 1957.

2. "If It's Good Enough for America, It's Good Enough for Us," cartoon, *New Africa*, October 1949, 3.

3. Ibid., caption.

4. Irwin, *Gordian Knot*, 59–62.

5. Borstelmann, *Apartheid's Reluctant Uncle*; Borstelmann, *Cold War and the Color Line*.

6. This publication is not to be confused with London's *Guardian*. "If It's Good Enough for America, It's Good Enough for Us," cartoon, *Guardian*, August 4, 1949. For work that has accounts of the demise of the Council on African Affairs (CAA) as a result of anticommunist harassment, see Lynch, *Black American Radicals*; Nesbitt, *Race for Sanctions*, chap. 1; Von Eschen, *Race against Empire*, esp. chap. 5.

7. Williams, *Concrete Demands*, chap. 2.

8. As Robin D. G. Kelley has commented in relation to the "global vision" of black history in the aftermath of World War II, "The fact is, no one could afford to ignore international politics during the decade of the 1950s. It was, after all, the era of the United Nations and its declarations of human rights, the era of decolonization, the crumbling of old empires and the rise of new ones; it was the age of the Mau Mau in Kenya, armed struggle in Cameroon, independence for Kwame Nkrumah's Ghana, the Bandung conference, the creation of the Organization of African Unity, the formation of the American Society of African Culture, the first International Congress of Negro Writers and Artists, and the appearance of the international black journals such as *Presence Africane*." See Kelley, " 'But a Local Phase of a World Problem,' " 1075–76.

9. Alfred Hutchinson, "Against the College Colour-Bar: A Letter to the Negro Woman Student Who Challenged the Alabama University Colour-Bar," *Fighting Talk*, May 1956, 9.

10. Kaplan, *Anarchy of Empire*, 1.

11. For similarities between nonviolent mass civil disobedience in the United States and South Africa in the 1950s, see Fredrickson, *Black Liberation*, chap. 6.

12. For an excellent overview of the rise of apartheid in the 1950s, see Dubow, *Apartheid, 1948–1994*, chap. 2.

13. Gerhart, *Black Power in South Africa*, chap. 4.

14. For how South African civil disobedience influenced black political thought in the United States, see Meriwether, *Proudly We Can Be Africans*, chap. 3.

15. The Campaign for the Defiance of Unjust Laws, more commonly known as the Defiance Campaign, was a large-scale act of nonviolent civil disobedience. It was announced on April 6, 1952, by the ANC, SAIC and Colored People's Congress. Dubow, *Apartheid, 1948–1994*, 43.

16. The Congress of the People included organizations such as the African National Congress, the South African Indian Congress, the South African Congress of Democrats, the South African Coloured People's Organisation, the Federation of South African Women, and the South African Congress of Trade Unions Communist Party of South Africa. For information on the Kliptown gathering, see Karis, "Revolution in the Making," 384.

17. Walker, *Women and Resistance in South Africa*, 189–203.

18. Brooks, *Boycotts, Buses, and Passes*, chap. 8.

19. Gerhart, *Black Power in South Africa*, chap. 6.

20. Bates, " 'Double V for Victory' "; Plummer, *Rising Wind*, chap. 3; Tuck and Kruse, *Fog of War*.

21. Gilmore, *Defying Dixie*; Jacquelyn Dowd Hall, "Long Civil Rights Movement."

22. Sullivan, "Movement Building during the World War II Era," 71–80; Sullivan, *Lift Every Voice*, chap. 7 and 8.

23. Gellman, *Death Blow to Jim Crow*; Horne, *Communist Front?*; Purnell, *Fighting Jim Crow*, 31–36; Swindall, *Path to the Greater*; Garrow, *Bearing the Cross*, esp. chap. 1 and 2.

24. For an interesting account of how Martin Luther King Jr. was inspired by anti-apartheid protest and nonviolence in South Africa, see Lewis Baldwin, *Toward the Beloved Community*.

25. Issued on June 25, 1955, at Kliptown. Extract from Worden, *Making of Modern South Africa*, 115.

26. George Fredrickson highlights the differences between racial politics in the United States and South Africa in this period; see Fredrickson, *Black Liberation*, chap. 6.

27. For a detailed discussion of the transition from segregation to apartheid, see Dubow, *Racial Segregation and the Origins of Apartheid*.

28. For a chronological list of apartheid legislation, see Lulat, *United States Relations*, xxxi–xxxvi.

29. See the Bantu Authorities Act (1951), the Native Laws Amendment Act (1952), and the Promotion of Bantu Self-Government Act (1959).

30. Dubow, *Apartheid, 1948–1994*, 58. For more on how the apartheid state was based around influx control and power over black movement, see Greenberg, *Legitimating the Illegitimate*.

31. The way in which concerns over America's global self-image shaped black protest in the Cold War period has been explored by a range of authors, including Borstelmann, *Cold War and the Color Line*; Dudziak, *Cold War Civil Rights*; Von Eschen, *Race Against Empire*, chap. 7.

32. George Fredrickson's *White Supremacy* and John Cell's *Highest Stage of White Supremacy* are landmark texts that established a comparative approach in tracing the racial histories of the United States and South Africa. Although these accounts are remarkable in both their quality and analysis, my research moves beyond a comparative approach by adopting a transnational approach that traces the interconnected racial histories of both countries. There have been a number of excellent studies that have traced transnational linkages between African Americans and South Africa, including Campbell, *Songs of Zion*; Engel, *Encountering Empire*; Nesbitt, *Race for Sanctions*; and Vinson, *Americans Are Coming!* However, there has so far been a lack of in-depth scholarly attention paid to how these transnational connections fared after 1948. It is my hope that this study is an effective first step in addressing this historiographical gap.

33. Paul Robeson, "A Lesson from Our South African Brothers and Sisters," *Freedom*, September 1952.

34. Chrisman, "Rethinking Black Atlanticism," 16.

35. Gilroy, *Black Atlantic*, 16.

36. Meriwether, *Proudly We Can Be Africans*, chap. 3. For an excellent account of the longer history of African American identification with Africa, see Corbould, *Becoming African Americans*.

37. For work that assesses the effect that the "Second Red Scare" had on the African American freedom struggle, see Horne, "Who Lost the Cold War?"; Manfred Berg, "Black Civil Rights and Liberal Anticommunism"; Lieberman and Lang,

Anticommunism and the African American Freedom Movement; Arnesen, "Civil Rights and the Cold War At Home"; Arnesen, "The Final Conflict?"; Gore, "The Danger of Being an Active Anti-Communist"; and Munro, "Imperial Anticommunism."

38. Von Eschen, *Race Against Empire*, 2. For an interesting case study of the extent to which African Americans embraced anti-imperialism in the 1940s, see Webb, "Reluctant Partners," 354–56.

39. Ibid., 112.

40. Gaines, *American Africans in Ghana*; Meriwether, *Proudly We Can Be Africans*, 177.

41. Von Eschen, *Race against Empire*, 124.

42. Carol Anderson, *Eyes off the Prize*; Borstelmann, *Cold War and the Color Line*; Dawson, *Blacks In and Out of the Left*, 78–86; Dudziak, *Cold War Civil Rights*; Horne, *Black and Red* and *Communist Front?*; McDuffie, "Black and Red," 236–47; Noer, *Cold War and Black Liberation*; Parker, "Decolonization, the Cold War, and the Post-Columbian Era"; Plummer, *Rising Wind*; Von Eschen, *Race Against Empire*.

43. This argument contradicts Saul Dubow's assertion that there was a "hiatus in transatlantic engagement between African American activists and the ANC in the decade after 1948." Dubow, *Apartheid, 1948–1994*, 50.

44. For work that explores radical black internationalism during the Cold War, see Davies, *Left of Karl Marx*; Gaines, *American Africans in Ghana*; Higashida, *Black Internationalist Feminism*; Gore, *Radicalism at the Crossroads*; Horne, *Black and Red* and *Black Revolutionary*; James, *George Padmore and Decolonization from Below*; McDuffie, *Sojourning for Freedom*; Von Eschen, *Race Against Empire*.

45. For more on the founding and early work of the CAA, including the influence of Max Yergan on the organization, see Johnson, "Re-Thinking the Emergence of the Struggle for South African Liberation," 171–92.

46. In 1953 the CAA was asked to register as a foreign agent under the McCarran Act before the Subversive Activities Control Board (SACB). See Council on African Affairs and Paul Robeson, "News Release," April 24, 1953, Paul and Eslanda Robeson Collection, Moorland-Spingarn Research Center (MSRC), Box 20. For a discussion of black responses to Popular Front politics during the 1930s, see Singh, *Black Is a Country*, 109–119.

47. Carol Anderson, introduction to *Bourgeois Radicals*.

48. Carol Anderson, *Bourgeois Radicals*, chap. 2; Carol Anderson, "International Conscience." Tillery, *Between Homeland and Motherland*, chap. 3.

49. For a detailed account of the ACOA's organizational origins, see Houser, interview with Lisa Brock.

50. For more on Houser's life and career, see Houser, *No One Can Stop the Rain*.

51. Martin Luther King Jr. was the ACOA national vice chairman in 1957; see American Committee on Africa, "Press Release: Declaration of Conscience," c. 1957, ACOA Records, Part 2, Reel 5, Frame 795–77.

52. For accounts that trace the ACOA's work with Africa, see Minter, Hovey, and Cobb, *No Easy Victories*; Hostetter, *Movement Matters*; Nesbitt, *Race for Sanctions*.

53. Mary McLeod Bethune, "A Message from Our President," *Telefact* 4, no. 2 (February 1946): 1; Mary McLeod Bethune to William Alphaeus Hunton, August 2, 1943, NCNW Records, Series 5, Box 10, Folder 1; Gallagher, "The National Council of Negro Women, Human Rights, and the Cold War"; Wells, "'She Pieced and Stitched and Quilted.'"

54. Minter and Hill, "Anti-Apartheid Solidarity," 748.

55. Borstelmann, *Apartheid's Reluctant Uncle*; Minter, *King Solomon's Mines Revisited*. The exception to this is Ryan M. Irwin's, *Gordian Knot*, 59–71.

56. Agence France-Presse, "Ex-CIA Spy Admits Tip Led to Nelson Mandela's Long Imprisonment," *Guardian* (London), May 15, 2016, https://www.theguardian .com/us-news/2016/may/15/cia-operative-nelson-mandela-1962-arrest; Adam Taylor, "The CIA's Mysterious Role in the Arrest of Nelson Mandela," *Washington Post*, May 16, 2015, https://www.washingtonpost.com/news/worldviews/wp/2016/05/16 /the-cias-mysterious-role-in-the-arrest-of-nelson-mandela/.

57. Horne, *End of Empires*, chap. 13; Slate, *Colored Cosmopolitanism*, chap. 6; "India, South Africa Set for Color Bar Test in UN," *Baltimore Afro-American*, November 2, 1946.

58. Carol Anderson, "International Conscience."

59. This represented a key flaw in terms of the anticolonial efforts of African American liberals, in that they were either unwilling or unable to question the insidious nature of the structural racism that continued to shape U.S. politics at the federal level.

60. This document was cosigned by James F. Carey of the AFL-CIO. James B. Carey and A. Philip Randolph, "International Sponsoring Campaign: Declaration of Conscience on South Africa and Day of Protest—December 10, 1957," c. November 1957, ACOA Records, Part 2, Reel 5, Frame 788–89.

61. Council on African Affairs, "Circular: Emergency Conference on the Present Crisis in South Africa," July 14, 1942, Du Bois Papers, Reel 68, Frame 197.

62. "Mass Protest as U.S. Lynchers Go Free: Apartheid in America," *New Age*, November 10, 1955.

63. As Marc Matera has commented, "Black internationalism connotes multiple formations, heterogeneous but unified in opposition to the racial order of empire and in a desire to transcend prevailing geopolitical divisions through an embrace of cultural differences. Black internationalism morphed and evolved not only in response to crises and the course of events but also in relation to different contexts and audiences." Matera, *Black London*, 17. For more on the variegated and contested nature of black internationalism, see Featherstone, "Black Internationalism," 1409–11.

64. West, Martin, and Wilkins, *From Toussaint to Tupac*, 1–2.

65. Minkah Makalani has explored the revolutionary potential of the black international left in the interwar period; see Makalani, *In the Cause of Freedom*.

66. W. E. B. Du Bois, *Negro*, 242.

67. As West, Martin, and Wilkins argue, "Civil rights gains for African Americans in the United States was inimical to black internationalism. As self-determination became equated with state sovereignty, black identities increasingly assumed a national, even nationalist, form." *From Toussaint to Tupac*, 22.

68. The authorities were particularly concerned by figures such as Nelson Mandela, who repeatedly criticized the United States' political and economic aspirations in Africa by arguing that, "It is American imperialism, which must be fought and decisively beaten down if the people of Asia and Africa are to preserve the vital gains they have won in their struggle against subjugation." Ewing, *Age of Garvey*; Makalani, *In the Cause of Freedom*; James, *George Padmore and Decolonization*.

69. Eslanda Goode Robeson, "The Cry Freedom Rings Through Africa," *New World Review*, September 1952, Paul and Eslanda Robeson Collection, Box 13.

70. Gore, *Radicalism at the Crossroads*, 5.

71. For an excellent discussion of the negative consequences of racial liberalism during the early Cold War, see Melamed, *Represent and Destroy*.

72. Paul Robeson to Oliver Tambo, December 4 1954, Paul and Eslanda Robeson Collection, Reel 7, Frame 47–48.

Chapter One

1. "U.S. Strikes at African Freedom: Council on African Affairs Called Subversive," *Advance*, May 28, 1953, 6.

2. For more information on anticommunism and the apartheid regime, see Miller, *An African Volk*, 35–47.

3. Minter, *King Solomon's Mines Revisited*, 132.

4. In his autobiography *Here I Stand*, Paul Robeson outlines how anticommunist legislation was used to prevent him calling for black freedom in the United States and Africa: "The State Department will tell you that the fact I am an advocate of Negro rights has nothing to do with the case, and to some people this might seem to be true since white persons as well as Negroes have been denied passports in this 'cold war' period. Nevertheless, there are facts—indisputable facts—which indicate that my concern for Negro rights is indeed at the heart of the case in which I am involved" (71).

5. Lieberman, " 'Another Side of the Story,' " 17–18.

6. Suppression of Communism Act, Act No. 44 of 1950.

7. Barber and Barratt, *South Africa's Foreign Policy*, chap. 4; Nolutshungu, *South Africa in Africa*, chap. 3; "Malan Asks African Charter to Maintain White Supremacy," *Jet*, April 29, 1954, 14–15.

8. Gerald Horne notes the international effects anticommunism had on black protest in Horne, *Black and Red*, 293.

9. A number of historians have traced the connections between the civil rights movement, African decolonization, and the Cold War, documenting how Cold War foreign policy interests shaped the domestic racial policies of the U.S. government. However, these studies been less forthcoming on the ways in which white governments in Africa responded to the Cold War concerns of American policymakers in order to maintain their political and economic ties with the United States. See Borstelmann, *Cold War and the Color Line*; Dudziak, *Cold War Civil Rights*; Von Eschen, *Race against Empire.*

10. Lake and Reynolds, *Drawing the Global Colour Line*; Stoler, "Tense and Tender Ties."

11. Lieberman and Lang, *Anticommunism and the African American Freedom Movement*, 2–5; Dudziak, "*Brown* as a Cold War Case," 41.

12. "Mass Protest as U.S. Lynchers Go Free: Apartheid in America," *New Age*, November 10, 1955.

13. For international significance of cases of racial violence in the American South, see Borstelmann, *Cold War and the Color Line*, 98; Miller, Pennybacker, and Rosenhaft, "Mother Ada Wright."

14. U.S. Department of State, Office of the Historian, "National Intelligence Estimate: Probable Developments in the Union of South Africa," October 20, 1952, Document 555-FRUS, 1952–1954. Africa and South Asia (in two parts): vol. 11, part 1, Historical Documents, https://history.state.gov/historicaldocuments/frus1952 -54v11p1/d555.

15. Minter, *King Solomon's Mines Revisited*, 133–135.

16. Borstelmann, *Cold War and the Color Line*, 124. For more information on South Africa's role in the establishment of the UN and the nation's subsequently troubled relationship with the international organization, see Dubow, "Smuts, the United Nations and the Rhetoric of Race and Rights," 45–77.

17. Minter, *King Solomon's Mines Revisited*, 76

18. William Alphaeus Hunton, *Resistance: Against Fascist Enslavement in South Africa* (1953), William Alphaeus Hunton Papers, Reel 2, 50.

19. Ibid., 77.

20. Borstelmann, *Apartheid's Reluctant Uncle*. 128; U.S. Department of State, Office of the Historian, "Memorandum of Conversation, 'Ambassador's Courtesy Calls on Acting Secretary for External Affairs, and on Prime Minister and Minister of External Affairs,'" September 27, 1950, Document 980, FRUS, 1950, The Near East, South Asia, and Africa, vol. 5, Historical Documents, https://history.state.gov /historicaldocuments/frus1950v05/d980.

21. Nattrass, *South African Economy*, 108.

22. M. Dickson, "Nats Look to United States for Protection," *New Age*, April 28, 1955.

23. Between 1949 and 1952 Kennecott Copper Corp. provided investments of over 15.5 million dollars in Orange Free State gold mine operations. See "S. Africa Tied to U.S. Imperialism: Uranium Production to Aid U.S. War Plans," *People's World*, October 16, 1952, 3.

24. Hunton, *Resistance*, 52.

25. The United States never represented more than 10 percent of South Africa's total export market in this period. However, even as the United States lagged behind Great Britain as a destination for South African goods (Britain regularly imported four times as many goods), exports were nevertheless increased markedly after the National Party came into power, jumping from $22 million in 1948 to $74 million in 1954. For statistics, see American Committee on Africa, "Exports of the Union of South Africa to the U.S." ACOA Records, Part 1, Reel 4, Frame 773.

26. Greenberg, *Legitimating the Illegitimate*, 39–44; Beinart, *Twentieth-Century South Africa*, 170, 173.

27. Borstelmann, *Apartheid's Reluctant Uncle*, 159.

28. Due to a combination of infighting, anticommunist persecution, and financial problems, the CAA folded in 1955. Despite the sizeable problems faced by the council during this period, its role in disseminating information and organizing on behalf of Africa was highly significant. In its heyday the CAA could fill Madison Square Garden for protest rallies, its publications were banned throughout colonial Africa, and it channeled money to various causes connected to the African struggle for liberation. For a history of the organization, see Lynch, *Black American Radicals*.

29. Brock, "The 1950s: Africa Solidarity Rising," 59–62; Johnson, "Re-Thinking the Emergence of the Struggle for South African Liberation," 186–91.

30. William Alphaeus Hunton, "American Trusts Bolster South African Racists."

31. "A U.S. Loan for South Africa?"

32. "U.S.A. Urged To Stop Buying S.A. Gold: Protest against Race Discrimination," *Guardian*, January 6, 1949.

33. Hunton, "American Trusts Bolster South African Racists," 6.

34. Hunton, *Resistance*, 48.

35. Nelson Mandela, "A New Menace in Africa," *Liberation*, March 1958, 23.

36. Ibid., 24.

37. Ibid.

38. A militant figure within the ANC, Mandela figures joined the South African Communist Party (SACP) in the early 1960s. His sympathy for communist opposition to apartheid helped facilitate his shift toward armed revolution with the emergence of Umkhonto we Sizwe. After being outlawed by the passing of the Suppression of Communism Act, the CPSA reformed clandestinely in 1953 as the South African Communist Party (SACP). The SACP entered into a formal alliance with the ANC in 1961. Ellis and Sechaba, *Comrades against Apartheid*, 24. For more on Mandela's involvement with the SACP, see Bonner, "The Antinomies of Nelson Mandela," 42; Ellis, *External Mission*, 22.

39. Borstelmann, *Cold War and the Color Line*, 155.

40. "South Africa Producing 20 Per Cent of World Uranium: Estimated Reserves Greater Than in North America," *South Africa Reports*, February 1, 1957, South African National Archives (SANA), BNY, 17/5 1–17/5/1, vol. 11.

41. "U.S. Atom Experts in South Africa: Investigating Uranium Sources," *Guardian*, October 24, 1949.

42. The rise of anticolonialism in the Congo, later symbolized by Patrice Lumumba and the Mouvement National Congolais (MNC), only added to the appeal of a South Africa openly opposed to communism of American investment. The Congo was increasingly viewed by the United States as a risky proposition in terms of trade in uranium and the State Department actively sought to develop alternative sources for the mineral. For an introductory overview of U.S. involvement in the Congo and the CIA's role in the assassination of Patrice Lumumba, see Blum, *Killing Hope*, chap. 26.

43. Holloway, *Stalin and the Bomb*. This agreement was finalized in December 1950 and was signed by the United States, South Africa, and the United Kingdom.

44. Jesse C. Johnson, "Report by the Director of Raw Materials (Johnson), Atomic Energy Commission," January 4, 1952, Document 524, FRUS, 1952–1954, Africa and South Asia (in two parts): vol. 11, part 1, Historical Documents, Office of the Historian, U.S. State Department, https://history.state.gov/historicaldocuments /frus1952-54v11p1/d524.

45. "US-SA Loan Agreement 1951," SANA, South Africa, BTS, 28/8/4, Loan from U.S., 1957–1958. A further $62,000,000 was then distributed to the South African government between 1951 and 1952 by the U.S. Export-Import Bank, acting at the behest of the Atomic Energy Commission. Hunton, *Resistance*, 61.

46. M. Dickson, "American Penetration in Our Industry," *New Age*, April 21, 1955.

47. "Arrests Continue in S. Africa; 5,600 Jailed," *New York Amsterdam News*, October 18, 1952, 42.

48. Ibid.

49. "Agreement for Co-operation Between the Government of the United States of America and the Government of the Union of South Africa Concerning Civil Uses of Atomic Energy," c. 1956, BWA, vol. 100 Z4/10, vol 1, 6; Anna-Mart Van Wyk, "Apartheid's Atomic Bomb," 104.

50. John Foster Dulles, "The Secretary of State to the Embassy in the Union of South Africa, at Pretoria," Document 576, FRUS, 1952–1954, Africa and South Asia (in two parts): vol. 11, part 1, Historical Documents, Office of the Historian, U.S. Department of State, https://history.state.gov/historicaldocuments/frus1952-54v11p1 /d576.

51. G. P. Jooste and Conrad Norton to Secretary for External Affairs, June 23, 1952, SANA, BTS, 35/4/3, U.S. perceptions of South West Africa, 1952–1956.

52. For how this played out throughout the Cold War, see Westad, *Global Cold War*.

53. Magubane, "From Détente to the Rise of the Garrison State," 47.

54. Borstelmann, *Apartheid's Reluctant Uncle*, 138. In addition to providing military assistance to the United States in the Korean War, the South African government also agreed to sell large quantities of uranium to the United States in 1950,

a move that Borstelmann argues was pivotal in securing foreign investment in the South African economy.

55. Minter, *King Solomon's Mines Revisited*, 135. "South Africa Will Recruit Air Squadron for Korea," *New York Times*, August 5, 1950.

56. Schraeder and Davis, "South Africa," 247.

57. John Pittman, "African Blood in the A-Bomb," *Daily Worker*, January 4, 1951.

58. Paul Robeson, "Struggle for Freedom in South Africa," Council on African Affairs, 1950, Paul and Eslanda Robeson Collection, Box 20, 1.

59. Dickson, "Nats Look to United States."

60. "S. Africa Tied to U.S. Imperialism: Uranium Production to Aid U.S. War Plans," *People's World*, October 16, 1952, 1.

61. PRIMSEC (Pretoria) to SALEG (Washington), November 7, 1951, SANA, BWA, vol. 97, C, 109.

62. Ryan M. Irwin makes this point in a short section in his excellent study, *Gordian Knot*, 59–71.

63. The historian Odd Arne Westad has made this point in *Global Cold War*.

64. Dudziak, *Cold War Civil Rights*.

65. Dongen, Roulin, and Scott-Smith, introduction to *Transnational Anti-Communism*.

Chapter Two

1. Waldemar J. Gallman (ambassador in the Union of South Africa) to the Department of State, "South Africa as Seen after Sixteen Months," March 2, 1953, Document 573, FRUS, 1952–1954, Africa and South Asia (in two parts): vol. 11, part 1, Historical Documents, Office of the Historian, U.S. Department of State, https://history.state.gov/historicaldocuments/frus1952-54v11p1/d573.

2. Waldemar J. Gallman (ambassador in the Union of South Africa) to the Department of State, "Final Summarization of Views on South Africa," August 6, 1954, Document 600, FRUS, 1952–1954, Africa and South Asia (in two parts): vol. 11, part 1, Historical Documents, Office of the Historian, U.S. Department of State, https://history.state.gov/historicaldocuments/frus1952-54v11p1/d600.

3. This sympathetic assessment of apartheid is symptomatic of how the language used by American state officials and policymakers was often compatible with Jim Crow. For an examination of how Southern Democrats shaped the racial politics of the New Deal and the Cold War, see Katznelson, *Fear Itself*.

4. Julius Klein Public Relations, Inc., "Preliminary Report: Public Relations for the Union of South Africa in the United State," in vol. 1, *South African Public Relations in USA*, November 1960, SANA, South Africa, BTS, 1/33/3/1, 2.

5. The amount of paperwork generated by the South African embassy and the consul general is testament to the importance the South African government placed on American racial politics.

6. The Defiance Campaign sparked widespread condemnation of South Africa in the United States. Organizations such as the CAA, ACOA, and NAACP repeatedly condemned apartheid in South Africa and contributed greatly to publicizing the racial discrimination in that country. Black newspapers also regularly reported on the campaign. Articles such as "White Supremacy in South Africa Finds Itself at the Crossroads," *Chicago Defender*, February 16, 1952, and Homer Jack, "South Africa Uncensored: America's Stake in South Africa," *Pittsburgh Courier*, February 14, 1953, and "Dixie Defiance Campaign Branded 'War' On Nation," *Norfolk Journal and Guide*, October 15, 1955, all made clear connections between black protest and white supremacy in South Africa and the United States.

7. G. P. Jooste to Secretary for External Affairs, Pretoria, June 23, 1952, SANA, BTS, 35/4/3, *U.S. Perceptions of SWA*, 1952–1956.

8. G. P. Jooste to Secretary for External Affairs, Pretoria, May 13, 1952, SANA, BTS, 35/4/3, *U.S. Perceptions of SWA*, 1952–1956.

9. The South African government would often blame any international criticism of its racial policies in the United States on negative media portrayals of the nation in the American media. Typical of this is the response of the South African press attaché at Washington to criticism of apartheid from Rabbi B. Gittelsohn, chairman of the Commission on Justice and Peace at the Central Commission of American Rabbis; see H. Moolman to Rabbi B. Gittelsohn, July 25, 1952, SANA, BTS, 35/4/3, *U.S. Perceptions of SWA*, 1952–1956.

10. "Maligning Malan," *New York Times*, May 31, 1955; "New Outrage in South Africa: Passes for Women," *New York Times*, October 31, 1958. For a detailed discussion of the "rise and fall" of the black international press with specific relevance to African American coverage of South Africa in the 1940s and 1950s, see Von Eschen, *Race against Empire*, esp. chap. 4 and 5.

11. This *Time* magazine piece is either mentioned explicitly or hinted at on numerous occasions by South African officials discussing public relations exercises in the United States; see "SOUTH AFRICA: Happy Birthday," *Time*, June 5, 1950; Mr. Coetzee to Ambassador Stewart, July 5, 1959, BWA, vol. 83, 165/1; Conrad Norton, "Report: Background Information Material for American Newspapers," South African Embassy, 1951, SANA, BWA, vol. 28, 39/1; Press attaché (South Africa Embassy, Washington), "The American Press and Africa," n.d., BNY, 1/1/1, vol. 1 and 2, *New York Consul, List S249*.

12. Conrad Norton, "Report: Background Information Material for American Newspapers," South African Embassy, 1951, SANA, BWA, vol. 28, 39/1.

13. This is highlighted in the same report in which Conrad Norton goes on to argue that *Time* magazine is one of the few—and unquestionably the most influential—sources from which most American derive their opinions of South Africa.

14. "Asks U.S. Sympathy in South African Race Problem," *Atlanta Daily World*, March 3, 1955.

15. Von Eschen, *Race against Empire*, 153–156.

16. Benjamin E. Mays, "My View," *Pittsburgh Courier*, April 18, 1959.

17. Other articles that stress the danger of communism in South Africa include "Reds Thrive On Racial Unrest in South Africa," *New Journal and Guide*, June 28, 1956, 9; "Africa to Communism," *Atlanta Daily World*, September 24, 1959; Sam Grant, "Racial Discrimination Worse than Communism, Says Cleric," *Philadelphia Tribune*, July 31, 1956; "Warning Now," *Chicago Defender*, February 19, 1949.

18. Carol Anderson, introduction to *Eyes off the Prize*; Von Eschen, *Race against Empire*, 155.

19. Melamed, *Represent and Destroy*, 53–61; Singh, *Black Is a Country*.

20. Homer Jack, "South Africa Uncensored!," *Pittsburgh Courier*, February 14, 1953.

21. Dudziak, *Cold War Civil Rights*; Plummer, *Rising Wind*.

22. For more on the relationship between American segregationists and the supporters of apartheid in South Africa, see Hyman, "American Segregationist Ideology."

23. "Public Reaction to South African Bantu Affairs—Favourable," 1952–1957, SANA, BWA, vol. 84, 183/2.

24. South African officials themselves also wrote in to newspapers to take issue with certain articles. See, for example, "Policies of South Africa: Positive Achievements of Union for Human Welfare," *New York Times*, December 3, 1949; "'Racism' in Union Denied: South Africa's Government Said to Work for Betterment of Non-Whites," *New York Times*, April 25, 1953; "South Africa Hits Matthews, Series," *New York Amsterdam News*, July 4, 1953; Conrad Norton, "Racial Ban of Segura Denied: Refusal of Visa Explained as Arising from Treasury Ruling," *New York Times*, September 7, 1953; Conrad Norton, "Position of South African," *New York Times*, March 24, 1955.

25. Anonymous letter to Mr. Russell Maguire, Chairman American Mercury Board, April 1, 1957, SANA, BWA, vol. 84, 183/2; J. R. Rousseau to G. P. Jooste, July 21, 1952, SANA. BWA, vol. 84, 183/2.

26. H. H. Moolman to J. G. Rousseau, July 24, 1952, SANA, BWA, vol. 84, 183/2.

27. Ibid.

28. Ibid.

29. Conrad Norton, "Report: Background Information Material for American Newspapers," c. 1951, SANA, BWA, vol. 28, 39/1, 1.

30. Ibid., 1–2.

31. Union of South Africa Government Information Office, New York, "South Africa: Facts for Filing," August 1950, SANA, BWA, vol. 28, 39/1, 4.

32. For a summary of Yergan's time in South Africa in the 1930s role in founding the CAA, see Johnson, "Re-Thinking the Emergence of the Struggle for South African Liberation in the United States," 171–192.

33. J. J. Coetzee to Commissioner for Immigration, "Re Communist—Max Yergan," April 14, 1938, SANA, South African Archives, Pretoria (hereafter SAB), NTS, 7601, 7/328, Max Yergan file, 1946–1957; Musser, "Presenting 'A True Idea of the African of To-day,'" 431.

34. Yergan's reputation as a communist agitator among South African officials can be seen in the following government reports: R. Webster, "Report: Council on African Affairs: New York Rally in Madison Square Garden," June 13, 1946, SANA, SAB, BTS, 1/33/13; *Negro Problem in USA, 1953–1958*; H. M. Moolman to Ambassador, Secretary for External Affairs, Secretary for the Interior, State Information Officer, Report No. 7, April 17, 1947, SANA, BWA, vol. 51, 58/19/1/1.

35. Gilmore, *Defying Dixie*, 434–437.

36. Ibid., 437.

37. South African Embassy (Washington) to secretary of external affairs (Pretoria), "Immigration and Cooperation with the FBI," August 18, 1951, SANA, BTS, 59/35, *Security Reports US Visitors*, 1951–1954, 1.

38. The deliberations surrounding Yergan's suitability for a South African visa is detailed in the following correspondence: Secretary of external affairs to secretary of native affairs, commissioner of police, and Justice Department, "Yergan Visit 1950," confidential telegram, March 28, 1949, SANA, SAB, NTS, 7601, 7/328, Max Yergan file, 1946–1957; Secretary of external affairs to secretary of interior, confidential telegram, September 13, 1949, SANA, SAB, NTS, 7601, 7/328, Max Yergan file, 1946–1957; Secretary of Native Affairs to Secretary of Interior, confidential telegram, June 1, 1950, SANA, SAB, NTS, 7601, 7/328, Max Yergan file, 1946–1957.

39. R. Webster (consul general) to South Africa ambassador H. T. Andrews, March 31, 1949, SANA, SAB, NTS, 7601, 7/328, Max Yergan file, 1946–1957.

40. Max Yergan to South African Embassy, memorandum, March 30 1949, SANA, SAB, NTS, 7601, 7/328, Max Yergan file, 1946–1957.

41. Borstelmann, *Apartheid's Reluctant Uncle*, 129.

42. G. P. Jooste to secretary for external affairs, Pretoria, May 29, 1952, SANA, NTS, 7601, 7/328, Max Yergan file, 1946–1957, 2.

43. Max Yergan, "Interview with Dr. Max Yergan. 'Africa: Next Goal of Communists,'" *U.S. News and World Report*, May 1, 1953, 52–63. "Max Yergan Trip to Africa, Itinerary," 1952, Max Yergan Papers, MSRC, Box 1, Folder 33.

44. G. P. Jooste to secretary for external affairs, Pretoria, May 29, 1952, 1–2.

45. Ibid., 2.

46. "U.S. Backs White Supremacy in Africa: Max Yergan Lets the Cat Out of the Bag," *Advance*, May 28, 1953, 7.

47. "South African Leaders Blast Max Yergan," *Freedom*, October 1952, 1, 7. Yergan was also criticized by his long-term friend and associate Z. K. Matthews for apparently betraying his core beliefs. See "An African Leader Exposes Max Yergan," *Freedom*, June 1953, 10.

48. Walter White, letter to the editor, *New York Times*, 3 July 1953, Max Yergan Papers, MSRC, SAS, Box 4, Folder 14.

49. Gilmore, *Defying Dixie*, 437; Anthony, *Max Yergan*, 275.

50. After 1948, the Justice Department also began compiling a perjury case against him as Yergan repeatedly denied under oath that he had ever been a member of the Communist Party. See Gilmore, *Defying Dixie*, 436–437.

51. Ibid., 437.

52. "Races Mix for First Time to View Film in Rhodesia," *Jet*, March 25, 1954, 13. The Moral Re-Armament movement was a strongly anticommunist organization involved in social and Christian activism. Nkomo attended his first Moral Re-Armament meeting in 1953 in Switzerland.

53. "Africa to Communism," *Atlanta Daily World*, September 24, 1959, 1, 3.

54. H. M. Moolman to Ambassador, Secretary for External Affairs, Secretary for the Interior, State Information Officer, Report No. 7, April 17, 1947, SANA, BWA, vol. 51, 58/19/1/1.

55. "South African Envoy Speaks," *New York Times*, April 8, 1949.

56. Throughout the box files of the BWA series I found copies and variations of the speech H. T. Andrews delivered to the English Speaking Union (eight speeches in total). Although it was often unclear to what audience these speeches were going to be delivered, the fact that they varied in date and were extensively circulated throughout South African governmental departments suggests that many of the themes addressed in Andrew's 1949 speech informed South African government perceptions of U.S.–South African relations.

57. Harry T. Andrews, "Address Delivered to the English-Speaking Union," April 7, 1949, SANA, BWA, vol. 1, 1/1/1, 1–2.

58. The English-Speaking Union (ESU) was dedicated to developing friendship between English-speaking peoples throughout the world. However, the organization's definition of "the world" appears to be largely limited to the white English-speaking world. The regular events put on by the ESU regularly featured appearances from government officials of the colonial nations, and in January 1956 the American branch was to sponsor an address by the social scientist and segregationist E. G. Malherbe. See "To Discuss South Africa," *New York Times*, January 1, 1956.

59. Andrews, "Address Delivered to the English-Speaking Union," 6.

60. Ibid., 16.

61. Ibid., 8.

62. Ibid., 4.

63. Ibid., 19.

64. Ernest Dichter, "Proposal for a Motivational Research Study on the Image of South Africa," Institute for a Motivational Research, New York, 1959, SANA, BTS, 1/33/3/1, vol. 1, *South African Public Relations in USA*.

65. Julius Klein Public Relations, Inc., "Preliminary Report: Public Relations for The Union of South Africa in the United States," November 1960, SANA, South Africa, BTS, 1/33/3/1, vol. 1, *South African Public Relations in USA*, 2.

66. Ibid., 3.

67. G. P. Jooste to Secretary for External Affairs, May 13, 1952, SANA, BTS, 35/4/3, *U.S. Perceptions of SWA*, 1952–1956.

68. Evidence of tensions between U.S. and South African government officials can be found in the following documents: Eric Louw and J. C. Satterthwaite,

"Memorandum of Conversation: Visit of the South African Minister of External Affairs," October 15, 1958, Document 354, FRUS, 1958–1960, Africa, vol. 14, Historical Documents, Office of the Historian, U.S. Department of State, https://history.state.gov/historicaldocuments/frus1958-60v14/d354; Christian Herter and Eric Louw, "Memorandum of Conversation: South African Attitudes at the United Nations," September 21, 1959, Document 340, FRUS, 1958–1960, Africa, vol. 14, Historical Documents, Office of the Historian, U.S. Department of State, https://history.state.gov/historicaldocuments/frus1958-60v14/d340; Counselor of the Embassy in South Africa (Maddox) to the Ambassador (Byroade), "Conversation on U.S.–South African Relations with Dr. W. C. Naude, Undersecretary for External Affairs," Document 319, FRUS, 1955–1957, Africa, vol. 18, Historical Documents, Office of the Historian, U.S. Department of State, https://history.state.gov/historicaldocuments/frus1955-57v18/d319.

69. "Question of Race Conflict in South Africa Resulting from Policies of Apartheid of the Government of the Union of South Africa," UN General Assembly Resolution 1248, October 30, 1958; Henry A. Byroade to the U.S. Department of State, telegram, November 7, 1958, Document 336, FRUS, 1958–1960, Africa, vol. 14, Historical Documents, Office of the Historian, U.S. Department of State, https://history.state.gov/historicaldocuments/frus1958-60v14/d336.

70. Henry Cabot Lodge Jr., "Telegram from the Mission at the United Nations to the Department of State," November 20, 1957, Document 321, FRUS, 1955–1957, Africa, vol. 18, Historical Documents, Office of the Historian, U.S. Department of State, https://history.state.gov/historicaldocuments/frus1955-57v18/d321; "National Intelligence Estimate: The Outlook for East, Central and South Africa," October 10, 1959, Document 18, FRUS, 1958–1960, Africa, vol. 14, Historical Documents, Office of the Historian, U.S. Department of State, https://history.state.gov/historicaldocuments/frus1958-60v14/d18; "National Intelligence Estimate: The Outlook for the Union of South Africa," July 19, 1960, Document 352, FRUS, 1958–1960, Africa, vol. 14, Historical Documents, Office of the Historian, U.S. Department of State, https://history.state.gov/historicaldocuments/frus1958-60v14/d352.

71. This can be seen in the following policy recommendation, which accepted the proposal that "it is in the interest of the United States that White leadership should be preserved, or at least indefinitely prolonged, in South Africa." See Dispatch from the Embassy in South Africa to the Department of State, "Embassy Staff Study on the South African Race Problem, II; Diplomatic Policy Recommendation," April 12, 1957, Document 314, FRUS, 1955–1957, Africa, vol. 18, Historical Documents, Office of the Historian, U.S. Department of State, https://history.state.gov/historicaldocuments/frus1955-57v18/d314.

72. Jason Parker, "Cold War II"; Parker, "Ideology, Race and Nonalignment"; Parker, "Decolonization, the Cold War, and the Post-Columbian Era," 129–130; Lawrence, "The Rise and Fall of Non-Alignment." See also Borstelmann, *Cold War and the Color Line*, 93.

73. W. C. Du Plessis (ambassador) to Secretary for External Affairs (Pretoria), c. 1957, SANA, SAB, BTS, 1/33/13, vol. 2, *Negro Problem in USA, 1953–1958*, 5.

74. Borstelmann, *Cold War and the Color Line*, 74.

75. Dudziak, *Cold War Civil Rights*, 249. Dudziak has perhaps been misrepresented by those who claim she largely ignores the oppressive sanctions placed on black protest as a result of Cold War politics in the United States. Although she sometimes fails to explore the full extent of negative effects anticommunism had on African American activism, she openly acknowledges its oppressive nature. In a subsequent article, Dudziak comments, "In *Cold War Civil Rights*, I did not argue, as has sometimes been suggested, that the Cold War was 'good' for the civil rights movement. Cold War–era red baiting activists harmed the movement and destroyed lives. Instead, I argue that while the Cold War narrowed acceptable civil rights discourse and led to sanctions against individuals who stepped outside those narrow bounds, within them it gave the movement important and effective leverage. . . . The Cold War *simultaneously* harmed the movement and created an opportunity for limited reform." See Dudziak, "*Brown* as a Cold War Case," 41.

76. "Legal Lynching in United States: Six Negroes Sentenced to Death," *Guardian*, April 14, 1949; "Legally Lynched," *Guardian*, February 8, 1951; "Race Terrorism against U.S. Negroes: Washington Charged with Genocide," *Guardian*, January 3, 1952.

77. Borstelmann, "Jim Crow's Coming Out: Race Relations and American Foreign Policy in the Truman Years," 549–569; Meriwether, *Proudly We Can Be Africans*, 131; Von Eschen, *Race against Empire*.

78. A particularly good example of this is Eslanda Goode Robeson, "Which Way for Africa?," *New World Review*, December 1952, Paul and Eslanda Robeson Collection, MSRC, Box 13.

79. "All African Peoples Conference Resolution on Colonialism and Imperialism," c. 1958, Brotherhood of Sleeping Car Porters Records, Box 97, Subject File, Africa, File 3; ANC leaders Alfred Hutchinson and Ezekiel Mphahlele managed to attend the All African People's Conference; see "ANC Will Be at Ghana Conference: Official Sponsor of African Freedom Talks Next Month," *New Age*, November 13, 1958; Eslanda Goode Robeson, "Africa for the Africans," c. 1958, Paul and Eslanda Robeson Collection, MSRC, Box 14.

80. "Accra Conference: A Milestone in African History," *New Age*, December 3, 1958.

81. Wentzel C. Du Plessis, "United States Foreign Policy in Africa—A Commentary," South Africa Embassy, Washington, DC, SANA, South Africa, BNY, 15/1, New York Consul, *Political Matters*, vol. 6–8, 6.

82. J. E. Holloway (ambassador) to Secretary for External Affairs, March 23 1956, SANA, SAB, BTS, 1/33/13, vol. 2, *Negro Problem in USA, 1953–1958*.

83. Department of External Affairs to all heads of mission, April 22, 1959, SANA, BWA, vol. 83, 165/1, 2.

84. Ibid.

85. Ibid.

86. Richard P. Hunt. "Views Defended by South Africa: Propaganda Unit Expanding in Efforts to Justify the Area's Racial Policy Distortions Are Charged, Irresponsibility Alleged," *New York Times*, February 2, 1957. For a public defense of apartheid by government officials, see "Policies of South Africa: Positive Achievements of Union for Human Welfare Emphasized," *New York Times*, December 3, 1949; "'Racism' in Union Denied: South Africa's Government Said to Work for Betterment of Non-Whites," *New York Times*, April 25, 1953.

87. Report of Washington embassy representative to D. F. Malan, November 18, 1948, SANA, BTS, 28/8/4, *Loan from US, 1957–1958*.

88. William Percy Maddox (counselor of the embassy in South Africa) to Palmer (deputy assistant secretary of state for African affairs), memorandum, "US Position on Apartheid," December 18, 1957, Document 322, FRUS, 1955–1957, Africa, vol. 18, Historical Documents, Office of the Historian, U.S. Department of State, https://history.state.gov/historicaldocuments/frus1955-57v18/d322.

89. J. J. Coetzee to Ambassador Stewart, July 5, 1959, SANA, South Africa, BWA, vol. 83, 165/1, 1.

90. Ibid., 10.

91. Alfred Hutchinson, "Against the College Colour-Bar: A Letter to the Negro Woman Student Who Challenged the Alabama University Colour-Bar," *Fighting Talk*, May 1956, 8.

92. Ibid., 9.

93. J. E. Holloway to secretary for external affairs, March 23, 1956, SANA, SAB, BTS, 1/33/13, vol. 2, *Negro Problem in USA, 1953–1958*, 5.

94. J. E. Holloway (ambassador) to secretary for external affairs (Pretoria), "Racial Segregation in Public Schools in the United States," June 17, 1955, SANA, SAB, BTS, 1/33/13, vol. 2, *Negro Problem in USA, 1953–1958*, 4.

95. The National Party combined its support for the South with criticisms of Northern race relations, which it cast as unnatural and the source of cross-racial "frustration." See "Strydom Says S. Africa Will Ignore New York," *Atlanta Daily World*, February 16, 1955, 2.

96. J. E. Holloway to Secretary for External Affairs, October 19, 1954, SANA, SAB, BTS, 1/33/13, vol. 2, *Negro Problem in USA, 1953–1958*, 3.

97. J. E. Holloway to Secretary for External Affairs, March 23, 1956, SANA, SAB, BTS, 1/33/13, vol. 2, *Negro Problem in USA, 1953–1958*, 3.

98. For the international impact of the Little Rock case, see Dudziak, "The Little Rock Crisis and Foreign Affairs."

99. Borstelmann, *Cold War and the Color Line*, 104; Dudziak, *Cold War Civil Rights*, chap. 4.

100. For more on the international reaction to Little Rock, see West, "Little Rock as America," 913–42.

101. For an example of the African response to the Little Rock Crisis, see "Minister Says Little Rock Talk in Africa," *Atlanta Daily World*, April 26, 1958.

102. Wentzel C. Du Plessis to Secretary for External Affairs, "The Closing of the Schools," December 12, 1958, BTS, 1/33/10, vol. 1, *U.S.A. Racial Policy 1958–1959*, 2.

103. Ibid., 2, 4.

104. William Alphaeus Hunton, "In South Africa Education for Slavery Is Government Plan," *Freedom*, March 1955, 4. For more on apartheid and Bantu education, see Kros, "W.W.M. Eiselen"; Giliomee, "A Note on Bantu Education."

105. Davenport and Saunders, *South Africa*, 674.

106. Du Plessis, "Memorandum: Little Rock," SANA, BWA, vol. 83, 165/1, 1.

107. Ibid., 3.

108. As Jamie Miller has noted, this strategy was also a feature of apartheid rule in the late 1960s and early 1970s; Miller, *An African Volk*, 69.

109. Secretary for external affairs to all South African representatives abroad, November 15, 1955, SANA, BNY, 15/3–16/1, vol. 9, 1.

110. W.C. Du Plessis to Secretary for External Affairs, October 3, 1957, SANA, SAB, BTS, 1/33/13, vol. 2, *Negro Problem in USA, 1953–1958*, 4.

111. Ibid., 4.

112. Borstelmann, *Apartheid's Reluctant Uncle*, 12.

113. In 1950, the Republican senator and U.S. ambassador to the United Nations Henry Cabot Lodge Jr. referred to American race relations as "our Achilles heel before the world." See Borstelmann, *Cold War and the Color Line*, 76.

Chapter Three

1. For an excellent discussion of the cultural and political significance of black South African jazz artists in exile, see Ansell, *Soweto Blues*, and Castledine, "Gender, Jazz, and Justice."

2. For more information on how travel enabled people of African descent to make black international connections in the Cold War world, see Von Eschen, *Satchmo Blows Up the World*.

3. Ansell, *Soweto Blues*, 226–227.

4. "Xhosa Songstress," *New York Times Magazine*, November 4, 1959, 34.

5. "South African Singer Set for TV Debut," *Los Angeles Sentinel*, May 5, 1960; Al Monroe, "Good, Yes! But Even Belafonte Can Flounder When Time Rules," *Chicago Defender*, December 17, 1960; Jesse H. Walker. "Theatricals," *New York Amsterdam*, November 28, 1959.

6. For Makeba's relationship with black activists and the civil rights movement in the United States, see Feldstein, *How It Feels to Be Free*, chap. 2, and Castledine, "Gender, Jazz, and Justice."

7. "Students Here Mourn South African Victims," *New York Amsterdam News*, April 23, 1960, 5; "Top Stars to Help African Students," *New York Amsterdam News*, April 23, 1960, 15; "One Day They'll Kill That South African Lion," *Washington Post*, April 25, 1960, 5; "Crossing the Culture Bridge between U.S. and Africa," *Chicago*

Defender Magazine, April 30, 1963, 9; "Miriam Makeba, at U.N., Scores South African Race 'Nightmare': Singer Moves Delegates with Plea to 'Open Jail Doors'—Asks Arms Boycott," *New York Times*, July 17, 1963; "Makeba Asks UN Boycott Against South Africa," *Atlanta Daily World*, March 26, 1963.

8. Iton, *In Search of the Black Fantastic*, 8.

9. Ibid.

10. Feldstein, *How It Feels to Be Free*, 54.

11. Ansell, *Soweto Blues*, 226.

12. Ibid.

13. This harassment was prompted, in Makeba's eyes, by the fact that she testified before the U.N. General Assembly against apartheid in 1963 and as a result of her controversial marriage to SNCC leader and Black Power icon Stokeley Carmichael; see Castledine, "Gender, Jazz, and Justice," 237.

14. For more on the State Department's regulation on black travel during the Cold War, see Lovelace, "William Worthy's Passport," 107–31.

15. The other non–South African actors included the African American Charles McCrae as well as the West Indian performers Edric Connor and Vivian Clinton. Goudsouzian, *Sidney Poitier*, 79; Paton, *Journey Continued*, 41.

16. Lee was known for playing strong, militant black characters such as Bigger Thomas and the Haitian General Christophe. Smith, *Becoming Something*, 63–65, 74–93, 147–150.

17. Ibid., 291–292.

18. Dolinar, *Black Cultural Front*, 64–68; Gill, *No Surrender! No Retreat!*, 124–125; Von Eschen, *Race against Empire*, 65.

19. Canada Lee to Frances Lee, August 3, 1950, Canada Lee Papers Microfilm, Reel 1, Folder 14.

20. "Canada Lee Surveys Life in Union," *Rand Daily Mail*, November 8, 1950; "South Africa Is Not a Bad Place, Actor Canada Lee Says in Letter," *Chicago Defender*, December 2, 1950, 21.

21. Pendennis, "Table Talk," *Observer*, December 17, 1950, 5.

22. "Special Bulletin: 'Cry, the Beloved Country,'" January 1, 1951, SANA, BWA, vol. 28, 39/1, 3.

23. Von Eschen, *Race against Empire*, 110–112.

24. Iton, *In Search of the Black Fantastic*, 38.

25. This is a reference to Paul Gilroy's framework of the black Atlantic, which he has used to identify how black culture and identities have been shaped by a range of transnational political and cultural exchanges throughout the Atlantic world. Gilroy, *Black Atlantic*.

26. Gill, *No Surrender! No Retreat!*, 128; Smith, *Becoming Something*, 248–250.

27. Lorraine Hansberry, "The Case of the Invisible Force: Images of the Negro in Hollywood Films," *New Foundations Student Magazine* (1952), Lorraine Hansberry Papers, Box 58, Folder 3.

28. The anti-apartheid press in South Africa were also highly critical of Paton's novel and Korda's subsequent film version. See "Cry, the Beloved Country," *Guardian*, November 2, 1950.

29. Hansberry, "The Case of the Invisible Force."

30. Nixon, *Homelands, Harlem, and Hollywood*, 26; Vlies, " 'Local' Writing, 'Global' Reading."

31. Horne, *Final Victim of the Blacklist*, 222–224.

32. Ellapen, "The Cinematic Township," 113–115.

33. Memo from secretary for native affairs to state information officer, c. January, 1949, SANA, Department of Native Affairs (hereafter NTS), vol. 9474, 16/400(23).

34. Ibid.

35. Sir Alexander Korda to Dr. A. L. Geyer, High Commissioner for the Union of South Africa, "Special Bulletin: 'Cry, the Beloved Country,' " SANA, BWA, vol. 28, 39/1, 2.

36. At this meeting it was also agreed that a finished version of the script would be sent to Pretoria for final approval; see Julian Mockford to chief of Film Services, May 3, 1950, SANA, BWA, vol. 26, 30/4/1, 30/5/2.

37. Robeson was still able to travel abroad at the time of filming, although the State Department would eventually revoke his passport from 1950 to 1958.

38. H. T. Andrews to D. D. Forsyth, secretary for external affairs, February 21, 1949, SANA, BWA, vol. 26, 30/4/1, 30/5/2.

39. Mockford to chief of Film Services, May 3, 1950.

40. Von Eschen, "Who's the Real Ambassador?," 120.

41. Poitier, *This Life*, 147–148.

42. Mitchell, *Black Drama*, 148.

43. bell hooks, "Representing Whiteness in the Black Imagination," 344.

44. Wright, *Black Power*; Thompson, *Africa, Land of My Fathers*.

45. Canada Lee to Frances Lee, August 2, 1950, Canada Lee Papers, Reel 1, Folder 14.

46. Canada Lee to Frances Lee, September 11, 1950, Canada Lee Papers, Reel 1, Folder 15.

47. Canada Lee to Frances Lee, August 4, 1950, Canada Lee Papers, Reel 1, Folder 14.

48. When shooting on location in Natal, Lee made regular trips with a number of nonwhite South African friends to Durban to watch local prizefights. Canada Lee to Frances Lee, September 9, 1950, Canada Lee Papers, Reel 1, Folder 15.

49. Jack Swinburne (British Lion Production Assets, Ltd.) to Zoltan Korda, "Special Bulletin: 'Cry, the Beloved Country,' " January 12, 1951, SANA, BWA, vol. 28, 39/1, 4; "Negro Actors Coming to S.A. for 'Cry' Film," *Rand Daily Mail*, July 20, 1950; "Negro Film Actor Speaks Up about South Africa," *Guardian*, June 14, 1951.

50. Poitier, *This Life*, 51.

51. Ibid., 151.

52. Ibid., 2.

53. Canada Lee to Frances Lee, October 3, 1950, Canada Lee Papers, Reel 1, Folder 15.

54. Walter Christmas, "Explosive Social Currents Hamper Movie Making in South Africa," *Freedom*, March 1951; "Negro Film Actor Speaks Up."

55. "Negro Film Actor Speaks Up."

56. Poitier, *This Life*, 167, 179; Fred Hift, "Negro Impressions of South Africa," *New York Times*, April 22, 1951, 97.

57. "Negro Film Actor Speaks Up."

58. Bosley Crowther, "The Screen in Review: Alan Paton's 'Cry, the Beloved Country,' with Canada Lee, Opens at Bijou Theatre," *New York Times*, January 14, 1952.

59. George Houser to Dr. J. S. Moroka, March 5, 1952, ACOA Records, Part 2, Reel 1, Frame 3; Smith, *Becoming Something*, 337–338.

60. American Committee on Africa, "Brush Off by South African Consul General—Demonstration to Be Held as Scheduled," c. 1952, ACOA Records, Part 2, Reel 10, Frame 802.

61. Meriwether, *Proudly We Can Be Africans*, chap. 3.

62. Z. K. Matthews, *Freedom for My People*, 160.

63. Masilela, "The 'Black Atlantic' and African Modernity"; Chrisman, "Rethinking Black Atlanticism," 16.

64. Frieda Matthews, interview, November 26, 1981, Gaborone, Botswana, South African Institute of Race Relations Oral History, AD1722, Historical Papers, University of Witwatersrand.

65. Z. K. Matthews, *Freedom for My People*, 95–97; Frieda Bokwe Matthews, *Remembrances*.

66. Z. K. Matthews, *Freedom for My People*, 95–97.

67. Walter Sisulu and Y. A. Cachalia to George Houser, July 21, 1952, ACOA Records, Part 2, Reel 1, Frame 62.

68. For Houser's correspondence with Matthews, see ACOA Records, Part 2, Reel 1.

69. For White's correspondence with Matthews, see NAACP Records, 1940–1955, Manuscripts Division, Library of Congress, Part 2, Box A7, General Office File, Africa, South Africa, Z. K. Matthews, 1952–1953.

70. Yergan was resident at Fort Hare, Alice, from 1922 to 1936; see J. J. Coetzee to Commissioner for Immigration, April 14, 1938, SANA, SAB, NTS, 7601, 7/328, Max Yergan file, 1946–1957; Anthony, *Max Yergan*, 100.

71. Betty Radford, "Grinding Poverty and Hunger in the Ciskei," *Guardian*, November 15, 1945; "Join the Council on African Affairs: You Can Help" (pamphlet, 1949), NAACP Records, 1940–1955, Part 2, Box A4, General Office File, Africa, General, 1947–1949.

72. William Alphaeus Hunton to W. E. B. Du Bois, December 1, 1952, Du Bois Papers, Manuscripts Division, Library of Congress, Reel 68, Frame 202. In this correspondence Hunton writes to Du Bois that Matthews is willing to accept his invitation to attend an evening at his home with close friends, an evening where it is hoped that guests will have the opportunity to meet the Matthewses and "contribute to the South African cause." Hunton also provides Du Bois with Matthews's address and telephone number in New York.

73. On the Matthewses' speaking engagements in the United States, see Richard Lincoln, "Black South African Forced Back Home," *New York Amsterdam News*, May 23, 1953; "African Leaders to Lecture at Institute," *Atlanta Daily World*, July 11, 1952; "Negro History Week Opens," *New York Amsterdam News*, February 7, 1953; Walter White, "Africa and Its People Are Far from Being as Primitive as Some Think," *Chicago Defender*, April 4, 1953; "Dinner Meet to Hear Dr. Z. K. Matthews," *New York Amsterdam News*, April 18, 1953; Americans for South African Resistance, "South African Elections and Resistance Campaign. Speaker: Z. K. Matthews," April 22, 1953, ACOA Records, Manuscripts Division, Library of Congress, Part 2, Reel 3, Frame 356.

74. Z. K. Matthews, *Freedom for My People*, 160.

75. Richard Lincoln, " 'This Century Belongs to Africa,' It's Warned," *New York Amsterdam News*, November 29, 1952.

76. "Says Malan Oppression Fires Revolt," *Chicago Defender*, December 13, 1952; Lincoln, " 'This Century Belongs to Africa' "; "Z. K. Matthews' Son Among Convicted S. Africans," *New York Amsterdam News*, April 11, 1953; Z. K. Matthews, "Special Issue on Africa," *Freedom*, June 1953; Z. K. Matthews, "The South African Crisis: Statement by Professor Z. K. Matthews," *AFSAR Bulletin*, October 1952, A. Philip Randolph Papers, Manuscripts Division, Library of Congress, Box 3, Subject File, *Americans for South African Resistance 1952–1953*.

77. "Rev. Scott Asks UN to Hear S. African," *New York Amsterdam News*, November 8, 1952; Paul Robeson and William Alphaeus Hunton to Alexis Kyrou, Chairman of the (Special) Political Committee of the UN, November 11, 1952, William Alphaeus Hunton Papers, Reel 1.

78. Frieda Matthews, *Remembrances*, 23–24.

79. Ibid., 27–28; Ransby, *Eslanda*, 106–7.

80. Gore, *Radicalism at the Crossroads*.

81. Castledine, " 'In a Solid Bond of Unity' "; McDuffie, *Sojourning for Freedom*, 178–181.

82. Higashida, *Black Internationalist Feminism*, 25.

83. Conrad Norton (Press Office, NY consul) to Secretary of External Affairs (Pretoria), January 13, 1953, SANA, BTS, 35/4/3, *U.S. Perceptions of SWA, 1952–1956*.

84. Special correspondent, "S.A. and US Govts. Tried to Bully Prof. Matthews: Frightened of Revelations Before United Nations," *Advance*, December 4, 1952, 7.

85. Ibid.

86. Houser, interview with Lisa Brock.

87. Ibid.

88. Robeson and Hunton to Kyrou, November 11, 1952.

89. Richard Lincoln, "Detectives Give S. African Educator Rough Welcome," *New York Amsterdam News*, May 20, 1953.

90. Department of Interior (Pretoria) to Consul General (New York), April 9, 1953. SANA, BNY, 8/1–12/17, vol. 4.

91. Lincoln, "Detectives Give S. African Educator Rough Welcome"; Z. K. Matthews to Mr. Whyte, April 1, 1954, Records of the SAIRR, Part 2, Manuscripts Division, Library of Congress, File 41; Americans for South African Resistance, "Bulletin: Americans for South African Resistance," July 7, 1953, ACOA Records, Part 2, Reel 3, Frame 326–331.

92. Ibid.

93. Walter White to NAACP Board Members, April 14, 1953, NAACP Records, 1940–1955, Part 2, Box A7, General Office File, Africa, South Africa, Matthews, Z. K., 1952–1953.

94. "No 'Welcome Home' for Prof. Matthews," *Advance*, May 28, 1953, 7.

95. Z. K. Matthews to George Houser, July 9, 1953, ACOA Records, Part 2, Reel 1, Frame 157–158; Z. K. Matthews to Walter White, August 18, 1953, NAACP Records, 1940–1955, Part 2, Box A7, General Office File, Africa, South Africa, General, 1950–1953.

96. Lincoln, "Detectives Give S. African Educator Rough Welcome."

97. Ibid.

98. Z. K. Matthews, *Freedom for My People*, 184.

99. Ibid.

100. In 1955 Z. K. was accused of high treason. He also lost his job at Fort Hare University, resigning his post in protest of government restrictions on black admissions at the institution; see ibid., 197.

101. For more on diaspora and black international history, see Edwards, *The Practice of Diaspora*; Gilroy, *Black Atlantic*; Patterson and Kelley, "Unfinished Migrations," 11–45.

102. Horne, *Black and Red*; Horne, *Cold War in a Hot Zone*.

103. As Robin D. G. Kelley has noted, "To conceive of hegemony without placing struggle at the center . . . is to reduce the concept to a theory of consensus"; see "An Archaeology of Resistance," 295.

104. Robeson was refused his passport between 1950 and 1958; Paul Robeson, "Passport Case Statement," c. 1955, Paul and Eslanda Robeson Collection, MSRC, Box 20, 2.

105. An oft-cited example of Robeson's criticism of the United States when abroad is his 1949 statement delivered at the World Peace Conference in Paris, in which he was reported to have claimed that it would have been "unthinkable" for African Americans to take up arms in any future war with the Soviet Union. "Robeson Assails Stettinius," *New York Times*, April 21, 1949. For a detailed account of

Eslanda Robeson's passport problems, see Ransby, *Eslanda*, esp. chap. 12. Jordan Goodman also offers a detailed analysis of Robeson's legal efforts to win back his passport from the State Department in *Paul Robeson*, 191–261.

106. Torpey, *Invention of the Passport*, 1–13.

107. Of course, the ability to access a passport hasn't always been, and indeed still isn't, a legal marker of citizenship. The obvious point to make here is that you can be born in a particular place, never claim a passport, and still be considered a citizen of that country. The U.S. government made this very point in response to Edward Snowden's claims that he has been left "stateless" following the withdrawal of his passport in 2013. Robeson, however, always insisted that the ability to claim a passport was indeed a key aspect of American citizenship.

108. "Robeson Offered Passport in Exchange for Silence Abroad," *California Eagle*, August 11, 1950, 2.

109. Lloyd L. Brown, "State Dept. Says African Freedom 'Against Best Interests of U.S.,'" *Freedom*, April 1952, 5; "Robeson Demands Passport: Cancelled Because of Support for African People," *New Age*, March 10, 1955; "A Lesson from Our South African Brothers and Sisters," *Freedom*, September 1952, in *Paul Robeson Speaks*, 326.

110. Paul Robeson, "Passport Case Statement," 2; Robeson, *Here I Stand*, 3–74.

111. Jordan Goodman, *Paul Robeson*, 222; Meriwether, *Proudly We Can Be Africans*, 85; Swindall, *Paul Robeson*, especially chap. 5; Horne, *Paul Robeson*, chap. 7.

112. Lloyd L. Brown, "State Dept. Says African Freedom 'Against Best Interests of U.S.,'" *Freedom*, April 1952, 5.

113. William L. Patterson to John Gates, June 11, 1956, Communist Party of the USA (CPUSA) Papers, Individual Records Group, William L. Patterson, Tamiment Library/Robert F. Wagner Labor Archives, New York University, TAM 132.4, Box 1, 1–2.

114. William L. Patterson, "Circular to Foreign Leaders," 1955, Paul and Eslanda Robeson Collection, Reel 6, Frame 132–134, 3. Robeson was invited to Bandung but was unable to attend due to his passport situation.

115. Paul Robeson, "Here's My Story: The Constitutional Right to Travel," *Freedom*, July–August 1955, in *Paul Robeson Speaks*, 406.

116. Paul Robeson, "Statement by Paul Robeson to the Peoples of Africa," n.d. Paul and Eslanda Robeson Collection, Reel 7, Frame 127–130, 1.

117. Lloyd L. Brown, "Lift Every Voice for Paul Robeson," November 1951, Doxey Wilkerson Papers, Schomburg Center for Research in Black Culture, Box 7, Folder 3.

118. Robeson, "A Lesson from Our South African Brothers and Sisters"; Robeson, "Here's My Story," 326.

119. Freedom of movement is not a right that is explicitly protected by the U.S. Constitution.

120. Robeson, *Here I Stand*, 74–75.

121. Ibid.

122. Paul Robeson, "Press Release: Importance of Travel," 1954, Paul and Eslanda Robeson Collection, Reel 6, Frame 933–935, 1.

123. Rodriguez, *Slavery in the United States*, 301–302; Horton and Horton, *Hard Road to Freedom*, 152; Harrold, *Rise of Aggressive Abolitionism*, chap. 5; Foner, *Free Soil, Free Labor, Free Men*, 134–135.

124. Paul Robeson, "Passport Case Statement."

125. Robeson, *Here I Stand*, 73–74.

126. Shirley Graham Du Bois, *Paul Robeson, Citizen of the World*. In his writings Robeson also regularly adopted Shirley Graham Du Bois's description and referred to himself as a both cosmopolitan figure and a "citizen of the world"; see Robeson, *Here I Stand*, 56–57, and Robeson, "Speech to the NCASF Rally," November 16, 1954, Paul and Eslanda Robeson Collection, Reel 8, Frame 769–775.

127. South African and West African students (London) to Paul Robeson, April 21, 1954, Paul and Eslanda Robeson Collection, Reel 6, Frame 558.

128. Robeson received messages of support and assistance from around the world in relation to his passport case. This included other nations of Africa, where emergent black states such as Ghana and Nigeria were particularly vocal in their support; see "Press Release: Planning Committee for a Cultural Salute to Paul Robeson," May 24, 1954, Paul and Eslanda Robeson Collection, Reel 6, Frame 944–945; Nnmandi Azikiwe to William Alphaeus Hunton, February 25, 1958, Paul and Eslanda Robeson Collection, MSRC, Box 39; Kwame Nkrumah to Eslanda Goode Robeson, September 7, 1960, Paul and Eslanda Robeson Collection, MSRC, Box 6, Correspondence, Mb–Pe.

129. In my archival research I came across the following articles in South African publications that heavily featured the political and cultural activities of Robeson: "Robeson to Aid Treason Fund," *New Age*, September 25, 1958; "Robeson Acclaimed All Over Britain," *New Age*, August 28, 1958; "Robeson Is Free," *New Age*, July 3, 1958; " 'Let Robeson Sing' Demand British People: American Negro Singer's Voice Heard by Cable," *New Age*, June 13, 1957; "Paul Robeson Faces Prison Sentence: Describes Interrogators as 'Murderers of My People,' " *Guardian*, June 28, 1956; A. M. Kathrada, "Towards A Cultural Boycott of South Africa," *Liberation*, June 1956, 18; "Editorial," *Liberation*, September 1955, 3; Sidney Finkelstein, "Africa and World Music," *Fighting Talk*, June 1955, 14; Paul Robeson, "Robeson 'Discovers' Africa," *Fighting Talk*, April 1955, 4; Paul Robeson, "Robeson's Message to the ANC," *New Age*, December 23, 1954; "World-Wide Campaign to Free Paul Robeson," *Advance*, June 10, 1954, 6; "Robeson Pledges U.S. Support for April 6," *Guardian*, March 13, 1952; "Robeson's Crime—He Sang," *Guardian*, September 22, 1949; Derek Kartun, "Paul Robeson Hits Back," *Guardian*, April 21, 1949; Sheila Lynd, "So Robeson Joined the People's Fight," *Guardian*, April 28, 1949; "Mrs. Paul Robeson," *Guardian*, October 18, 1945; "Robeson Cables Atlee," *Guardian*, September 17, 1945.

130. Kay, "Robeson Popular in Prague," *Guardian*, June 9, 1949; "Robeson Demands Passport: Cancelled Because of Support for African People," *New Age*, March 10, 1955; Paul Robeson, "Robeson 'Discovers' Africa," *Fighting Talk*, April 1955, 4; "Editorial," *Liberation*, September 1955, 3; "Paul Robeson Faces Prison

Sentence: Describes Interrogators as 'Murderers of My People,'" 7; "Robeson Is Free," *New Age*, July 3, 1958.

131. Eslanda Goode Robeson, "Robeson: The World's Symbol of Freedom," *Freedom*, April 1952, 1.

132. The Committee to Restore Paul Robeson's Passport, "The People of the World Want to See and Hear Paul Robeson," n.d., Paul and Eslanda Robeson Collection, Reel 8, Frame 908, 1.

133. ANC and South African Congress to Paul Robeson, c. 1954, Paul and Eslanda Robeson Collection, Reel 6, Frame 560. The signatories included Walter Sisulu, J. L. Patse, T. T. Govenho, Ivan Scheombaucher, G. Broola, Arnold Selby, A. M. Kathrada, W. Kramer, S. I. Gangat, Sulman Esakjee, Ursula Goodgall, Hoosu Hoolla, E. Hoodle, G. Pochie, A. Jassat, R. M. Pillay, H. Joseph, Ismael Noola, Jack Hodgson, H. Hoydon, T. Tandui, Barmey Desai, A. Sulioson, G. W. Berry, Y. Sachalio, and Poppy Ransat.

134. "World-Wide Campaign to Free Paul Robeson," *Advance*, June 10, 1954, 6.

135. Singh, *Black Is a Country*; Melamed, *Represent and Destroy*, introduction and chap. 1.

136. World-Wide Campaign to Free Paul Robeson," *Advance*, June 10, 1954, 6.

137. Council on African Affairs, "CAA Statement: On Paul Robeson's Passport," n.d., Paul and Eslanda Robeson Collection, Reel 2, Frame 583–564, 1.

138. Simon Hall, *American Patriotism, American Protest*.

139. Robeson, *Here I Stand*, 63.

140. Derek Kartun, "Paul Robeson Hits Back," *Guardian*, April 21, 1949.

141. "The Annual Report of the National Executive Committee to the 42nd Annual Conference of the African National Congress Held at the Bantu Social Centre, Durban on the 16th to the 19th December, 1954," December 1954, Jack and Ray Simons Collection, Manuscripts and Archives, University of Cape Town, Folder P13.1, 3.

142. "Defiance of Malan Over 'Unjust' Laws Set in South Africa," *New York Times*, April 7, 1952.

143. "We Can Learn from the Struggle in South Africa," *Freedom*, July 1952.

144. Paul Robeson, "The Annual Report of the National Executive Committee to the 42nd Annual Conference of the African National Congress," 1954, Jack and Ray Simons Collection, Manuscripts and Archives, University of Cape Town, Folder P13.1.

Chapter Four

1. As the historian James Campbell has noted, cultural transactions between the United States and South Africa enabled individuals in both countries to develop "new ways of understanding and acting upon their worlds." See *Race, Nation, & Empire*, 235.

2. Sonja Laden and Tsitsi Ella Jaji are the notable exceptions here. Laden's work on the importance of consumer magazines to black South African culture in the

twentieth century includes an excellent analysis of *Zonk!* magazine in the 1950s. See Laden, "'Making the Paper Speak Well,'" and Jaji, *Africa in Stereo*, chap. 4.

3. Chapman, *The "Drum" Decade*, 194. For recent work on *Drum* magazine, see Clowes, "'Are You Going to Be MISS (or MR) Africa?'"; Clowes, "Masculinity, Matrimony and Generation"; Helgesson, "Shifting Fields"; Odhiambo, "Inventing Africa in the Twentieth Century"; Rauwerda, "Whitewashing *Drum* Magazine (1951–1959)"; Vlies, "'Local' Writing, 'Global' Reading, and the Demands of the 'Canon.'"

4. *Zonk!* was owned by the Jewish businessman Ike Baruch Brooks.

5. Abrahams, *Return to Goli*, 143.

6. South African Library Association, *Suid-Afrikaanse Biblioteke*, 88.

7. Recent studies have begun to explore how African American culture in *Zonk!* influenced definitions of what it meant to be both black and modern in South Africa. While this work has started to trace the ways in which these key cultural exchanges shaped black responses to apartheid, there is still a general need to assess how this consumerist form of internationalism shaped the relationship between black South Africans and black America during the 1950s. See Jaji, *Africa in Stereo*; Laden, "'Making the Paper Speak Well'"; and Laden, "Who's Afraid of a Black Bourgeoisie?"

8. Thomas, "Skin Lighteners," 264.

9. Laden, "Who's Afraid of a Black Bourgeoisie?," 196–197.

10. Jaji, *Africa in Stereo*, chap. 4.

11. Ibid., 117. Jaji's concept of "sheen reading" as an interpretative strategy that emphasizes the agency of the reader in relation to African consumer magazines is important here.

12. By consuming these images black South Africans were not simply buying into notions of white privilege, as Antje M. Rauwerda suggests in her discussion of the "whitewashing" effect of advertisements in *Drum* magazine. While it is important to account for the power differentials and racial hierarchies that shaped the black print media in South Africa, such a view underplays the reader's capacity for critical engagement with this material that could lead to a questioning of the structural frameworks that allowed racial inequalities to flourish under apartheid. See Rauwerda, "Whitewashing *Drum* Magazine (1951–1959)."

13. As Jaji concludes her discussion of black consumer culture in the pages of *Zonk!* magazine, "The promised fruits of development were offered with the supplemental glare of a requirement to accommodate the demands of racist capitalist exploitation as domestic and industrial labor. All that glittered was not gold, nor did all sheen shine true," *Africa in Stereo*, 123.

14. Ibid., 119.

15. "Be really refreshed—sparkle with Coca-Cola," *Zonk!*, February 1960, 36.

16. Luthuli, *Let My People Go*, 82.

17. Nixon, *Homelands, Harlem, and Hollywood*.

18. Davarian Baldwin, *Chicago's New Negroes*, 7–8; Wilson, "Race in Commodity Exchange and Consumption," 603.

19. Crankshaw, "Class, Race and Residence," 355.

20. Beinart and Dubow, *Segregation and Apartheid*, 11; Rodney Davenport, "African Townsmen?"

21. Ibid., 220.

22. Beinart and Dubow, *Segregation and Apartheid*, 16; Grubbs, " 'Workshop of a Continent,' " 411; Maylam, "The Rise and Decline of Urban Apartheid," 70.

23. Dubow, *Scientific Racism*, 170; Ferguson, "Formalities of Poverty," 73; Hickel, "Engineering the Township Home," 132–133.

24. Cell, *Highest Stage of White Supremacy*, 224.

25. Dubow, *Scientific Racism*, 170.

26. Ibid., 249; Bonner, "African Urbanisation on the Rand."

27. Hickel, "Engineering the Township Home," 153.

28. Alan Baldwin, "Mass Removals and Separate Development," 215; Mabin, "Comprehensive Segregation"; Maylam, "The Rise and Decline of Urban Apartheid."

29. Hickel, "Engineering the Township Home," 132–133.

30. Demissie, "Controlling and 'Civilising Natives,' " 485; Parnell and Mabin, "Rethinking Urban South Africa"; Hickel, "Engineering the Township Home," 142–143.

31. Hickel, "Social Engineering and Revolutionary Consciousness," 309.

32. Ibid., 314–315.

33. Demissie, "Controlling and 'Civilising Natives,' " 493, 501.

34. W. W. M. Eiselen, cited in Haarhoff, "Appropriating Modernism," 5.

35. Hickel, "Engineering the Township Home," 143, 153.

36. "The American Family Insists on the Very Best," *Hi-Note*, August 1956.

37. "Meet Clifford Brown: American Businessman," *Drum*, April 17, 1956; "Meet Clara Brown: American Housewife," *Drum*, April 17, 1956; "The American Family," *Hi-Note*, August 1956; "This Young American Medical Student Knows What's Good," *World*, February 2, 1952.

38. Demissie, "Controlling and 'Civilising' Natives," 494.

39. Indeed, when it came to the issues of urban housing and the African family, government officials stressed the "effectiveness" of their scientific development policies in order to defend apartheid overseas. See South African Government Information Office, *The Union of South Africa*, (1957); H. F. Verwoerd, "Uplifting the Bantu: The Blueprint for Self-Realisation as a Nation," *South African-American Survey*, 1955–1956.

40. Jaji, *Africa in Stereo*, 119.

41. *Zonk!* was also available in the United States. In a report that compared Howard University to Fort Hare, Mordecai Johnson, Howard's president, stated, "I have read your issues with very great interest and I am making it available in the library of the University so that our students may become acquainted with ZONK! and her friends." See "Howard University Is to American Negroes What Fort Hare Is to African Students," *Zonk!*, November 1949, 24–25. For more on the

racial politics of *Ebony* and Johnson Publishing, see Green, *Selling the Race*, chap. 4.

42. "Zonk! Director Visits Ebony," *Zonk!*, December 1957, 29.

43. "A Future in America, Not Africa," *Ebony*, July 1947, 40.

44. Some of the magazine's stories that focused on the "exoticism" and "mystery" of Africa include "Kings of Jump," *Ebony*, March 1946, 26–27; "African Influence on Fashion," *Ebony*, June 1948, 50; Griffith Davis, "The Private Life of Emperor Selassie," *Ebony*, November 1950, 14–19; Era Bell Thompson, "Kings of the Tallest Men by Era Bell Thompson," *Ebony*, October 1954, 116–118.

45. "African Art for Americans," *Ebony*, November 1945, 10–12; "Africa's Greatest Artist," *Ebony*, 27–29.

46. "African Art for Americans," *Ebony*, November 1945, 10.

47. "His Majesty Jim Crow: Race Discrimination in South Africa Is Worst in the World," *Ebony*, April 1946, 13–15; "A Spectre Haunts the Empire Builders," *Ebony*, June 1946, 40–41; Seretse Khama, "Why I Gave Up My Throne for Love," *Ebony*, June 1951, 32–29; "Africa's Quiet Revolution," *Ebony*, June 1952, 94–98; "How to Stop the Mau Mau," *Ebony*, March 1953, 88–89; "The World's No. 1 Race Problem, South Africa," *Ebony*, May 1954, 90–91; Peter Abrahams, "Death of a College," *Ebony*, May 1955, 49–56; "Ten Biggest Lies about Africa," *Ebony*, May 1957, 58–59; "Dark Leaders of the World," *Ebony*, March 1958, 24–26, 29; "Dr Aggrey: Father of African Education," *Ebony*, April 1959, 45–49; "Nigeria Unshackled," *Ebony*, October 1960, 25–32.

48. First black Wimbledon champion—Althea Gibson; First black Major League Baseball player—Jackie Robinson; First African American Nobel Prize winner—Ralph Bunche. "Althea Is World's No. 1 Woman Tennis Player: New York Gives Her Traditional 'Hero's Welcome,'" *Zonk!*, August 1957, 15; "American Personality: Meet Jackie Robinson," *Zonk!*, June 1950, 3; "First Negro Wins Nobel Peace Prize," *Zonk!*, December 1950, 42–43.

49. George B. Evans, "Lena Horne Is a Great Artist," *Zonk!*, August 1949, 40.

50. "Jet Pilot!," *Zonk!*, December 1955, 27.

51. "Wonder Boy of Baseball," *Zonk!*, November 1954, 25–26.

52. Joe Louis, "How to Box by Joe Louis," *Zonk!*, July, 1950, 14–15; Joe Louis, "How to Box," *Zonk!*, August 1950, 14–15; "News from Abroad," *Zonk!*, April 1953, 11.

53. Nixon, *Homelands, Harlem, and Hollywood*, 4, 30; Campbell, "The Americanization of South Africa," 35; Matshikiza, *Chocolates for My Wife*; Modisane, *Blame Me on History*; Themba, *The Will to Die*.

54. Glaser, *Bo Tsotsi*, 69, 177.

55. Campbell, "The Americanization of South Africa," 35.

56. Chrisman, "Rethinking Black Atlanticism," 14.

57. Ibid.

58. Gaines, *American Africans in Ghana*, 29.

59. Chrisman, *Postcolonial Contraventions*, 90–91.

60. Masilela, "The 'Black Atlantic' and African Modernity," 90. Kemp and Vinson, "'Poking Holes in the Sky.'" See also Vinson's work on how Garveyism influenced the lives of black South Africans in the 1930s and 1950s, in *Americans Are Coming!*, esp. chap. 5 and 6.

61. Chrisman, *Postcolonial Contraventions*, 90–92.

62. Gilroy, *Black Atlantic*.

63. Hanchard, "Afro-Modernity," 253.

64. Ibid., 247.

65. Ibid., 267–268.

66. "Picture News from the U.S.A.," *Zonk!*, October 1952, 14.

67. Ibid.; "Picture News from the U.S.A.," *Zonk!*, June 1952, 15.

68. For scholarship on racial respectability in the American context, see Davarian Baldwin, *Chicago's New Negroes*, esp. chap. 1; Harris, "Gatekeeping and Remaking"; Higginbotham, *Righteous Discontent*, esp. chap. 7; Wolcott, *Remaking Respectability*.

69. Goodhew, "Working-Class Respectability"; Goodhew, *Respectability and Resistance*, 168.

70. Thomas, "The Modern Girl and Racial Respectability," 467.

71. "American Letter: Lena Horne," *Zonk!*, August 1949, 4.

72. Feldstein, *How It Feels to Be Free*.

73. C. B. Powell, "American Letter," *Zonk!*, September 1949, 5; Adam Clayton Powell, "American Letter: Adam Clayton Powell and Hazel Scott," *Zonk!*, December 1949, 3.

74. For some background on Marian Anderson's opposition to segregation, see Sandage, "A Marble House Divided." For more on Adam Clayton Powell Jr.'s political career at home and abroad, see Hamilton, *Adam Clayton Powell, Jr.*, esp. chap. 7–15; Matthew Jones, "A 'Segregated' Asia?," 863–865. For an overview of Hazel Scott's career and political activism, see Mack, "Hazel Scott."

75. Keiler, *Marian Anderson*, chap. 10.

76. Marian Anderson, "American Letter," *Zonk!*, October 1949, 5.

77. Gonny Govender, "Wimbledon's Tennis Queen Talks to Zonk!! Gonny Govender Interviews Althea Gibson," *Zonk!*, September 1958, 17.

78. Pinocchio Mokaleng was a regular on the Sophiatown jazz scene and founder of the Odin Cinema's Modern Jazz Sessions. He left South Africa in 1958 after the authorities refused to renew his pass. See Ansell, *Soweto Blues*, 134; Mattera, *Memory Is the Weapon*, 94–98.

79. Von Eschen, *Satchmo Blows Up the World*, chap. 3.

80. Ibid., 250.

81. Gonny Govender, "Satchmo Interviewed by Zonk!'s Gonny Govender," *Zonk!*, June 1959, 36.

82. Huddleston, *Naught for Your Comfort*, chap. 7.

83. Govender, "Satchmo Interviewed," 57.

84. Gilroy, *Black Atlantic*, 36.

85. Von Eschen, *Satchmo Blows Up the World*, 20; Lemke, *Primitivist Modernism*, chap. 3.

86. Kelley, *Africa Speaks, America Answers*, 4–5.

87. Von Eschen, *Satchmo Blows Up the World*, 256.

88. Modisane, *Blame Me on History*, 174.

89. Ibid.

90. Titlestad, "Traveling Jazz," 73.

91. Muller, "Musical Echoes of American Jazz," 62. Also see Kelley, *Africa Speaks, America Answers*.

92. P. G. Makaza, "Originality in Jazz?," *Zonk!*, July 1954, 53.

93. Ibid.

94. Ibid.

95. Ibid.

96. Davarian Baldwin, *Chicago's New Negroes*, 9.

97. Wilson, "Race in Commodity Exchange and Consumption," 594.

98. Masilela, "The 'Black Atlantic' and African Modernity," 90.

99. Hanchard, "Afro-Modernity," 248.

100. Makaza, "Originality in Jazz?," 53.

101. Chrisman, "Rethinking Black Atlanticism," 16.

102. This observation is influenced by Tsitsi Ella Jaji's concept of "Sheen Reading": "Sheen lay at the heart of modernity's stress on the new and consumer capitalism's fetishization of clean, shiny, polished surfaces. Indeed, advertising new technologies was one of the primary functions of the 'African pictorial magazine,' and the authoritative voice of the consumer advocates which spoke from its pages was constitutive of the popular print form. . . . At the same time, the periodicity of the magazine form betrayed the impossibility of maintaining such fetishized surfaces: in constantly advertising new products, magazines were signs of potential or rather *planned* obsolescence," *Africa in Stereo*, 117. Italics in original.

103. "Crossing the Culture Bridge between U. S. and Africa," *Chicago Defender Magazine*, April 30, 1963, 9.

Chapter Five

1. Mandela, *Long Walk to Freedom*, 233. In his autobiographical account of his life Mandela uses the evolving story of his own incarceration is an effective indicator of the changing nature of the apartheid state. Through the prison the reader is informed about the intricacies of apartheid rule and black resistance in South Africa.

2. Incarceration has been central to the operation of state power. See Foucault, *Discipline and Punish*; Rodriguez, "A Reign of Penal Terror," 202.

3. Lichtenstein, *Twice the Work of Free Labor*, esp. chap. 1 and 2; Curtin, *Black Prisoners and Their World*; Alexander, *New Jim Crow*, 22–35; Blackmon, *Slavery by Another Name*, esp. chap. 2.

4. Lichtenstein, *Twice the Work of Free Labor*, 17–18.

5. Heather Ann Thompson, "Why Mass Incarceration Matters"; Wacquant, "From Slavery to Mass Incarceration."

6. Worger, "Convict Labour, Industrialists and the State," 68.

7. Ibid., 78.

8. Ruth First, "Jo'Burg's 'Slave Market': Arrested Men 'Persuaded: To Take Farm Work,'" *Guardian*, June 2, 1945; Ruth First, "He Escaped from Slavery: Horror Conditions on Bethal Farm," *Advance*, April 16, 1953, 1, 8; Ruth First, "The Farm Labour Scandal," 1959, FSAW Records, Historical Papers, William Cullen Library, University of Witwatersrand, G2.

9. Worger, "Convict Labour, Industrialists and the State," 68.

10. Bernault, *History of Prison and Confinement*, 16.

11. Political prisoners were segregated according to their race. However, they were often housed together in different racial groups. As a result, they were sometimes able to form close personal ties and deep political solidarities while incarcerated. See Alexander, "Political Prisoners' Memoirs in Zimbabwe"; Caine, "Prisons as Spaces of Friendships"; Suttner, "Rethinking and Re-Remembering Prison."

12. Thinking of the prison in terms of a borderland, Mary Bosworth observes that "borders define who may come and who may go. . . . They are both inclusive and exclusive sites that sort the deserving from the undeserving. They set out who belongs, and who is an outsider." Bosworth, "Identity, Citizenship, and Punishment," 135.

13. Caster, *Prisons, Race, and Masculinity*, 15; Dubow, "Afrikaner Nationalism, Apartheid," 223.

14. The NAACP officially supported the Defiance Campaign and wrote to the ANC to express the organization's solidarity with the protests. See Walter White to Dr. James Moroka, April 8, 1952, NAACP Records, 1940–1955, Part 2, Box A7, General Office File, Africa, South Africa, General, 1950–1953. For more on the NAACP's anti-apartheid efforts, see Carol Anderson, *Bourgeois Radicals*, chap. 2.

15. Council on African Affairs, "An Appeal from South Africa—And How We Can Answer It," 1952, NAACP Records, 1940–1955, Part 2, Box A373; Council on African Affairs, "Campaign of the Council on African Affairs—In Aid of the Arrested Volunteers and Their Dependents in the Campaign of the Defiance of Unjust Laws in South Africa," January 20, 1953, NAACP Records, 1940–1955, Part 2, Box A373, General Office File, Leagues, Council on African Affairs, Inc. 1948–1955; William Alphaeus Hunton, "Here Are the Facts . . . You Be the Judge! The Council on African Affairs Answers Attorney General Brownell," c. November 1953, NAACP Records, 1940–1955, Part 2, Box A373, 3.

16. Ibid.

17. Ibid.

18. "World Action against S.A. Mooted: Humanity's Conscience Outraged by Apartheid," *Clarion*, August 7, 1952, 5.

19. George M. Houser to J. L. Njongwe, November 3, 1952, ACOA Records, Part 2, Reel 1, Frame 85; R. T. Bokwe to George Houser, December 30, 1952, ACOA Rec-

ords, Part 2, Reel 1, Frame 112–113; George Houser to R. T. Bokwe, April 24, 1953, ACOA Records, Part 2, Reel 1, Frame 123; "Bulletin: Americans for South African Resistance," January 14, 1953, ACOA Records, Part 2, Reel 3, Frame 312–316, 1; "Bulletin: Americans for South African Resistance," April 14, 1953, ACOA Records, Part 2, Reel 3, Frame 323–325, 3.

20. Meriwether, *Proudly We Can Be Africans*, 103.

21. Walter White to Dr. James Moroka, April 8, 1952, NAACP Records, 1940–1955. Part 2, Box A7, General Office File, Africa, South Africa, General, 1950–1953.

22. "Brush Off by South African Consul General—Demonstration to Be Held as Scheduled," c. April, ACOA Records, Part 2, Reel 10, Frame 799–803. James Lawson's United African Nationalist Movement also maintained a presence at the protest and wrote to James Moroka outlining their support for the militant action of the ANC in trying to secure freedom of black South Africans; see A. H. Mertsch, consul general to G. P. Jooste, ambassador, April 5, 1952, SANA, BTS, 35/4/3, *U.S. Perceptions of SWA*, 1952–1956.

23. Meriwether, *Proudly We Can Be Africans*, 113.

24. "World Action against S.A. Mooted: Humanity's Conscience Outraged by Apartheid," *Clarion*, August 7, 1952, 5; "Dollars Sent to Help Resistance Victims," *People's World*, October 30, 1952, 3.

25. Walter Sisulu to William Alphaeus Hunton, September 1, 1952, William Alphaeus Hunton Papers, Box 1, Frame 16; "Walter Sisulu: Message to the Negro People of the USA from the African National Congress," *Spotlight on Africa*, October 17, 1952, Schomburg Center, Robeson Papers, Reel 7, Frame 175.

26. American Committee on Africa, "Support the Non-Violent Campaign against Unjust Laws in South Africa," c. April 1953, NAACP Records, 1940–1955, Box A7, General Office File, South Africa General.

27. Martin Luther King Jr., "Circular Letter: Martin Luther King, ACOA and African Imprisonment," 1957, NCNW Records, Series 7, Box 1, Folder 2.

28. American Committee on Africa, "Apartheid Takes Ever Greater Toll in Union of South Africa," n.d., A. Philip Randolph Papers, Box 3, Subject File, Africa, American Committee on Africa, 1954–1969.

29. Frieda Matthews to George Houser, December 10, 1956, A. Philip Randolph Papers, Box 3, Subject File, Africa, American Committee on Africa, 1954–1969; Frieda Matthews to George Houser, January 17, 1957, ACOA Records, Part 2, Reel 1, Frame 552; Frieda Matthews to George Houser, March 12, 1957, ACOA Records, Part 2, Reel 1, Frame 552. Frieda Matthews also wrote to Walter White of the NAACP to appeal for assistance while Z. K. was imprisoned; see Frieda Matthews to Walter White, c. 1953, NAACP Records, 1940–1955, Part 2, Box A7, General Office File, Africa, South Africa, Matthews, Z. K., 1952–1953.

30. Luthuli, *Let My People Go*, 169.

31. Lichtenstein, "One Struggle," 3–4; Nesbitt, *Race for Sanctions*, 33–34. The ACOA's Declaration of Conscience on South Africa campaign and day of protest played an important role in mobilizing international opposition against the

Treason Trial; see James B. Carey and A. Philip Randolph, "International Sponsoring Campaign: Declaration of Conscience on South Africa and Day of Protest—December 10, 1957," 1957, ACOA Records, Part 2, Reel 5, Frame 788–789.

32. John Munro recognizes the importance of accounting for the ways in which African Americans understood anticommunism as a manifestation of imperialism "at home" in the United States. See Munro, "Imperial Anticommunism."

33. Dawson, *Blacks In and Out of the Left*, 78–86; Lieberman and Lang, *Anticommunism and the African American Freedom Movement*; Zeigler, *Red Scare Racism*.

34. Gerald Horne makes this point in his article "Race from Power," 454. Work that has gone on to examine this topic includes Kim, *Ends of Empire*, esp. chap. 1 and 2; Kwon, *Other Cold War*; Masuda, *Cold War Crucible*; Colleen Woods, "Bombs, Bureaucrats, and Rosary Beads."

35. Wald, *Writing from the Left*, chap. 6.

36. Munro, "Imperial Anticommunism," 58–59.

37. For just some of the work that emphasizes the negative effects that Cold War anticommunism had on the black freedom struggle, see Carol Anderson, *Eyes off the Prize*, 273–274; Biondi, *To Stand and Fight*, esp. chap. 7; Jacquelyn Dowd Hall, "The Long Civil Rights Movement"; Horne, "Who Lost the Cold War?"; Horne, *Black and Red*; Horne, *Black Liberation/Red Scare*; Lieberman and Lang, *Anticommunism and the African American Freedom Movement*, 5–6; McDuffie, "Black and Red," 236; McDuffie, *Sojourning for Freedom*, 163–164; Marable, *Race, Reform and Rebellion*, 18; Sugrue, *Sweet Land of Liberty*, 83; Von Eschen, *Race against Empire*, chap. 5; Washington, *Other Blacklist*, esp. the introduction; Zeigler, *Red Scare Racism*. For a dissenting voice that downplays the disruptive influence of anticommunism on the African American freedom struggle, see Arnesen, "Civil Rights and the Cold War At Home."

38. As demonstrated by the Dies Committee investigation of Mary McLeod Bethune in 1943 for suspected subversive activities. See Hanson, *Mary McLeod Bethune*, 187–188.

39. See Davies, "Deportable Subjects"; Schrecker, *Many Are the Crimes*, 292–294.

40. Winston skipped bail and went underground following the verdict. He eventually surrendered, and was released in 1961 after serving his sentence in full. Ben Davis served three years and four months of his sentence, and was later indicted under the McCarran Act in 1962. He died before the case could go to trial. Horne, *Black Liberation/Red Scare*, 265.

41. National Committee to Defend Negro Leadership, "An Appeal in Defense of Negro Leadership," n.d., Du Bois Papers, Reel 68, Frame 619–621, 2. Among the African American leaders listed as having suffered at the hands of anticommunist suppression were Benjamin L. Careathers, former vice chairman of the CPUSA in western Pennsylvania, indicted under the Smith Act at age 73; Rev. Charles A. Hill,

pastor of Hartford Avenue Baptist Church, called before HUAC in 1952; and C.I.O. organizer Coleman Young, who appeared before HUAC in 1952.

42. Brock, "The 1950s: Africa Solidarity Rising"; Adi and Sherwood, *Pan-African History*, 93.

43. Alongside the Smith Act, the McCarran Act, which was introduced in 1950 and required members of communist organizations to officially register with government, the immigration authorities, and the local police, also had important consequences for black leaders in the United States. Schrecker, *Many Are the Crimes*, 141.

44. C. L. R. James, the noted Pan-Africanist, Trotskyist writer, and activist, who had first left Britain for the United States in 1938, was arrested in 1952 and held on Ellis Island before being deported in the autumn of the following year. Claudia Jones, a CPUSA leader and staunch advocate for black women's rights, was deported from the United States in December 1955, having served a one-year prison sentence at Alderson prison, West Virginia. See Worcester, *C.L.R. James*, 109–110; Stephens, *Black Empire*, 273; Davies, "Deportable Subjects," 134–136; Pease, "Doing Justice to C. L. R. James's *Mariners, Renegades, and Castaways*."

45. Walter Goodman, *Committee*. The SACB played a prominent role in the demise of the CAA; see Von Eschen, *Race against Empire*, 135.

46. Jeff Woods, *Black Struggle, Red Scare*, 6–7. For more on the relationship between anticommunism and massive resistance, see George Lewis, *White South and the Red Menace*. For research on Southern segregationists, anticommunism, and U.S. foreign relations, see Noer, "Segregationists and the World."

47. Duberman, *Paul Robeson*, 373; Nollen, *Paul Robeson: Film Pioneer*, 164.

48. Plummer, *Rising Wind*, 196. For how antisegregationist activists Carl Braden and Theodore Gibson were threatened with contempt of Congress, see Jeff Woods, *Black Struggle, Red Scare*, 19–45.

49. Louise Thompson Patterson Circular, July 29, 1954, William L. Patterson Papers, MSRC, Collection 208, Box 5, Folder 7; Horne, *Black Revolutionary*, esp. chap. 8–10.

50. "Lynch Charge Resented by Georgia Congressman," *Atlanta Daily World*, August 5, 1950; Paul P. Kennedy, "Police Restrain House Georgian from Attacking a Negro Witness," *New York Times*, August 5, 1950; "Police Quell Rep. Lanham in Probe Clash," *Washington Post*, August 5, 1950; "Record Fails to Disclose Lanham Language Threat," *Atlanta Daily World*, August 11, 1950; "William L. Patterson Freed of Contempt Charges," *Jet*, April 3, 1952, 9; Horne, *Black Revolutionary*, 122–123.

51. Carol Anderson, *Eyes off the Prize*, 273; Manfred Berg, "Black Civil Rights and Liberal Anticommunism," 76; Horne, *Black and Red*, 234; Horne, *Black Liberation/ Red Scare*, 228; Schrecker, *Many Are the Crimes*, 393.

52. For a brilliant analysis of how anticommunism and liberalism limited the possibilities of antiracist discourse, see Melamed, *Represent and Destroy*, esp. chap. 1;

Melamed, "The Spirit of Neoliberalism"; Melamed, "W. E. B. Du Bois's UnAmerican End"; Melamed, "The Killing Joke of Sympathy," 770–772.

53. Seymour, "The Cold War, American Anticommunism," 170–171.

54. "Turning All South Africa into a Prison," *Guardian*, July 15, 1954.

55. Cited in Visser, "Afrikaner Anti-communist History Production in South African Historiography," 307.

56. Bunting, *Rise of the South African Reich*, 198.

57. For a brief summary of the legal power of the Suppression of Communism Act, see Clark and Worger, *South Africa*, 58–59; Gerhart, *Black Power in South Africa*, 90n3; Worden, *Making of Modern South Africa*, 106–107.

58. For the numbers of those arrested during the Defiance Campaign, see Bunting, *Rise of the South African Reich*, 202–203; "South African Jails Bulge with Defiers," *Chicago Defender*, August 23, 1952.

59. James Moroka and Yusuf Dadoo were among the twenty Defiance Campaign leaders charged under the Suppression of Communism Act. Each leader received a two-year suspended sentence to be invoked upon any evidence of further political organizing. "African Court Frees 20 Defying Race Law," *Chicago Defender*, December 13, 1952.

60. The task of linking black activists to "subversive" communist organizations was a relatively easy one in South Africa, as communists played a prominent role in the anti-apartheid movement; see Beinart, *Twentieth-Century South Africa*, chap. 6; Ellis and Sechaba, *Comrades against Apartheid*.

61. "Defiance Action at New Peak Answering Trial of Leaders," *Spotlight on Africa*, September 18, 1952, 1.

62. "African Court Frees 20," 9.

63. Albert J. Luthuli, "An Urgent Call . . . by Chief A. J. Luthuli," July 1, 1953, SAIRR Political Documents, F1.

64. The Suppression of Communism Act was much broader than the Smith Act in terms of defining communism and foreign subversion. However, both acts shared an ideological focus and were constructed in relation to one another throughout this period.

65. Union of South Africa Government Information Office, New York, "South Africa: Facts for Filing," 1950, SANA, BWA, vol. 28, 39/1; ANC and SAIC, Walter Sisulu and Y. A. Cachalia, "Bulletin of the Campaign for the Defiance of Unjust Laws: Bulletin No. 1," July 2, 1952, ACOA Records, Part 2, Reel 1, Frame 47, 3; "Communism and South Africa," *Africa Today*, October–November 1954, 11.

66. Bunting, *Rise of the South African Reich*, 201.

67. See correspondence: Department of External Affairs, Cape Town to South African Embassy, Washington, DC, May 21, 1957, SANA, BWA, vol. 82, 158/1; South African Embassy, Washington, DC, to G. P. Jooste, Department of External Affairs, Cape Town, May 22, 1957, SANA, BWA, vol. 82, 158/1.

68. John R. Sims to Honorable Herbert Brownell Jr., "For the Attention of Mr. Nathan B. Lenvin, Chief Foreign Agents Registration Section," May 27, 1957, SANA, BWA, vol. 82, 158/1.

69. Ibid. For Sims's work on this survey of U.S. anticommunist prosecutions, Dow, Lohnes, and Albertson were paid $2,083.42 by the South African government; see Wilmat Theunissen (Secretary of Embassy) to John. R. Sims, September 15, 1957, SANA, BWA, vol. 82, 158/1.

70. Fast, "Why the Fifth Amendment?," 46; Pederson, "Memories of the Red Decade," 183.

71. Internal Affairs to South African Embassy, Washington, DC, confidential document, November 1, 1957, SANA, BWA, vol. 82, 158/1, 1.

72. Ibid.

73. Confidential memo, South African Embassy Files, October 21, 1957, BWA, vol. 82, 158/1, 1. For the questionnaire and Lautner's answers, see "Answers to a Draft Questionnaire," October 21, 1957, SANA, BWA, vol. 82, 158/1, 1–21. There is no record of John Lautner appearing at the Treason Trial or indeed traveling to South Africa at this time. Professor Józef Maria Bocheński, who had held a number of visiting positions in the United States, did appear, along with Professor Murray, as an expert on communism and Marxist theory in 1958. See "Statement by Joseph Bockenski," Records of the 1956 Treason Trial, AD182.A1.

74. Horne, "Race from Power," 441–442.

75. Nancy MacLean shows how Southern Democrats and conservative Republicans used the language of anticommunism in the 1940s and 1950s to restrict freedoms for African Americans; see *Freedom Is Not Enough*, 30–33, 50.

76. Flyer, "Ben Davis: RAILROADED!," n.d. CPUSA Papers, TAM 132.02, Biographical Files on Communist Leaders and Activists, 1907–1909, Davis, Benjamin J., Box 2, Folder 19.

77. "Negro Leader Called Black S.O.B. Gets Jail Threat, No Apology," *California Eagle*, September 1, 1950, 4.

78. "Lanham Offers Backhand Apology for Slur to Negro," *Atlanta Daily World*, August 15, 1950; "Better Late Than Never," *Atlanta Daily World*, August 6, 1950; "Congressman Curses, Tries To Fight Negro Witness during House Probe," *Chicago Defender*, August 12, 1950.

79. "Stigmatizing Witness Admitted by Lanham," *New York Times*, April 10, 1951; "Better Late Than Never," *Atlanta Daily World*, August 6, 1950; "Record Fails to Disclose Lanham Language Threat," *Atlanta Daily World*, August 11, 1950; "Congressman Curses, Tries to Fight Negro Witness during House Probe," *Chicago Defender*, August 12, 1950; "Negro Leader Called Black S.O.B.," 1; Horne, *Black Revolutionary*, 123.

80. Patterson, "Prison Figures Show 'Brand of Criminality,'" 5.

81. Louise Thompson Patterson Circular, July 29, 1954, William L. Patterson Papers, MSRC, Box 5, Folder 7.

82. "Defiance Action at New Peak Answering Trial of Leaders," *Spotlight on Africa*, September 18, 1952, 1–2; "Police Fire at African Trial Demonstrators," *Los Angeles Sentinel*, December 15, 1956.

83. Treason Trial Defence Fund, *South Africa's Treason Trial*, July 1958, National Library of South Africa, Cape Town, 5.

84. Alfred Hutchinson, "It Could Never Be in Vain," *Fighting Talk*, February 1957, 3.

85. Albert Luthuli, *Let My People Go*, 167.

86. Suttner, "Rethinking and Re-Remembering Prison," 4–5.

87. Caine, "Prisons as Spaces of Friendships"; Jocelyn Alexander, "Political Prisoners' Memoirs," 395–396.

88. Z. K. Matthews to George Houser, January 3, 1957, ACOA Records, Part 2, Reel 1, Frame 571–574, 1.

89. "There's No Ethnic Grouping in Jail!," *New Age*, July 5, 1956.

90. Luthuli, *Let My People Go*, 171.

91. Z. K. Matthews made a similar point to Luthuli in relation to the Treason Trial in a letter to George Houser, observing that "in this country where the colour line is so rigidly drawn in every sphere of life, the accused in this trial sit together as a mixed group without regard to race." Z. K. Matthews to George Houser, January 3, 1957, ACOA Records, Part 2, Reel 1, Frame 571–574.

92. Jocelyn Alexander, "Political Prisoners' Memoirs," 303, 407.

93. Gready, "Autobiography and the 'Power of Writing,'" 501.

94. Horne, *Black and Red*, 152–153; David L. Lewis, *W. E. B. Du Bois*, 156, 546–47.

95. Spraggs, "DuBois, Humiliated By Court, Denies Charge," *Chicago Defender*, February 24, 1951; Alice A. Dunnigan, "Dr. Du Bois, 3 Others Win Freedom on $1,000 Bonds," *Atlanta Daily World*, February 22, 1951; Louis Loutier, "Capital Spotlight," *Atlanta Daily World*, February 27, 1951; "Court Indicts Dr. W. E. B. Du Bois," *Atlanta Daily World*, February 15, 1951; "Silhouette of Tragedy," *Chicago Defender*, February 24, 1951; "The Strange Case of Dr. DuBois," *Chicago Defender*, March 3, 1951.

96. Langston Hughes, "The Accusers' Names Nobody Will Remember. But History Records Du Bois," CPUSA Papers, TAM 132.02, Biographical Files on Communist Leaders and Activists, 1907–1909, Du Bois, W.E.B., Box 2, Folder 47. This writing was published in the *Chicago Defender* on October 6, 1951.

97. Patterson, "Prison Figures Show 'Brand of Criminality,'" 5.

98. Eslanda Goode Robeson, "Let's Go! (The Du Bois Case)," c. 1951, Paul and Eslanda Robeson Collection, MSRC, Box 13, 2.

99. "'Peace on Trial in U.S.': Dr. Du Bois Indicted," *Guardian*, July 5, 1951. For more on the Food and Canning Workers Union, which was made up of predominantly African and "colored" workers, see Gasa, *Women in South African History*, 196–205.

100. Special correspondent, "It's Un-American: Record of U.S. Red-Baiting Committee," *Guardian*, June 26, 1947; "Legal Lynching in United States: Six Negroes Sentenced to Death," *Guardian*, April 14, 1949; "'Peace on Trial in U.S.'" ; "Race Terrorism against U.S. Negroes: Washington Charged with Genocide," *Guardian*, January 3, 1952; "Negro Tortured in U.S. Southern Jail," *Clarion*, August 14, 1952, 8; "U.S. Prisoners Sent to Asylum, Protest at Dirty Deal: Negroes See 'Freedom' in Action," *Advance*, May 21, 1953, 5; "Paul Robeson Faces Prison Sentence: Describes Interrogators as 'Murderers of My People,'" *Guardian*, June 28, 1956.

101. John Duffy, "Seven Men Died Because They Were Black," *Guardian*, February 15, 1951.

102. Kramer, "Power and Connection," 1352.

103. "'A Lesson from Our South African Brothers and Sisters,' 'Here's My Story,'" *Freedom*, September 1952. In *Paul Robeson Speaks*, 326.

104. Ibid.

105. Council on African Affairs and William Alphaeus Hunton, "Here Are the Facts . . . You Be the Judge! The Council on African Affairs Answers Attorney General Brownell," November 1953, NAACP Records, 1940–1955, Part 2, Box A373, 6.

106. This is important to remember as many traditional historical accounts of black organizing on the left cast the Communist Party as an organization that exploited gullible African Americans. For example, Theodore Draper comments that "Negroes counted least of all in the early communist movement." *Roots of American Communism*, 192, 387.

107. For a revisionist view of African American engagement with the Communist Party and the left, see Kate Baldwin, *Beyond the Color Line*; Gilmore, *Defying Dixie*; Kelley, "'Afric's Sons with Banner Red'"; Kelley, *Hammer and Hoe*; Kelley, *Race Rebels*; Naison, *Communists in Harlem*; Singh, "Retracing the Black-Red Thread."

108. Ellis and Sechaba, *Comrades against Apartheid*, 25.

109. "Campaign of Defiance Spreads; Arrests Now Total 2750," *Spotlight on Africa*, August 21, 1952, 2. The links between American and South African anticommunism were also made in relation to the use of "stool pigeon" witnesses in another *Spotlight* article, "Defiance Action at New Peak Answering Trial of Leaders," *Spotlight on Africa*, September 18, 1952, 2.

110. "The African National Congress in South Africa Speaks Out in Praise of the Council's Work," *Spotlight on Africa*, July 14, 1953, 1.

111. Hunton, "Here Are the Facts . . . You Be the Judge!," 8.

112. Paul Robeson to Dr. G. M. Naicker, January 22, 1954, Robeson Papers, Reel 1, Frame 313–314, 2.

113. Munro, "Imperial Anticommunism," 54.

Chapter Six

1. "South African Honor Roll," *Spotlight on Africa*, c. 1952, Robeson Papers, Reel 7, Frame 222–223, 2.

2. Ibid.

3. Iliffe, *Honour in African History*.

4. "South African Honor Roll," 2.

5. Ibid., 2–3.

6. Walker, *Women and Resistance in South Africa*.

7. "South African Honor Roll," 2.

8. Kuumba, "'You've Struck a Rock,'" 517; Hassim, "Texts and Tests of Equality," 11.

9. The lack of reporting on the activism of African women in African American publications was out of step with the coverage their efforts received in South Africa. In *Women and Resistance in South Africa*, Cherryl Walker documents how *Dum* magazine reported on the upsurge in women's membership of the ANC throughout the 1950s; see *Women and Resistance in South Africa*, 27. The *Guardian* and *New Age* also emphasized the activism of black women in this period. For example, see "Women's Mighty Protest against Passes: 'We Shall Not Rest Until We Have Won Our Freedom for Our Children,'" *New Age*, August 8, 1957; "600 Women Not Downhearted," *New Age*, December 27, 1958. "'Let the People Live in Peace,'" *New Age*, November 19, 1959; and "They Could Not Break Us," *New Age*, October 22, 1959.

10. Unterhalter, "The Work of the Nation," 163.

11. Ibid., 163–172.

12. Ibid., 163.

13. This masculinist framing of the national liberation struggle is discussed in Erlank, "Gender and Masculinity in South African Nationalist Discourse."

14. Unterhalter, "The Work of the Nation," 172–174; Erlank, "Gender and Masculinity in South African Nationalist Discourse," 663; Enloe, *Bananas, Beaches and Bases*, esp. chap. 3.

15. Gillespie, "Containing the 'Wandering Native,'" 499, 504; Bonner, "Family, Crime and Political Consciousness."

16. Evans, *Bureaucracy and Race*, 60–62.

17. W. W. M. Eiselen, "The Meaning of Apartheid," lecture given to the SAIRR Winter School, 1948, 4. Cited in Gillespie, "Containing the 'Wandering Native,'" 506.

18. Letter to the editor, *The Star*, November 4, 1941; Goodhew, "Working-Class Respectability," 251; Nauright, "'The Mecca of Native Scum,'" 65, 75.

19. The phrase 'Tsotsi' was used to refer to young black men living in urban areas who were potentially violent and involved in gangsterism. Fourchard, "The Making of the Juvenile Delinquent"; Goodhew, "The People's Police-Force."

20. Gillespie, "Containing the 'Wandering Native,'" 504; Chanock, *Making of South African Legal Culture*, 62–63.

21. "Turning All South Africa into a Prison," *Guardian*, July 15, 1954.

22. Unterhalter, "The Work of the Nation," 162.

23. Homer Jack, "South Africa Uncensored!," *Pittsburgh Courier*, January 24, 1953.

24. Nagel, "Masculinity and Nationalism," 251–252.

25. Paul Robeson, "Here's My Story: A Lesson from Our South African Brothers and Sisters," *Freedom*, September 1952, in *Paul Robeson Speaks*, 326.

26. Richard Lincoln, "'This Century Belongs to Africa,' It's Warned," *New York Amsterdam News*, November 29, 1952.

27. The National Action Committee of the African National Congress and the South African Indian Congress, "Bulletin of the Campaign for the Defiance of Un-

just Laws," No. 3, July 18, 1952, NAACP Record, 1940–1955, Part 2, Box A7, General Office File, Africa, South Africa, General, 1950–1953, 2.

28. "Bulletin of the Campaign for the Defiance of Unjust Laws," No. 1, July 2, 1952, ACOA Records, Part 2, Reel 1, Frame 47, 2. The *Bulletin* was published by the National Action Committee of the ANC and SAIC and was circulated widely. The CAA, AFSAR, and NAACP received copies.

29. Enloe, *Bananas, Beaches and Bases*, 44.

30. The National Action Committee of the African National Congress and the South African Indian Congress, "Bulletin of the Campaign for the Defiance of Unjust Laws," No. 2, July 9, 1952, NAACP Records, 1940–1955, Part 2, Box A7, General Office File, Africa, South Africa, General, 1950–1953, 1.

31. Sam Raditlhalo notes that "redemptive suffering is . . . that form of suffering in which the autobiographical subject accepts such suffering in order to relieve the larger suffering experienced by those with whom he or she identifies." See "Unzima Lomthwalo—'This Load Is Heavy,'" 31.

32. "Bulletin of the Campaign for the Defiance of Unjust Laws," No. 1, July 2, 1952, ACOA Records, Part 2, Reel 1, Frame 47, 2.

33. William Patterson's criticisms of race and the American prison system show how black leftists linked political imprisonment to the prison experiences of the African American population as a whole; see Patterson, "Prison Figures Show 'Brand of Criminality,'" 5; Horne, *Black Revolutionary*, chap. 8–10.

34. John Pittman, "What's Behind the Jailing of Dr. W. A. Hunton?," *Daily Worker*, n.d.; Council on African Affairs, "CAA News Release: Alphaeus Hunton Imprisonment," November 6, 1951, NAACP Records, 1940–1955, Part 2, Box A373.

35. Paul Robeson, "Circular: A Petition By Negro Americans to the President Attorney General of the United States," n.d., Robeson Papers, Reel 1, Frame 226–227, 1. This declaration is reminiscent of Erik S. McDuffie's work on Esther Cooper Jackson that shows how the Red Scare occasionally required black leftists "to appropriate the discourse of conservative postwar domesticity as a political strategy of resistance to McCarthyism." See McDuffie, "The March of Young Southern Black Women," 84.

36. "CAA News Release: Alphaeus Hunton Imprisonment," November 6, 1951, Records of the NAACP, 1940–1955, Part 2, Box A373, 1.

37. Ibid.

38. John Pittman, "What's Behind the Jailing of Dr. W.A. Hunton?"

39. For the number of autobiographies published by South African anti-apartheid activists, see Unterhalter, "The Work of the Nation," 177–178.

40. Alfred Hutchinson, "The Night Marching to the Morrow," in *South Africa's Treason Trial* (Afrika! Publications, 1958), National Library of South Africa, Cape Town, 4.

41. Alex La Guma, "Treason Trial Diary: 'A Time to Think,'" *Fighting Talk*, September 1958, 8–9.

42. Alfred Hutchinson, "The Night Marching to the Morrow," 4.

43. Mandela, *Long Walk to Freedom*, 233–234.

44. A notable exception is a report in the CAA's *Spotlight on Africa* that briefly noted the role of black women in the Defiance Campaign; see "Campaign of Defiance Spreads; Arrests Now Total 2750," *Spotlight on Africa*, August 21, 1952, 2.

45. Unterhalter, "The Work of the Nation," 172.

46. Nagel, "Masculinity and Nationalism," 254.

47. Gaines, *Uplifting the Race*, 5.

48. Paul Robeson's *Freedom* newspaper represented an important forum where black women such as Vicki Garvin and Lorraine Hansberry challenged masculinist narratives of black protest, addressing issues of race and gender discrimination. See Gore, *Radicalism at the Crossroads*, 115–116; Higashida, *Black Internationalist Feminism*, 48–58.

49. "Pregnant Women Beaten in Gaol," *Guardian*, September 3, 1953; "Inhuman Jail Treatment of African Women Alleged," *Guardian*, January 1, 1947; "Women, Juveniles Must Now Carry Passes: Thousands of 'Criminals' Created by New Act," *Advance*, January 1, 1953, 1; "'Widows, Yet Our Husbands Live': Women Prepare Anti-Pass Campaign," *New Age*, January 13, 1955; "'We Have No Other Home': Women Fight Back against Inhuman Expulsion Act," *New Age*, February 10, 1955; "Pregnant Women Battoned by Police in Uitenhage," *New Age*, August 1, 1957; "Women's Mighty Protest against Passes: 'We Shall Not Rest Until We Have Won Our Freedom for Our Children,'" *New Age*, August 8, 1957; "Freedom Babies Born in Jail," *New Age*, August 19, 1957; "600 Women Not Downhearted," *New Age*, December 27, 1958; "Police Baton Women, Babies," *New Age*, March 5, 1959. "Batons, Gas Again Used on Women," *New Age*, September 3, 1959; "They Could Not Break Us," *New Age*, October 22, 1959; "'Let the People Live in Peace': Women Condemn Pass Laws," *New Age*, November 19, 1959.

50. "Pregnant Women Battoned by Police in Uitenhage"; "Police Baton Women, Babies."

51. "Pregnant Women Battoned by Police in Uitenhage," 5.

52. Unterhalter, "The Work of the Nation," 167.

53. Morrell, introduction to *Changing Men in Southern Africa*.

54. "Inhuman Jail Treatment of African Women Alleged," *Guardian*, January 1, 1947.

55. William Alphaeus Hunton, *Resistance: Against Fascist Enslavement in South Africa*, 1953, William Alphaeus Hunton Papers, Reel 2, Frame 37.

56. Ibid.

57. Lincoln, "'This Century Belongs to Africa,'" 1.

58. ACOA, "Apartheid Takes Ever Greater Toll in Union of South Africa," c. 1959, A. Philip Randolph Papers, Box 3, Subject File, Africa, American Committee on Africa, 1954–1969, 1.

59. Luthuli, *Let My People Go*, 169–170.

60. "Support the Non-Violent Campaign against Unjust Laws in South Africa," c. April 1953, NAACP Records, 1940–1955, Part 2, Box A7, General Office File, South Africa General, 3.

61. Z. K. Matthews, "From South Africa a Distinguished Leader Writes," c. 1953. Du Bois Papers, Reel 69, Frame 736.

62. Lincoln, " 'This Century Belongs to Africa,' " 1.

63. Further evidence of the political importance of the black family can be found in Hutchinson's description of police raids in an internationally circulated pamphlet about the Treason Trial. Commenting on the arrest of Lawrence Nkosi, Hutchinson comments, "Twelve year old Mandhla and nine year old Bongi were still sleeping. Divorced some years ago, Lawrence had no option but to leave the children alone in the house. So he kissed them goodbye and locked the door behind him, for safety. It was late that afternoon before Congressmen visiting the raided homes could retrieve the children and move them to their grandmother's home. . . . The dawn thump of the Special Branch was heard on doors throughout the country that Wednesday morning." Treason Trial Defence Fund, "South Africa's Treason Trial," (Afrika! Publications, 1958), ACOA Records, Part 2, Reel 10, Frame 83–100, 2.

64. Erlank, "Gender and Masculinity," 667–668.

65. Federation of South African Women, "Correspondence and Press Statements. Johannesburg Statement on Treason Trial Police Raids," n.d., FSAW Records, B6.1.

66. Wolcott, *Remaking Respectability*, 4. For work on the motherhood and anti-apartheid protest, see Pam Brooks, "Crossing Borders," 7; Castledine, " 'In a Solid Bond of Unity,' " 58–64; Collins, *Black Feminist Thought*, 192–193; Geisler, " 'Parliament Is Another Terrain of Struggle,' " 608; McClintock, "Family Feuds," 72–73; Wells, "Maternal Politics."

67. Federation of South African, "Document Presented to the Native Commissioner for Johannesburg on Tuesday March 5, 1959 Re. Women's Anti-pass Protests," March 5, 1959, FSAW Records, Cb2.6.3.

68. Ibid.

69. Federation of South African Women, African National Congress Women's League, "Women in Chains," September 1956, National Library of South Africa, Cape Town, 12.

70. Federation of South African Women, "Report, FSAW, August 1955 to 9th August 1956," August 9, 1956, FSAW Records, Cb1.4.

71. Federation of South African Women, African National Congress Women's League, "Women in Chains," 11.

Chapter Seven

1. Collins, *Black Feminist Thought*, 192–193; hooks, *Yearning: Race, Gender, and Cultural Politics*, 45.

2. For more on how motherhood has provided an important political platform for African American and black South African women, see Pam Brooks, "Crossing Borders," 7; McClintock, "Family Feuds," 73–74.

3. Anne McClintock makes this argument by pointing to how black South African women "have embraced, transmuted and transformed the ideology [of motherhood] in a variety of ways, working strategically within traditional ideology to justify untraditional public militancy." However, McClintock ignores the way in which this was often invested with a transnational meaning for black women seeking to alter race, gender, and class hierarchies across national borders. See McClintock, "Family Feuds," 73–74.

4. Hassim, *Women's Organizations and Democracy in South Africa*, 28.

5. Collins, *Black Feminist Thought*, 175–176.

6. Ibid., 175.

7. Boris, "Power of Motherhood," 32.

8. hooks, "Homeplace," *Yearning: Race, Gender, and Cultural Politics*, 42.

9. Ibid., 42.

10. Leeds, " 'Toward the 'Higher Type of Womanhood.' "

11. Writing in 1954, Era Bell Thompson of *Ebony* magazine captured this somewhat ambiguous relationship between African Americans and the "African Motherland," noting that, in this period, "Along with a few million other American Negroes, I began to take new interest and a growing pride in the Motherland. If my heathen relatives were about to re-inherit their father's Kingdoms, I would be among the first to congratulate them." See Thompson, *Africa, Land of My Fathers*, 17–18.

12. Michelle Stephens's work on the way black masculinist politics influenced transnational racial politics between the United States and the Caribbean demonstrates the centrality of gender to black internationalism; see Stephens, *Black Empire*.

13. A. Philip Randolph, "Statement by A. Philip Randolph upon the Occasion of Africa Freedom Day, Carnegie Hall, New York City, April 15, 1959," A. Philip Randolph Papers, Box 40, Speeches & Writings File, February 7 to September 6 1959.

14. Ibid.

15. The ordering of intimate relationships was central to the development of imperialist and white supremacist systems of rule. These themes are discussed in detail in Ann Laura Stoler's edited collection, *Haunted by Empire*. Stoler's own essay helps to clarify this emphasis on the intimacies of colonial and imperial rule. See "Intimidations of Empire: Predicaments of the Tactile and Unseen," 4.

16. Essie Robeson visited South Africa in 1936 as part of an African tour with her son, Paul Robeson Jr. Her travel notes were subsequently turned into a book: Robeson, *African Journey*. See also Mahon, "Eslanda Goode Robeson's African Journey"; Ransby, *Eslanda*, chap. 7.

17. Kathleen A. Brown, "The 'Savagely Fathered and Un-Mothered World' of the Communist Party."

18. Eslanda Goode Robeson, "Speech: The Freedom Family," October 1951, Victims of the Smith Act Meeting, Paul and Eslanda Robeson Collection, MSRC, Box 13, 2.

19. For a detailed exploration of African American connections with Ghana, see Gaines, *American Africans in Ghana*. For information on the U.S. presence at the All-African People's Conference, see chap. 3. Eslanda was accompanied by her husband Paul Robeson on this trip after his passport was returned to him.

20. Eslanda Goode Robeson, "African Family Affair," December 11, 1958, Paul and Eslanda Robeson Collection, MSRC, Box 14, 1.

21. Eslanda Robeson frequently used the metaphor of the "extended family" in her African writing. Another example of this can be found in "Goings on in the World Family," *New World Review*, December 1955, Paul and Eslanda Robeson Collection, MSRC, Box. 9.

22. Ibid.

23. Paul Maylam, "The Rise and Decline of Urban Apartheid," 67–79.

24. This argument has been influenced by Laura Briggs's work on the visual iconography of rescue that informed American transnational and transracial adoption during the Cold War. While Briggs argues that images of vulnerability were used to justify U.S. imperial interventions abroad, I would argue that these images had a different meaning for African Americans who had been denied full citizenship rights. See Briggs, "Mother, Child, Race, Nation."

25. Linda Gordon, "Internal Colonialism and Gender," 437–438.

26. Ibid.

27. Collins, *Black Feminist Thought*, 109; Higginbotham, *Righteous Discontent*, 187–188; Chappell, Hutchinson, and Ward, " 'Dress modestly, neatly," 77–78.

28. Homer Jack, "South Africa Uncensored!," *Pittsburgh Courier*, January 17, 1953; Homer Jack, "South Africa Uncensored!," *Pittsburgh Courier*, January 24, 1953; Homer Jack, "South Africa Uncensored!," *Pittsburgh Courier*, January 31, 1953; "Police Arrest 2000 Natives in Bus Strike," *Los Angeles Sentinel*, February 21, 1957; "South African Women Beaten by Policemen," *Norfolk Journal and Guide*, November 8, 1958, 1.

29. Homer Jack, 'South Africa Uncensored!," *Pittsburgh Courier*, January 17, 1953.

30. On the decline of black transnational press in the United States, see Penny Von Eschen, *Race against Empire*, 118–121.

31. Homer Jack, "South Africa Uncensored!," *Pittsburgh Courier*, January 31, 1953.

32. Waetjen, "The 'Home' in Homeland," 656.

33. Homer Jack, "South Africa Uncensored!," *Pittsburgh Courier*, January 31, 1953.

34. See Frazier, *Negro Family in the United States.*

35. "African Women Fight Back," *Chicago Defender*, August 25, 1959.

36. Ibid.

37. "Campaign of Defiance Spreads; Arrests Now Total 2750," *Spotlight on Africa*, October 21, 1952, 2; "Women in Africa Vanguard of Liberation Struggle," *Spotlight on Africa*, February 20, 1954; "Voices for Freedom," *Spotlight on Africa*, September 15, 1954. 1.

38. A similar image also appeared on the front page of same publication in October 1954, depicting a woman from French Equatorial Africa feeding her child. See front cover, *Spotlight on Africa*, 28 October 1954, 1.

39. Ibid.

40. Walker, *Women and Resistance in South Africa*, 228–229.

41. Ibid.

42. Mafeking's situation also fueled anti-apartheid sentiment in Britain, and in 1959 she was heralded in Claudia Jones's *West Indian Gazette* as the newspaper's "Heroine of the Year." See Schwarz, "'Claudia Jones and the West Indian Gazette,'" 271.

43. Among the few articles that went into detail concerning Mafeking's political activities was "Banishments: Elizabeth Mafeking and 80 More," *Fighting Talk*, December 1959, 2–3.

44. The forced deportation of other prominent black women leaders elucidated similar responses. For example, when police forcibly deported ANC and FSAW organizer Annie Silinga from her Langa home in Cape Town to the Transkei under the Urban Areas Act, newspaper reports focused on her upheaval from the home as well as her separation from her family and three children. As one report commented, "She has no 'home' there, no family to shelter her." Emphasizing the notoriety of the Transkei region for drought and famine, the article added, "For all Verwoerd cares, Mrs. Silinga may also starve in the Transkei. She will get no help from the Government to start her life again there. She has no land to till, no hut to sleep in. Only the charity of her fellow Africans will keep her from destitution." See Brian Bunting, "Three Children Motherless: Annie Silinga Deported to the Transkei," *New Age*, March 1, 1956.

45. American Committee on Africa, "Press Release: Woman Banished by South African Government Receives American Aid Through Africa Defense Fund," September 2, 1960, ACOA Records, Part 2, Reel 10, Frame 818.

46. Jackie Robinson, "Opening Speech by Jackie Robinson for South Africa Emergency Conference," June 1, 1960, Papers of Jackie Robinson, Container 6, File 4, 3–4.

47. George M. Houser to Duma Nokwe, November 23, 1959, ACOA Records, Part 2, Reel 2, Frame 75.

48. Adler, "Gendering Histories."

49. Switzer, "*Bantu World* and the Origins of a Captive Commercial Press," 189–190.

50. Both Thema and Nhlapo expressed admiration for African American educators and missionaries. Thema was a product of the Lovedale Missionary School. Thema cited Booker T. Washington as a role model, commenting "I wanted to be like him in every respect. I wanted to be a great orator as he was, to be able to speak before European audiences on behalf of my people as he did on behalf of the Negroes in the United States. This became the burning passion of my life." Quoted in Switzer, "*Bantu World* and the Origins of a Captive Commercial Press," 193. Nhlapo traveled to the United States and received a doctorate in psychology from the University of Chicago's McKinley-Roosevelt Extension College in 1944. While in the United States he developed an awareness and admiration for the African American educators Booker T. Washington, Washington Carver, and J. E. K. Aggrey. See "Dr. Jacob Mfaniselwa Nhlapo," South African History Online, accessed March 30, 2011, http://www.sahistory.org.za/pages/people/bios/nhlapo-j.htm.

51. The *Bantu World* reached a large section of the literate black population in South Africa, accounting for around 25 percent of the total newspaper circulation among Africans. It regularly ran letters and editorials that aired African grievances against the white state and employed writers who would go on to radically condemn apartheid in the 1950s and beyond, such as Peter Abrahams and Henry Nxumalo. In relation to the readership of the *Bantu World*, circulation peaked at around 24,000 copies a week, although there is evidence to suggest that the newspaper was read much more widely and sellers claimed that every copy sold would be circulated to at least five others, who in turned shared its contents with friends and family members. Switzer, "*Bantu World* and the Origins of a Captive Commercial Press," 190, 200, 202.

52. This poem was penned by the white American author Grace Noll Crowell. "Home Corner for African Women," *Bantu World*, March 29, 1947, 8.

53. Goodhew, *Respectability and Resistance*, 168.

54. Bickford-Smith, *Ethnic Pride and Racial Prejudice*, 118–119.

55. "Letter to African Womanhood: Our Children," *Bantu World*, September 11, 1943, 8.

56. hooks, "Homeplace," *Yearning: Race, Gender, and Cultural Politics*.

57. "Letter to African Womanhood: Self-Reliance," *Bantu World*, March 11, 1944, 8.

58. "Letter to African Womanhood: Teaching Children Self-Confidence," *Bantu World*, November 20, 1943.

59. Ibid.

60. See chapter 4 for a detailed discussion of *Zonk!* magazine.

61. "Looking after Baby," *Zonk!* September 9, 1949, 48. South African women were also encouraged not to fall behind the standards of care set by mothers in "overseas countries," including "in American homes."

62. "Looking after Baby," *Zonk!*, June 1950, 22–23.

63. "Front Cover," *Zonk!*, May 1951, 1, 3.

64. Another excellent example of the reoccurring African child image can be found in the article "Portrait of a Lucky Girl," *Zonk!*, January 1952, 14–15. Commenting on a picture of baby Ntombethamsanqa sent in by a reader, the article observes that "she is indeed a Lucky girl, for her parents, her four sisters and her brother all do what they can to make her life a very happy one, and they succeed very well."

65. McClintock, "Family Feuds," 63.

66. "Front Cover," *Zonk!*, December 1951, 1, 3.

67. Mary Helen Washington highlights how it is important to read newspaper articles in relation to the content and themes raised by the other reports, images, and advertisements that also appeared in the publication. She argues that the meaning of certain stories can be "dramatically transformed by their position on the page and by their dialogic relationship to their audience and to the other stories within the paper." See Washington, "Alice Childress, Lorraine Hansberry, and Claudia Jones," 189.

68. For an excellent account of *tsotsi* culture see Glaser, *Bo Tsotsi*. Goodhew questions Glaser's assertion that *tsotsi* crime was a form of political resistance against apartheid, documenting how black leaders used respectable ideas to challenge *tsotsi* violence within the community. See Goodhew, *Respectability and Resistance*, 107.

69. Clowes, "Men and Children," 108; Erlank, "Gender and Masculinity in South African Nationalist Discourse," 660–665.

70. "Portrait of a Family: A Study in Misery and Courage," *Zonk!*, May 1956, 11–13.

71. Ibid., 11–12.

72. Ibid., 13.

73. Ibid.

74. This was especially significant given that African women weren't required to carry passes up until 1952 and the introduction of reference books with the passing of the Natives Abolition of Passes and Coordination of Documents Act. This had allowed many women to move into factory jobs where they could secure more pay. See Gasa, "Feminisms, Motherisms, Patriarchies," 208.

75. Hickel, "Social Engineering and Revolutionary Consciousness," 308–311.

76. Walker, *Women and Resistance in South Africa*, 189. The apartheid government passed the Natives Abolition of Passes and Coordination of Documents Act in 1952, which saw the introduction of reference books that contained information on racial classification as well as an individual's place of birth, legal residence, and employment. This act was used to restrict Africans from urban areas and made it clear that—at some point in the future—African women would also be required to carry reference books. In 1954, the government began issuing permits to African women, defining where an individual could live and work, and in 1956, it started the process of issuing reference books to women.

77. Hassim, *Women's Organizations and Democracy in South Africa*, 25.

78. Hilda Bernstein and Ray Alexander, "Draft Constitution: Federation of South African Women," 1954, FSAW Records, Aa1, 1.

79. As Shireen Hassim and Cherryl Walker have noted a significant tension often existed between national liberation movements and women involved in FSAW. This tension was ultimately resolved, they argue, by South African women acknowledging the pre-eminence of the national liberation struggle. See Hassim, *Women's Organizations and Democracy in South Africa*; Walker, *Women and Resistance in South Africa*.

80. Shireen Hassim, "Texts and Tests of Equality," 7–18.

81. Federation of South African Women, "Women's Charter and Aims. Adopted 17th April 1954," April 16, 1954, Jack and Ray Simons Papers, Manuscripts and Archives, University of Cape Town, Folder R9.3.1.

82. Gasa, "Feminisms, Motherisms, Patriarchies," 213–223; Geisler, *Women and the Remaking of Politics*, 66–68.

83. Walker, *Women and Resistance in South Africa*, 125.

84. Ibid., 32–35, 40–43, and 125–126.

85. Gaitskell and Unterhalter, "Mothers of the Nation," 69.

86. Lilian Ngoyi, "FSAW: Inaugural Conference 1954, Addresses," April 1954, FSAW Records, AC1.5.2, 6.

87. Ida Mtwana, "FSAW: Inaugural Conference 1954, Addresses," April 1954, FSAW Records, AC1.5.1, 3.

88. This report also appeared in slightly modified form in the same year as *The Life of the Child in South Africa*, 1955, FSAW Records, Ai7. The original report acted as the federation's report to the WIDF in advance of the World Congress of Mothers due to be held in the same year.

89. *Children of South Africa: A Report Compiled by the Federation of South African Women,* 1955, Jack and Ray Simons Collection, Manuscripts and Archives, University of Cape Town, Folder R9.3.2, 7.

90. Ibid., 2, 19.

91. This was the second time the FSAW had organized a protest in Pretoria. The first, in 1955, attracted between one thousand and two thousand women.

92. Press estimates of attendance varied from six thousand to twenty thousand, depending on the political viewpoint of the publication, although all agreed that the meeting represented mass action on a hitherto unprecedented scale. Walker, *Women and Resistance in South Africa*, 195.

93. Federation of South African Women, "Strijdom—You Have Struck a Rock," 1956, National Library of South Africa, Cape Town, South Africa.

94. McClintock, "Family Feuds," 66.

95. Hassim, *Women's Organizations and Democracy in South Africa*, 28; Ginwala, "Women and the African National Congress," 90.

96. A similar point has been made by Nomboniso Gasa, *Women in South African History*, chap. 5.

97. Ida Mtwana, "FSAW: Inaugural Conference 1954, Addresses," April 1954, FSAW Records, AC1.5.1.

98. Frances Baard interview, July 15, 1982, SAIRR, Oral History.

99. Federation of South African Women, "Conference to Promote Women's Rights. To Be Held on Saturday 17th April 1954, Johannesburg, Trades Hall," March 16, 1954, FSAW Records, Ac1.1, 1.

100. Lilian Ngoyi, "FSAW: Transvaal Region Rent Increases Conference Report," November 14, 1954, FSAW Records, Ba4.1.5, 6.

101. In her work on Sojourners for Truth and Justice and their links with black South African women, Jacqueline Castledine argues that the commitment of these women to "both women's emancipation and the black nationalist goal of self-determination challenges the claims of many that 'nowhere has feminism in its own right been allowed to be more than a maidservant to nationalism.'" See Castledine, "'In a Solid Bond of Unity,'" 58.

102. Albert J. Luthuli, "The African Women's Demonstration in Natal," *Liberation*, October 1959, 22.

103. Ibid.

104. Albert J. Luthuli, "Chief Speaks: A Message by Albert J. Luthuli (President-General, African National Congress) to South African Women on the Occasion of the 3rd Anniversary, August 9, 1959, of the Mass Demonstrations at Union Buildings Pretoria," August 9, 1959, FSAW Records, CB1.5.3, 3–4.

105. "FSAW Congress of Mothers, Transvaal," March 1955, FSAW Records, Ae2.1, 1.

106. Rupp, *Worlds of Women*, 80. Between 1945 and 1975 more than fifty African American women joined the Women's International League for Peace and Freedom (WILPF). The organization's African American delegates were instrumental in urging WILPF delegates to protest the treatment of black South Africans before the UN. See Blackwell, *No Peace without Freedom*, 152.

107. Laville, *Cold War Women*, chap. 2. For more on how African women engaged with the structures of the WIDF, see Martin, "'More Power to Your Great Self,'" 66–67.

108. Helen Joseph circular, "Letter, Regarding FSAW and WIDF Connections," c. 1955, FSAW Records, Db2.2; Women's International Democratic Federation, "For Their Rights as Mothers, Workers, Citizens," 1952, Jack and Ray Simons Papers, Manuscripts and Archives, University of Cape Town, Folder R14.4.5; Women's International Democratic Federation, *That They May Live*, 20.

109. Gladys Smith of the Cape Housewives League also attended the World Congress of Mothers with Ngoyi and Tamana. See Smith, "World Conference of Mothers: Four South African Delegates," *New Age*, August 4, 1955.

110. Helen Joseph circular, "FSAW and the WIDF," c. 1955, FSAW Records, Db2.2, 2.

111. Women's International Democratic Federation, "For Their Rights as Mothers, Workers, Citizens," 1952, Jack and Ray Simons Papers, Manuscripts and Archives, University of Cape Town, Folder R14.4.5, 4, 33. The WIDF was also involved in American politics and openly condemned the exploitation of African American

women workers in the South as well as publicizing the cause of black women such as Rosa Lee Ingram. See Charles H. Martin, "Race, Gender, and Southern Justice."

112. "Lilian Ngoyi Biographical writing," 1972, Lilian Masediba Ngoyi Collection, Historical Papers, William Cullen Library, University of Witwatersrand, A2551, 7–10.

113. Federation of South African Women, *The Life of the Child in South Africa,* c. 1955, FSAW Records, Ai7.

114. Scanlon, *Representation and Reality,* 266.

115. Dora Tamana, "Biographical Writing," n.d., Jack and Ray Simons Papers, Folder R1.9, 11.

116. Ibid., 10.

117. "Elizabeth Mafeking, Biographical Writing," n.d., FSAW Records, Ai1.

118. Dora Tamana, "Speech: WIDF Conference Geneva," February 1955, Jack and Ray Simons Papers, R9.3.2, 4.

119. Lilian Ngoyi, "My Knees Shook, and I Realised What an Honour to My People It Was When I Presided Over a Meeting of Mothers from 66 Nations," *New Age,* August 25, 1955.

120. Hassim, *Women's Organizations and Democracy in South Africa,* 28.

Chapter Eight

1. Lilian Ngoyi, "My Knees Shook."

2. Ibid.

3. Robeson outlined the WIDF's condemnation of American foreign policy and demonstrates the pivotal role played by the U.S. government in securing its removal from the list of UN consultant organizations. See Eslanda Goode Robeson, "140,000,000 Women Can't Be Wrong," *New World Review,* 1954, Paul and Eslanda Robeson Collection, MSRC, Box 13; Weigand, *Red Feminism,* 64.

4. For more on Sojourners for Truth and Justice see McDuffie, *Sojourning for Freedom.*

5. Ibid., 174.

6. Ibid., 176–179. Jacqueline Castledine has noted that the Sojourners' policies on South Africa were largely based on resolutions formulated by the CAA; see Castledine, " 'In a Solid Bond of Unity,' " 69.

7. McDuffie, *Sojourning for Freedom,* 179. This second quote is taken from Jacqueline Castledine's article published in the *Journal of Women's History.* According to her footnotes it comes from a letter Thompson Patterson and Bass sent to Minah T. Soga in South Africa. Soga was the longtime leader of the National Council of African Women (NCAW) in South Africa, a "nonpolitical" organization that distanced itself from the mass civil disobedience of the 1950s. It is unclear from Castledine's references whether the quote was used in other letters sent to more radical black South African women such as Mkize; however, that the STJ made approaches to black South African women with diverse political backgrounds is significant with

regard to the international outlook of African American women. See Castledine, " 'In a Solid Bond of Unity,' " 58.

8. McDuffie, *Sojourning for Freedom*, 179.

9. Ibid., 183–184.

10. Ibid., 184.

11. Vivian Carter Mason, "Report of Meeting in Paris of the Women's International Democratic Federation," *Aframerican Woman's Journal*, March 1946, 3.

12. Ibid., 17.

13. Perhaps the clearest example of this was a letter to the white labor organizer and trade unionist Dorothy J. Bellanca, in which Mason wrote:

> Recently I returned from the International Congress held in Paris and was extremely regretful that there were no women at this Congress from the West Indian Islands, the Virgin Islands, Haiti, Panama, or Africa. It was a stimulating and extraordinarily informative and educational Congress, so that it caused real concern among the American Delegation that our women from so many of these countries did not participate in this great meeting. We are therefore extremely anxious to make contact with women in the countries indicated above in order that we might inform them about the plans for the International Assembly and submit their names for official invitations to this international meeting. We should very much like the addresses of the women who head up women's organisations such as trade unions, workers' groups, welfare and charity organizations, etc.

Vivian Carter Mason to Dorothy J. Bellanca, January 30, 1946, NCNW Records, Series 5, Box 18, Folder 13, 1. Mason, "Report of Meeting in Paris of the Women's International Democratic Federation," 3.

14. For information on the NACW's international politics, see Byrd, "The Transnational Work of Moral Elevation," 128–150.

15. Hanson, *Mary McLeod Bethune*, 164–165.

16. Collier-Thomas, *N.C.N.W., 1935–1980*, 148–150.

17. *Annual Report of the National Council of Negro Women, 1954–1955*, November 11, 1955, NCNW Records, Series 2, Box 8, Folder 85, 26.

18. Hanson, *Mary McLeod Bethune*, 168; Brandy T. Wells argues that the NCNW often exaggerated the extent of its ties to women's groups in the Caribbean and Latin America. See Wells, " 'She Pieced and Stitched and Quilted,' " 378.

19. In 1941, the NCNW held a conference on the theme of "Women Facing New Frontiers." At this conference the need for "closer cooperation" with countries with a "large Negro Population" was discussed, while it was noted that there was a particular need to work "with the women of closely allied ethnic groups in Cuba, Haiti, South America and the Orient." See "High Lighting the Conference," *Aframerican Woman's Journal* 4 (1941): 6–12. Accounts of the NCNW's organizing often ignore the council's international focus. For example, see White, *Too Heavy a Load*, esp. chap. 5.

20. Mary McLeod Bethune to William Alphaeus Hunton, August 2, 1943, NCNW Records, Series 5, Box 10, Folder 1.

21. "Another Dream Realized," *Telefact*, January 1952, 1.

22. Lynch, *Black American Radicals*; Von Eschen, *Race against Empire*.

23. Mary McLeod Bethune to Max Yergan and Paul Robeson, June 14, 1948, Max Yergan Papers, MSRC, Box 3, Folder 12.

24. Hanson, *Mary McLeod Bethune*, 187–188.

25. Mary McLeod Bethune, "The President's Message: Without Flinching," *Aframerican Woman's Journal* (Winter 1947), 3.

26. Mary McLeod Bethune, "The President's Message: Without Flinching," *Aframerican Woman's Journal* (Winter 1947), NCNW Records, Series 13, Box 1, Folder 23, 3.

27. Vivian Carter Mason, "Letter of Thanks for Workshop on Africa—19th Annual Convention 1954," December 8, 1954, NCNW Records, National Archives for Black Women's History (NABWH), Washington, DC, Series 2, Box 6, Folder 70. The flags of these independent African nations were also displayed for the duration of the workshop and convention; see National Council of Negro Women, 19th Annual Convention, Workshop Summaries, November 8–13, 1954, NCNW Records, Series 2, Box 6, Folder 12, 7.

28. "National Council of Negro Women, Inc. 19th Annual Convention, 8–13 November 1954, Washington, DC, Workshop Summaries," NCNW Records, Series 2, Box 6, Folder 72, 1–7.

29. *Annual Report of the National Council of Negro Women, 1954–1955*, November 11, 1955, NCNW Records, Series 2, Box 8, Folder 85, 13; "Highlight Review—19th Annual Convention," *Telefact*, December 1954, 3.

30. *Annual Report of the National Council of Negro Women, 1954–1955*, November 11, 1955, 7.

31. Hanson, *Mary McLeod Bethune*, 188.

32. "NCNW International Committee Meeting Minutes," January 28, 1946, NCNW Records, NABWH, Washington, DC, Series 5, Box 18, Folder 14, 1–2.

33. For more on the life of Dorothy Ferebee and her work with the NCNW, see Kiesel, *She Can Bring Us Home*.

34. "Annual Report of the National Council of Negro Women, 1954–1955," NCNW Records, Series 2, Box 8, Folder 85.

35. "President's Address," *Telefact*, January 1955, 1.

36. "Resolutions Passed in Biennial Convention," *Telefact*, December 1953, 2.

37. Madie Hall first met Mary McLeod Bethune when she was in her twenties and maintained a close personal relationship with the NCNW leader up until Bethune's death in 1955. Berger, "An African American 'Mother of the Nation,'" 127.

38. Walker, *Women and Resistance in South Africa*, 89; Berger, "An African American 'Mother of the Nation,'" 125–156.

39. Madie Hall Xuma to NCNW, c. 1946, NCNW Records, Series 5, Box 18, Folder 13, 1; Walker, *Women and Resistance in South Africa*, 89.

40. Walker, *Women and Resistance in South Africa*, 35.

41. Mary McLeod Bethune to Miss M. Soga, September 28, 1940, NCNW Records, Series 5, Box 18, Folder 14.

42. Vivian Carter Mason to Minah Soga, June 30, 1955, NCNW Records, Series 7, Box 1, Folder 2, 1.

43. "Minutes of the NCNW Annual Convention," November 15, 1956, NCNW Records, Series 2, Box 9, Folder 102.

44. "Minutes of the 21st Annual Convention 14–17 November 1956," NCNW Records, Series 2, Box 9, Folder 102, 11.

45. Vivian Carter Mason to Edith Nono Msezane, June 29, 1955, NCNW Records, Series 7, Box 1, Folder 2, 1–2.

46. Although Feeding Scheme officials claim in their correspondence with the National Council of Negro Women that the initiative started in 1947, Father Trevor Huddleston has claimed he first started the ACFS in June 1945. See Trevor Huddleston, "Holiday Feeding for African Children," *Bantu World*, July 14, 1945, 4; "Feeding of African Children during Holidays," *Bantu World*, October 13, 1945, 1; "School Feeding Scandal Exposed: African Children Get Less," *Guardian*, June 30, 1946.

47. At this time, as a result of the deliberate policies of the ruling National Party, the average African child was receiving a school meal that cost just one-sixth of the price of those provided for white children. See Pat Sutten to Mary McLeod Bethune, July 4, 1955, NCNW Records, Series 7, Box 1, Folder 3, 3; "School Feeding: Grant for White Children to Be Doubled?," *Guardian*, July 21, 1949.

48. The ACFS relied heavily on financial donations and struggled to balance the books throughout this period. See Pat Sutten to Mary McLeod Bethune, July 4, 1955, NCNW Records, Series 7, Box 1, Folder 3, 2. In the financial year 1954–1955, the ACFS spent at total of £6,452.5s.5d.; food that was largely covered by charitable donations amounted to £5,833 9s.7d. See "African Children's Feeding Scheme Income and Expenditure Account for the Year Ended 28th February, 1955," June 1, 1955, NCNW Records, Series 7, Box 1, Folder 3. The dismantling of state provision for black education was enshrined in the 1953 Bantu Education Act.

49. Pat Sutten to Mary McLeod Bethune, July 4, 1955, 1–3.

50. Vivian Carter Mason to William McKinley Johnson Jr., South African Desk, State Department, December 19, 1955, NCNW Records, Series 7, Box 1, Folder 3; John L. Kuhn to Vivian Carter Mason, February 2, 1956, Series 7, Box 1, Folder 3; Margaret Simms to NCNW members, January 12, 1955, NCNW Records, Series 7, Box 1, Folder 3.

51. "With Our Councils," *Telefact*, May 1956, 6; Trevor Huddleston to Vivian Carter Mason, March 22, 1956, NCNW Records, Series 7, Box 1, Folder 3.

52. Vivian Carter Mason to Pat Sutten, 12 June 1955, NCNW Records, Series 7, Box 1, Folder 3.

53. Vivian Carter Mason to William McKinley Johnson Jr., South African Desk, State Department, December 12, 1955, NCNW Records, Series 7, Box 1, Folder 3.

54. John L. Kuhn to Vivian Carter Mason, February 2, 1956, Series 7, Box 1, Folder 3.

55. Laville and Lucas, "The American Way," 567.

56. Dudziak, *Cold War Civil Rights*; Anderson, *Eyes off the Prize*; Borstelmann, *Cold War and the Color Line*.

57. "National Council of Negro Women, Inc., 19th Annual Convention, November 8–13, 1954, Washington, DC, Workshop Summaries," NCNW Records, Series 2, Box 6, Folder 72, 2–4.

58. "African Children's Feeding Scheme: Chairman's Report 1953–1954," 1954, Community of the Resurrection Records, Historical Papers, William Cullen Library, University of Witwatersrand, B10, 4; "Feeding of African Children during Holidays," *Bantu World*, October 13, 1945, 1.

59. Sutten to Bethune, July 4, 1955, 1–2.

60. Ibid., 5.

61. Ibid., 2.

62. The decision to request a one-penny contribution from parents may also have been a way of identifying the most at-risk children. As Pat Sutten stated when writing to Mary McLeod Bethune: "Should the child come without its penny, particulars are taken by the workers, and if necessary the case is handed over to Child Welfare, who investigate it and help the family." Sutten to Bethune, July 4, 1955, 2.

63. Pat Sutten to Vivian Carter Mason, December 13, 1955, NCNW Records, Series 7, Box 1, Folder 3, 2.

64. Ibid., 1.

65. "African Children's Feeding Scheme: Chairman's Report 1953–1954," 1954, Community of the Resurrection Records, B10, 2.

66. Ibid., 5. See also Berghe, *South Africa, a Study in Conflict*, 184.

67. Pippa Stein, "Father Trevor Huddleston Interview," January 1986, Sophiatown Interviews, Historical Papers, William Cullen Library, University of Witwatersrand, 9.

68. Margaret Simms to NCNW members, December 1, 1955, NCNW Records, Series 7, Box 1, Folder 3.

69. Margaret Simms, "Circular Re. African Children's Feeding Scheme," December 1, 1955, NCNW Records, Series 7, Box 9, Folder 8.

70. There is evidence that junior council members occasionally resented the level of control that the NCNW executive exerted over their activities. This sometimes resulted in the slow uptake of official NCNW initiatives. For example, the response to the Feeding Scheme among junior council members in New York City was hampered by these tensions, specifically the belief that junior council members were being asked to make too large a financial contribution to activities that were conceived of at a national level. See Daisy S. George to Vivian Carter Mason, March 20, 1956, NCNW Records, Series 6, Box 4, Folder 33. I am indebted to Brandy T. Wells for providing me with a copy of this letter.

71. Margaret Simms, "Memo to Local Councils and Junior Councils," February 20, 1956, NCNW Records, Series 7, Box 1, Folder 3.

72. "Junior Council Assists Needy African Children," *Norfolk Journal and Guide*, December 29, 1956, 3.

73. "With Our Councils," *Telefact*, May 1956, 6; Trevor Huddleston to Vivian Carter Mason, March 22, 1956, NCNW Records, Series 7, Box 1, Folder 3.

74. Vivian Carter Mason to Trevor Huddleston, January 26, 1956, NCNW Records, Series 7, Box 1, Folder 3.

75. Artishia Jordan to the NCNW, April 16, 1956, NCNW Records, Series 7, Box 1, Folder 3; "Bishop Jordan Finally Admitted to South Africa," *Atlanta Daily World*, August 1, 1954; "Bishop Jordan to Defy So. Africa Ban on AMEs," *Chicago Defender*, August 4, 1953; "Bishop Jordan Leaves for South Africa," *Los Angeles Sentinel*, November 4, 1954; "Bishop Closes AME Conference in South Africa," *Atlanta Daily World*, December 21, 1954.

76. Margaret Simms, "Annual Report of Junior Councils Presented by National Director at the Annual Convention at the Willard House, November 14–18," 1956, NCNW Records, Series 2, Box 10, Folder 103, 2.

77. "Minutes of the 21st Annual Convention, November 14–17," 1956, including the minutes of the board of directors meeting, November 14 and 18, 1956, NCNW Records, Series 2, Box 9, Folder 102, 3; Vivian Carter Mason to Eleanor Ponsonby, August 14, 1956, NCNW Records, Series 7, Box 1, Folder 3.

78. Vivian Carter Mason to Margaret Simms, April 30, 1956, NCNW Records, Series 7, Box 1, Folder 3, 1; Margaret Simms to Vivian Carter Mason, December 17, 1956, NCNW Records, Series 7, Box 9, Folder 8.

79. Jacqueline Nassy Brown, "Black Liverpool, Black America," 301.

80. Blassingame, *Slave Community*; Gutman, *Black Family*. For more recent work that assesses the historical significance of the black family for African Americans, see hooks, *Yearning*, 42; Yellin, *Harriet Jacobs*, 9; Jones, *Labor of Love, Labor of Sorrow*.

81. Feldstein, *Motherhood in Black and White*.

82. Frazier, *Negro Family in the United States*; Frazier, *Black Bourgeoisie*.

83. May, *Homeward Bound*; McDuffie, "The March of Young Southern Black Women."

84. Feldstein, "'I Wanted the Whole World to See,'" 265.

85. "Goodbye Mammy, Hello Mom," *Ebony*, March 1947, 36. Jones, *Labor of Love, Labor of Sorrow*, 224.

86. Hanson, *Mary McLeod Bethune*, 168.

87. National Council of Negro Women, "Annual Report of the National Council of Negro Women, 1954–1955," November 11, 1955, NCNW Records, Series 2, Box 8, Folder 85, 26–27.

88. Collins, *Black Feminist Thought*, 175–176; Boris, "Power of Motherhood," 25.

89. Stavney, "'Mothers of Tomorrow,'" 535. For more on the gendered "politics of respectability," see Higginbotham, *Righteous Discontent*.

90. Mintz, *Sweetness and Power*, 151.

91. Witt, *Black Hunger*.

92. Warnes, *Hunger Overcome?*, 3.

93. Wylie, *Starving on a Full Stomach*, 234.

94. Ibid., 59, 127.

95. *Children of South Africa: A Report Compiled by the Federation of South African Women*, 1955, Jack and Ray Simons Papers, Folder R9.3.2, 9–10.

96. Wylie, *Starving on a Full Stomach*, 217–218; Wylie, "The Changing Face of Hunger," 159.

97. Lilian Ngoyi speech, "FSAW Report: Transvaal Region Rent Increases Conference," 1954, Records of FSAW, Ba4.1.5, 5–7.

98. Vivian Carter Mason to Artishia W. Jordon, AME Church, 5 March 1956, NCNW Records, Series 7, Box 1, Folder 3.

99. Margaret Simms was directed to use pictures provided by the ACFS in national press releases that detailed the NCNW's work with the Feeding Scheme. See Vivian Carter Mason to Margaret Simms, January 26, 1956, NCNW Records, Series 7, Box 1, Folder 3. In January 1956 Vivian Carter Mason wrote to Pat Sutten requesting that she send one hundred copies of the ACFS pamphlets and yearly reports for circulation throughout the local NCNW councils: "Please remit by airmail about one hundred of the pamphlets and yearly reports."

100. Briggs, "Mother, Child, Race, Nation," 180–181.

101. Ibid., 191–193.

102. Anderson, *Bourgeois Radicals*, chap. 2.

103. Collins, *Black Feminist Thought*, 189–190.

104. The NCNW has been involved in a range of charitable activities in Africa from the mid-1950s to the present day. The NCNW records at the NABWH in Washington, DC, are a testament to the organization's African organizing.

Conclusion

1. The Reid family owned the *New York Herald Tribune*. The newspaper held a committed anticommunist stance and ran campaigns against the "communist influence" in the press. William Gordon arrived in Africa in 1958 and would eventually join the U.S. Information Agency. See William Gordon, interview by John Egerton, January 19, 1991, Interview A-0364, Southern Oral History Program Collection (#4007), http://docsouth.unc.edu/sohp/html_use/A-0364.html.

2. "American Journalist in Union: City Editor of 'Atlantic Daily World' on Two-Weeks Visit to South Africa," *Zonk!*, February 1959, 25; "U.S. Negro Editor Visits *New Age* Office," *New Age*, January 22, 1959.

3. Von Eschen, *Race against Empire*, chap. 4.

4. Rhonda Williams has emphasized how anticolonial activism in the 1950s helped lay the groundwork for the politics of Black Power, *Concrete Demands*, 48–70.

5. Though her focus is on tracing the increased reluctance of black liberals to challenge U.S. foreign policy, *Race against Empire* sometimes gives the impression that African Americans were either unable or unwilling to support anticolonial liberation struggles and shied away from condemning the U.S. government's relationship with South Africa; see Von Eschen, *Race against Empire*, esp. chap. 5.

6. Mary Helen Washington makes the case for the extension of leftist politics and the "black popular front" into the 1950s with her work on African American writers and artists following the World War II. Washington, *Other Blacklist*, 1–33.

7. Davies, *Left of Karl Marx*; Gore, Theoharis, and Woodard, *Want to Start a Revolution?*; Gore, *Radicalism at the Crossroads*; Higashida, *Black Internationalist Feminism*; McDuffie, *Sojourning for Freedom*; Washington, *Other Blacklist*.

8. Jake Hodder refers to this as a form of "(African) American Internationalism" in his excellent assessment of Bayard Rustin's political work in Africa in the 1950s; see Hodder, "Toward a Geography of Black Internationalism."

9. Anderson, *Bourgeois Radicals*. Tillery, Between Homeland and Motherland, chap. 3.

10. As Nikhil Pal Singh reminds us, if there was a "great divide" in the twentieth-century black freedom struggle, "it was between black activists and intellectuals who gravitated toward an identification with the U.S. state and social policy as the answer to black discontent, and those who eyed the rhetorical professions of American universality and inclusiveness from the more exacting and worldly standpoint of subjection to racializing power." See Singh, *Black Is a Country*, 109.

11. This is true of whiteness and blackness as political categories: Lake and Reynolds, *Drawing the Global Colour Line*; West, Martin, and Wilkins, *From Toussaint to Tupac*.

12. Patterson and Kelley, "Unfinished Migrations," 20.

13. Stuart Hall, "Cultural Identity and Diaspora," 224.

14. Stephens, "Disarticulating Black Internationalisms," 105.

15. Jacqueline Nassy Brown, "Black Liverpool, Black America," 291–325; Lao-Montes, "Decolonial Moves"; Stephens, *Black Empire*; Summers, "Diasporic Brotherhood"; Gunning, Hunter, and Mitchell, "Gender, Sexuality, and African Diasporas."

16. Unterhalter, "The Work of the Nation," 157–158; Onishi, "The New Negro of the Pacific," 207–209.

17. Onishi, "The New Negro of the Pacific," 207.

18. Leeds, "Toward the 'Higher Type of Womanhood,'" 3.

19. Weinbaum, "Reproducing Racial Globality," 23.

20. Ibid., 30–13, 37.

21. Mahon, "Eslanda Goode Robeson's African Journey"; Stephens, *Black Empire*. Robin D. G. Kelley discusses this in relation to the gender politics of Garveyism: "Defending Africa from imperialism was tantamount to defending black womanhood from rape; black men were called upon to redeem this oppressed and

degraded black woman, our mother of civilization, in a bold, chivalrous act." Kelley, *Freedom Dreams*, 27.

22. Higashida, *Black Internationalist Feminism*, 2; Blain, "'[F]or the Rights of Dark People in Every Part of the World.'"

23. Eslanda Goode Robeson, "Interview: African Women," n.d., Paul and Eslanda Robeson Collection, MSRC, Box 9, 4.

24. Mandela, foreword to *No Easy Victories*.

25. James Meriwether traces the effects that the Defiance Campaign had on African American protest in the early 1950s; see *Proudly We Can Be Africans*, chap. 3.

26. "We Can Learn from the Struggle in South Africa," *Freedom*, July 1952, 1.

27. Ibid.

28. C. L. R James, *Black Jacobins*, 314.

29. Hall's frequently quoted observation that "hegemonizing is hard work" is quoted in Kelley, "An Archaeology of Resistance," 295.

Bibliography

Manuscript Collections and Microfilm

South Africa
    Historical Papers, William Cullen Library, University of the Witwatersrand
        African Advertisements
        African National Congress Records, 1928–1975
        Community of the Resurrection Records
        Federation of South African Women Records
        Gerhart Interviews
        History Workshop Photographs
        Lilian Masediba Ngoyi Collection
        Pan-Africanist Records
        Records of the 1956 Treason Trial
        Records of the South African Institute of Race Relations, Oral History
            Project, 1981–1982
        Records of the South African Institute of Race Relations, Part 1
        Records of the South African Institute of Race Relations, Part 2
        Records of the South African Institute of Race Relations, Photographs
        Records of the South African Institute of Race Relations, Political Documents
        Records of the South African Institute of Race Relations, Political Publications
        Sophiatown Interviews, 1985–1987
    Manuscripts and Archives, University of Cape Town
        Jack and Ray Simons Collection
    South African National Archives, Pretoria
        Records of the South African Consul General, New York
        Records of the South African Embassy, Washington, DC
United States
    Foreign Relations of the United States Collection. Available at the
        U.S.Department of State Office of the Historian website, http://history
        .state.gov/historicaldocuments
        Foreign Relations of the United States, 1950, the Near East, South Asia, and
            Africa, Volume 5
        Foreign Relations of the United States, 1952–1954, Africa and South Asia (in
            two parts), Volume 11, Part 1
        Foreign Relations of the United States, 1955–1957, Africa, Volume 18
        Foreign Relations of the United States, Africa, 1958–1960, Africa, Volume 14

Manuscripts Division, Library of Congress, Washington, DC
  Mary McLeod Bethune Papers, Microfilm, Bethesda, MD, University
    Publications of America
  Papers of the NAACP, Frederick, MD, University Publications of America
  Papers of the National Negro Congress, Microfilm, Frederick, MD,
    University Publications of America
  Papers of Jackie Robinson
  A. Philip Randolph Papers
  Records of the American Committee on Africa, Microfilm, Bethesda, MD,
    University Publications of America
  Records of the Brotherhood of Sleeping Car Porters
  W.E.B. Du Bois Papers, Microfilm, Amherst, MA, University of Massachusetts
Moorland-Spingarn Research Center, Howard University, Washington, DC
  E. Franklin Frazier Papers
  Rayford W. Logan Papers
  Kwame Nkrumah Papers
  William L. Patterson Papers
  Paul and Eslanda Robeson Collection
  Max Yergan Papers
National Archives for Black Women's History, NCNW Council House,
    Washington, DC
  NABWH Photographic Collection
  Records of the National Council of Negro Women
Schomburg Center for Research in Black Culture, New York City
  Black Women's Oral History Project
  Louis E. Burnham Newspaper Collection
  Alice Childress Papers
  Eugene Gordon Papers
  Lorraine Hansberry Papers
  William Alphaeus Hunton Papers
  Canada Lee Papers, Microfilm
  Paul Robeson Papers
  Doxey A. Wilkerson Papers
Tamiment Library/Robert F. Wagner Labor Archives, New York University,
    New York City
  Communist Party of the USA Records
  James and Esther Cooper Jackson Papers
  John Pittman Papers

Newspapers and Journals

United States

Aframerican Women's Journal
Africa Today

Baltimore Afro-American
California Eagle
Chicago Defender
Crisis
Ebony
Freedom
New Africa
New York Age
New York Amsterdam News
New York Times
Norfolk Journal and Guide
Observer
Pittsburgh Courier
South African-American Survey
Spotlight on Africa
Telefact
Washington Post

South Africa

Bantu World
Clarion
Drum
Fighting Talk
Guardian
Hi-Note
International Bulletin of the Defiance Campaign
Liberation
New Age
People's World
Rand Daily Mail
Zonk!

Published Primary Sources

Abrahams, Peter. *Return to Goli*. London: Faber and Faber, 1953.

Bunting, Brian. *The Rise of the South African Reich*. London: Harmondsworth Penguin, 1969.

Du Bois, Shirley Graham. *Paul Robeson, Citizen of the World*. New York: J. Messner, 1946.

Du Bois, W. E. B. *The Negro*. New York: Henry Holt, 1915.

Fast, Howard. "Why the Fifth Amendment?" *Masses & Mainstream* 7, no. 2 (1954): 44–50.

Frazier, E. Franklin. *Black Bourgeoisie: The Rise of a New Middle Class*, 2nd ed. New York: Free Press, 1965.

——. *The Negro Family in the United States*. Chicago: University of Chicago Press, 1939.

Houser, George M. *No One Can Stop the Rain: Glimpses of Africa's Liberation Struggle*. New York: Pilgrim, 1989.

Huddleston, Trevor. *Naught for Your Comfort: An Account of Racial Relations in the Union of South Africa*. London: Collins, 1956.

James, C. L. R. *The Black Jacobins: Toussaint L'Ouverture and the San Domingo Revolution*. With introduction by James Walvin. London: Penguin, 2001.

Karis, Thomas, and Gwendolen Margaret Carter, eds. *From Protest to Challenge: A Documentary History of African Politics in South Africa 1882–1964*. Vol. 4. Stanford, CA: Hoover Institution Press, 1977.

Luthuli, Albert. *Let My People Go: An Autobiography*. London: Collins, 1962.

Mandela, Nelson. *Long Walk to Freedom: The Autobiography of Nelson Mandela*. Boston: Little, Brown, 1994.

Matthews, Frieda Bokwe. *Remembrances*. Bellville, South Africa: Mayibuye Books, 1995.

Matthews, Z. K. *Freedom for My People: The Autobiography of Z. K. Matthews, Southern Africa 1901 to 1968*. Cape Town: David Philip, 1981.

Matshikiza, Todd. *Chocolates for My Wife*. London: Hodder and Stoughton, 1961.

Modisane, Bloke. *Blame Me on History*. London: Penguin, 1990. First published 1963 by E. P. Dutton.

Paton, Alan. *Journey Continued: An Autobiography*. New York: Scribner, 1988.

Poitier, Sidney. *This Life*. New York: Knopf, 1980.

Robeson, Eslanda Goode. *African Journey*. London: Victor Gollancz, 1946.

Robeson, Paul. *Here I Stand*. Boston: Beacon, 1988.

——. *Paul Robeson Speaks: Writings, Speeches, Interviews, 1918–1974*. Edited by Philip Sheldon Foner. New York: Brunner/Mazel, 1978.

South Africa's Treason Trial. Johannesburg: Afrika! Publications, 1958.

Suid-Afrikaanse Biblioteke. Cape Town: South African Library Association, 1959.

Themba, Can. *The Will to Die*. London: Heinemann, 1972.

Thompson, Era Bell. *Africa, Land of My Fathers*. Garden City, NY: Doubleday, 1954.

The Union of South Africa. New York: South African Government Information Office, 1957.

Women's International Democratic Federation. *That They May Live, African Women Arise*. Berlin: Author, 1954.

Wright, Richard. *Black Power: Three Books from Exile: Black Power, The Color Curtain, and White Man, Listen!* New York: Harper Perennial Modern Classics, 2008.

Books

Adi, Hakim, and Marika Sherwood. *Pan-African History: Political Figures from Africa and the Diaspora since 1787*. London: Routledge, 2003.

Alexander, Michelle. *The New Jim Crow: Mass Incarceration in the Age of Colorblindness*. New York: New Press, 2012.

Anderson, Carol. *Bourgeois Radicals: The NAACP and the Struggle for Colonial Liberation, 1941–1960*. New York: Cambridge University Press, 2014.

———. *Eyes off the Prize: The United Nations and the African American Struggle for Human Rights, 1944–1955*. New York: Cambridge University Press, 2003.

Ansell, Gwen. *Soweto Blues: Jazz, Popular Music, and Politics in South Africa*. New York: Continuum, 2004.

Anthony, David Henry. *Max Yergan: Race Man, Internationalist, Cold Warrior*. New York: New York University Press, 2006.

Baldwin, Davarian L. *Chicago's New Negroes: Modernity, the Great Migration, and Black Urban Life*. Chapel Hill: University of North Carolina Press, 2007.

Baldwin, Kate A. *Beyond the Color Line and the Iron Curtain: Reading Encounters between Black and Red, 1922–1963*. Durham, NC: Duke University Press, 2003.

Baldwin, Lewis V. *Toward the Beloved Community: Martin Luther King Jr. and South Africa*. Cleveland: Pilgrim Press, 1995.

Barber, James, and John Barratt. *South Africa's Foreign Policy: The Search for Status and Security, 1945–1988*. Cambridge: Cambridge University Press, 1990.

Beinart, William. *Twentieth-Century South Africa*. Oxford: Oxford University Press, 2001.

Beinart, William, and Saul Dubow, eds. *Segregation and Apartheid in Twentieth-Century South Africa*. London: Routledge, 1995.

Benjamin, Walter. *Illuminations: Essays and Reflections*. Edited with an introduction by Hannah Arendt. Translated by Harry Zohn. New York: Schocken, 1969.

Berghe, Pierre L. van den. *South Africa, a Study in Conflict*. Berkeley: University of California Press, 1967.

Bernault, Florence, ed. *A History of Prison and Confinement in Africa*. Portsmouth, NH: Heinemann, 2003.

Bickford-Smith, Vivian. *Ethnic Pride and Racial Prejudice in Victorian Cape Town*. Cambridge: Cambridge University Press, 2004.

Biondi, Martha. *To Stand and Fight: The Struggle for Civil Rights in Postwar New York City*. Cambridge, MA: Harvard University Press, 2003.

Blackmon, Douglas A. *Slavery by Another Name: The Re-Enslavement of Black People in America from the Civil War to World War II*. New York: Doubleday, 2008.

Blackwell, Joyce. *No Peace without Freedom: Race and the Women's International League for Peace and Freedom, 1915–1975*. Carbondale: Southern Illinois University Press, 2004.

Blassingame, John W. *The Slave Community: Plantation Life in the Antebellum South*. rev., enl. ed. New York: Oxford University Press, 1979.

Blum, William. *Killing Hope: U.S. Military and CIA Interventions since World War II*. London: Zed Books, 2003.

Borstelmann, Thomas. *Apartheid's Reluctant Uncle: The United States and Southern Africa in the Early Cold War.* Oxford: Oxford University Press, 1993.

———. *The Cold War and the Color Line: American Race Relations in the Global Arena.* Cambridge, MA: Harvard University Press, 2003.

Brooks, Pamela E. *Boycotts, Buses, and Passes: Black Women's Resistance in the U.S. South and South Africa.* Amherst: University of Massachusetts Press, 2008.

Campbell, James T. *Middle Passages: African American Journeys to Africa, 1787–2005.* New York: Penguin, 2006.

———. *Race, Nation, & Empire in American History.* Chapel Hill: University of North Carolina Press, 2007.

———. *Songs of Zion: The African Methodist Episcopal Church in the United States and South Africa.* Chapel Hill: University of North Carolina Press, 1998.

Caster, Peter. *Prisons, Race, and Masculinity in Twentieth-Century U.S. Literature and Film.* Columbus: Ohio State University Press, 2008.

Cell, John Whitson. *The Highest Stage of White Supremacy: The Origins of Segregation in South Africa and the American South.* Cambridge: Cambridge University Press, 1982.

Chanock, Martin. *The Making of South African Legal Culture 1902–1936: Fear, Favour and Prejudice.* Cambridge: Cambridge University Press, 2001.

Chapman, Michael. *The "Drum" Decade: Stories from the 1950s.* Pietermaritzburg: University of KwaZulu-Natal Press, 1996.

Chrisman, Laura. *Postcolonial Contraventions: Cultural Readings of Race, Imperialism, and Transnationalism.* Manchester: Manchester University Press, 2003.

Clark, Nancy L., and William H. Worger. *South Africa: The Rise and Fall of Apartheid.* London: Routledge, 2016.

Collier-Thomas, Bettye, and National Council of Negro Women. *N.C.N.W., 1935–1980.* Washington, DC: National Council of Negro Women, 1981.

Collins, Patricia Hill. *Black Feminist Thought: Knowledge, Consciousness, and the Politics of Empowerment.* 2nd ed. New York: Routledge, 2000.

Corbould, Clare. *Becoming African Americans: Black Public Life in Harlem, 1919–1939.* Cambridge, MA: Harvard University Press, 2009.

Curtin, Mary Ellen. *Black Prisoners and Their World, Alabama, 1865–1900.* Charlottesville: University of Virginia Press, 2000.

Davenport, T. R. H., and Christopher Saunders. *South Africa: A Modern History.* 5th ed. Basingstoke, UK: Macmillan, 2000.

Davies, Carole Boyce. *Left of Karl Marx: The Political Life of Black Communist Claudia Jones.* Durham, NC: Duke University Press, 2007.

Dawson, Michael C. *Blacks In and Out of the Left.* Cambridge, MA: Harvard University Press, 2013.

Dolinar, Brian. *The Black Cultural Front: Black Writers and Artists of the Depression Generation.* Jackson: University Press of Mississippi, 2012.

Dongen, Luc van, Stéphanie Roulin, and Giles Scott-Smith, eds. *Transnational Anti-Communism and the Cold War: Agents, Activities, and Networks.* New York: Palgrave Macmillan, 2014.

Draper, Theodore. *The Roots of American Communism.* New York: Viking Press, 1957.

Duberman, Martin B. *Paul Robeson: A Biography.* London: New Press, 2005.

Dubow, Saul. *Apartheid, 1948–1994.* Oxford: Oxford University Press, 2014.

———. *Racial Segregation and the Origins of Apartheid in South Africa, 1919–1936.* London: Macmillan, 1989.

———. *Scientific Racism in Modern South Africa.* Cambridge: Cambridge University Press, 1995.

Dudziak, Mary L. *Cold War Civil Rights: Race and the Image of American Democracy.* Princeton, NJ: Princeton University Press, 2002.

Edwards, Brent Hayes. *The Practice of Diaspora: Literature, Translation, and the Rise of Black Internationalism.* Cambridge, MA: Harvard University Press, 2003.

Ellis, Stephen. *External Mission: The ANC in Exile, 1960–1990.* Oxford: Oxford University Press, 2013.

Ellis, Stephen, and Tsepho Sechaba. *Comrades against Apartheid: The ANC and the South African Communist Party in Exile.* Bloomington: Indiana University Press, 1992.

Engel, Elisabeth. *Encountering Empire: African American Missionaries in Colonial Africa, 1900–1939.* Stuttgart: Franz Steiner, 2015.

Enloe, Cynthia H. *Bananas, Beaches and Bases: Making Feminist Sense of International Politics.* Berkeley: University of California Press, 2000.

Evans, Ivan Thomas. *Bureaucracy and Race: Native Administration in South Africa.* Berkeley : University of California Press, 1997.

Ewing, Adam. *The Age of Garvey: How a Jamaican Activist Created a Mass Movement and Changed Global Black Politics.* Princeton, NJ: Princeton University Press, 2014.

Feldstein, Ruth. *How It Feels to Be Free: Black Women Entertainers and the Civil Rights Movement.* New York: Oxford University Press, 2014.

———. *Motherhood in Black and White: Race and Sex in American Liberalism, 1930–1965.* Ithaca, NY: Cornell University Press, 2000.

Foner, Eric. *Free Soil, Free Labor, Free Men: The Ideology of the Republican Party before the Civil War.* New York: Oxford University Press, 1995.

Foucault, Michel. *Discipline and Punish: The Birth of the Prison.* Translated by Alan Sheridan. New edition. London: Penguin, 1991.

Fredrickson, George M. *Black Liberation: A Comparative History of Black Ideologies in the United States and South Africa.* Oxford: Oxford University Press, 1995.

———. *White Supremacy: A Comparative Study in American and South African History.* Oxford: Oxford University Press, 1981.

Gaines, Kevin K. *American Africans in Ghana: Black Expatriates and the Civil Rights Era*. Chapel Hill: The University of North Carolina Press, 2008.

———. *Uplifting the Race: Black Leadership, Politics, and Culture in the Twentieth Century*. Chapel Hill: University of North Carolina Press, 1998.

Garrow, David J. *Bearing the Cross: Martin Luther King, Jr., and the Southern Christian Leadership Conference*. New York: Open Road Integrated Media, 2015.

Gasa, Nomboniso. *Women in South African History: They Remove Boulders and Cross Rivers*. Cape Town: HSRC Press, 2007.

Geisler, Gisela G. *Women and the Remaking of Politics in Southern Africa: Negotiating Autonomy, Incorporation, and Representation*. Uppsala, Sweden: Nordic Africa Institute, 2004.

Gellman, Erik S. *Death Blow to Jim Crow: The National Negro Congress and the Rise of Militant Civil Rights*. repr. Chapel Hill: The University of North Carolina Press, 2014.

Gerhart, Gail M. *Black Power in South Africa: The Evolution of an Ideology*. Berkeley: University of California Press, 1978.

Gill, Glenda Eloise. *No Surrender! No Retreat!: African-American Pioneer Performers of Twentieth-Century American Theater*. New York: St. Martin's, 2000.

Gilmore, Glenda Elizabeth. *Defying Dixie: The Radical Roots of Civil Rights, 1919–1950*. New York: W. W. Norton, 2008.

Gilroy, Paul. *The Black Atlantic: Modernity and Double Consciousness*. Cambridge, MA: Harvard University Press, 1993.

Glaser, Clive L. *Bo-Tsotsi: The Youth Gangs of Soweto, 1935–1976*. Portsmouth, NH: Heinemann, 2000.

Goodhew, David. *Respectability and Resistance: A History of Sophiatown*. Westport, CT: Praeger, 2004.

Goodman, Jordan. *Paul Robeson: A Watched Man*. London: Verso, 2013.

Goodman, Walter. *The Committee: The Extraordinary Career of the House Committee on Un-American Activities*. London: Secker and Warburg, 1969.

Gore, Dayo F. *Radicalism at the Crossroads: African American Women Activists in the Cold War*. New York: New York University Press, 2011.

Gore, Dayo F., Jeanne Theoharis, and Komozi Woodard, eds. *Want to Start a Revolution?: Radical Women in the Black Freedom Struggle*. New York: New York University Press, 2009.

Goudsouzian, Aram. *Sidney Poitier: Man, Actor, Icon*. Chapel Hill: University of North Carolina Press, 2004.

Green, Adam. *Selling the Race: Culture, Community, and Black Chicago, 1940–1955*. Chicago: University of Chicago Press, 2007.

Greenberg, Stanley B. *Legitimating the Illegitimate: States, Markets, and Resistance in South Africa*. Berkeley: University of California Press, 1987.

Gutman, Herbert George. *The Black Family in Slavery and Freedom, 1750–1925*. New York: Vintage, 1977.

Hall, Simon. *American Patriotism, American Protest: Social Movements since the Sixties*. Philadelphia: University of Pennsylvania Press, 2011.

Hamilton, Charles V. *Adam Clayton Powell, Jr.: The Political Biography of an American Dilemma*. New York: Cooper Square, 2001.

Hanson, Joyce Ann. *Mary McLeod Bethune and Black Women's Political Activism*. Columbia: University of Missouri Press, 2003.

Harrold, Stanley. *The Rise of Aggressive Abolitionism: Addresses to the Slaves*. Lexington: University Press of Kentucky, 2004.

Hassim, Shireen. *Women's Organizations and Democracy in South Africa: Contesting Authority*. Madison: University of Wisconsin Press, 2006.

Higashida, Cheryl. *Black Internationalist Feminism: Women Writers of the Black Left, 1945–1995*. Urbana: University of Illinois Press, 2011.

Higginbotham, Evelyn Brooks. *Righteous Discontent: The Women's Movement in the Black Baptist Church, 1880–1920*. Cambridge, MA: Harvard University Press, 1994.

Holloway, David. *Stalin and the Bomb: The Soviet Union and Atomic Energy, 1939–1956*. New Haven, CT: Yale University Press, 1994.

hooks, bell. *Yearning: Race, Gender, and Cultural Politics*. Toronto: Between-the-Lines, 1990.

Horne, Gerald. *Black and Red: W.E.B. Du Bois and the Afro-American Response to the Cold War, 1944–1963*. Albany: State University of New York Press, 1986.

———. *Black Liberation/Red Scare: Ben Davis and the Communist Party*. Newark: University of Delaware Press, 1993.

———. *Black Revolutionary: William Patterson and the Globalization of the African American Freedom Struggle*. Urbana: University of Illinois Press, 2013.

———. *Cold War in a Hot Zone: The United States Confronts Labor and Independence Struggles in the British West Indies*. Philadelphia: Temple University Press, 2007.

———. *Communist Front?: The Civil Rights Congress, 1946–1956*. Madison, NJ: Fairleigh Dickinson University Press, 1988.

———. *The End of Empires: African Americans and India*. Philadelphia: Temple University Press, 2009.

———. *The Final Victim of the Blacklist: John Howard Lawson, Dean of the Hollywood Ten*. Berkeley: University of California Press, 2006.

———. *Paul Robeson: The Artist as Revolutionary*. London: Pluto Press, 2016.

Horton, James Oliver, and Lois E. Horton. *Hard Road to Freedom: The Story of African America*. Vol. 1, *From African Roots through the Civil War*. New Brunswick, NJ: Rutgers University Press, 2002.

Hostetter, David. *Movement Matters: American Antiapartheid Activism and the Rise of Multicultural Politics*. New York: Routledge, 2006.

Iliffe, John. *Honour in African History*. Cambridge: Cambridge University Press, 2004.

Irwin, Ryan M. *Gordian Knot: Apartheid and the Unmaking of the Liberal World Order*. New York: Oxford University Press, 2012.

Iton, Richard. *In Search of the Black Fantastic: Politics and Popular Culture in the Post-Civil Rights Era*. New York: Oxford University Press, 2008.

Jaji, Tsitsi Ella. *Africa in Stereo: Modernism, Music, and Pan-African Solidarity*. New York: Oxford University Press, 2014.

James, Leslie. *George Padmore and Decolonization from Below: Pan-Africanism, the Cold War, and the End of Empire*. New York: Palgrave Macmillan, 2014.

Jones, Jacqueline. *Labor of Love, Labor of Sorrow: Black Women, Work, and the Family from Slavery to the Present*. New York: Vintage, 1995.

Kaplan, Amy. *The Anarchy of Empire in the Making of U.S. Culture*. Cambridge, MA: Harvard University Press, 2002.

Katznelson, Ira. *Fear Itself: The New Deal and the Origins of Our Time*. New York: W.W. Norton, 2013.

Keiler, Allan R. *Marian Anderson: A Singer's Journey*. Urbana: University of Illinois Press, 2002.

Kelley, Robin D. G. *Africa Speaks, America Answers: Modern Jazz in Revolutionary Times*. Cambridge, MA: Harvard University Press, 2012.

——. *Freedom Dreams: The Black Radical Imagination*. Boston: Beacon Press, 2002.

——. *Hammer and Hoe: Alabama Communists during the Great Depression*. Chapel Hill: University of North Carolina Press, 1990.

——. *Race Rebels: Culture, Politics, and the Black Working Class*. New York: Free Press, 1994.

Kiesel, Diane. *She Can Bring Us Home: Dr. Dorothy Boulding Ferebee, Civil Rights Pioneer*. Lincoln: University of Nebraska Press, 2015.

Kim, Jodi. *Ends of Empire: Asian American Critique and the Cold War*. Minneapolis: University of Minnesota Press, 2010.

Kwon, Heonik. *The Other Cold War*. New York: Columbia University Press, 2010.

Lake, Marilyn, and Henry Reynolds. *Drawing the Global Colour Line: White Men's Countries and the International Challenge of Racial Equality*. Cambridge: Cambridge University Press, 2008.

Laville, Helen. *Cold War Women: The International Activities of American Women's Organisations*. Manchester: Manchester University Press, 2002.

Lemke, Sieglinde. *Primitivist Modernism: Black Culture and the Origins of Transatlantic Modernism*. Oxford: Oxford University Press, 1998.

Lewis, David L. *W.E.B. Du Bois: The Fight for Equality and the American Century, 1919–1963*. New York: Henry Holt, 2001.

Lewis, George. *The White South and the Red Menace: Segregationists, Anticommunism, and Massive Resistance, 1945–1965*. Gainesville: University Press of Florida, 2004.

Lichtenstein, Alexander C. *Twice the Work of Free Labor: The Political Economy of Convict Labor in the New South*. London: Verso, 1996.

Lieberman, Robbie, and Clarence Lang, eds. *Anticommunism and the African American Freedom Movement: 'Another Side of the Story.'* New York: Palgrave Macmillan, 2009.

Lulat, Y. G. M. *United States Relations with South Africa: A Critical Overview from the Colonial Period to the Present.* New York: Peter Lang, 2008.

Lynch, Hollis Ralph. *Black American Radicals and the Liberation of Africa: The Council on African Affairs 1937–1955.* Ithaca, NY: Africana Studies and Research Center, 1978.

MacLean, Nancy. *Freedom Is Not Enough: The Opening of the American Workplace.* Cambridge, MA: Harvard University Press, 2008.

Makalani, Minkah. *In the Cause of Freedom Radical Black Internationalism from Harlem to London, 1917–1939.* Chapel Hill: University of North Carolina Press, 2011.

Marable, Manning. *Race, Reform, and Rebellion: The Second Reconstruction and Beyond in Black America, 1945–2006.* 3rd ed. Jackson: University Press of Mississippi, 2007.

Masuda, Hajimu. *Cold War Crucible: The Korean Conflict and the Postwar World.* Cambridge, MA: Harvard University Press, 2015.

Matera, Marc. *Black London: The Imperial Metropolis and Decolonization in the Twentieth Century.* Oakland: University of California Press, 2015.

Mattera, Don. *Memory Is the Weapon.* Oxford: African Books Collective, 2009.

May, Elaine Tyler. *Homeward Bound: American Families in the Cold War Era.* New York: Basic, 1988.

McDuffie, Erik S. *Sojourning for Freedom: Black Women, American Communism, and the Making of Black Left Feminism.* Durham, NC: Duke University Press, 2011.

Melamed, Jodi. *Represent and Destroy: Rationalizing Violence in the New Racial Capitalism.* Minneapolis: University of Minnesota Press, 2011.

Meriwether, James H. *Proudly We Can Be Africans: Black Americans and Africa, 1935–1961.* Chapel Hill: University of North Carolina Press, 2002.

Miller, Jamie. *An African Volk: The Apartheid Regime and Its Search for Survival.* New York: Oxford University Press, 2016.

Minter, William. *King Solomon's Mines Revisited: Western Interests and the Burdened History of Southern Africa.* New York: Basic, 1986.

Minter, William, Gail Hovey, and Charles Cobb Jr. *No Easy Victories: African Liberation and American Activists over a Half-Century, 1950–2000.* Trenton, NJ: Africa World Press, 2007.

Mintz, Sidney W. *Sweetness and Power: The Place of Sugar in Modern History.* Reprint, New York: Penguin, 1986.

Mitchell, Loften. *Black Drama: The Story of the American Negro in the Theatre.* New York: Hawthorn, 1967.

Morrell, Robert. *Changing Men in Southern Africa.* London: Zed, 2001.

Naison, Mark. *Communists in Harlem during the Depression.* Urbana: University of Illinois Press, 1983.

Nattrass, Jill. *The South African Economy: Its Growth and Change*. Cape Town: Oxford University Press, 1981.

Nesbitt, Francis Njubi. *Race for Sanctions: African Americans against Apartheid, 1946–1994*. Bloomington: Indiana University Press, 2004.

Nixon, Rob. *Homelands, Harlem and Hollywood: South African Culture and the World Beyond*. New York: Routledge, 1994.

Noer, Thomas. *Cold War and Black Liberation: The United States and White Africa, 1948–1968*. Columbia: University of Missouri Press, 1985.

Nollen, Scott Allen. *Paul Robeson: Film Pioneer*. Jefferson, NC: McFarland, 2010.

Nolutshungu, Sam C. *South Africa in Africa: A Study in Ideology and Foreign Policy*. Manchester: Manchester University Press, 1975.

Plummer, Brenda Gayle. *Rising Wind: Black Americans and U.S. Foreign Affairs, 1935–1960*. Chapel Hill: University of North Carolina Press, 1996.

Purnell, Brian. *Fighting Jim Crow in the County of Kings: The Congress of Racial Equality in Brooklyn*. Lexington: University Press of Kentucky, 2013.

Ransby, Barbara. *Eslanda: The Large and Unconventional Life of Mrs. Paul Robeson*. New Haven, CT: Yale University Press, 2013.

Rodriguez, Junius P. *Slavery in the United States: A Social, Political, and Historical Encyclopedia*. Santa Barbara, CA: ABC-CLIO, 2007.

Rupp, Leila J. *Worlds of Women: The Making of an International Women's Movement*. Princeton, NJ: Princeton University Press, 1997.

Scanlon, Helen. *Representation and Reality: Portraits of Women's Lives in the Western Cape, 1948–1976*. Cape Town: HSRC Press, 2007.

Schrecker, Ellen W. *Many Are the Crimes: McCarthyism in America*. Princeton, NJ: Princeton University Press, 1999.

Singh, Nikhil Pal. *Black Is a Country: Race and the Unfinished Struggle for Democracy*. Cambridge, MA: Harvard University Press, 2004.

Slate, Nico. *Colored Cosmopolitanism: The Shared Struggle for Freedom in the United States and India*. Cambridge, MA: Harvard University Press, 2012.

Smith, Mona Z. *Becoming Something: The Story of Canada Lee*. New York: Faber and Faber, 2004.

Stephens, Michelle Ann. *Black Empire: The Masculine Global Imaginary of Caribbean Intellectuals in the United States, 1914–1962*. Durham, NC: Duke University Press, 2005.

Stoler, Ann Laura, ed. *Haunted by Empire: Geographies of Intimacy in North American History*. Durham, NC: Duke University Press, 2006.

Sugrue, Thomas J. *Sweet Land of Liberty: The Forgotten Struggle for Civil Rights in the North*. New York: Random House, 2008.

Sullivan, Patricia. *Lift Every Voice: The NAACP and the Making of the Civil Rights Movement*. New York: New Press, 2009.

Swindall, Lindsey R. *The Path to the Greater, Freer, Truer World: Southern Civil Rights and Anticolonialism, 1937–1955*. Gainesville: University Press of Florida, 2014.

———. *Paul Robeson: A Life of Activism and Art.* Lanham, MD: Rowman & Littlefield Publishers, 2013.

Tillery, Alvin B., Jr., *Between Homeland and Motherland: Africa, U.S. Foreign Policy, and Black Leadership in America.* Ithaca, NY: Cornell University Press, 2011.

Torpey, John C. *The Invention of the Passport: Surveillance, Citizenship and the State.* Cambridge: Cambridge University Press, 2010.

Tuck, Stephen, and Kevin M. Kruse, eds. *Fog of War: The Second World War and the Civil Rights Movement.* New York: Oxford University Press, 2012.

Vinson, Robert Trent. *The Americans Are Coming! Dreams of African American Liberation in Segregationist South Africa.* Athens: Ohio University Press, 2012.

Von Eschen, Penny M. *Race against Empire: Black Americans and Anticolonialism, 1937–1957.* Ithaca, NY: Cornell University Press, 1997.

———. *Satchmo Blows Up the World: Jazz Ambassadors Play the Cold War.* Cambridge, MA: Harvard University Press, 2004.

Wald, Alan M. *Writing from the Left: New Essays on Radical Culture and Politics.* London: Verso, 1994.

Walker, Cherryl. *Women and Resistance in South Africa.* Cape Town: David Philip, 1991.

Warnes, Andrew. *Hunger Overcome?: Food and Resistance in Twentieth-Century African American Literature.* Athens: University of Georgia Press, 2004.

Washington, Mary Helen. *The Other Blacklist: The African American Literary and Cultural Left of the 1950s.* New York: Columbia University Press, 2014.

Weigand, Kate. *Red Feminism: American Communism and the Making of Women's Liberation.* Baltimore, MD: Johns Hopkins University Press, 2001.

West, Michael O., William G. Martin, and Fanon Che Wilkins. *From Toussaint to Tupac: The Black International since the Age of Revolution.* Chapel Hill: University of North Carolina Press, 2009.

Westad, Odd Arne. *The Global Cold War: Third World Interventions and the Making of Our Times.* New York: Cambridge University Press, 2005.

White, Deborah. *Too Heavy a Load: Black Women in Defense of Themselves, 1894–1994.* New York: W.W. Norton, 1999.

Witt, Doris. *Black Hunger: Food and the Politics of U.S. Identity.* New York: Oxford University Press, 1999.

Wolcott, Victoria W. *Remaking Respectability: African American Women in Interwar Detroit.* Chapel Hill: University of North Carolina Press, 2001.

Woods, Jeff. *Black Struggle, Red Scare: Segregation and Anti-Communism in the South, 1948–1968.* Baton Rouge: Louisiana State University Press, 2004.

Worcester, Kent. *C.L.R. James: A Political Biography.* Albany: State University of New York Press, 1996.

Worden, Nigel. *The Making of Modern South Africa: Conquest, Apartheid, Democracy.* 4th ed. Oxford: Blackwell, 2007.

Wylie, Diana. *Starving on a Full Stomach: Hunger and the Triumph of Cultural Racism in Modern South Africa.* Charlottesville: University of Virginia Press, 2001.

Yellin, Jean Fagan. *Harriet Jacobs: A Life*. New York: Basic Civitas, 2004.

Zeigler, James. *Red Scare Racism and Cold War Black Radicalism*. Jackson: University Press of Mississippi, 2015.

Articles and Book Chapters

Adler, K. H. "Gendering Histories of Homes and Homecomings." *Gender & History* 21, no. 3 (2009): 455–464.

Alexander, Jocelyn. "Political Prisoners' Memoirs in Zimbabwe: Narratives of Self and Nation." *Cultural and Social History* 5, no. 4 (2008): 395–409.

Anderson, Carol. "International Conscience, the Cold War, and Apartheid: The NAACP's Alliance with the Reverend Michael Scott for South West Africa's Liberation, 1946–1951." *Journal of World History* 19, no. 3 (2008): 297–325.

Arnesen, Eric. "Civil Rights and the Cold War at Home: Postwar Activism, Anticommunism, and the Decline of the Left." *American Communist History* 11, no. 1 (2012): 5–44.

———. "The Final Conflict? On the Scholarship of Civil Rights, the Left and the Cold War." *American Communist History* 11, no. 1 (2012): 63–80.

Baldwin, Alan. "Mass Removals and Separate Development." *Journal of Southern African Studies* 1, no. 2 (1975): 215–227.

Bates, Beth T. " 'Double V for Victory' Mobilizes Black Detroit, 1941–1946." In *Freedom North: Black Freedom Struggles outside the South, 1940–1980*, edited by Jeanne F. Theoharis and Komozi Woodard, 17–39. New York: Palgrave Macmillan, 2003.

Berg, Manfred. "Black Civil Rights and Liberal Anticommunism: The NAACP in the Early Cold War." *Journal of American History* 94, no. 1 (2007): 75–96.

Berger, Iris. "An African American 'Mother of the Nation': Madie Hall Xuma in South Africa, 1940–1963." In *Extending the Diaspora: New Histories of Black People*, edited by Dawne Y. Curry, Eric D. Duke, and Marshanda A. Smith, 125–156. Champaign: University of Illinois Press, 2009.

Blain, Keisha N. " '[F]or the Rights of Dark People in Every Part of the World': Pearl Sherrod, Black Internationalist Feminism, and Afro-Asian Politics during the 1930s." *Souls* 17, nos. 1–2 (2015): 90–112.

Bonner, Philip L. "African Urbanisation on the Rand between the 1930s and 1960s: Its Social Character and Political Consequences." *Journal of Southern African Studies* 21, no. 1 (1995): 115–129.

———. "The Antinomies of Nelson Mandela." In *The Cambridge Companion to Nelson Mandela*, edited by Rita Barnard, 29–49. New York: Cambridge University Press, 2014.

———. "Family, Crime and Political Consciousness on the East Rand, 1939–1955." *Journal of Southern African Studies* 14, no. 3 (1988): 393–420.

Boris, Eileen. "Power of Motherhood: Black and White Activist Women Redefine the 'Political.' " *Yale Journal of Law and Feminism* 2, no. 1 (1989): 25–49.

Borstelmann, Thomas. "Jim Crow's Coming Out: Race Relations and American Foreign Policy in the Truman Years." *Presidential Studies Quarterly* 29, no. 3 (1999): 549–569.

Bosworth, Mary. "Identity, Citizenship, and Punishment." In *Race, Gender, and Punishment: From Colonialism to the War on Terror*, edited by Jeanne Flavin and Mary Bosworth, 134–148. New Brunswick, NJ: Rutgers University Press, 2007.

Briggs, Laura. "Mother, Child, Race, Nation: The Visual Iconography of Rescue and the Politics of Transnational and Transracial Adoption." *Gender & History* 15, no. 2 (2003): 179–200.

Brock, Lisa. "The 1950s: Africa Solidarity Rising." In *No Easy Victories: African Liberation and American Activists over a Half-Century, 1950–2000*, edited by William Minter, Gail Hovey, and Charles Cobb Jr., 59–72. Trenton, NJ: Africa World Press, 2007.

Brooks, Pam. "Crossing Borders: A Black Feminist Approach to Researching the Comparative Histories of Black Women's Resistance in the U.S. South and South Africa." *Safundi* 4, no. 1 (2003): 1–16.

Brown, Jacqueline Nassy. "Black Liverpool, Black America, and the Gendering of Diasporic Space." *Cultural Anthropology* 13, no. 3 (1998): 291–325.

Brown, Kathleen A. "The 'Savagely Fathered and Un-Mothered World' of the Communist Party, U.S.A.: Feminism, Maternalism, and 'Mother Bloor.'" *Feminist Studies* 25, no. 3 (1999): 537–570.

Byrd, Brandon R. "Prisons as Spaces of Friendships in Apartheid South Africa." *History Australia* 3, no. 2 (2006): 1–13.

———. "The Transnational Work of Moral Elevation: African American Women and the Reformation of Haiti, 1874–1950." *Palimpsest: A Journal on Women, Gender, and the Black International* 5, no. 2 (2016): 128–50.

Campbell, James T. "The Americanization of South Africa." In *"Here, There and Everywhere": The Foreign Politics of American Popular Culture*, edited by Reinhold Wagnleitner and Elaine Tyler May, 34–63. Lebanon, NH: University Press of New England, 2000.

Castledine, Jacqueline. "Gender, Jazz, and Justice in Cold War Freedom Movements." In *Freedom Rights: New Perspectives on the Civil Rights Movement*, edited by Danielle L. McGuire and John Dittmer, 223–246. Lexington: University Press of Kentucky, 2011.

———. "'In a Solid Bond of Unity': Anticolonial Feminism in the Cold War Era." *Journal of Women's History* 20, no. 4 (2008): 57–81.

Chappell, Marisa, Jenny Hutchinson, and Brian Ward. "'Dress modestly, neatly . . . as if you were going to church': Respectability, Class, and Gender in the Montgomery Bus Boycott and the Early Civil Rights Movement." In *Gender and the Civil Rights Movement*, edited by Peter John Ling and Sharon Monteith, 69–100. New Brunswick, NJ: Rutgers University Press, 2004.

Chrisman, Laura, "Rethinking Black Atlanticism." *Black Scholar* 30, nos. 3–4 (2000): 12–17.

Clowes, Lindsay. "'Are You Going to Be MISS (or MR) Africa?' Contesting Masculinity in Drum Magazine 1951–1953." *Gender & History* 13, no. 1 (2001): 1–20.

——. "Masculinity, Matrimony and Generation: Reconfiguring Patriarchy in Drum 1951–1983*." *Journal of Southern African Studies* 34, no. 1 (2008): 179–192.

——. "Men and Children: Changing Constructions of Fatherhood in Drum Magazine, 1951–1965." In *Baba: Men and Fatherhood in South Africa*, edited by Linda M. Richter and Robert Morrell, 108–119. Cape Town: HSRC Press, 2006.

Crankshaw, Owen. "Class, Race and Residence in Black Johannesburg, 1923–1970." *Journal of Historical Sociology* 18, no. 4 (2005): 353–393.

Davenport, Rodney. "African Townsmen? South African Natives (Urban Areas) Legislation through the Years." *African Affairs* 68, no. 271 (1969): 95–109.

Davies, Carole Boyce. "Deportable Subjects: U.S. Immigration Laws and the Criminalizing of Communism." *South Atlantic Quarterly* 100, no. 4 (2001): 949–966.

Demissie, Fassil. "Controlling and 'Civilising Natives' through Architecture and Town Planning in South Africa." *Social Identities* 10, no. 4 (2004): 483–507.

Dubow, Saul. "Afrikaner Nationalism, Apartheid and the Conceptualization of 'Race.'" *Journal of African History* 33, no. 2 (1992): 209–237.

——. "Smuts, the United Nations and the Rhetoric of Race and Rights." *Journal of Contemporary History* 43, no.1 (2008): 45–74.

Dudziak, Mary L. "*Brown* as a Cold War Case." *Journal of American History* 91, no. 1 (2004): 32–42.

——. "The Little Rock Crisis and Foreign Affairs: Race, Resistance and the Image of American Democracy." *Southern California Law Review* 70, no. 6 (1997): 1641–1716.

Ellapen, Jordache Abner. "The Cinematic Township: Cinematic Representations of the 'Township Space' and Who Can Claim the Rights to Representation in Post-apartheid South African Cinema." *Journal of African Cultural Studies* 19, no. 1 (2007): 113–138.

Erlank, Natasha. "Gender and Masculinity in South African Nationalist Discourse, 1912–1950." *Feminist Studies* 29, no. 3 (2003): 653–671.

Featherstone, David. "Black Internationalism, Subaltern Cosmopolitanism, and the Spatial Politics of Antifascism." *Annals of the Association of American Geographers* 103, no. 6 (2013): 1406–20.

Feldstein, Ruth. "'I Wanted the Whole World to See': Race, Gender and Constructions of Motherhood in the Death of Emmett Till." In *Not June Cleaver: Women and Gender in Postwar America, 1945–1960*, edited by Joanne Jay Meyerowitz, 263–303. Philadelphia: Temple University Press, 1994.

Ferguson, James. "Formalities of Poverty: Thinking about Social Assistance in Neoliberal South Africa." *African Studies Review* 50, no. 2 (2007): 71–86.

Fourchard, Laurent. "The Making of the Juvenile Delinquent in Nigeria and South Africa, 1930–1970." *History Compass* 8, no. 2 (2010): 129–142.

Gaitskell, Deborah, and Elaine Unterhalter. "Mothers of the Nation: A Comparative Analysis of Nation, Race and Motherhood in Afrikaner

Nationalism and the African National Congress." In *Woman-Nation-State*, edited by Nira Yuval-Davis and Floya Anthias, 58–78. London: Palgrave Macmillan, 1989.

Gallagher, Julie A. "The National Council of Negro Women, Human Rights, and the Cold War." In *Breaking the Wave: Women, Their Organizations, and Feminism, 1945–1985*, edited by Kathleen A. Laughlin and Jacqueline L. Castledine, 80–98. New York: Routledge, 2011.

Gasa, Nomboniso. "Feminisms, Motherisms, Patriarchies and Women's Voices in the 1950s." In *Women in South African History: They Remove Boulders and Cross Rivers*, edited by Nomboniso Gasa, 207–231. Cape Town: HSRC Press, 2007.

Geisler, Gisela. "'Parliament Is Another Terrain of Struggle': Women, Men and Politics in South Africa." *Journal of Modern African Studies* 38, no. 4 (2000): 605–630.

Giliomee, Hermann. "A Note on Bantu Education, 1953 to 1970." *South African Journal of Economics* 77, no. 1 (2009): 190–198.

Gillespie, Kelly. "Containing the 'Wandering Native': Racial Jurisdiction and the Liberal Politics of Prison Reform in 1940s South Africa." *Journal of Southern African Studies* 37, no. 3 (2011): 499–515.

Ginwala, Frene. "Women and the African National Congress, 1912–1943." *Agenda: Empowering Women for Gender Equity* 8 (1990): 77–93.

Goodhew, David. "The People's Police-Force: Communal Policing Initiatives in the Western Areas of Johannesburg, circa 1930–62." *Journal of Southern African Studies* 19, no. 3 (1993): 447–470.

———. "Working-Class Respectability: The Example of the Western Areas of Johannesburg, 1930–55." *Journal of African History* 41, no. 2 (2000): 241–266.

Gordon, Linda. "Internal Colonialism and Gender." In *Haunted by Empire: Geographies of Intimacy in North American History*, edited by Ann Laura Stoler, 427–451. Durham, NC: Duke University Press, 2006.

Gore, Dayo F. "'The Danger of Being an Active Anti-Communist': Expansive Black Left Politics and the Long Civil Rights Movement." *American Communist History* 11, no. 1 (2012): 45–48.

Gready, Paul. "Autobiography and the 'Power of Writing': Political Prison Writing in the Apartheid Era." *Journal of Southern African Studies* 19, no. 3 (1993): 489–523.

Grubbs, Larry. "'Workshop of a Continent': American Representations of Whiteness and Modernity in 1960s South Africa." *Diplomatic History* 32, no. 3 (2008): 405–439.

Gunning, Sandra, Tera W. Hunter, and Michele Mitchell. "Gender, Sexuality, and African Diasporas." *Gender & History* 15, no. 3 (2003): 397–408.

Haarhoff, Errol J. "Appropriating Modernism: Apartheid and the South African Township." *ITU Journal of the Faculty of Architecture* 8, no. 1 (2011): 184–195.

Hall, Jacquelyn Dowd. "The Long Civil Rights Movement and the Political Uses of the Past." *Journal of American History* 91, no. 4 (2005): 1233–1263.

Hall, Stuart. "Cultural Identity and Diaspora." In *Identity: Community, Culture and Difference,* edited by Jonathan Rutherford, 222–237. London: Lawrence and Wishart, 2003.

Hanchard, Michael. "Afro-Modernity: Temporality, Politics, and the African Diaspora." *Public Culture* 11, no. 1 (1999): 245–268.

Harris, Paisley Jane. "Gatekeeping and Remaking: The Politics of Respectability in African American Women's History and Black Feminism." *Journal of Women's History* 15, no. 1 (2003): 212–220.

Hassim, Shireen. "Texts and Tests of Equality: The Women's Charters and the Demand for Equality in South African Political History." *Agenda* 28, no. 2 (2014): 7–18.

Helgesson, Stefan. "Shifting Fields: Imagining Literary Renewal in Itinerário and Drum." *Research in African Literatures* 38, no. 2 (2007): 206–226.

Hernández, Kelly Lytle, Khalil Gibran Muhammad, and Heather Ann Thompson. "Introduction: Constructing the Carceral State." *Journal of American History* 102, no. 1 (2015): 18–24.

Hickel, Jason. "Engineering the Township Home: Domestic Transformations and Urban Revolutionary Consciousness." In *Ekhaya: The Politics of Home in KwaZulu-Natal,* edited by Jason Hickel and Meghan Healy-Clancy, 131–161. Pietermaritzburg, South Africa: University of KwaZulu-Natal Press, 2014.

———. "Social Engineering and Revolutionary Consciousness: Domestic Transformations in Colonial South Africa." *History and Anthropology* 23, no. 3 (2012): 301–322.

Hodder, Jake. "Toward a Geography of Black Internationalism: Bayard Rustin, Nonviolence, and the Promise of Africa." *Annals of the American Association of Geographers* 106, no. 6 (2016): 1360–1377.

hooks, bell. "Representing Whiteness in the Black Imagination." In *Cultural Studies,* edited by Lawrence Grossberg, Cary Nelson, and Paula A Treichler, 338–346. New York: Routledge, 1992.

Horne, Gerald. "Race from Power: U.S. Foreign Policy and the General Crisis of 'WhiteSupremacy.'" *Diplomatic History* 23, no. 3 (1999): 437–461.

———. "Who Lost the Cold War? Africans and African Americans." *Diplomatic History* 20, no. 4 (1996): 613–626.

Hunton, William Alphaeus. "American Trusts Bolster South African Racists." *Freedom* 1, no. 3 (1951): 6.

Johnson, Charles Denton. "Re-Thinking the Emergence of the Struggle for South African Liberation in the United States: Max Yergan and the Council on African Affairs, 1922–1946." *Journal of Southern African Studies* 39, no. 1 (2013): 171–92.

Jones, Matthew. "A 'Segregated' Asia?: Race, the Bandung Conference, and Pan-Asianist Fears in American Thought and Policy, 1954–1955." *Diplomatic History* 29, no. 5 (2005): 841–868.

Karis, Thomas G. "Revolution in the Making: Black Politics in South Africa." *Foreign Affairs* 62, no. 2 (1983): 378–406.

Kelley, Robin D. G. "'Afric's Sons with Banner Red': African American Communists and the Politics of Culture, 1919–1934." In *Imagining Home: Class, Culture, and Nationalism in the African Diaspora*, edited by Sidney J. Lemelle and Robin D. G. Kelley, 35–54. London: Verso, 1994.

———. "An Archaeology of Resistance." Review of *Domination and the Arts of Resistance: Hidden Transcripts* by James C. Scott. *American Quarterly* 44, no. 2 (1992): 292–298.

———. "'But a Local Phase of a World Problem': Black History's Global Vision, 1883–1950." *Journal of American History* 86, no. 3 (1999): 1045–1077.

Kemp, Amanda D., and Robert Trent Vinson. "'Poking Holes in the Sky': Professor James Thaele, American Negroes, and Modernity in 1920s Segregationist South Africa." *African Studies Review* 43, no. 1 (2000): 141–159.

Kramer, Paul A. "Power and Connection: Imperial Histories of the United States in the World." *American Historical Review* 116, no. 5 (2011): 1348–1391.

Kros, Cynthia. "W.W.M. Eiselen: Architect of Apartheid Education." In *The History of Education under Apartheid, 1948–1994: The Doors of Learning and Culture Shall Be Opened*, edited by Peter Kallaway, 53–73. Cape Town: Pearson Education South Africa, 2002.

Kuumba, M. Bahati. "'You've Struck a Rock': Comparing Gender, Social Movements, and Transformation in the United States and South Africa." *Gender & Society* 16, no. 4 (2002): 504–523.

Laden, Sonja. "'Making the Paper Speak Well,' or, the Pace of Change in Consumer Magazines for Black South Africans." *Poetics Today* 22, no. 2 (2001): 515–548.

———. "Who's Afraid of a Black Bourgeoisie?" *Journal of Consumer Culture* 3, no. 2 (2003): 191–216.

Lao-Montes, Agustin. "Decolonial Moves: Trans-locating African Diaspora Spaces." *Cultural Studies* 21, nos. 2–3 (2007): 309–338.

Laville, Helen, and Scott Lucas. "The American Way: Edith Sampson, the NAACP, and African American Identity in the Cold War." *Diplomatic History* 20, no. 4 (1996): 565–590.

Lawrence, Mark Atwood. "The Rise and Fall of Non-Alignment." In *The Cold War in the Third World*, edited by Robert J. McMahon, 139–155. New York: Oxford University Press, 2013.

Leeds, Asia. "Toward the 'Higher Type of Womanhood': The Gendered Contours of Garveyism and the Making of Redemptive Geographies in Costa Rica, 1922–1941." *Palimpsest: A Journal on Women, Gender, and the Black International* 2, no. 1 (2013): 1–27.

Lieberman, Robbie. "'Another Side of the Story': African American Intellectuals Speak Out for Peace and Freedom during the Early Cold War Years." In *Anticommunism and the African American Freedom Movement*, edited by

Robbie Lieberman and Clarence Lang, 17–49. New York: Palgrave Macmillan, 2009.

Lichtenstein, Alex. "One Struggle: Legitimating Anti-Apartheid Discourse." Review of *Race for Sanctions*, by Francis Nesbitt. *Safundi* 5, no. 3 (2004): 1–6.

Lovelace, H. Timothy. "William Worthy's Passport: Travel Restrictions and the Cold War Struggle for Civil and Human Rights." *Journal of American History* 103, no. 1 (2016): 107–31.

Mabin, Alan. "Comprehensive Segregation: The Origins of the Group Areas Act and Its Planning Apparatuses." *Journal of Southern African Studies* 18, no. 2 (1992): 405–429.

Mack, Dwayne. "Hazel Scott: A Career Curtailed." *Journal of African American History* 91, no. 2 (2006): 153–170.

Magubane, Bernard. "From Détente to the Rise of the Garrison State." In *The Road to Democracy in South Africa,* vol. 2, *1970–1980*, edited by the South African Democracy Education Trust, 37–98. Pretoria: Unisa Press, 2006.

Mahon, Maureen. "Eslanda Goode Robeson's *African Journey*: The Politics of Identification and Representation in the African Diaspora." *Souls* 8, no. 3 (2006): 101–118.

Martin, Charles H. "Race, Gender, and Southern Justice: The Rosa Lee Ingram Case." *American Journal of Legal History* 29, no. 3 (1985): 251–268.

Martin, Maria. " 'More Power to Your Great Self': Nigerian Women's Activism and the Pan-African Transnationalist Construction of Black Feminism." *Phylon* (1960-) 53, no. 2 (2016): 54–78.

Masilela, Ntongela. "The 'Black Atlantic' and African Modernity in South Africa." *Research in African Literatures* 27, no. 4 (1996): 88–96.

Maylam, Paul. "The Rise and Decline of Urban Apartheid in South Africa." *African Affairs* 89, no. 354 (1990): 57–84.

McClintock, Anne. "Family Feuds: Gender, Nationalism and the Family." *Feminist Review* no. 44 (1993): 61–80.

McDuffie, Erik S. "Black and Red: Black Liberation, the Cold War, and the Horne Thesis." *Journal of African American History* 96, no. 2 (2011): 236–247.

——. "The March of Young Southern Black Women: Esther Cooper Jackson, Black Left Feminism, and the Personal and Political Costs of Cold War Depression." In *Anticommunism and the African American Freedom Movement*, edited by Robbie Lieberman and Clarence Lang, 81–114. New York: Palgrave Macmillan, 2009.

Melamed, Jodi. "The Killing Joke of Sympathy: Chester Himes's *End of a Primitive* Sounds the Limits of Midcentury Racial Liberalism." *American Literature* 80, no. 4 (2008): 769–797.

——. "The Spirit of Neoliberalism: From Racial Liberalism to Neoliberal Multiculturalism." *Social Text* 24, no. 4 (2006): 1–24.

——. "W. E. B. Du Bois's UnAmerican End." *African American Review* 40, no. 3 (2006): 533–550.

Miller, James A., Susan D. Pennybacker, and Eve Rosenhaft. "Mother Ada Wright and the International Campaign to Free the Scottsboro Boys, 1931–1934." *American Historical Review* 106, no. 2 (2001): 387–430.

Minter, William, and Sylvia Hill. "Anti-Apartheid Solidarity in United States–South Africa Relations: From the Margins to the Mainstream." In *The Road to Democracy in South Africa*, vol. 3, *International Solidarity Part 2*, edited by the South African Democracy Education Trust, 745–822. Pretoria: University of South Africa Press, 2008.

Muller, Carol. "Musical Echoes of American Jazz: Towards a Comparative Historiography." *Safundi* 8, no. 1 (2007): 57–71.

Munro, John. "Imperial Anticommunism and the African American Freedom Movement in the Early Cold War." *History Workshop Journal* 79, no. 1 (2015): 52–75.

Musser, Charles. "Presenting 'A True Idea of the African of To-Day': Two Documentary Forays by Paul and Eslanda Robeson." *Film History: An International Journal* 18, no. 4 (2006): 412–439.

Nagel, Joane. "Masculinity and Nationalism: Gender and Sexuality in the Making of Nations." *Ethnic and Racial Studies* 21, no. 2 (1998): 242–269.

Nauright, John. " 'The Mecca of Native Scum' and 'A Running Sore of Evil': White Johannesburg and the Alexandra Township Removal Debate, 1935–1945." *Kleio* 30, no. 1 (1998): 64–88.

Noer, Thomas. "Segregationists and the World: The Foreign Policy of the White Resistance." In *Window on Freedom: Race, Civil Rights, and Foreign Affairs, 1945–1988*, edited by Brenda Gayle Plummer, 141–162. Chapel Hill: University of North Carolina Press, 2003.

Odhiambo, Tom. "Inventing Africa in the Twentieth Century: Cultural Imagination, Politics and Transnationalism in *Drum* Magazine." *African Studies* 65, no. 2 (2006): 157–174.

Onishi, Yuichiro. "The New Negro of the Pacific: How African Americans Forged Cross-Racial Solidarity with Japan, 1917–1922." *Journal of African American History* 92, no. 2 (2007): 191–213.

Parker, Jason. "Cold War II: The Eisenhower Administration, the Bandung Conference, and the Reperiodization of the Postwar Era." *Diplomatic History* 30, no. 5 (2006): 867–892.

———. "Decolonization, the Cold War, and the Post-Columbian Era." In *The Cold War in the Third World*, edited by Robert J. McMahon, 124–138. New York: Oxford University Press, 2013.

———. "Ideology, Race and Nonalignment in US Cold War Foreign Relations: or, How the Cold War Racialized Neutralism without Neutralizing Race." In *Challenging US Foreign Policy: America and the World in the Long Twentieth Century*, edited by Bevan Sewell and Scott Lucas, 75–98. Basingstoke, UK: Palgrave Macmillan, 2011.

Parnell, Susan, and Alan Mabin. "Rethinking Urban South Africa." *Journal of Southern African Studies* 21, no. 1 (1995): 39–61.

Patterson, Tiffany Ruby, and Robin D. G. Kelley. "Unfinished Migrations: Reflections on the African Diaspora and the Making of the Modern World." *African Studies Review* 43, no. 1 (2000): 11–45.

Pease, Donald E. "Doing Justice to C. L. R. James's *Mariners, Renegades, and Castaways.*" *Boundary* 2 27, no. 2 (2000): 1–19.

Pederson, Vernon L. "Memories of the Red Decade: HUAC Investigations in Maryland." In *American Labor and the Cold War: Grassroots Politics and Postwar Political Culture*, edited by Robert W. Cherny, William Issel, and Kieran Walsh Taylor, 177–189. New Brunswick, NJ: Rutgers University Press, 2004.

Raditlhalo, Sam. "Unzima Lomthwalo—'This Load Is Heavy': A Selection of South African Prison and Exile Life Writings." *Life Writing* 1, no. 2 (2004): 27–54.

Rauwerda, Antje M. "Whitewashing *Drum* Magazine (1951–1959): Advertising Race and Gender." *Continuum* 21, no. 3 (2007): 393–404.

Rodriguez, Dylan. "A Reign of Penal Terror: United States Global Statecraft and the Technology of Punishment and Capture." In *The Violence of Incarceration*, edited by Phil Scraton and Jude McCulloch, 187–208. New York: Routledge, 2008.

Sandage, Scott A. "A Marble House Divided: The Lincoln Memorial, the Civil Rights Movement, and the Politics of Memory, 1939–1963." *Journal of American History* 80, no. 1 (1993): 135–167.

Schraeder, Peter J., and R. Hunt Davis. "South Africa." In *Intervention into the 1990s: U.S. Foreign Policy in the Third World*, edited by Peter J. Schraeder, 247–267. Boulder: Lynne Rienner, 1992.

Schwarz, Bill. " 'Claudia Jones and the West Indian Gazette': Reflections on the Emergence of Post-colonial Britain." *Twentieth Century British History* 14, no. 3 (2003): 264–285.

Seymour, Richard. "The Cold War, American Anticommunism and the Global 'Colour Line.' " In *Race and Racism in International Relations: Confronting the Global Colour Line*, edited by Alexander Anievas, Nivi Manchanda, and Robbie Shilliam, 157–174. London: Routledge, 2014.

Singh, Nikhil Pal. "Retracing the Black-Red Thread." *American Literary History* 15, no. 4 (2003): 830–840.

Stavney, Anne. " 'Mothers of Tomorrow': The New Negro Renaissance and the Politics of Maternal Representation." *African American Review* 32, no. 4 (1998): 533–561.

Stephens, Michelle Ann. "Disarticulating Black Internationalisms: West Indian Radicals and The Practice of Diaspora." *Small Axe* 9, no. 1 (2005): 100–111.

Stoler, Ann Laura. "Intimidations of Empire: Predicaments of the Tactile and Unseen." In *Haunted by Empire*, 1–22.

——. "Tense and Tender Ties: The Politics of Comparison in North American History and (Post) Colonial Studies." *Journal of American History* 88, no. 3 (2001): 829–865.

Sullivan, Patricia. "Movement Building during the World War II Era: The NAACP's Legal Insurgency in the South." In *Fog of War: The Second World War and the Civil Rights Movement*, edited by Kevin M. Kruse and Stephen Tuck, 70–86. New York: Oxford University Press, 2012.

Summers, Martin. "Diasporic Brotherhood: Freemasonry and the Transnational Production of Black Middle-Class Masculinity." *Gender & History* 15, no. 3 (2003): 550–574.

Suttner, Raymond. "Rethinking and Re-Remembering Prison: Reification, Agency and Liminality." *Psychology in Society* no. 39 (2010): 3–20.

Switzer, Les. "*Bantu World* and the Origins of a Captive Commercial Press." In *South Africa's Alternative Press: Voices of Protest and Resistance, 1880–1960*, edited by Les Switzer, 189–212. Cambridge: Cambridge University Press, 1997.

Thomas, Lynn M. "The Modern Girl and Racial Respectability in 1930s South Africa." *Journal of African History* 47, no. 3 (2006): 461–490.

———. "Skin Lighteners, Black Consumers and Jewish Entrepreneurs in South Africa." *History Workshop Journal* 73, no. 1 (2012): 259–283.

Thompson, Heather Ann. "Why Mass Incarceration Matters: Rethinking Crisis, Decline, and Transformation in Postwar American History." *Journal of American History* 97, no. 3 (2010): 703–734.

Titlestad, Michael. "Traveling Jazz: Themes and Riffs." *Safundi* 8, no. 1 (2007): 73–82.

Unterhalter, Elaine. "The Work of the Nation: Heroic Masculinity in South African Autobiographical Writing of the Anti-apartheid Struggle." *European Journal of Development Research* 12, no. 2 (2000): 157–178.

"A U.S. Loan for South Africa?" *New Africa* 7, no. 3 (1948): 1–2.

Van Wyk, Anna-Mart. "Apartheid's Atomic Bomb: Cold War Perspectives." *South African Historical Journal* 62, no. 1 (2010): 100–120.

Visser, Wessel. "Afrikaner Anti-communist History Production in South African Historiography." In *History Making and Present Day Politics: The Meaning of Collective Memory in South Africa*, edited by Hans Erik Stolten, 306–333. Uppsala, Sweden: Nordic Africa Institute, 2007.

Vlies, Andrew van der. " 'Local' Writing, 'Global' Reading, and the Demands of the 'Canon': The Case of Alan Paton's *Cry, the Beloved Country*." *South African Historical Journal* 139, no. 55 (2006): 20–32.

Von Eschen, Penny M. "Who's the Real Ambassador? Exploding Cold War Racial Ideology." In *Cold War Constructions: The Political Culture of United States Imperialism, 1945–1966*, edited by Christian G. Appy, 110–131. Amherst: University of Massachusetts Press, 2000.

Wacquant, Loïc. "From Slavery to Mass Incarceration: Rethinking the 'Race Question' in the US." *New Left Review* 13 (2002): 41–60.

Waetjen, Thembisa. "The 'Home' in Homeland: Gender, National Space, and Inkatha's Politics of Ethnicity." *Ethnic and Racial Studies* 22, no. 4 (1999): 653–678.

Washington, Mary Helen. "Alice Childress, Lorraine Hansberry, and Claudia Jones: Black Women Write the Popular Front." In *Left of the Color Line: Race, Radicalism, and Twentieth-Century Literature of the United States*, edited by Bill V. Mullen and James Smethurst, 183–204. Chapel Hill: University of North Carolina Press, 2003.

Webb, Clive. "Reluctant Partners: African Americans and the Origins of the Special Relationship." *Journal of Transatlantic Studies* 14, no. 4 (2016): 350–64.

Weinbaum, Alys Eve. "Reproducing Racial Globality: W. E. B. DuBois and the Sexual Politics of Black Nationalism." *Social Text* 19, no. 2 (2001): 15–41.

Wells, Julia. "Maternal Politics in Organizing Black South African Women: The Historical Lessons." In *Sisterhood, Feminisms, and Power: From Africa to the Diaspora*, edited by Obioma Nnaemeka, 251–262. Trenton, NJ: Africa World Press, 1998.

West, Michael O. "Little Rock as America: Hoyt Fuller, Europe, and the Little Rock Racial Crisis of 1957." *Journal of Social History* 78, no. 4 (2012): 913–42.

Wilson, Bobby M. "Race in Commodity Exchange and Consumption: Separate but Equal." *Annals of the Association of American Geographers* 95, no. 3 (2005): 587–606.

Worger, William H. "Convict Labour, Industrialists and the State in the US South and South Africa, 1870–1930." *Journal of Southern African Studies* 30, no. 1 (2004): 63–86.

Wylie, Diana. "The Changing Face of Hunger in Southern African History 1880–1980." *Past & Present* no. 122 (1989): 159–199.

PhD Dissertations

Hyman, Zoe Laura. "American Segregationist Ideology and White Southern Africa, 1948–1975." PhD diss., Sussex University, 2012.

Wells, Brandy T. " 'She Pieced and Stitched and Quilted, Never Wavering nor Doubting': A Historical Tapestry of African American Women's Internationalism, 1890s–1960s." PhD diss., Ohio State University, 2015.

Woods, Colleen P. "Bombs, Bureaucrats, and Rosary Beads: The United States, the Philippines, and the Making of Global Anti-Communism, 1945–1960." PhD diss., University of Michigan, 2012.

Interviews

Gordon, William. Interview by John Egerton, January 19, 1991, Southern Oral History Program Collection (#4007), interview A-0364, transcript, http://docsouth.unc.edu/sohp/html_use/A-0364.html.

Houser, George M. Interview by Lisa Brock, July 19, 2004, transcript, http://www.noeasyvictories.org/interviews/int02_houser.php.

Index

Maddox, William, 54–55

Mafeking, Elizabeth, 140, 165–167, 173, 182

Makaza, P. G., 110–112

Makeba, Miriam, 65–66, 99, 113, 233n13

Malan, Daniel François: African Charter, 24; apartheid policies, 4, 43; criticism of, 40, 46, 70, 137–138, 201; involvement with *Cry, the Beloved Country* (film), 71; U.S. government, relationship with, 32–35, 39

Mandela, Nelson, 11, 14, 30–31, 46, 117, 140, 149, 212, 222n38, 245n1

Marks, J. B., 140, 145–146

Marshall, Thurgood, 4

Martinsville Seven, 135

Masekela, Hugh, 65–66

Masilela, Ntongela, 100

Mason, Vivian Carter, 9, 185–186, 190–193, 195, 198, 201, 212

Matomela, Florence, 140

Matthews, Frieda, 44, 66, 76–82, 121, 212

Matthews, Joe, 144–145

Matthews, Z. K., 9, 44, 66, 76–82, 121, 132, 149, 152–153, 237n100

Mays, Benjamin E., 40–41

Mays, Willie, 99

McCarran Internal Security Act, 23–24, 80, 123, 138, 249n43

McCarran-Walter Act, 24, 42, 124

McClintock, Ann, 176–177

McDuffie, Erik S., 79, 185

Mdledle, Gertrude, 192–193

Meadowlands, 95

Meriwether, James H., 7, 76

Mhlaba, Raymond M., 139–140

Mini, Vuyisile, 149

Mkhize, Bertha, 140

Mockford, Julian, 71

Modisane, Bloke, 99, 109

Modise, Joe, 147

Mokaleng, Pinocchio, 108

Montgomery Bus Boycott, 3–4

Monyake, Chief Berung, 198

Moolman, H., 42–43

Moral Re-Armament, 47, 228n52

Moroka, James S., 126, 144–145

Motherhood, 96, 150, 153–155, 159–183, 199–206; and global black motherhood, 159–167, 180–183, 199–206, 211; and Mother Africa symbolism, 161; nationalism and, 169–170; postwar image of, 199; and the preservation of the home, 168–173; politicization of, 149–155, 165–167, 171–173, 199–206; respectability of, 91, 102–105, 142 168, 171, 190, 200, 206; separate spheres of, 96, 171–172, 179; and traditional values, 169. *See also Bantu World*; Federation of South African Women (FSAW); National Council of Negro Women (NCNW)

Moton, Robert, 77

Msezane, Edith Nono, 192–193

Mtwana, Ida, 173, 175, 177

Muller, Carol, 110

Mundt-Nixon Bill, 24

Murray, Andrew, 128

Mutual Defense Assistance Act (MDAA), 32–33

Naicker, G. M., 137, 149

National Association for the Advancement of Colored People (NAACP), 4, 55, 129; anti-apartheid politics of, 8–9, 13, 46, 120, 145; and Z. K. and Frieda Matthews U.S. visit, 77–78. *See also* Anderson, Carol; White, Walter

National Association of Colored Women (NACW), 186

National Council of African Women (NCAW), 192–193

National Council of Negro Women
(NCNW), 8–9, 13, 17, 185–206, 210;
African Children's Feeding Scheme
(ACFS), cooperation with, 193–206;
anti-apartheid position of, 191–193;
anticommunist position of, 187–189,
194; child welfare position of,
194–195; founding, 186–187; internationalism, 187–193, 266n13; junior
councils, 193, 197; motherhood, view
of, 199–206; State Department,
relationship with, 186, 197; Women's
International Democratic Federation
(WIDF) ties, 185–186. *See also*
Mason, Vivian Carter; Bethune,
Mary McLeod

National Negro Congress (NNC), 4

National Party: anticommunism, 1,
10–11, 24–26, 34–36, 42–44, 60–62,
126–128, 135–137, 180–181; civil rights
movement, monitoring of, 25, 38–62,
208; *Cry, the Beloved Country* (film),
party views reflected in, 70–72;
foreign investment as support of,
27–28; foreign policy, influence on,
10–11, 226n24 16–17, 26–36, 38–62.
See also Apartheid

National Union of South African
Students (NUSAS), 1

Native Affairs Department, 5, 70, 95,
207

New Africa, 1, 7, 29

New Age, 132

New York Amsterdam News, 78, 105,
144, 163

New York Times, 40, 89

Ngakane, Lionel, 73

Ngoyi, Lilian, 140, 155, 173–175, 178,
181–186, 201, 204, 212

Ngwevela, Johnson, 145

Nhlapo, Jacob M., 168

Njongwe, J. L., 120, 163–164

Njongwe, Nomple, 163–164

Nkomo, William, 47

Nkrumah, Kwame, 188, 190

Nokwe, Duma, 167

Norton, Conrad, 43–44, 225n13

Pan-Africanism, 7, 14, 17–18, 53, 102,
105, 108–109, 120–121; and gender
politics, 159–183, 205–206, 211–212.
See also Black internationalism;
Diaspora; Motherhood

Pan-Africanist Congress (PAC), 3

Parker, Jason, 51–52

Paton, Alan, 67, 69–70

Patterson, Louise Thompson, 79,
184–185

Patterson, Tiffany, 210

Patterson, William L., 83–84, 124,
129–130, 134, 147

Peace Information Center (PIC), 133

Perry, Pettis, 124

Pittman, John, 33, 147

Pittsburgh Courier, 41, 142, 163–164

Plaatje, Solomon, 100

Poitier, Sidney, 66–76, 79–83, 98

Powell, Adam Clayton, 75–76, 98, 105,
120–121

Powell, C. B., 105

Prison system: of South Africa, 117–118;
of United States, 118, 129–130. *See
also* Incarceration

Race and crime, 118–119, 141–142

Randolph, A. Philip, 8, 12–13, 121, 161,
163

Rankin, John Elliot, 124

Red Scare. *See* Anticommunism

Resha, Robert, 149

Richardson, Beulah, 79, 184

Rickard, Donald, 11

Robeson, Eslanda Goode, 15, 78–79, 82,
87, 134, 161–163, 184, 212

Verwoerd, Hendrik, 5, 94
Von Eschen, Penny M., 6–7, 108–109

Walcott, Joe, 102
Walker, Cherryl, 174
Waller, Fats, 110
Wesley, Charles H., 77
White "civilization," 47–49, 94
White, Walter, 46, 77
Winston, Henry, 123, 248n40
Witt, Doris, 200
Women's Day Protest, Pretoria (1956), 3, 176
Women's International Democratic Federation (WIDF), 180–182, 184–186, 190. *See also* Federation of South African Women (FSAW); National Council of Negro Women (NCNW)
Woods, Jeff, 124
World Congress of Mothers, 180–183, 184–185. *See also* Federation of South African Women (FSAW); Lilian

Ngoyi; Dora Tamana; Women's International Democratic Federation (WIDF)
Wright, Richard, 72
Wylie, Diana, 200

Xuma, Alfred Bitini, 191
Xuma, Madie Hall, 191–193

Yergan, Max: South Africa, tour, 44–47; and Z. K. Matthews, 44, 77

Zenzele Clubs, 192. *See also* Xuma, Madie Hall; National Council of Negro Women (NCNW)
Zonk!: African Americans and modernity, 91–93, 95–96, 98–113, 241n12; and consumer culture, 92–93, 95–96, 245n102; and gender politics, 92–93; jazz, coverage of, 108–113; production and circulation, 91–92, 242n41; respectability, defining, 102–104

Made in United States
North Haven, CT
08 October 2024

58563840R00195